NATO ASI Series

Advanced Science Institutes Series

A series presenting the results of activities sponsored by the NATO Science Committee, which aims at the dissemination of advanced scientific and technological knowledge, with a view to strengthening links between scientific communities.

The Series is published by an international board of publishers in conjunction with the NATO Scientific Affairs Division

A	Life Sciences	Plenum Publishing Corporation
B	Physics	London and New York
C	Mathematical and Physical Sciences	Kluwer Academic Publishers Dordrecht, Boston and London
D	Behavioural and Social Sciences	
E	Applied Sciences	
F	Computer and Systems Sciences	Springer-Verlag Berlin Heidelberg New York
G	Ecological Sciences	London Paris Tokyo Hong Kong
H	Cell Biology	Barcelona

The ASI Series Books Published as a Result of
Activities of the Special Programme on
ADVANCED EDUCATIONAL TECHNOLOGY

This book contains the proceedings of a NATO Advanced Research Workshop held within the activities of the NATO Special Programme on Advanced Educational Technology, running from 1988 to 1993 under the auspices of the NATO Science Committee.

Designing Hypermedia for Learning

Edited by

David H. Jonassen

Instructional Technology
University of Colorado
Denver, CO 80217-3364, USA

Heinz Mandl

Deutsches Institut für Fernstudien (DIFF)
University of Tübingen
D-7400 Tübingen, FRG

With the assistance of
Sherwood Wang and Peter M. Fischer

Springer-Verlag Berlin Heidelberg New York
London Paris Tokyo Hong Kong Barcelona
Published in cooperation with NATO Scientific Affairs Division

Proceedings of the NATO Advanced Research Workshop on Designing
Hypertext/Hypermedia for Learning, held in Rottenburg/Neckar, FRG, July 3—8, 1989.

ISBN 3-540-52958-6 Springer-Verlag Berlin Heidelberg New York
ISBN 0-387-52958-6 Springer-Verlag New York Berlin Heidelberg

Printing: Druckhaus Beltz, Hemsbach; Binding: J. Schäffer GmbH & Co. KG, Grünstadt
2145/3140-543210 – Printed on acid-free-paper

Table of Contents

Part 5: Hypermedia Design Process

Part 6: Conceptual Foundations for Designing Hypermedia Systems for Learning

Preface

This most unusual book results from the NATO Advanced Research Workshop, "Designing Hypertext/Hypermedia for Learning", held in Rottenburg am Neckar, FRG, from July 3-8, 1989. The idea for the workshop resulted from the burgeoning interest in hypertext combined with the frustrating lack of literature on learning applications for hypertext. There was little evidence in 1988 that hypertext could successfully support learning outcomes. A few projects were investigating hypertext for learning, but few conclusions were available and little if any advice on how to design hypertext for learning applications was available. Could hypertext support learning objectives? What mental processing requirements are unique to learning outcomes? How would the processing requirements of learning outcomes interact with unique user processing requirements of browsing and constructing hypertext? Should hypertext information bases be restructured to accommodate learning outcomes? Should the user interface be manipulated in order to support the task functionality of learning outcomes? Does the hypertext structure reflect the intellectual requirements of learning outcomes? What kinds of learning-oriented hypertext systems were being developed and what kinds of assumptions were these systems making? These and other questions demonstrated the need for this workshop.

The workshop included presentations, hardware demonstrations, sharing and browsing of hypertexts, and much discussion about all of the above. These were the experiences that you, the reader of this book, unfortunately did not experience. We have tried in the format of this book to share some of those experiences with you. This book is more than a compilation of papers. It is a textual implementation of the workshop constrained by the limitations of print-on-paper text.

Following the workshop, we asked each of the contributors to revise their papers to reflect the ideas and discussion shared at the workshop. Each paper needed to make heavier use of headings and to include a list of keywords. Each paper needed to state its assumptions about learning, characteristics of hypertext (one of the conclusions of the workshop was that we should use the more generic term, hypermedia, rather than hypertext), and provide some advice or guidelines for designing hypermedia for learning. These papers were collected and edited. They were organized into sections that reflected some of the themes of the workshop. The text of each paper was allocated to the larger inside column of each page. A copy of the entire book was then sent to each participant. Each participant then read and commented on the other papers. Most comments were submitted in the form of qualified annotations (McAleese & Duncan, 1983). These predefined relations connect the text next to the annotation with other text in the book. Qualified annotations included:

example - specific instances of current topic
recommendation - principle for designing hypermedia
background - conceptual/theoretical foundations
explanation - expands or elaborates on current topic
corroboration - supports current topic
illustration - visual illustration of topic
contrast - contradictory interpretation or description
definition - definition of idea or topic
results - relevant research results
parallel - similar interpretation or description
implication - inferential conclusion
methodology - description of relevant research or design
methodology

By following these built-in links, you may read additional information (for example, explanation) about the topic that is defined by the link. So, an annotation such as "DJ explanation 4.13" means that DJ (see the following list of participants for the identity of each participant) claims that there is an explanation of the idea(s) adjacent to the annotation that can be found on page 4.13. Participants could also add non-qualified comments or other references to external documents that the author did not include in the paper to the annotation column. These annotations were shared with all of the participants via an electronic mail conference. This provided each author with the opportunity to read how other workshop participants reacted to their chapter and to amend their works to accommodate the pertinent slings and arrows of their peers. These annotations, comments, and references were then added to the outside column of the book, which was then printed out in its final form. And since this book repeatedly claims that annotation is such an important part of the hypermedia process, we invite you to add your own annotations and comments to the columns. This will contribute to the meaningfulness of the book for you by personalizing and contextual-izing it. If you are one of those people who cannot bear the thought of marking in a textbook, then think of this as a hypertext, not a textBOOK.

The elaborate and iterative process was undertaken for a number of reasons. First, we hoped that the quality of the ideas and writing would improve if subjected to the scrutiny of peers. Second, we wanted the book to exhibit some of the characteristics of hypermedia. The annotations represent internal links. The references represent external links to other documents. Were this a true hypermedium, the references would consist of links that transport you directly to the relevant portion of the referenced document. That is not possible in print without aggregating all of the relevant references in one book. Page and copyright restrictions preclude that.

In order to help you access, compare, and contrast ideas, other common hypermedia access tools, such as contents lists and keywords for each chapter, are provided. Third, we wanted the book to reflect some of the themes, issues, and opinions discussed but not resolved at the workshop — to engage you in some of the dialogues that engaged us. To clarify some of the issues (if not the resolutions), some of the participants were asked to write chapters (Chapters 8, 11, 18, 19) summarizing the concerns relevant to the different themes of the workshop. Finally, we wanted to continue the dialogue begun at the workshop, so the electronic mail conference enabled us to do that.

We trust that you will profit from these additional labors (they were laborious). They may impose additional processing on your part. We hope that they do. So does hypermedia.

References
McAleese, R. & Duncan, E.B. (1983). *Meaning and use of qualifying terms in citation indexing for education.* Aberdeen, UK: University of Aberdeen, University Teaching Centre.

Participants ————————————————

The following people participated in the workshop in Rottenburg. Their highlighted initials are the referents in the annotations on the following pages.

Eric Bruillard is an Associate Researcher at the National Institute of Pedagogical Research where he has studied Logo micro-worlds, robotics and intelligent tutoring systems. He is currently completing his Ph.D. thesis on intelligent tutoring systems in mathematics using hypermedia and diagnosis systems from the Universite du Maine, Le Mans, France. **EB**

Andrew Dillon studied psychology at University College Cork (BA 1984, MA 1986). In his latter two years there he worked on a project investigating user development with adaptable interfaces. He joined the HUSAT Research Institute, Loughborough University, in 1986 and is currently researching readers' models of texts and the usability of hypertext. **AD**

Dr. Philippe Duchastel is a researcher in the field of artificial intelligence — intelligent tutoring systems and other knowledge-based systems, such as instructional games and advisory systems. He is currently engaged in **PD** research and technological strategy planning at McAir Corporation in Denver, Colorado. His Ph.D. from Florida State University involved R&D experience in computer science and cognitive psychology (human learning). He has studied instructional techniques, new technologies in teaching, distance teaching procedures, textual learning, instructional illustrations, professional education, methods of evaluation, and various forms of intelligent systems. His many publications and presentations at scientific and professional meetings illustrate this wide range of interests. Dr. Duchastel has worked in various countries outside the U.S., including Canada, England, France, and Switzerland. Dr. Duchastel is a member of the NATO Scientific Committee Panel on Advanced Educational Technology, which organizes international summer institutes and advanced research workshops.

TD Thomas M. Duffy is an associate professor in Instructional Systems Technology and a research associate in Learning Resources at Indiana University. His work has focused on document design and his current work is on the design of learning environments. He is the co-editor of *Designing Usable Texts* and co-author of *Designing Online Help Systems: Research and Practice.*

PF Peter Michael Fischer is a cognitive research scientist at the Deutsches Institut für Fernstudien (DIFF) at the University of Tübingen. At this time he is actively engaged in the development and experimental investigation of interactive teaching/learning systems and in the development of diagnostic tools and feedback for online tutoring.

OF Otmar Foelsche heads a language learning project at Dartmouth College. His primary research interest includes the use of hypermedia for language learning.

SG R. Scott Grabinger is an Assistant Professor of Instructional Technology at the University of Colorado. He completed his doctorate at Indiana University where he began researching screen design. His current research interests include hypermedia, expert systems, and screen design. He has published numerous articles and a book on expert systems in education.

RH Rainer Hammwöhner is a professor and researcher in the Fachgruppe Informationswissenschaft at the University of Konstanz. His research interests include the structuring of hypertext using rhetorical models.

DJ David H. Jonassen is Professor and Chair of Instructional Technology at the University of Colorado. His doctorate was from Temple University in educational psychology and technology. Dr. Jonassen has taught previously at the University of North Carolina, Syracuse University, and Temple University. His current research interests include knowledge representation, hypertext, and intelligent computer based instruction. He has published ten books and numerous articles, chapters, and reports on different aspects of instructional technology.

Piet Kommers studied Pedagogy, Psychology and Computer Science at the State University in Utrecht (The Netherlands). After his doctorate degree he specialized in Knowledge Engineering, Hypertext and interaction metaphors for explorative learning. From 1982 he has been appointed as assistant professor in the Faculty of Educational Technology at Twente University. His current research is into 'Hypertext and the acquisition of Knowledge'. The key issue in it is the design and evaluation of conceptual mapping techniques for learning situations. He has developed a prototype TEXTVISION, which is a knowledge representation tool used in many Dutch schools . He participates in the DELTA research project called HYPERATE. He has written extensively on the topic of hypertext.

PK

George P. Landow, Professor of English and Art at Brown University, holds the AB, MA, and PhD from Princeton University and an MA from Brandeis University. Landow has published on nineteenth-century literature, art, and religion as well as on educational hypertext. He has taught at Columbia, the University of Chicago, Brasenose College, Oxford, and Brown Universities. He has been a Fulbright Scholar (1963-4), twice a Guggenheim Fellow (1973, 1978), and a Fellow of the Society for the Humanities, Cornell University, and he has received numerous grants and awards from the National Endowment for the Humanities and the National Endowment for the Arts. Since 1984 he has worked as a member of the team at the Institute for Research in Information and Scholarship that developed *Intermedia* at Brown. He supervised, edited, and partially wrote *Context32*, a body of hypermedia documents used to support English literature courses.

GL

John J. Leggett earned his M.C.S and Ph.D. in Computing Science from Texas A&M University where he is currently an Assistant Professor. His research interests include hypertext/hypermedia systems, computer-supported collaborative systems, human-computer interface, and distributed and object-oriented computation. He has several publications in the areas of human-computer interface and hypertext/hypermedia systems. As director of the Hypertext Research Laboratory, Dr. Leggett is directing research on next generation hypermedia systems, collaborative information systems and the use of hypertext in education and traditional scholarship. He teaches a graduate course on hypertext and is the principle investigator on several funded hypertext research projects. Dr. Leggett is a member of Honor Societies including Alpha Chi, Phi Kappa Phi, Upsilon Pi.

JL

Anja Lkoundi studied pedagogy at the University of Utrecht and the University of Paris. For several years she filled teaching positions and conducted research in the field of education of ethnic minority groups in the

AL

Netherlands. The last few years she has held a position at the Dutch Open University in the development of courses, where she participates in a research project that is concerned with hypertext applications.

HM Heinz Mandl is professor for Educational Psychology and Pedagogics at the University of Tübingen. He is also director of the Deutsches Institut für Fernstudien (DIFF) at the University of Tübingen and head of the Department of Learning Research at DIFF. Presently he is concerned with the Psychology of Learning, Cognitive Science, Educational Psychology, Media Research, Intelligent Learning & Tutoring Systems.

GM Gary Marchionini is an Associate Professor in the College of Library and Information Services at he University of Maryland at College Park where he teaches courses in computer applications and research methods. He received his PhD from Wayne State University in mathematics education and conducts research related to information seeking in electronic environments. He has published numerous articles related to hypertext and serves as the General Editor of Hypertext Publications for the Association of Computing Machinery.

TM Terry Mayes completed a degree in Psychology at the University of Bristol, before going to the University of Newcastle where he completed a PhD in human memory. During his time at Newcastle he also became involved in the development and manufacture of teaching machines. This early interest in educational technology has been subsequently developed in his personal research while lecturing in cognitive psychology at the University of Strathclyde. In 1986 he was appointed Deputy Director of

RM theScottish HCI Centre at Strathclyde. A major strand of research at the Centre is in hypertext and its role in interactive learning.

Ray McAleese is Director of the University Teaching Centre in the University of Aberdeen. His major research interests are cognitive aspects of hypermedia. His research work has involved him in the design of graphical interfaces to hypermedia systems. He has used NoteCards and SemNet as knowledge acquisition tools in a number of projects. He is co-editor of *Hypertext Theory into Practice: State of the Art.*

CM Cliff McKnight served an engineering apprenticeship and worked as a design draughtsman before reading psychology at Brunel University (BTech 1973, PhD 1976). As a lecturer and later senior lecturer, he taught psychology at the University of London Goldsmiths' College for several years. After two years as editor of various computer magazines, he returned to academic life and is currently a Principal Scientist at the HUSAT Research Institute, Loughborough University. A member of the editorial board of the journal 'Hypermedia', he has a book entitled 'Hypertext in Context' (written with Andrew Dillon and John Richardson) published later this year by Cambridge University Press.

Max Mühlhauser received his Diploma and his Doctorate in Informatics (Computer Science) from the University of Karlsruhe, West Germany. He has worked as a senior researcher at the Institute for Telematics at the University of Karlsruhe. Since 1986, he has managed the CEC, a research facility of Digital Equipment Corporation and two joint projects of German universities and the industry: one on software engineering and languages for distributed applications and one on the use of networked multimedia workstations in computer-assisted instruction. He has become a Professor in Telematics at the University of Kaiserslautern, at the same time continuing and expanding the technical supervision of the aforementioned projects from his new location.

MM

Jakob Nielsen is Assistant Professor of user interface design at the Technical University of Denmark. He is responsible for the human factors/user interface program at this university, manager of the user interface subproject of the European Community DELTA SAFE project, and a user interface consultant for several Danish and international companies. His research interests include usability engineering and hypertext. Dr. Nielsen's earlier affiliations include the IBM User Interface Institute in Yorktown Heights, NY and Aarhus University, Denmark. He is the author of the book *Hypertext and Hypermedia*, the European Editor for the ACM SIGCHI Bulletin, and on the editorial boards of *Behaviour and Information Technology*, *Hypermedia*, and *Interacting with Computers*.

JN

Martin Richartz received his Diploma in Informatics (Computer Science) from the University of Karlsruhe in 1986. He had been working in several large software projects before he joined the CEC research center of Digital Equipment in Karlsruhe, W. Germany, in 1988. He is a member of the Telematics Group of the University of Kaiserslautern, West Germany. His main research interests are Collaborative Hypermedia Systems, Human-Machine Interaction, and Software Engineering for Distributed Applications.

MR

Alexander Joseph Romiszowski is Professor of Instructional Design Development and Evaluation at Syracuse University. He has been a professor at several universities including Concordia University, the State University of Rio de Janeiro, the Federal University of Bahia, Salvador and Middlesex Polytechnic, London. His major research interests include instructional design and development, distance education, the education of adults, skills training, the effective use of new technologies in education and training and

AR

the skills of management of innovation in the field of education. He has worked as an educational technology expert or as project manager on a number of international projects in developing countries. He has published over 100 papers in scholarly journals and ten books. His interest in hypertext/hypermedia focuses on the benefits that can be gained through the structuring and storage of information as a network of interconnected nodes and instructional design aspects of hypertext information bases which are destined for instructional applications.

DR Daniel M. Russell is a Member of the Research Staff at the Xerox Palo Alto Research Center where for the past six years he led the "Instructional Design Environment" (IDE) project, a hypertext-based design environment targeted for instructional materials analysis, development and synthesis. Dr. Russell recently joined the User Interface Research (UIR) where he pursues mechanisms for accessing, using and searching large, heterogenous, multimedia knowledge bases, studying how these techniques will operate in the growing information-access milieu. He is also an adjunct lecturer on the Engineering and Computer Science faculty of the University of Santa Clara, California. His research interests revolve around intelligent tutoring based upon sophisticated student models, intelligent computer-aided design environments, knowledge manipulation systems, intelligent retrieval from heterogenous databases, knowledge-based synthesis of responses to queries, together with automatic problem-solving and planning systems. Dan received his B.S. in Information and Computer Science from U.C. Irvine, and his M.S. and Ph.D. degrees in Computer Science from the University of Rochester, New York.

NS Norbert Streitz earned a Ph.D. in theoretical physics from the University of Kiel and a Ph.D. in psychology from the Technical University of Aachen. Since then, he has spent a year as a post-doctoral fellow at the University of California at Berkeley, has been an Assistant Professor at the Technical University of Aachen, and has headed the Aachen Cognitive Ergonomics Project. Since 1987, he has headed the knowledge-based authoring and hypertext department at the Integrated Publication and Information Systems Institute in Darmstadt. Dr. Streitz has been a leader in the German Society of Computer Science. His research interests focus on cognitive science and computer science applied to user-oriented, task-driven, and ergonomic system design, human computer interactions, and hypertext systems. He has co-edited volumes and contributed several papers on these topics.

WV Wil Verreck studied psychology at the University of Leiden, taught for several years in social psychology at that university, and then shifted to a position in educational research at the Technological University Eindhoven. He has written a Ph.D. on individualized instruction and published several papers on the topic. Interests shifted again to informatics and information technology. After several years in the executive board of the TUE, he resumed a research position at the Dutch Open University, where he is running a project directed at the utilization of hypertext in distance education.

Patricia Wright is a member of the scientific staff of the Medical Research Council working at the Applied Psychology Unit in Cambridge, England. Her research concerns the cognitive processes of reading, particularly the strategic options that readers exercise, and the cognitive problems of writing/designing written information. She has published journal articles and book chapters on materials as diverse as medical forms, data graphics, signposting within buildings and technical documentation. Among her current hypermedia projects are studies of people's use of diagrams while reading, readers' willingness to access glossary information, writers' decisions about the representational forms for giving instructions, people's information-seeking behavior while problem-solving and cognitive issues relating to hypertext navigation. She is a Fellow of Churchill College at Cambridge University, of the British Psychological Society and of the Institute of Scientific and Technical Communicators.

PWr

Peter Whalley is a Research Fellow in the Centre for Information Technology in Education at the Open University. He has a BSc and a PhD in Psychology. His main research interests concern the the development of simulation environments, and the general use of hypertext within distance education. Other interests include models of learning from text, and the development of object-oriented control environments for children.

PWh

Acknowledgements

First, we should like to acknowledge each of the participants at the workshop and any other co-contributors to this book. We appreciate their stimulating ideas and engaging colloquy.

More importantly, there are two people without whom the workshop would not have succeeded and the book would not have been completed. We express our sincerest gratitude to Peter Fischer who was responsible for the computer support and many of the other arrangements in Rottenburg. His sensitivity, intelligence, and tenacity made the experience more meaningful for all of us. He also contributed very substantial ideas to the discussion. We also express gratitude to Sherwood Wang for his editorial, communication, and production expertise in the completion of the manuscript. This very unusual book could not have been completed without his help.

We should also like to acknowledge Ray McAleese for his ideas, discussion, and confirmation of the annotation process that makes this book so effective.

Dedication

To James Hartley, a friend, colleague, and fellow text design researcher.

Introduction

Toward a Psychophysics of Hypermedia

Peter Michael Fischer and Heinz Mandl

Deutsches Institut für Fernstudien, FRG

Hypermedia as virtual media ⸻

Hypermedia are *virtual* media. The prefix "hyper" in hypermedia distinguishes this type of media from multimedia. The difference is based upon the depth and richness of the information contained. Hypermedia are also different from multimedia because the learner decides how much of this virtual richness he or she wants to use. Thus the effectiveness of hypermedia depends upon the accessibility of the given *hypermedium* as the source of information and the willingness and ability of the user to use the information in an efficient and meaningful manner based upon his/her prior knowledge and learning skills. Hypermedia as an information source is composed of *hypersource*, user interface, and the characteristics of the content.

Hypermedia are *virtual media* for the simple reason that their information value or outcome is the product of an interpretative act. Consequently we need a psychophysics of hypermedia which views the resulting interpretation as being dependent upon the *stimulus attributes* of the *hypersource* and the *responder attributes* of the *user*. While the former are determined by the domain and media characteristics, the latter are determined by the characteristics of the hypermedia setting and task. Such *psychophysics of hypermedia* can be illustrated by a tetrahedral model of the interrelationships and interactions of the relevant variables involved (Fig. 1). Hypermedia are not only fuzzy concepts from an epistemological point of view, but they also include fuzzy entities (for instance, do we include the user as a hypermedia entity?). Thus, hypermedia per se have the status of *platonic ideas*. As such they are idealistic entities. They come into existence only if their users perceive them; they exist through the users' interpretative acts. In other words hypermedia without users are as dead as print media without readers or movies without viewers. Without such an interpretation they are simply galleries of wisdom without visitors.

A model of hypermedia interactions ⸻

The model of hypermedia interactions (illustrated in Fig. 1) includes the *user* or *learner*, *tasks*, *goals*, *intentions* and *motives* or *purposes* applicable in hypermedia use, the domain in question and the materials used, including the intellectual and/or learning activities involved.

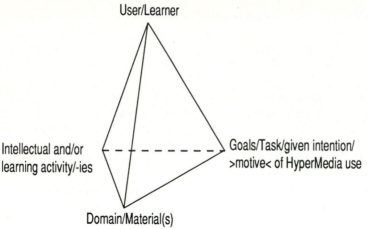

Fig. 1

The tetrahedral model of possible influences on the hypermedia can be viewed from different planes (Figures 2 to 5), illustrating the possible perspectives of hypermedia. We used the tetrahedral model intentionally in order to show that none of the four views or planes provide a holistic, unreduced picture.

User characteristics include intellectual abilities, learning skills, metacognitive abilities, motivation, plans, intentions and objectives. Users may also differ as to computer literacy in general or hypermedia literacy specifically.

Goal or *task characteristics* are typically imposed by an external agent; however, they may be imposed by the user himself. Goals or tasks may originate internally (e.g. the user decides to collect more information on specific topics which interest him) or they may be determined externally (e.g. following the instructions of a teacher). These tasks and goals may comprise information extraction (simply collecting new facts) or they may be aimed at comprehension/understanding and/or acquisition of new skills and knowledge. Their purpose may also be the direct application of this newly acquired knowledge and skill including knowledge transfer to other areas.

The domain and the materials used may vary as in format (textual or pictorial), domain characteristics (e.g. abstractness vs. concreteness), topic complexity and topical hierarchical structure. The structure of the materials affects accessibility to the user. The user employs them as a tool with which he/she extracts the needed information from the hypermedium. However, intellectual activities vary depending upon how the user interfaces with the hypermedium. Users may employ creative ideas, structural experiences, or new insights. Intellectual activities are *learning activities* if the user behaves as an intentional learner.

Possible interactions

User x goal x domain interactions

The user's prior knowledge of the content domain determines his/her interest and motivation to browse through the hypermedium when no explicitly defined tasks or external instructions are involved . If we do not conceive the user as an unintentional idler who simply uses the hypermedium for entertainment purposes, then he or she is an active, goal-directed agent. The user's goals or intentions add partial structure to the hypermedium by overlaying expectations onto the hypermedium and its data, a structure which guides the user's browsing. This imposed structure on the hypermedium by the user is only one part of the final structure. Further structure is added by the domain in question, i.e. the knowledge domain as it was intended to appear in this hypermedium by the original authors, contributors, and designers. It would be misleading to think of hypermedia as being nothing more than an information source or multi-media database. Several sources contribute to the final structure of hypermedia. At least one part of the structure inherent in a hypermedium should resemble the structure of its original content, i.e. resemble the structure of the sub-sources which contributed to the hypermedium. On a textual level this structure could be conceived as a network of interconnected micro- or macropropositions which once again could be mapped as an interconnected, associative network of nodes and linkages. To some degree this particular structure resembles the theoretical organization of the world. This structure is modified by the *characteristics* of the media which carry the information (e.g. print with more or less formatted text, graphs with a given structure, animated video). At present we do not possess sufficient knowledge about the structural relations between the different informational sources that constitute a hypermedium. Is the whole more than the sum of its parts?

Figure 2 illustrates the possible interactions between the user, goal and domain characteristics. The structure and meaning given to hypermedia is dependent upon the interplay between user/learner, domain and goal characteristics.

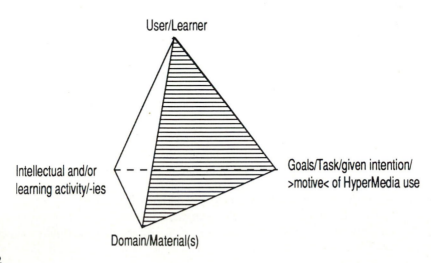

Fig. 2

Interactions of user x goal x intellectual activities

Curiosity or the need for intellectual stimulation may be sufficient to motivate the user to browse through a hypermedia knowledge base, but rarely are they the aim itself. Most of the time, at least for adults, a need to satisfy some goal or external task drives the access. Figure 3 shows the extrapolation of a *learner x intellectual activities x goal interaction.*

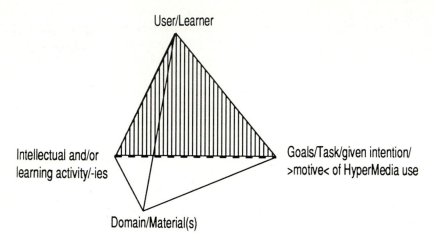

Fig. 3

With respect to the information processing in hypermedia, the user's intellectual activities function as a kind of filter: The user has certain beliefs and expectations about hypermedia itself and their application and benefits. Users' approaches to hypermedia will vary with their beliefs. Since users also have different interests, motivations and needs their use of a given hypermedium will depend upon their current situation and their corresponding goal-structure. Finally, users' prior knowledge and metacognitive skills vary. As we have argued, the *perceived structure* of a hypermedium relies on the structure added by the user.

A psychophysics of hypermedia includes the (*objective*) structure of the hypertext source and the user's subsequent knowledge structure which results from an interaction of the hypermedia knowledge base and his/her prior knowledge and skills. The structure derive from a given hypermedium can only be as sophisticated as the user's prior knowledge and intellectual skills and the constraints of the hypermedia structure and interface.

Interactions of user x domain x intellectual activities

Figure 4 shows that the structure a user projects onto the hypermedium is dependent upon the domain itself, the user's prior knowledge about that domain, the user's intellectual and/ or information processing skills, his/her motivation, and the task involved.

In addition to the user's prior declarative and procedural knowledge and his/her metacognitive ability to monitor and to control activities, the domain characteristics of the hypermedia affect the structure and accessibility of the hypermedia. Although the respective topics may contain some inherent *explicitness* and clarity which may or may not be utilized by the

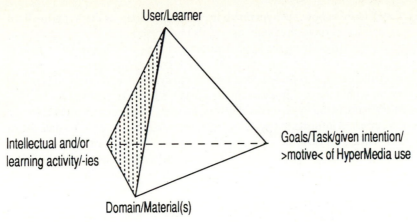

User/Learner

Intellectual and/or
learning activity/-ies

Goals/Task/given intention/
>motive< of HyperMedia use

Domain/Material(s)

Fig.4

user, they are still embedded within the hypermedium. As discussed previously, different
structural sources are responsible for different structural components of the complete
hypermedia structure. However, this objective structure is contained within the surface
structure of a given hypermedium and its underlying relational and associative structure. At
the same time there is also the subjective structure imposed by the user. While the objective
structure represents the virtual features of a hypermedium, the subjective structure consists
of those hypermedia features experienced by the user. This can be explained with an
analogy from psychophysics. In psychophysics we distinguish between an objective
stimulus or stimulus event and its *subjective* perception (the hypermedium as an 'abstract'
entity), as well as between inference or interpretation (the hypermedium as it is actually
perceived).

Interactions of intellectual activities x task x domain characteristics

Figure 5 shows that task characteristics, goal structure, domain and content may influence
the user's intellectual activities when interacting with a hypermedium, including the modality in which the contents are processed. Furthermore, the epistemological predilections of

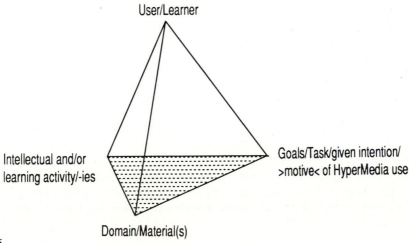

User/Learner

Intellectual and/or
learning activity/-ies

Goals/Task/given intention/
>motive< of HyperMedia use

Domain/Material(s)

Fig. 5

the user may also determine how the hypermedium is used. As long as the hypermedium does not serve an explicit purpose then only the user's understanding and willingness to extract meaningful information from the hypermedium and the *overtness* and *accessibility* of the hypermedium govern the nature of the resulting *hypermedia percept*.

As long as hypermedia use is self-guided, the user has to synthesize not only the content but also that content within the multimedia compound as well as that imposed by the computer which operates as the hypermedia delivery system. The user understands that he/she modifies this extracted information with his/her own perceptual filters. To date we do not have any have models for how the user accomplishes this. We are lacking the appropriate information extraction and information-processing models which could explain how users process information from hypersources.

Learning with hypersources

As long as hypermedia are not constrained by pedagogic means or as long as they are not specifically designed to operate as teaching/learning tools, we should try to discover how hypersources can facilitate learning. For example, is *incidental learning* an adequate paradigm? Can we support and advance such a concept as *discovery learning*? Is browsing equivalent to discovery learning? Can individuals process information in a trial and error manner? To find answers to these questions, we must develop a model of learning with hypermedia, i.e. find a learning modality that is capable of using unconstrained/unrestricted sources of information in a motivating, effective and economic way. Until we have a clearer picture about knowledge acquisition from hypermedia, we must include diagnostic assessment tools capable of recording the user's browsing trail. Analysis and systematization tools are needed to model such travels.

Hypermedia systems as explicit teaching/learning tools

If we intend to use a hypermedium as a deliberate teaching/learning tool, then the interactions become even more complex. If we consider the hypermedium to be *stand-alone*, i.e. as a system without a personal tutor, supervisor, advisor or teacher, then we must either place the responsibility on the learner or on the delivery system. In the first case, the user/learner's success in gaining information from the hypermedium depends mostly upon prior knowledge, learning and thinking skills, and the degree of usable organization within the hypermedium. If we cannot rely on the internal structure of hypermedia as the *deus benignus* that prevents the user from making mistakes, then we must develop a delivery system which is as *intelligent* as possible. Since the pedagogic use of hypermedia implies a goal structure or even a hierarchical arrangement of learning goals, we must make certain that these learning goals can be reached. In addition to the *domain/content/media x user x task interaction*, instructional hypermedia should contain a tutorial and/or pedagogical component which facilitates this interaction. In order to achieve these learning goals the hyper-teaching system must be able to diagnose the user's prior knowledge and possibly operational and meta-operational learning skills, current state of comprehension as well as the user's misconceptions about the respective learning criterion. Furthermore, the hyperteaching system must also be able to match an estimated learner or *student model* against an *expert model* and allocate the system's tutoring measures appropriately. Investigation and analysis of intelligent hypermedia must utilize the theories and concepts already available in information processing and artificial intelligence research.

The need for hypermedia research

Since the use of hypermedia is such a multifaceted endeavour, there is an urgent need to develop an adequate systematic framework for the extraction of information from hypermedia both in a free, unrestricted manner and in a systematic, guided way as is the case in learning from hypermedia. The same holds for purposeful use of hypermedia for specific tasks beyond learning. Future research should also include appropriate learner/user models on information processing of hypermedia. In addition to modeling the learners/users, we should model the use of hypermedia for different purposes. Only by a systematic variation of the possible uses of hypermedia can we gain insight and user data.

A lot of scientific research is needed. The tetrahedral model sketched above can assist in the systematic derivation of research questions related to hypermedia use. Our hypermedia research materials should be designed carefully. Without a clear picture of the stimulus we cannot hope to get a noise-free picture of user responses. With respect to navigational issues, our hypermedia and their user interfaces should accommodate Barbara Allen's (1985) five ET(*H*)IC commandments: The user should always be able to answer the following questions:

(1) Where am I ?
(2) How did I get here ?
(3) What can I do here ?
(4) Where can I go to ?
(5) How do I get there ?

We can get rid of noise in user data only if our materials help the user to answer these questions rationally. Then we can acquire naturalistic data on hypermedia use and users with which to model new hypermedia knowledge bases.

The contributions presented at this conference and in this book show that the initial results of our scientific research on hypermedia are promising. Gaps in our research agenda can be identified by systematic views such as the tetrahedral model. If puzzles are the motor of proliferative theorizing, then our first insights into the nature of hypermedia use are indeed quite promising.

PART 1

HYPERMEDIA
AND LEARNING

Chapter 1
Problems and Issues in Designing Hypertext/Hypermedia for Learning

David H. Jonassen and R. Scott Grabinger
University of Colorado, USA

Keywords

Hypertext; hypermedia; instructional design; human computer interaction; computer based instruction; knowledge representation

Contents

NATO ASI Series, Vol. F 67
Designing Hypermedia for Learning
Edited by D. H. Jonassen and H. Mandl
© Springer-Verlag Berlin Heidelberg 1990

Introduction ───────────

The growth in interest in hypertext and hypermedia (hereafter referred to by the more generic term, hypermedia) in recent years has been staggering. Hypermedia systems are being used extensively in software engineering and collaborative problem solving applications, for online documentation and information retrieval and help systems, as writing aids, and more recently as authoring tools for instruction and learning. Although hypermedia promises great potential for instruction, its efficacy is neither established nor without likely problems. Hypermedia learning systems will place more responsibility on the learner for accessing, sequencing and deriving meaning from the information. This added responsibility will entail added cognitive processing requirements on the learners. In many ways, this increased processing load appears consistent with constructive conceptions of learning and therefore desirable. Yet, it is not clear whether users will be able to assume this additional responsibility and processing load. The issues that this Advanced Research Workshop considered were how the hypermedia information and environment should be organized and displayed and how the information processing requirements specific to learning outcomes can be facilitated by hypermedia.

The primary purpose of this introduction to the book is to provide an overview for the remaining sections and chapters.

DJ explanation 1.18

PK recommendation 7.3

In order to accomplish this, we shall begin by defining general characteristics of hypermedia and our assumptions about learning that can be effected by hypermedia. Each of the chapters should also define hypermedia from their perspective, as well as defining their assumptions about learning that may be facilitated by hypermedia. Another of the important aims of this introduction to the book is to enumerate the problems in using and designing hypermedia for learning. Problems in designing hypermedia for learning cluster in five general areas: designing the information model, designing the user interface, designing the intellectual interface, the design process that should be used, and hypermedia delivery system requirements. The enumeration of these problems provides a context for the principles and guidelines for designing hypermedia systems for learning should emerge in each part of the book and each chapter. The primary purpose of this Advanced Research Workshop was to discuss and develop possible solutions to problems in designing hypermedia for learning.

Characteristics of Hypermedia ⎯⎯⎯⎯

We will begin by defining generalized characteristics of hypermedia. Not every hypermedia knowledge base or system possesses every characteristic. Each chapter will define hypermedia in terms of its most important characteristics.

WVparallel 22

Nodes
Probably the most pervasive characteristic of hypermedia is the node, which consists of chunks or fragments of text, graphics, video or other information. Nodes may also be conceived as learner tranactions. The size of a node (granularity) varies from a single picture or a few words to the size of a large document. Nodes, also referred to as frames, are the basic unit of information storage. Russell describes them as resources (packets of computation). Rather than encountering a continuous flow of information, such as a book or a motion picture film, hypermedia places information into nodes that are interrelated to each other in some way. Modularizing information enables the user of the information system to determine what node of information to access next. It may be a node that consists of an elaboration, an opposing point of view, or an example or illustration of the information in the original node.

JL recommendation 6.17

DJ definition 6.3 See granularity, DJ exp 6.4-5

PK parallel 7.3, DJ example 5.7

The most popular metaphor for nodes are note-cards, which

typically limits the amount of information in a node to a single screen. Perhaps the most important characteristic of nodes (in some systems) is that they may be amended or modified by the user. The user may add to or change the information in a node or create his or her own node of information for the hypermedia knowledgebase. Many *browsing systems*, however, provide a set of predetermined nodes that may not be amended. Nodes may be unalterable, because they reflect the information processing requirements of a task as defined by the goal of the system.

DJ methodology 6.5

Links

The interrelationships between nodes of information are defined by links, the interconnections between the nodes. Links in hypermedia systems are typically associative, that is, they define an associative relationship between the node pairs that they connect. The links transport the user through the information space to the nodes that he or she selects. Links enable the user to navigate through the hypermedia knowledge base. Links also provide organizational information, typically stating explicitly the nature of the relationship between the interconnected nodes. Linked transfers are activated by a pointing device (eg. mouse, keystroke, light pen, finger on a touchscreen) being directed at a *hot button* on the screen. Many hypermedia systems permit the user to either amend the existing links or to create new ones.

DJ explanation 11.2

DJ recommendation 10.13, 11.8-9

Links may be embedded in the text or picture, so that simply pointing at a word or part of a picture will transport the user to another node or location within a node. Links may be placed in a dedicated screen area outside the information space . Links may be referential or or organizational [1]. Referential links refer to information in another node and then permit the user to return via the same link. Organizational links are typically organized in a network of related nodes. Links may also be value, text, or lexical links [2]. Value links point from one node to another. Text links connect text to nodes. Lexical links connect regions of text to nodes.

DJ definition 7.10

Network of ideas: Organizational structure

Nodes are linked together in meaningful ways. The node structure and the link structure form a network of ideas. A network is an interrelated and interconnected group or system of ideas. The ideas in a hypermedia network are the nodes which are interconnected by the links. Nodes may be linked together based upon semantic relationships in the subject

DJ methodology 7.12

matter or the information processing required by a task. The network may also emanate from the user, who imposes his or her own structure on the information.

The organizational structure of any hypermedia system determines the information model of the hypermedia knowledge base. The information model describes the organization of ideas and their interrelationships which, if explicitly signalled, may help the user comprehend better the information or problem that is embedded in the system. The information model also facilitates the location and retrieval of information in the system. Once again, the information model may be amended by the user, in which case it reflects (to some extent) the semantic network of the user.

DJ parallel 3.8

Database
Many consider hypermedia only a glorified database of information that facilitates searching and accessing information in an associative manner. The organizational structure of many hypermedia knowledge bases does, in fact, resemble a database. Some hypermedia systems even store nodes of information in a database. Links become coded search strategies. Hypermedia differs from databases in the associative information structure and the dynamic control provided to users. The data structure and query capabilities of databases are more constrained than those in hypermedia.

DJ implication 12.4

PK contrast 7.4

Interactivity: Dynamic control
Hypermedia permits the user to determine the sequence in which to acess information (browsing), to add or amend the information in order to make it more personally meaningful (collaboration), or to build and structure their own knowledge base. The level of user control varies with the system and its purpose. What is important is that the user is meaningfully interacting with and dynamically controling the information. They can accelerate/decelerate, change directions, expand their information horizons, argue/fight back, or even switch intellectual vehicles. Unlike most information systems, hypermedia users *must* be mentally active while interacting with the information. Interaction is a hallmark of most information systems. Hypermedia permits a higher level of dynamic user control.

DJ corroboration 3.2

Paths
Paths may be determined by the author, the user/learner, or by shared responsibility. Author generated paths refer to predetermined links within the informaton space, "guided tours"

JL example17.15, 21.5, 23.19

PK comment The logic that the learner uses to traverse 'logic' suggests a rather rational component in the readers mental process. I would prefer to say that the paths reflect a 'pre-attentive' preference due to a variety of associations.

through the knowledge base. Users who do not wish to determine the sequence of access to information frequently traverse systems in this linear manner. Users or learners may also create their own paths. These paths are typically individualized reflections of the logic that a learner uses to traverse the knowledge base. Some systems enable the user to save these paths for later review and annotation. Users and learners also may share these paths in collaborative systems or add their paths to the knowledge base.

PD contrast 8.2

Annotation and collaboration

Many hypermedia systems permit simultaneous access to the information in the knowledge base by several users through a distributed network of computers.   Users in stand-alone and distributed systems are usually provided editing capabilities for annotating or ammending the information in the knowledge base. Large hypermedia systems often require multiple, collaborative authorship because of the size of the corpus of information. While this characteristic implies dynamic control, it also implies a level of collaboration not typically available in other, individually oriented information systems.

PK comment 'Collaborative' suggests 'working together against something or someone'. 'Cooperative' authorship reflects the superordinate character of its goal.

Authoring environment

Hypermedia systems are typically flexible and adaptive tools for authoring and browsing. Some hypermedia systems have become popular and commonly used authoring environments for creating computer based instruction, personal notetaking or information management, communications with peers, or as cognitive learning tools for organizing and storing their own knowledge. Many of these applications do not exhibit other characteristics of hypermedia. They are nonetheless important and useful information applications. Therefore, the broadest conception of hypermedia is a software environment for building or conveying knowledge, collaborating, or problem solving.

DJ parallel 3.18

Hypermedia and learning _____

There are many conceptions of learning, far too many to review in this introduction. Descriptive theories of learning include cognitive/information processing, behavioral, cybernetic, and others. For the purpose of designing instructional systems, learning is thought of in terms of tasks or learning outcomes, such as Gagne [3], Bloom and his colleagues [4], and Merrill [5]. When designing hypermedia for learning, three learning processes seem to be best supported by hypermedia — information seeking, knowledge acquisition, and problem solving.

Information seeking

An important step in any learning process is satisfying information needs — seeking information that answers a question, makes a decision, solves a problem, or helps to comprehend. Information about any domain of knowledge is stored in a variety of forms in many places and is organized in different ways. When seeking information, what most people are concerned about is accuracy, understandability, and access time [6]. Information is a fundamental learning activity, precursive to many others.

PK definition 12.2

The distinct advantage of hypermedia for information seeking is its ability to integrate large corpi of information in alternative representations. Access to the information is facilitated by the associative organization of the information in hypermedia, which may resemble the associative structure of human memory. Hypermedia is capable of providing different organizational structures for libraries of information, thereby providing access to information in ways that more closely resemble the information seeking behaviors and needs of users.

Knowledge acquisition

Conceptually, learning is the reorganization of knowledge structures. Knowledge structures refer to the organization of ideas in semantic memory. Ideas are referred to as "schema." A schema for an object, event, or idea is comprised of a set of attributes. Attributes are the associations that an individual forms around an idea. These schema are arranged in a network of interrelated concepts known as our semantic network. Schemata in our semantic network are linked together by attributes or associations. These interconnections enable learners to combine ideas, infer, extrapolate or otherwise reason from them. Structured networks, like hypermedia, are composed of nodes and ordered, labelled relationships (links) connecting them . These networks describe what a learner knows, which provides the foundations for learning new ideas, that is, expanding the learner's semantic network. This is the richest conceptual model of learning from hypermedia. Learning, then results from the interactive processes of accretion, restructuring and tuning [7].

SH background 23.8

Accretion. Accretion describes the accumulation of information in order to fill existing schemas. The learner adds information (arguments or attributes) to the knowledge structure that exists.

DJ explanation 6.10-11

Restructuring. As knowledge is acquired, the learner's schemas expand to a point where they are unable to adequately accommodate or interrelate all of the information. The learner begins to restructure his or her knowledge by adding schemas or developing new conceptualizations for existing ones. The results of restructuring are new knowledge structures, which enable the learner to interpret or access their knowledge in new ways. The ideas are rearranged sufficiently to provide new meanings to ideas.

Tuning. After all of the schemas have been developed and reorganized by the learner into a coherent knowledge base, minor adaptations are made in order to make performance more efficient. Through practice or consistent use of new knowledge structures, they are tuned or finely adjusted. Schemas are modified to meet specific task demands or adapted to particular knowledge domains or contexts. Tuning might entail the refining of a procedure, filling-in of inferences, or adapting the schemas to new situations.

Learning vis-a-vis hypermedia is a process of accretion, restructuring, and tuning. Hypermedia is the ultimate accretion medium, a knowledge base of interrelated ideas that can be readability accessed and assimilated. Restructuring is permitted by the dynamic control capabilities of creating and reorganizing links in the system. Tuning is provided by the authoring and collaborative characteristics of hypermedia.

Problem solving

From an information processing perspective, problem solving starts with a problem, which includes a goal state, a starting state, and solution paths to reaching the goal, all of which constitute the problem space [8]. Problem solving assumes an unsatisfied goal state. When the starting state and goal state are consonant, no problem exists. Problem solving entails three processes — problem representation, knowledge transfer, and evaluation [9].

Problem representation. Regardless of the nature of the problem space, the problem solver first must represent the problem in a meaningful way. This requires accessing enough relevant schemata to make sense out of the problem. The problem must be stated in terms that the solver understands. This stage is the most important to the problem solving process, because it determines what knowledge will be activated by the solver. One of the strengths of hypermedia is its ability to alternatively represent the problem. Problem solving applications such as IBIS represent information in the system in constrained nodes, such as issue, position, and argument nodes [10].

SH example 23.15

Transfer. The problem representation, be it a formal statement such as a formula or an informal description of the problem, activates relevant knowledge. This knowledge is then applied to the problem as possible solutions. Problem solvers typically apply some strategy to the solution of a problem, such as means-ends analysis, brainstorming or analogical reasoning. Hypermedia may facilitate the transfer process by providing alternative representations of information, such as analogical links. The collaborative nature of many hypermedia environments facilitate brainstorming and means-ends activities.

Evaluation. The problem solver evaluates a solution by whether it produces the goal state with a reasonable amount of effort in a reasonable amount of time. Solutions that do not meet minimal criteria reactivate the knowledge retrieval process in search of alternative solutions. Collaborative environments can facilitate this process.

Designing the information model ⎯⎯⎯⎯

The major issue in designing the information model is how structured the information in the hypermedia knowledge base should be and, assuming some structure is desirable, then what type of structure is most appropriate for the application, and how should that structure be imposed on the information? This section of the book will address these questions.

DJ parallel 3.8

Getting started
Starting a linearly structured paper is difficult for most people. Organizing your thoughts, developing an outline for the paper, and collecting your ideas is difficult. It can be an even greater problem if there is no apparent structure to the information; or, even more difficult, if you must transcend the basic structure of the content to permit hypermedia applications.

The following questions related to getting started need answers.

How do you identify the kind of information to be included in the hypermedia system (excluding Xanadu, which seeks to include everything)?

How should the separate pieces of information (e.g., cards, frames, screens, nodes) be identified and separated?

How should the information be sequenced?

Structuring the information

WV, SH contrast 3.8, PD implication 8.7

The most significant problem in creating hypermedia is deciding how to structure the information. The answer to this question depends, in part, upon how the hypermedia will be used. The various applications of hypermedia require different access and information structures. Several approaches include:

DJ methodology 6.14-16

- *Semantic structures* reflect the knowledge structure of the author or an expert.
- *Conceptual structures* include pre-determined content relationships such as taxonomies.
- *Task-related structures* are those that resemble or facilitate the completion of a task. Primary tasks include retrieving information, such as in information retrieval

DJ methodology 7.10-14

  systems, and learning from instructional systems.
- *Knowledge-related structures* are those that are based upon the knowledge structures of the expert or the learner.
- *Problem-related structures* simulate problems or decision making.

The following questions related to structuring the information need answers.

How can we identify and represent the knowledge structure necessary to achieve the purpose for which the hypermedia is designed?

What type of structures are most appropriate for what types of tasks?

How do we assess learning from hypermedia?

How do you assess structural knowledge? Structural knowledge is the knowledge of the interrelationships between ideas, how they are linked or associated.

What methods are available for developing a task-related or conceptual structures?

Unstructured hypermedia

Unstructured hypermedia is random, node-link hypermedia in which only referential links are used. This type of hypermedia provides random access directly from any node to any other node that is linked to it. Two nodes are linked because one node contains a reference to the information in the other. The user jumps immediately to any topics within the hypermedia by pointing at the item.

The major task in designing an unstructured hypermedia system is to identify the concepts or information fragments that will point to and comprise each node. This may be accomplished by analyzing textbooks (especially the table of contents and index) for important terms or ideas and the co-occurrence of the ideas in other nodes. Whenever ideas co-occur, develop an associative link to connect the ideas. No overall conceptual structure is implied necessarily by this type of hypermedia.

DJ parallel 3.8

The following questions related to unstructured hypermedia need answers.

> What are the effects of unstructured browsing on achieving the purpose for the browsing?
> For what kinds of learners is an unstructured design most suitable?
> What kinds of learner control techniques are most appropriate for unstructured hypermedia systems?
> What kinds of purposes are best served with an unstructured hypermedia system?
> What types of list structures are most appropriate — referential or structured?
> How do we identify the concepts or nodes to be included in such a hypermedia?

Structured hypermedia

Structured hypermedia implies an explicit organization or arrangement of nodes and associative links. In designing structured hypermedia, the designer is saying that there is a subject matter structure or a knowledge structure that ought to be conveyed in the links between the nodes. Structured hypermedia consists of sets of nodes, each set accessible from any other set. Each set is explicitly arranged to depict the structure of the information. Hypermedia structures assume various conceptual models.

PK contrast 8.6

SH example 23.15

From the study of reading and rhetoric, several possible structures for organizing hypermedia emerge:
- •Problem-solution
- •Chronological, sequential
- •Parts-whole
- •Cause-effect, antecedent-consequent, and many others.

The following questions related to structured hypermedia need answers.

Are multiple structures possible within the same knowledge base? desirable?

Can learners accomodate multiple structures within the same knowledge base?

What kinds of learner control techniques are most appropriate for structured hypermedia systems?

What kinds of purposes are best served with a structured hypermedia system?

How explicitly should the structure be signalled?

What types of structures are most effectively used in hypermedia?

Hierarchical hypermedia

Hierarchical hypermedia represents a highly structured design. The arrangement of content within the hypermedia is hierarchical, with more detailed concepts (and the text and iconics describing them) subsumed under more general concepts. That is, general concepts are broken down into more detailed concepts which are instantiated by individual events or objects in hypermedia.

Certain content (especially in the sciences) are frequently represented by a hierarchy. Hierarchical hypermedia should model the hierarchy, requiring users to move up and down through the hierarchy in order to access related concepts (e.g. plant kingdom). The individual blocks or screens prompt various pre-defined hierarchical relationships (superordinate/subordinate). For example, each concept or information block would consist of screens showing the key terms, synonym (for lateral movement), definitions, broader terms (information blocks on the next block up the hierarchy), narrower terms (more detailed down a level on the hierarchy), and any other related information (e.g. analogies, descriptions of links between various screens, etc.). Users would move up and down the hierarchy in order to explore subordinate and superordinate relationships.

The following questions related to structured hypermedia
need answers.

> Is learner control more important for hierarchical
>   systems?
> What content or tasks are best structured hierarchi-
>   cally?
> What kinds of learners benefit most from hierarchical
>   systems?
> Will hypermedia constrain the users too much?

Designing the user interface ─────────

Navigating through hypermedia

The most commonly identified user problem is *navigating
through hypermedia*. Many hypermedia systems consist of
hundreds and even thousands of nodes with a potentially
confusing array of links connecting them. It is well documented that in such systems, users can easily become lost, not
knowing where they came from, where they should go, or
even how to exit the part of the program they are in. Users are
frustrated by this experience, frequently losing sight of their
original purpose in using the hypermedia. Often, they give up
without acquiring any information from the hypermedia. User
interface solutions will be addressed in this section of the
book

WV contrast 3.10

RK contrast 2.9
JL contrast 3.10, 13.10, 13.19,
parallel 13.7

The following questions related to navigation need answers.

> How do users navigate, unaided, through unstructured
>   hypermedia systems?
> What individual differences will predict the paths they
>   choose to follow?
> How much navigational guidance should the users re-
>   ceive?
> What form of structural cues are most effective in
>   aiding navigation?
> How structured should the hypermedia be?
> How should this structure be represented?
> How important is knowing the "purpose" in helping
>   the hypermedia user?

How much learner control?

Learner control is an instructional strategy that permits the
learner to direct the sequence of instruction, that is, too make
decisions about the type and amount of instructional support

1.14

JL definition 1.13, corroboration
15.3, background 16.12

that he/she thinks is necessary. Rather than the instruction
directing the learner, the learner is allowed to adapt the instruction to personal preferences or abiltities. Learner control
is justified by the beliefs that learners knows what is best for
them and that if learners are in control of instruction, they will
invest more mental effort in their learning. Hypermedia use
is premised on learner control.

Unfortunately, the research on learner control has not generaly
supported any learning benefits. This is especially true with
average and below-average learners. Research has shown
consistently that learners, when given control over instructional variables, do not make the best decisions. Those who
need the most instructional support (underachievers) frequently select the least, and those who need the least (over-
achievers) frequently select the most. Learners in learner
control treatments have regularly learned less than those in
treatments controlled by the the instructor or by an adaptive
instructional design. When compared with teacher-directed or
computer-programmed decision making, learner control has
generally yielded less learning. Since hypermedia use de-

WV contrast 3.4, 13.11
JL corroboration 19.2

pends extensively on learner control, its potential for learning
is questionable.

The following questions related to learner control need answers.

What kinds of learner control are essential for hypermedia use?

How can an instructional hypermedia system discriminate between learners who benefit from learner control
and those who do not benefit?

Who or what decides how much learner control should
be provided to the learner?

What kinds of learner control devices and techniques
are most successful?

Searching for information

Many implementations of hypermedia provide the user with
the capability of searching through the document to find nodes
that contain specific information. This is usually accomplished by doing a "string search", that is, searching for a
string of characters through the entire document. This is a
slow and inefficient method of searching, especially if the
hypermedia knowledge baseis very large. Also, if the
knowledgebase is contained in several files, the search may
not extend to those other files so important information would

not be accessed. String searches are useful however. When the user is not familiar with the structure of the document or is not adept at navigation, they can go directly to needed information.

The following questions related to searching and finding information need answers.

> What information processing processes are required to search for information? Is there a way to measure it? How can a "train of thought" be maintained through several "irrelevant hits?"
> What structural devices, besides indexes, support searching/finding?

Structured searching

Since string searching a document is inefficient and often ineffective, some researchers are working on the capability of providing structured searches. Structured searches would look for strings but only in a specified pattern of nodes and only if certain information conditions are met. For instance, a structured search for the term "index" might look for the term only in nodes related to designing the information model. In order to develop algorithms to do this kind of searching, the system would have to have a "virtual structure". Since no systems have such a structure as yet, sophisticated structured searches are not yet possible but should be soon.

The following questions related to structured searching need answers.

> What system can be used to create structured searches? Expert systems?
> What types of organizational components should be used to structure the search? Should they be content cues or functional markers?

Designing the learning interface ⸻

The user interface acts like a navigational filter that either clarifies and facilitates the use of the system or acts as an impediment, preventing effective use of the system. Hypermedia that is designed to facilitate learning outcomes has another set of design problems — how to facilitate the information processing requirements that are specific to learning outcomes. What type of processing aids can help the learner seek information, acquire knowledge and solve problems, for instance. The intellectual problems of using hypermedia for learning, such as cognitive overhead, integration, and synthesis of information, will be addressed in this section of the book.

Where does the user begin?

When hypermedia is less structured with no obvious beginning or when no guided tours are available, users may be perplexed about where to begin accessing information from the hypermedia.

The following questions related to entering hypermedia need answers.

> At what node do users enter the hypermedia?
> Who determines the starting node — user or hypermedia?
> How do users know what they need to know and how to find it?
> How will the access point affect user understanding?
> What sorts of access structures are needed to guide the user?
> How overt do these access-aids need to be?

PK results 12.9

Integrating information

A problem related to navigation and equally important is integration of new knowledge by the learners into their own cognitive structures. Learning is the creation or reorganization of the learners' knowledge structures. Learning entails the acquisition of information and the re-organization or re-structuring of that information to make it more meaningful. The less structured the hypermedia is, the less likely users are to integrate what they have learned into their own knowledge structures, because the hypermedia facilitates only the acquisition part of learning.

SH parallel 23.10

If hypermedia can be structured to replicate content or knowledge structures, then it should provide the necessary anchors for re-structuring the learner's knowledge. What is not known is how likely users are to assimilate these structures or to use them to integrate what they have learned. The attempt to replicate effective stimuli (users' knowledge structures) with the nominal stimulus (e.g., written word, page, or screen) has met with little success. This is primarily due to the fact that no picture of the effective stimulus is available to replicate. The effective stimulus is also in a constant state of change both within an individual and among individuals.

The following questions related to integrating information need answers.

> What kinds of aids do hypermedia users need to integrate the hypermedia into their own cognitive structures?
>
> Do these aids need to be covert or overt?
>
> Do users' navigation within the hypermedia reflect their own cognitive structure?
>
> Are there techniques that we can use to map the users' cognitive structures?
>
> What effect does prior knowledge have on the nodes selected within the hypermedia?

PK methodology 7.3

Synthesizing information

Learning requires another process in addition to the processes of acquisition and integration — *synthesis* of the information into smooth and automated behavior. Synthesis is similar to the cognitive process of *tuning* in Norman's model of learning (accretion, restructuring, and tuning). Once a learner has acquired information and integrated it into his/her knowledge structure, a new structure evolves. The learner fine-tunes the new knowledge structure by practicing with it and generalizing it to novel situations. As with integration, unstructured, node-link hypermedia would not facilitate the process of synthesis.

The following questions related to synthesizing information need answers.

> How can hypermedia be structured to facilitate synthesis of a new knowledge structure?
>
> What kinds of overt hypermedia design features will facilitate synthesis?
>
> What kinds of covert hypermedia design features will facilitate synthesis?
>
> Do practice and transfer activities need to be included in the hypermedia to facilitate tuning?
>
> If tuning activities are included in the hypermedia, how can the learner be encouraged to use them?

1.18

JL corroboration 13.16, 23.4,
example 6.16, background 13.11,
recommendation 23.11

Cognitive overhead

The number of learning options available to learners places increased cognitive demands upon the learners that they are often unable to fulfill. Hypermedia browsers must be able to monitor their own comprehension of the information presented in the hypermedia, select appropriate strategies for correcting any misconceptions, and develop information seeking strategies that facilitate integrating information and synthesizing information from the hypermedia. These are known as meta-cognitive strategies, and they require additional effort on the part of the browser. We know that good learners use them and that poor learners do not. "The richness of non-linear representation carries a risk of potential intellectual indigestion, loss of goal-directness, and cognitive entropy" [11]. Browsing hypermedia places significant demands upon the user, demands that may take energy from the more important process of learning.

The following questions related to cognitive overhead need answers.

> What devices and techniques can be used to reduce cognitive overhead?
> Should strategies be suggested directly to the learner?
> Would a "library of strategies" be an effective part of the hypermedia?
> Should testing opportunities be provided so users may check their progress and understanding?
> Will the additional cognitive load imposed by hypermedia lead to the intellectual and information rich getting richer and the information poor getting poorer?

Hypermedia learning strategies

Since hypermedia is a new information source, users have not developed skills in navigating, integrating information, and so on. Most novice browsers report discomfort. Many browsers are afraid and don't want to commit the effort or they select the default, linear route through the knowledge base. The most frequently selected button is typically "Next Screen". This is partially because users do not have a schema for using hypermedia, that is, they are not used to the information processing requirements of hypermedia. It is novel form of study.

If large amounts of our reading in the future will be by unguided and unconstrained electronic text, new strategies (a
hypermedia literacy) will be needed. Use with college students has shown that they soon adapt. Sophisticated browsers
develop strategies for searching, comparing information, and
solving problems. Effective browsers need to develop hypermedia processing strategies in order to effectively use hypermedia. Users vary in the extent to which they develop these
habits. Effective users develop hyper-thinking strategies.

The following questions related to user strategies need answers.

> What are hypermedia strategies? What replicable
> skills do hypermedia users need?
> Can a simple, logical taxonomy of hypermedia strate-
> gies be created?
> How easily can these strategies be taught? How much
> experience is needed in order to stabilize these strate-
> gies?
> Can a hypermedia system be so well structured and
> presented as to eliminate the need for any instruction
> in its use?
> Is there a "type" of student who can be identified who
> more easily learns (or already possesses) the hyperme-
> dia strategies?
> Will hypermedia processing strategies become the in-
> formation literacy of the 1990's?

Hypermedia design process

Designing hypermedia is not like designing other forms of
computer based instruction. Hypermedia is structured differently. The roles of the developers differ. Users interact with it
differently. This section of the book will be concerned with
the hypermedia design process. There are at least three
general approaches to structuring and developing hypermedia
— deductive and inductive and instructional systems development.

Deductively developed hypermedia

A deductive or top-down approach to designing the information model and other components of hypermedia requires
starting with a content structure or expert's knowledge structure. Many subject matter domains have well prescribed
content structures, so that the arrangement of ideas in the

content domains dermines the structure. If we assume that learning is the process of replicating the expert's knowledge structure in the learner's knowledge structure, then learning should be facilitated by hypermedia that replicates the expert's knowledge structure in the structure of the hypermedia and that explicitly conveys that structure.

The following questions related to deductively design hypermedia need answers.

> How do we define that ideal knowledge structure?
> What is the relationship between an expert's knowledge structure and a new learner's structure?
> Can a learner comprehend an expert's knowledge structure?
> Can the expert's knowledge structure be mapped directly or indirectly onto the learner's?
> How can the structure be represented?

Inductively developed hypermedia

Another approach to designing hypermedia is to observe how users navigate through unstructured hypermedia. How do they assimilate information from hypermedia? Are there patterns of access? Do those patterns relate to individual differences that may be used as predictor variables for designing hypermedia? Then hypermedia structures must be designed to support the verified patterns of access and use. This method is a bottom-up or inductive approach to hypermedia design.

The following questions related to inductively designing hypermedia need answers.

> How do users assimilate information from hypermedia?
> Do users exhibit distinctly different patterns of access?
> Do those patterns relate to individual differences that may be used as predictor variables?
> Do the paths created by the users reflect a specific type of learner?

Instructional systems development

The instructional systems development (ISD) process is a systematic process for designing and producing instructional materials. This process may be useful in designing hypermedia and typically includes:

Needs Assessment. The first step in the ISD process is to determine what it is that students need to be able to do when they have completed the instructional unit. This is expressed as a need or goal through an informal or formal analysis of needs.

Task Analysis. Task analysis inventories and selects tasks for development, describes in detail and sequences sub-tasks, and classifies the learning outcomes of each. The need is analyzed to identify the subordinate skills or procedural steps that must be learned for the student to achieve a specific objective. The results of the analysis are used to write performance objectives, specific statements of what it is the learners will do when they complete the instructional sequence.

Test Item Construction. Assessment items that parallel the objectives are developed. The items are designed to measure the learner's ability to meet the prescribed objectives. Test items must be as closely related to the desired performance as is practically possible.

Selection of Instructional Strategies. Information from the preceding steps is used to identify a set of instructional activities that are used to meet the identified need. The strategy describes how information will be presented to the students, selects the types of examples and non-examples, specifies the types of practice activities students will use to practice and consolidate their learning.

Selection of Delivery System. Most instruction involves the presentation of information to the learner. Technology has made possible a wide variety of presentation formats, such as lecture, film, video, audiotape, computer, book, job aid, etc. The selection of the delivery system also has implications for strategy selection.

ISD and hypermedia. ISD is a fairly prescriptive approach to designing materials. Although many critics feel that ISD and hypermdia are inconsistent, they actually are mutually supportive. Because of the malleable structure of hypermedia, virtually any instructional design can be mapped onto the knowledge base. Hypermedia systems, such as IDE running under NoteCards, provides a rich and powerful instructional design environment. Because of the collaborative capabilities of many hypermedia systems, users become designers of instruction themselves, so that the gap between users and designers disappears.

DJ example 24.14-17

DR reference   DR, D. M., Moran, T., & Jordan, D. (1988). "The Instructional Design Environment" In J. Psotka, D. Massey Jr., & S. Mutter (Eds.), Intelligent Tutoring Systems: Lessons Learned. Hillsdale, NJ: Lawrence Erlbaum Associates Inc.

JL parallel 20.3, 22.9, 12.22

The following questions related to ISD and hypermedia design need answers.

> How useful is the ISD process for designing hypermedia?
>
> Is the ISD process too restrictive for a content oriented technology like hypermedia?
>
> Will user-generated design affect learning differently than ISD?

Hypermedia Delivery Systems ⎯⎯⎯⎯⎯

The final section of this introduction and of the book is concerned with designing computer systems for delivering hypermedia. What are the hardware requirements of hypermedia learning systems? What problems are encountered in a large distributed hypermedia system as opposed to stand-alone personal computer systems? Many researchers are examining the the problems in storing the information base, providing networked access, and display systems for visually complex hypermedia. Developers of online help and information retrieval hypermedia systems are impelled by reducing information access and screen rewriting time. Other developers concentrate on screen resoultion and producing large knowledge bases. How important these characteristics are to various learning outcomes is the crucial question. What are the system requirements for an integrated authoring and learning environment as opposed to a browsing-only system? The general issue that is addressed in this last section of the book is the necessary configuration for various hyperworlds?

The following questions related to hypermedia delivery systems need answers.

> How important are delivery characteristics like wait state, access time, screen resolution to learning from hypertext?
>
> How important is simulataneous access to knowledge bases in a distributed, collaborative hypermedia system?
>
> What are the physical and intellectual requirements for a hyperworld?
>
> What are the information management/file serving requirements for various hypermedia systems?

References ———————————————

[1] Conklin, J. (1987). Hypertext: An introduction and survey. *Computer*, *20*(9), 17-41.

[2] Collier, G.H. (1987). Thoth-II: Hypertext with explicit semantics. In *Proceedings of Hypertext '87 Conference*. Chapel Hill, NC: University of North Carolina, Computer Science Department.

[3] Gagne, R.M. (1985). *The conditions of learning*, 4th Ed. New York: Holt, Rinehart, & Winston.

[4] Bloom, B.S., Englehart, M.D., Furst, E.J., Hill, W.H., & Krathwohl, D.R. (1956). *Taxonomy of educational objectives: Hanbook I. The cognitive domain*. New York: Longman.

[5] Merrill, M.D. (1983). Component display theory. In C.M. Reigeluth (Ed.), *Instructional designing theoies and models: An overview of their current status*. Hillsdale, NJ: Lawrence Erlbaum Associates.

[6] Chen, C. (1982). *Information seeking: Assessing and anticipating user needs*. New Yor: Neal-Schuman.

[7] Rumelhart, D.E. & Norman, D.A. (1978). Accretion, tuning and restructuring: Three modes of learning. In J.W. Cotton & R. Klatzky (Eds.), *Semantic factors in cognition*. Hllsdale, NJ: Lwrence Erlbaum Associates.

[8] Newell, A. & Simon, H.A. (1972). *Human problem solving*. Englewood Cliffs, NJ: Prentice Hall.

[9] Gagne, E.D. (1985) *The cognitive psychology of school learning*. Boston: Little, Brown & Co.

[10] Conklin, J. & Begeman, M. (1987). IBIS: A hypertext tool for team design deliberation. In *Proceedings of Hypertext '87*. Chapel Hill, NC: University of North Carolina, Computer Science Department.

[11] Dede, C. (1988). *The role of hypertext in transforming information into knowledge*. Paper presented at the annual meeting of NECC, Dallas, Texas, June, 1988.

Chapter 2
Hypertext for Learning

John J. Leggett, John L. Schnase, Charles J. Kacmar
Department of Computer Science
Texas A&M University, USA

Keywords

Hypertext; hypermedia; learning; definitions; taxonomy

Contents

Introduction

Bush [1], Engelbart [2], and Nelson [3] were among the first
to propose systems that augment the human intellect by
managing information stored in what is now called hypertext.
These early proponents had a strong sense that the connections in hypertext were linked ideas, that associations could be
easily and arbitrarily forged, and that information could be
personalized, freely annotated, freely viewed, and readily
accessed. They proposed systems that offer a direct manipulation approach to information management and rely heavily on
the user's increased use of visual cues, spatial reasoning, and
associative thought. The revolutionary content of their ideas
was, and continues to be, the extent to which these systems
engage the user as an active participant in interactions with
information.

NATO ASI Series, Vol. F 67
Designing Hypermedia for Learning
Edited by D. H. Jonassen and H. Mandl
© Springer-Verlag Berlin Heidelberg 1990

Hypertext systems for the educational community have recently become technologically feasible. The widespread availability of personal computers, workstations and local area networking is making hypertext use at the university level possible. Hypertext systems built on these platforms are struggling to provide the vision of hypertext layed down by the pioneers. Existing systems provide minimal support for personalization, free annotation, and free viewing which are essential to providing a hypertext learning environment.

Research efforts on hypertext in education are now underway at several Universities [4,5,6]. The broader educational community has also embraced hypertext and hypertext systems for the delivery of educational media [7,8]. Although there is much activity, the literature is lacking in theoretical findings, empirical results, and practical experiences in using hypertext for learning.

In this paper, a conceptual model of hypertext and a taxonomy of hypertext systems is proposed that helps to identify the characteristics necessary for particular styles of hypertext presentation. Three case studies in the use of hypertext for learning at the university level are discussed. The main thesis of the paper is that a particular hypertext system, and more importantly the hypertext model it implements, defines the bounds of what can be learned through the medium. The thesis is supported through practical examples from the use of existing hypertext systems in a university curriculum. From these experiences, several conclusions are drawn and recommendations are given to designers of hypertext and hypertext systems for learning.

Conceptual Model and Definitions

In this section, a conceptual model of hypertext (Figure 1) and set of definitions for hypertext systems [9] is presented. The model and definitions provide a framework for conceptualizing hypertext architectures.

Components of Hypertext

There are four basic components of hypertext: information elements, abstractions, anchors, and links. Each instance of these components may be typed and named.

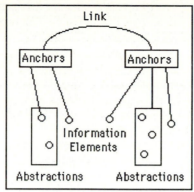

Figure 1. A conceptual model of hypertext.

Information element. Information elements are the objects created and manipulated by the user. These include such things as thoughts, diagrams, drawings, ideas, discussions, lesson plans, arguments, algorithms, etc. Their physical manifestations can be text, bit-mapped images, graphics, sound clips, animations, processes, etc.

DJ parallel 1.3

Abstraction. An abstraction is an object that allows information elements and other abstractions to be structured, grouped, or otherwise related. It may or may not be possible for users to manipulate abstractions directly. Some example abstractions from existing hypertext systems include: cards and fileboxes (NoteCards); frames and framesets (KMS); articles and encyclopedias (HyperTIES); and documents and journals (NLS/Augment). *@i*(Node) is a generic term for an abstraction.

PWr parallel 10.4

Anchor. Anchors designate information elements or abstractions that may be the source or destination of a link.

Link. A connector among anchors.

Basic Associations of Hypertext

In the simplest case, links may connect anchors that are attached to a single information element or abstraction. Four basic associations are thus possible as shown in Figure 2.

An example of an existing hypertext system in this model is given in Figure 3 for KMS.

Hypertext System Definitions

Hypertext model. A set of abstractions that provide a conceptual framework for creating, storing, and retrieving information in a hypertext.

DJ parallel 1.13

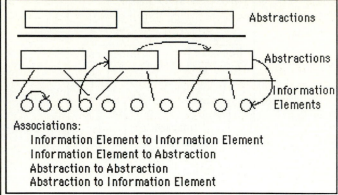

Figure 2. Basic associations in hypertext.

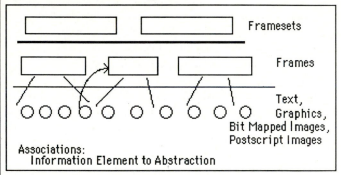

Figure 3. The possible associations supported by the KMS hypertext system presented in terms of the conceptual model.

Hypertext system. A functionally related set of computer hardware and software components that implement a hypertext model.

Author. A component of a hypertext system that creates hypertext.

Browser. A component of a hypertext system that retrieves information contained in hypertext.

Other Definitions

Trail. A path of associations through hypertext.

History. The trail created while browsing hypertext.

Overview. A graphical representation of hypertext.

Extensible. The ability to extend the functionality of a hypertext system through the use of a programming language.

Tailorable. The ability to customize a hypertext system by changing attributes of the system.

View. The components of a hypertext that are accessible. *A web.*

Filter. The process of generating a view.
Collateral display. The ability to display two or more disparate parts of the information space in parallel.

Taxonomy of Hypertext Systems ─────

An application-oriented taxonomy of hypertext systems is now provided to characterize existing and future systems. Any taxonomy of hypertext systems is somewhat arbitrary since a particular system can be used (or misused) for many purposes. The taxonomy presented here consists of the following five classes of hypertext systems: Literary, Structural, Presentational, Collaborative, and Explorative. Each class is described by giving its main characteristics and listing example applications and systems. Existing hypertext systems comprise only the first three classes. The latter two classes represent future hypertext system design and, as such, are not represented well by any existing system. The few existing hypertext systems having limited functionality of the Collaborative and Explorative classes are listed below. This taxonomy in no way indicates the "power" or appropriateness of a given hypertext system for a particular application.

Literary

 In the Literary class, links are relatively more important than nodes. That is, associations among information elements are very important while structuring of information elements is not as important. Links have a smaller granularity of referent, and these systems have information element to information element associations. Literary hypertext systems should allow free annotation. Example applications include reading, writing, publishing, critiquing, education, and scholarship. Example systems include Augment, Xanadu, and Intermedia.

Structural

In the Structural class, nodes are relatively more important than links. That is, associations among information elements are not as important as structuring of information elements. Links have a larger granularity of referent, and these systems do not have information element to information element associations. Structural hypertext systems have limited or no annotation capabilities. Example applications include information management and argumentation. Example systems include KMS, gIBIS, NoteCards, and HyperCard.

Presentational

The Presentational class has the same characteristics as the Structural class with the additional restriction of separate author and browser components. Example applications include information kiosks, reference material, and documentation. HyperTIES is an example of this class.

Collaborative

DJ example 18.4-6

In the Collaborative class, links and nodes are equally important. That is, both associations among information elements and structuring of information elements are important. Links have a small granularity of referent, and these systems have information element to information element associations. Collaborative hypertext systems allow free annotation, are distributed, and provide security. Example applications include software engineering environments and organizational information management. Example systems with limited Collaborative class functionality include DIF and Augment.

Explorative

The Explorative class has the same characteristics as the Collaborative class with the additional requirement of a spatial metaphor in the user interface. The concept of "space" allows the display screen to be used like a painter's canvas for recording and manipulating information elements and abstractions. Example applications include early activities of writing and thinking, and problem formulation and exploration. Example systems with limited Explorative class functionality include Intermedia and KMS.

Case Studies ————————————————

This section presents experiential evaluations of student learning from hypertext based upon responses from student questionnaires (see [10] for details). Three levels of university students interacted with different hypertexts in order to study information presented at various levels of complexity. Group one consisted of undergraduate Sophomores learning a very low-level, detailed lesson on constructing loops in an assembler programming language. The hypertext tutorial was presented in the HyperTIES hypertext system [11] and was used for four semesters. A summary of student responses is presented in Table 1.

Table 1

Responses of Sophomores using a hypertext tutorial on assembly language programming

In general:
1) the students found books easier to read and more accessible than the hypertext tutorial
2) they were divided on which method, books or hypertext, was more enjoyable
3) disorientation was a minor problem
4) navigational access to information was well-liked
5) they felt that they understood the material presented in the hypertext tutorial

The top 5 comments have been:
1) "Want bookmark facility"
2) "Want to annotate"
3) "Want an overview diagram"
4) "Want trails through the information"
5) "Want an active system"

PK parallel 7.12

Group two consisted of undergraduate Seniors learning the programming language Modula-2 in an operating systems class. This hypertext tutorial was also presented in Hyper-TIES. The tutorial has been used for four semesters. Results are shown in Table 2.

Table 2

Responses of Seniors using a hypertext tutorial on Modula-2 systems programming

In general:
1) the students found books easier to read and more accessible than the hypertext tutorial
2) they were divided on which method, books or hypertext, was more enjoyable
3) disorientation was not a problem
4) navigational access to information was well-liked
5) they felt that they understood the material presented in the hypertext tutorial

The top 4 comments have been:
1) "Want to annotate"
2) "Want mouse selection"
3) "Want bookmark facility"
4) "Want the tutorial integrated directly into the programming environment"

Group three consisted of master and doctoral level graduate students learning about hypertext and the use of hypertext systems for design and collaboration [12,13,14]. The medium itself was the object of learning and the subject of readings and lectures in the class. In this case study, the KMS [15,16] hypertext system was used. The class has been taught twice. Results are shown in Table 3.

Table 3
Responses of graduate students using a hypertext system for design and collaboration

In general:
1) the students like being able to precisely annotate each other's work
2) they liked the capability of collateral display
3) they liked having "space" to jot things down while browsing
4) disorientation was not a problem
5) navigational access to information was well-liked

The top 5 comments have been:
1) "Want better collaboration support when working in the same area of the hypertext"
2) "Want a distributed communication facility"
3) "Want to be able to link inside a frame"
4) "Want to personalize system functionality"
5) "Want bookmark facility"

WV results 15.10

Discussion

A Presentational class hypertext system was used in case studies one and two. In case study one, it was used to teach a small, detailed lesson to less mature students. In case study two, a larger, more general lesson was taught to more mature students. Both groups found books easier to read and more accessible than a computer screen, enjoyed hypertext and navigational access to information, and felt they understood the material presented in the hypertext. The one difference was the less mature group became disoriented as they browsed the tutorial, while the more mature group did not.

More importantly, comments from both groups are similar. Both groups would like the capability to personalize material in the tutorial through annotation, a bookmarking facility [17] to allow quick review of disparate parts of the information space, and to have the hypertext system integrated into their normal computing environment. Additionally, the less mature group wanted an overview facility and trails (paths) to help with their disorientation.

A Structural class hypertext system (with features of the Explorative class) was used in case study three. KMS is distributed, has a spatial metaphor in the user interface that allows annotation, provides collateral display, and has one kind of link - information element to abstraction.

The students in case study three enjoyed hypertext and navigational access to information and felt they understood the lesson to be learned from the hypertext. These students did not become disoriented, and they particularly liked the spatial metaphor of the user interface. Like the students in case studies one and two, students in case study three wanted a bookmarking facility. They also requested links of finer granularity, better support for distributed collaboration and communication, and they expressed a desire to personalize the hypertext system as well as the hypertext.

2.9

DJ explanation 6.3-6

Conclusions _____

Several common threads are apparent in the remarks of students in these case studies. First, the capability to personalize information through annotation is a paramount requirement for use of hypertext systems in learning at this level. Second, a bookmarking facility is very desirable even when the hypertext system allows collateral display. Third, the hypertext system should be integrated into the typical working environment of the user. Fourth, for collaboration, information element to information element links are highly desirable along with supporting mechanisms for communication and security. Finally, advanced users will demand the hypertext system be tailorable and extensible [18].

JL example 21.7, 24.9,12.13, corroboration 15.11

JL example 16.2

Recommendations _____

The implication for use of hypertext in learning environments is that we should at least use a Literary class hypertext system for the delivery of educational material. Also, since scholarship (reading, writing, critiquing, learning) is both collaborative and explorative, we should look toward Collaborative and Explorative class hypertext systems for future learning environments. Using a Structural or Presentational class hypertext system for learning is like using a slide show. The slide show

WV example 3.3

JL parallel 18.1, 18.7, 22.14, RK parallel 12.14, WV example 3.4

would be non-linear and under user control, but it is a slide show just the same. The students should be able to personalize the information in order to deeply integrate it with their existing knowledge. We should allow scribbling in the information space, "bending" of node corners, copying of pertinent passages, restructuring of the hypertext, and integration of existing work environments. We should never give the learner less with this medium, but much, much more.

References

[1] Bush, V. (1945). As We May Think. *Atlantic Monthly, 176, (July)*, 101-108.

[2] Engelbart, D. (1962). *Augmenting human intellect: A conceptual framework.* SRI Technical Report AFOSR-3223, Contract AF 49(638)-1024..

[3] Nelson, T. H. (1965). A file structure for the complex, the changing, and the indeterminate. *Proceedings of the 20th National ACM Conference*, (pp. 84-100).

[4] Crane, G. (1987). From the old to the new: Integrating hypertext into traditional scholarship. *Hypertext '87 Papers,* (pp. 51-56), Chapel Hill, North Carolina.

[5] Jonassen, D. H. (1986). Hypertext principles for text and courseware design. *Educational Psychologist, 21,* 269-292.

[6] Yankelovich, N., Landow, G., and Heywood, P. (1987). *Designing hypermedia "ideabases" - The Intermedia experience.* Brown University IRIS Technical Report 87-4, Providence, Rhode Island.

[7] Beck, J. R. and Spicer, D. Z. (1988). Hypermedia in Academia. *Academic Comptuting. 22.*

[8] Por, G. (1987). Hypermedia and higher education. *Computer Currents, (August)*, 14-16.

[9] Leggett, J., Schnase, J. L, and Kacmar, C. J. (1988). *Working definitions of hypertext.* Department of Computer Science Technical Report No. TAMU 88-020, Texas A&M University, College Station, Texas.

[10] Leggett, J., Schnase, J. L, and Kacmar, C. J. (1989). *Practical experiences with hypertext for learning*. Department of Computer Science Technical Report No. TAMU 89-016, Texas A&M University, College Station, Texas.

[11] Shneiderman, B. and Morariu, J. (1986). *The Interactive Encyclopedia System (TIES)*. University of Maryland, College Park, Md.

[12] Foster, G., and Stefik, M. (1986). Cognoter, Theory and practice of a colab-orative tool. *Proceedings of the CSCW '86 Conference,* (pp. 7-15), Austin, Texas..

[13] Kraemer, K., and King, J. (1988). Computer-based systems for cooperative work and group decision making. *ACM Computer Survey, 20,* 2, 115-146.

[14] Trigg, R., Suchman, L., and Halasz, F. (1986). Supporting collaboration in NoteCards. *Proceedings of the CSCW '86 Conference.*, (pp. 153-162), Austin, Texas.

[15] Akscyn, R., McCracken D., and Yoder, E. (1988). KMS: A distributed hypermedia system for managing knowledge in organizations. *Communication of the ACM, 31,* (7), 820-835.

[16] Yoder, E., Akscyn, R., and McCracken, D. (1989) Collaboration in KMS, A shared hypermedia system. *Proceedings of the CHI' 89 Conference*, (pp. 37-42), Austin, Texas.

[17] Bernstein, M. (1988). The Bookmark and the Compass: Orientation Tools for Hypertext Users. *SIGOIS Bulletin, 9,*(4), 34-45.

[18] Halasz, F. (1988). Reflections on NoteCards: Seven issues for the next generation of hypermedia systems. *Communications of the ACM, 31*, (7), 836-852.

Chapter 3
Popular Fallacies About Hypertext

George P. Landow
Brown University, USA

Keywords

Hypertext; hypermedia; rhetoric; stylistics; education; design principles; concept maps; navigation; information retrieval; interface design

Contents

Introduction

Some writers on educational hypertext appear to be reinventing the wheel, and others insist on using a square or polygonal one when perfectly good round, rubber ones have been available for several years. Many dogmatic pronouncements one encounters at conferences and in published discussions of hypertext incorporate a few popular fallacies. Having taught with a hypertext system for four years, I have become convinced that some of these fallacies arise, quite understandably, because so few people have worked with growing, expanding bodies of hypertext materials that students actually use and to which they contribute.

NATO ASI Series, Vol. F 67
Designing Hypermedia for Learning
Edited by D. H. Jonassen and H. Mandl
© Springer-Verlag Berlin Heidelberg 1990

Fallacy: Hypertext can do it all for teacher and learner

The first fallacy, which has prompted now common skeptical grumblings about the hype in hypertext, takes the form that merely linking documents has major educational effects, that hypertext systems will solve most, if not all, educational problems, and that, therefore, once students have access to hypertext they will dramatically improve in some almost magical way.

PD contrast 8.4, DJ results 15.10

My criticism of some excessive expectations of advantages of hypertext hardly derives from any essential skepticism about this information technology itself. Indeed, I have made broad claims myself about the advantages that educational hypertext confers on student and teacher alike. More than four years' experience teaching with Intermedia, the hypertext system developed and Brown University's Institute for Research in Information and Scholarship (IRIS), convinces me that networked hypertext systems in which reader and writer work in the same environment do in fact dramatically improve critical, relational thinking [1]. Quantitative studies and more impressionistic data alike confirm that use of hypermedia habituates students making their own connections, just as it also dramatically improves class discussion, reading habits, and general ability to handle large amounts of difficult information [2, 3]. Similarly, my experience convinces me that hypertext does encourage some kinds of collaborative work [4]. Hypertext systems that employ large multi-author databases (or collections of documents) also, I would argue, have other capacities to change education in fundamental ways, one of which lies in its ability to encourage interdisciplinary teaching and learning. Another potential of hypertext to effect educational change lies in its ability to change our basic conceptions of a university curriculum [5].

DJ explanation 18.2-3

However, none of these advantages comes without the instructor's expenditure of time and energy, even if he already has developed or obtained suitable hypertext materials. First of all, the instructor must decide how the hypertext component meshes with others in a particular course, and there are many possibilities. For example, when developing the Intermedia version of English 32, the Brown University *Survey of English Literature, 1700 to the Present,* I made several key decisions. First, *Context32,* the hypermedia segment, would supplement, rather than replace, primary readings, and it would take the form of biographical, historical, critical, and other crucial information that instructors have difficulty including in lectures and discussions. Finally, since this survey was intended to be one of the university's Modes of Analysis courses, these hypertext materials would both permit students to obtain large amounts of factual information and model ways of summoning that information to make explanatory hypotheses. Like many participants in the NATO workshop on educational hypertext, I began with a model of learning that stressed the learner's active construction of ideas and concepts rather than passive acquisition of factual data. Recognizing that beginning American undergraduates possess neither adequate information nor skills necessary to processs that information, I wished to determine if hypertext would help them acquire both. By linking various bodies of information, the hypertext corpus could encourage students to ask questions, explore relations, and formulate their own explanations. By linking information, the hypertext corpus could also habituate students to compare works found throughout the course with each other in a way uncommon in courses based on print technology.

In English 32, therefore, students read the usual anthologies plus additional texts, such as Dickens's *Great Expectations* and Austen's *Pride and Prejudice,* and they also receive copious reading questions. The classes, which generally have between thirty and fifty students, emphasize student-directed discussions, and Intermedia provides materials students can use to answer these reading questions and to provide other information necessary for exercises. (In contrast, Professor Peter Heywood's Biology 106, *Plant Cell Biology,* which employs a conventional lecture format, from the beginning used its Intermedia module to present much of the primary reading. Drawing upon the connectivity intrinsic to hypertext, Professor Heywood wanted it to integrate the course and thereby support writing of research papers.)

To produce some of the potential educational advantages of hypertext, the instructor, having determined what role it will play in a course, must self-consciously teach with it. That principle implies, first of all, that I had to find some way to have students unacquainted with this new information medium use it from the beginning of the course. At the same time, I had to make clear both the goals of the course and the role of Intermedia in meeting them. As Peter Whalley correctly points out, "the most successful uses of hypertext will

RK contrast 1.7, parallel 12.20

SH parallel 23.10

SH example 23.22

AR constast 19.16

involve learners and lead them to adopt the most appropriate learning strategy for their task. They must allow the learner to develop higher level skills, rather than simply become the passive recipients of a slick new technology." Instructors, I soon realized, therefore must create assignments that emphasize precisely those qualities and features of hypertext that furnish the greatest educational advantages. I have elsewhere described in detail such an initial assignment and will summarize it below before providing the example of a more complex exercise.

GM recommendation 12.7

Whether true or not that readers retain less information they encounter while reading text on a screen than that they read on the printed page, electronically linked text and printed text have different advantages. One should therefore have an initial assignment that provides the student with experience of its advantages — the advantages of connectivity. If instructors wish to introduce students to the capacity of hypertext to choose their own reading paths and hence construct their own document, then assignments from the very beginning must encourage students to do so.

SH parallel 23.21

The first Intermedia assignment in all my courses instructs students to follow links from the same location or link marker and then report what they encounter. Similarly, since I employ a corpus of linked documents to accustom students to discovering or constructing contexts for individual blocks of text or data, my assignments require multiple answers to the same question or multiple parts to the same answer. If one wishes to accustom students to the fact that complex phenomena involve complex causation, one must arrange assignments in such a way to make students summon different kinds of information to explain them. Since my courses have increasingly taken advantage of Intermedia's capacity to promote collaborative learning, from the beginning of the course my assignments require students to comment upon the materials and links they find, suggest new ones, and add materials.

Instructors employing educational hypertext must also reconfigure examinations and other forms of evaluation to see if they have fulfilled their stated educational goals. If hypertext's greatest educational strength as well as most characteristic feature is connectivity, then tests and other evaluative exercises must measure the results of using that connectivity to develop the ability to make connections. Independent of hypertext, dissatisfaction with American secondary school students' ability to think critically has recently led to a new willingness to try evaluative methods that emphasize conceptual skills — chiefly making connections — rather than those that stress simple data acquisition [7].

Taking advantage of the full potential of hypertext obviously forces instructors to rethink the goals and methods of education. If hypertext can in fact accustom students to synthesize answers from large amounts of varying kinds of information, then one must employ both assignments and evaluative methodologies that place greatest importance on such skills. If one wishes to develop student skills in critical thinking in this manner, then one might have to make the goal elegance of approach rather than simple quantitative answer. Particularly when dealing with beginning students, instructors will have to recognize that several correct answers may exist for a single problem — and that such multiplicity of answers does not indicate that the assigned problem is subjective or that any answer will do. If, for example, one asks students to provide a context in contemporary philosophy or religion for a literary technique or historical event, one can expect to receive a range of correct solutions.

Several of the courses that I teach with hypertext employ the following exercise, which may take the form of either an in-class exercise or a take-home exam that students have a week or more to complete. The exercise consists of a series of passages from the assigned readings that students have to identify and then relate in brief essays to a single work; in the past, these exercises have used Wordsworth's "Tintern Abbey," *Great Expectations,* and Austen's *Pride and Prejudice* as the central text. The directions for the exercise asking students to relate passages to "Tintern Abbey" instructs:

> Begin each essay by identifying the full name, exact title, and date of the passage, after which you should explain at least three ways in which the passage relates (whatever you take that term to mean) to the poem. One of these connections should concern theme, a second should concern technique, and a third some aspect of the religious, philosophical, historical, or scientific context. . . . Not all the relations you discover or create will turn out to be obvious ones, such as matters of influence

or analogous ideas and techniques. Some
may take the form of contrasts or opposi-
tions that tell us something interesting
about the authors, literary forms, or times
in which these works appeared.

To emphasize that demonstrating skill at formulating possible
explanations and hypothesizing significant relations counts as
much as factual knowledge alone, the directions explain that
some subjects, "particularly matters of context, may require
you to use materials in *Context32* on Intermedia to formulate
an hypothesis. In many cases *Context32* provides the materials
to create an answer but not answers themselves."

Using this exercise in four iterations of the survey course as
well as in two other courses convinces me that it provides a
useful, accurate means of evaluation that has several additional beneficial effects. Although the exercise does not
directly ask for specific factual information other than titles,
authors, and dates, students soon recognize that without such
information they cannot effectively demonstrate connections
between works. In comparing a passage from Pope's "Essay
on Man" with "Tintern Abbey," for example, they soon realize
that only specific examples and specific comments on those
examples produce effective discussion. Gary Marchionni
points out that "hypermedia is an enabling technology rather
than a directive one, offering high levels of user control.
Learners can construct their own knowledge by browsing
hyperdocuments according to the associations in their own
cognitive structures. As with access, however, control requires responsibility and decision making." By making students choose which literary techniques, themes, or aspects of
context they wish to relate, the exercise emphasizes the major
role of student choice.

DJ corroboration 20.3

This assignment itself also proves an effective educational
tool because while attempting to carry it out many students
realize that they have difficulty handling matters of context,
which at the beginning they often confuse with the theme or
main idea of the passage under discussion. Such discussions
of context require one to posit a connection between some
phenomenon, say, the imagery in a poem, and some other,
often more general, phenomenon, such as conceptions of the
human mind contemporaneous with that imagery. Perceiving
possible connections and then arguing for their validity is a
high-level intellectual skill. Since students are permitted and

in fact encouraged to redo these exercises as many times as they wish, these exercises simultaneously furnish students the opportunity to make conceptual breakthroughs and teachers the opportunity to encourage and then measure them.

Two additional advantages of this exercise for the courses in which it appears involve writing. Since both the survey and more advanced course are intended to be intensive writing courses, the opportunity for a large amount of writing (and rewriting) supports one of the goals of these courses, though, of course, it might prove a hindrance in other kinds of courses, particularly those with large enrollments. Second, the structure of the assignment, which requires writing a number of short essays, seems to accomplish more than single long essays. At the same time that students find writing many short essays easier than constructing much longer single ones, they both cover far more material than that possible with a more usual assignment and they cover different approaches, each demanding the kind of materials generally available only in our hypermedia corpus.

Another advantage of this exercise, which I find well suited to courses with hypertext supplements, lies in the fact that, particularly in its take-home version, it demonstrates the usefulness of the hypertext system at the same time that it draws on skills encouraged by using it. The materials in *Context32* show students possible connections they might wish to make and furnish information to make their own connections. Our hypermedia corpus also permits them to range back and forth throughout the course, thereby effecting their own syntheses of the materials.

A final utility of this exercise lies in the fact that it creates more materials for *Context32* and thereby encourages students to take a more active, collaborative approach to learning. This past year approximately one third of the students in my survey wrote their answers to these exercises directly on Intermedia, and the writers of the most successful ones later linked them to relevant documents. Other students almost all wrote their essays on Intermedia-compatible word processors, such as Microsoft Word, documents in which can be placed directly on Intermedia. Integrating new student materials into *Context32* is therefore easy and efficient. and hence requires little support.

RK parallel 12.14

Fallacy: Structuring the database is everything

One frequently encounters pronouncements that hypertext requires lavishing enormous amounts of time to arrange the data in one's database. Another version of this approach, which seems to misunderstand a basic capacity of hypertext, takes the form that the designer of hypertext systems must create some universal data system. Neither of these approaches take into account the fundamental principle that hypertext's intrinsic open-endedness removes both the need to create some final universalizing approach to arranging data or even the possibility that one can do so at all. In hypertext organization of data, although important, is not crucial because any one arrangement of data is not finally defining or confining.

Links allow the multiple arrangement of the same data. Intermedia's potentially reductive or limiting folder system provides a good example of what I mean. Let us look at what happens when we place a particular document set, which can include images, animation, and numerical data, in a folder. In the course of developing a group of materials on, say, the economic foundations of Dickens's novels, my assistants and I create several essays on serial publication, the economics of Victorian publication methods, and the economic class and religious allegiance of his readers. Since we have developed these materials to support teaching several of Dickens's novels, we placed them within a folder entitled "Economic Background" that resides within the Dickens folder. Later, another instructor either at the author's own university or at another institution realizes that these materials also connect to materials on technology, specifically to those on the history of printing.

What do later developers (whether the original creators of the materials at a later time or a different people) do at this point? They have a choice. First of all, after conferring with the original author, hypertext editor, or someone else with authority, they can move the materials from the "Dickens" folder in the literature section to the "Printing" folder in "Technology." Such an approach, occasionally necessary in the early expansion of a hypertext corpus, becomes increasingly difficult as different users and developers justify different locations — really classifications — of the same materials.

GL example 1.9
DJ parallel 1.5

AR contrast 19.26

In most cases linking, the central concept of hypertext, provides the second, more common, and superior solution. When I encountered precisely this apparent problem when working with the materials on Intermedia that support my courses, I did not move the materials on serial publication to the "Technology" folder. Instead, I linked them not only to overview (or directory) documents and to an essay on Dickens's career but also to relevant documents in the "Technology" folder.

3.9

PWr comment Adding more links could make it harder for readers to know which links to follow.

Linking is not in any sense a stop-gap measure one takes instead of another course of action, such as moving or duplicating one's materials, just as the presence of multiple valid connections is not problem or annoyance but an essential, positive feature of hypertext, one that produces many of its most important educational effects. In fact any hypertext corpus, or metatext, demands multiple linkages, for if such were not required, then why employ hypertext when a more linear information medium would do?

Fallacy: One can study the nature and effect of hypertext with small document sets

To determine if the education potential claimed for hypertext can ever be realized, one must work with large enough hypermedia metatexts. One frequently encounters the notion that the nature and effect of hypertext can be studied with small document sets despite the fact that in any university-level course students encounter the equivalent of thousands of documents per set. Many problems concerning both system design and principles of author-generated rhetoric do not appear until the hypermedia corpus (or metatext) reaches a particular size. For example, although I conceived of using *intellectual mapping* to create overview documents before Intermedia was designed and implemented, I did not encounter the need to formulate working rules about number and variety of materials linked to each block within an overview until several iterations of the course produced substantially more documents than had originally linked to these directory documents.

GL example 15.9

Fallacy: Navigation and orientation are serious and as yet unresolved problems of hypertext and media systems ⎯⎯⎯⎯

GL example 1.13

Many authors who take the position that navigation remains an unresolved problem follow that assertion by suggesting two solutions, global maps and artificial intelligence. The first, however, does not work as a navigation tool with any but the smallest hypermedia corpora, and the second does not exist at the moment in any usable form. My experience with Intermedia suggests that navigation and orientation are not in fact a major problem: Using system features, the reader can locate something or travel to it by means of full text searches, folders, links, web views, and menus of link choices from a particular marker. One always knows what documents "surround" the document one is reading, and one can always travel to an overview document, which in most cases gets one off in the direction one wishes to head.

RK contrast 1.13
GL example 13.7
DR contrast 24.2

Since IRIS has published numerous accounts of actual sessions on Intermedia, and a video of Intermedia sessions is available, I shall not narrate how one uses all the features of the system [1,2]. Instead, I wish to emphasize the crucial importance of a local tracking map or similar device in orienting readers and permitting them to find the information they wish. The idea of a dynamic system-generated tracking map has evolved considerably since IRIS developers first proposed a feature that provided readers with a visual image of the links that join visual and text documents on Intermedia. This basic idea evolved through three stages. The first, the Global Tracking Map, provided graphic information about all links and documents in a particular body of linked documents. Activating the icon for a particular hypertext corpus, such as *Context32, Nuclear Arms,* or *Biology,* simultaneously activated that hypertext web and generated a document in which icons representing each document in the web were joined by lines representing links between pairs of documents. This Global Tracking Map, which functioned only during early stages of Intermedia's development, immediately demonstrated that such a device was virtually useless for all but the smallest documents sets or webs. Although pictures of it have appeared in articles on hypertext, the Global Tracking Map was never used educationally and was never part of any released version of Intermedia.

PWr definition 3.11
DJ parallel 13.7

GL contrast 4.3

Instead, IRIS developed the Local Tracking Map, which presented icons for all documents linked to that one currently activated. As before, the reader chooses a particular web and opens it by double clicking upon its icon or by first activating it and then choosing "open" from the Intermedia menu. The reader then moves the Local Tracking Map to one side of the screen, which permits her to work with an individual document and the tracking map it generates open side by side. Each time the reader opens a new document or acticates a previously opened one, the Local Tracking Map transforms itself, thus informing the reader about where she can go. This information alone serves to remove much potential disorientation from the reader's experience.

In its third instantiation, the Local Tracking Map, which now bears the name "Web View," adds two chief features: First, double-clicking on any icon in the Web View opens the document represented by that icon, thereby adding another way of making one's way through materials on Intermedia.

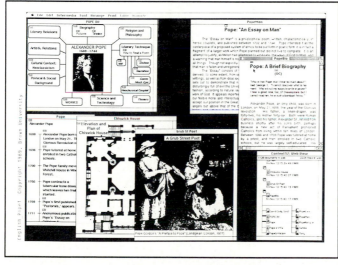

Figure 1. This illustration shows a selection of materials from *Contexct 32: English Literature in Context*. This is the largest collection of Intermedia materials to date (notice the Web View shows that there are 1,238 documents in the collection with 2,224 links). A typical author overview document is open (upper left), providing an entry point for students wishing to find more information about Alexander Pope. Also shown are a sampling of materials typically connected to author overview documents: a biographical timeline, a brief prose biography, an essay about one of the author's works and several illustrations. the Web View (bottom right), shows the user's path through the materials as well as the links emanating from the current document (in this case "PopeBio").

Second, the Web View presents a history of the reader's path by means of a vertical array of icons that indicate the titles of documents previously opened; additional smaller icons show that the document was opened from a folder, by following a link, or by reactivating a document previously opened on the desktop [8].

Although this Intermedia system feature succeeds well in orienting the reader, it works even better when combined with author-generated overview files or other forms of intellectual mapping. A *Context32* overview surrounds one concept (Victorianism, Darwinism) or entity (Joyce, Lawrence) by a series of others (literary relations, cultural context, economic background) to each of which many documents may link. Whereas the Web View presents all documents attached to the entire overview, the overview has a hierarchical organization, but does not reveal the nature or number of documents link to each block (whose presence is indicated by a link marker). Intermedia provides two ways of obtaining this information — a menu which following links from a particular link marker activates and the Web View. Clicking upon a particular link and thus activating it darkens all the links attached to that block in the Web View. Thus, working together, individual documents and the Web View continually inform the reader what information lies one jump away from the current text. This combination of materials generated by authors and Intermedia well exemplifies the way hypertext authors employ what are essentially stylistic and rhetorical devices to supplement system design and work synergistically with it. Intermedia 4.0, which saw completion in time for Hypertext '89 in November 1989, includes full-text searching, a feature that promises to change readers' habits of working with materials on Intermedia. Since it has not yet been used in the Intermedia classroom at Brown, I concentrate above on features in use for several iterations of my survey course.

Fallacy: Analogies of navigation, narration, and space help us think accurately about hypertext

The analogy of navigation, with its associated and possibly misleading spatial assumptions, has become widespread in writings on hypertext. I am one of those who first introduced this analogy into discussions of hypertext and now face its shortcomings [9,10]. Unfortunately, no analogy maps reality with complete accuracy, and relying too heavily on them risks leading one to false assumptions. In a recent talk at Brown University, Tim Orren from Apple Computing proposed a second paradigm, that of the narrative, as a means of finding the information one wishes to encounter (or retrieve). In Orren's description of a current Apple experiment, agents in the form of virtual people or personages guide the reader, presenting as major choice the items that the reader would be most likely to want to see based on the nature of the chosen guide or other means of determining reader preferences. This model, which has some potentially troubling political implications, reveals that narrative and navigation share similar shortcomings as overarching paradigms for hypertext systems.

3.13

DR parallel 24.8

Navigation, the art of controlling the course of a plane or ship, presupposes a spatial world, but hypertext is not experienced as a spatial world. Or rather one does not entirely experience hypertext as a spatial world. In navigation, we remember, one must determine one's spatial position in relation to landmarks or astral locations and then decide upon a means of moving toward one's goal, which lies out of sight at some spatial distance from one. Because it takes time to move across the separating distance, one also experiences that distance as time: one's ship lies so many nautical miles and therefore so many days and hours from one's goal. The reader, however, does not experience hypertext in this way. The reader of *Paradise Lost,* for example, experiences as equally close the linked parts of Homer and Vergil to which the poem's opening section allude and linked lines on the next page or in the next book. Because hypertext linking takes relatively the same amount of time to traverse, all linked texts are experienced as lying at the same "distance" from the point of departure. Thus, whereas navigation presupposes that one finds oneself at the center of a spatial world in which desired items lie at varying distances from one's own location, hypertext presupposes an experiential world in which the goal is always but one jump or link away.

PWr comment This may be interface dependent - e.g. pop-up displays may be psychologically closer than replacement windows.

JL comment Not true - rarely one jump away.

Hypertext positions one in a continuing present in which something is about to happen. Bringing a desired bit of text or data into view always happens next and not at some, often long-deferred temporal interval. All of this is in part just another way of emphasizing that in a hypertext system, one is always at the center and that one's current area of interest, the document presently under examination, always becomes the temporary center of the entire system and the point from which one departs — or more literally, the text from which one acts to make another text appear.

Narrative offers no better explanatory analogy for the experience of hypertext than does navigation, for it too relies upon an unsuitable temporal association and assumption. In the first place, when living in the middle of a story, one does not experience it as such, because one's experience cannot have the formal coherence of narrative, which possesses a beginning, conflict, resolution, and satisfying closure. One can experience reading a story, but one cannot experience living a story. Narratives, as recent theorists have pointed out, are delightful, but they also have certain totalitarian implications for people as opposed to characters, who are just literary constructs that in some ways are recognized as resembling people. In order to call a particular set of actions or events a narrative requires that one not only consider that action complete but also that to make this judgment, one step back from that sequence and see it as a whole. Such is precisely what one cannot do from within the experience of bringing up text.

One finds avoiding such spatial analogies all but impossible. One naturally speaks of one's present "location" in a text, and one equally naturally speaks of obtaining a second text, image, or collection of data as "moving" to it. Even the phrase "bringing up" or "opening" the linked document falsely implies its existence in a uniform, rational space. Part of the reason one so easily falls into such spatial analogies derives from the fact that most texts we encounter exist on the printed page, which does exist in space, and with reasonable accuracy one speaks of "bringing" that text to us or "moving" to it. A second reason, however, lies in the probability that our minds work in spatial terms, most easily assigning spatial locations or falling into habits of spatialization when organizing ideas.

DJ comment Research often assumes that semantic distance can be depicted as geometric space.

WV reference Hammond, N., and Allinson, L., 1988. The travel metaphor as design principle and training aid for navigating around complex system. In D. Diaper and R. Winder, (Eds.). People and Computers III.

Fallacy: Hypertext is just another publication system

Although many researchers tell funding agencies (and their departmental chairs) that hypertext has the capacity to revolutionize reading, writing, and publication, they seemingly forget such claims of novelty as soon as they work with hypertext systems. Part of the problem lies in the fact that many of us depend so completely on habits developed by print technology that we assume hypertext is just like a book — but better when we want it to be so. A corollary of these ingrained attitudes appears in the assumption one can in fact simply transfer to hypertext articles and full-length works created for and by book (print) technology. If one cannot make that transference easily, so the feeling goes, then there is something wrong either with our system or with hypertext in general. Too many writers on the subject of hypertext start with the assumption that it is merely another publication system. They therefore necessarily begin, most of the time, with print documents and try the best way to adapt them to the system and the system to them. This assumption, which is shaky and unexamined to say the least, further leads to treating the chunk, grain, reading unit, or lexia as a fairly large block to begin with. In fact, as Ray McAleese points out, "Granularity of information in hypertext is not determined by the system but by the way information is presented by the designer [i.e. author]. Hypertext systems allow the size of nodes to vary from large chunks of text, graphics and pictures to concept labels." The lexia or text block is whatever size the author wishes it to be.

Instead of blurring the notion of hypertext, we would do better to recognize that we have several problems or several different kinds of hypertext involved, one of which consists of materials created originally on hypertext systems and the other, transitional hypertext, is the result of translating materials originally created for print into another medium. We have two different sets of problems here. When adapting materials from print technology to hypertext one must take care not to violate their original organization and form, but such care intrinsically places important, and possibly distorting, limits on the hypertext system itself.

One can learn from the fate of manuscript materials during the early stages of the age of printing. The first and most obvious result of printing, as Marshall McCluhan pointed out, was that it promulgated manuscript culture [11]. When printers looked for materials to publish, they naturally and inevitably turned to manuscripts, which had been produced according to very different economic, ideological, and technological systems, and only later did they publish works originally created for the new information medium. We can expect that hypertext will similarly draw upon the hoard of printed works that it encounters, and we can also expect that hypertext and print will constrain each other in the same ways that manuscript and print did centuries earlier.

Printing manuscripts radically changed their nature and purpose, even when the printer reproduced them with a high standard of accuracy. Printing, as Elizabeth Eisenstein points

3.15

JL contrast 6.5

JL recommendation 6.17

PWh contrast 4.2, 19.3

RH contrast 5.3,16.4

out, produces many identical copies of a single work that can then be distributed over a wide geographical area, and these characteristics of print, which she argues provided one of the fundamental conditions of the Renaissance, also changed the role of scholarship [12]. In a manuscript culture the scholar's chief task involved preserving texts:

> Of all the new features introduced by the duplicative powers of print, preservation is possibly the most important. . . . No manuscript, however useful as a reference guide, could be preserved for long without undergoing corruption by copyists. . . . Insofar as records were seen and used, they were vulnerable to wear and tear. Stored documents were vulnerable to moisture and vermin, theft and fire. However they might be collected or guarded within some great message center, their ultimate dispersal and loss was inevitable. To be transmitted by writing from one generation tot he next, information had to be conveyed by drifting texts and vanishing manuscripts.

In contrast, "the notion that valuable data could be preserved best by being made public, rather than being kept secret," which is a product of print technology, "ran counter to tradition, led to clashes with new censors, and was central both to early-modern science and to Enlightenment thought." Whereas the primary function of the scholar in the age of manuscripts was to preserve fragile, scarce, often unique items, the scholar in an age of books spends a far greater portion of his energies relating individual works to each other.

Print, as various authors have pointed out, also produced increased use of the vernacular, standardized spelling and grammar, conceptions of authorial property and resulting copyright laws, and radical changes in the theory and practice of education at all levels. Relatively inexpensive copies that could easily be disseminated — inexpensive, that is, in relation to the cost of manuscripts — ultimately contributed to an explosion of scientific and technological knowledge and also to major religious conflict as well. Whether or not one considers the changes effected by print beneficial or pernicious, print changed the experience of text and data, the way they were used, and the individuals and institutions who used them.

Nonetheless, although the introduction of printing had these major effects, the remains of manuscript culture long acted to constrain the cultural effects of print technology. Not only did the products of this earlier culture long provide the materials for printers to publish, the habits of mind associated with unique texts kept printers from realizing the implications of their new technology. It took, for example, more than a century for publishers to include pagination, tables of contents, and indices in their printed books. Such devices of information retrieval become particularly helpful only when multiple copies exist so that spatially separated readers can cite to each other specific portions of the texts they read. The evidence provided by the first century of printing suggests that a transition stage will exist for hypertext in which it similarly works under constraints created by habits of mind induced by an earlier form of writing technology.

Fallacy: Text is primarily alphanumeric ——

Failure to distinguish carefully between these different stages leads one to base one's assumptions and expectations of hypertext upon printing. One such assumption is that text is primarily and inevitably verbal. Although from the earliest days of printing books occasionally mixed word and images on the same page in imitation of illuminated manuscripts, print culture eventually cast out illustrations as anything but supplements to the main text. Readers became accustomed to reading solid pages of print, and although books have seen several great ages of illustration, the modern age generally segregates word and image. By mid-twentieth century, in fact, serious works of literarature rarely appeared with illustrations.

Desk top publishing has made integrating word and image easier than ever before, and now hypertext, which links images as easily as it does linguistic texts, prompts a redefinition of text and reading. The use of visual clues has always proved important in books, and hypertext promises to make even greater use of them. Visual information appears in the form of concept maps, flow charts, and other forms of intellectual mapping and not merely as supplements — not, that is, as illustrations of some other concept — but as a major element of the text. Intermedia, for example, makes use of author-generated intellectual maps as directory documents that inform the reader about the arrangement of a set of

PWh contrast 4.5

hypermedia documents. These overview documents, which we have created for authors (Austen, Joyce), concepts (Biblical Typology), and movements in history and literature (Romanticism, Darwinism, Feminism), have an additional advantage when employed on a system that features a web view or local tracking map. Using an author-generated document as a directory or organizing center of a body of materials allows the reader to see all the linked documents in the web view, something particularly useful when multiple documents link to each portion of the overview document.

Furthermore, because hypertext (or hypermedia) can just as easily link one or two dozen images to a particular text node, hypermedia permits the convenient and efficient organizing of a far larger body of information than might be possible with print media. The need for sequence, like the high cost of reproducing images in print, makes problematic the copious

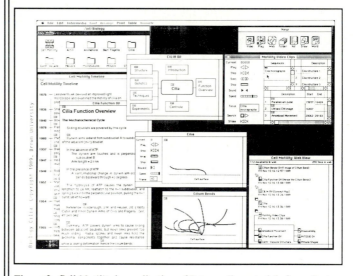

Figure 2. *Cell Motility* is a collection of Intermedia materials for a plant cell biology course. Shown here is one of every type of Intermedia document. The InterVal timeline (left) provides students with an overivew of important developments int he field. The InterWord document (second from left) gives students an overview of one of the topics covered in this collection. It provides much of the same information, in more detail, that is found int the InterDraw overview diagram. Below The overview diagram is an animated InterPlay diagram and below that is a still image explaining the animation. An InterVideo table (middle right) provides students with access to video stills, clips, and sequencescontained on a cell biology videodisk. The New window (upper right) provides access to all of the Intermedia applications and the Web View (bottom right) shows the user's path through the material and the documents that are linked to the current one (in this case the Intervideo document).

use of images in this medium. Hypertext, in contrast, permits linking of any materials already online, and because hypertext permits the reader to choose both her own reading path and the level or depth at which she wishes to consult basic or additional information, the inclusion of a large number of linked documents does not clutter the main argument or hinder exposition.

Fallacy: The hypertext or the hypertext system does it all for the author ⎯⎯⎯⎯⎯

The mistaken assumption that hypertext or any particular hypertext system will produce all the substantial intellectual connections implies that the author working with a hypertext system does not have to create text substantially differently than he would for print technology. Such a conception of hypertext fails to see the need for new rhetoric and stylistics. True, the system generates aspects of such a stylistics, such as Intermedia's folder system and web view, but other aspects require a new stylistics, perhaps the most important part of which is the intellectual mapping described by Alexander Romiszowski.

DJ corroboration 15.11

Fallacy: Hypertext is a form of text that does not contain more information than regular print text ⎯⎯⎯⎯⎯⎯

At the same time that many authors express grandiose expectations of hypertext as an educational and general information technology, others assume that it does not contain more information than regular print text. Rainer Hammwöhner, however, quite accurately points out that hypertexts are not "a more or less arbitrary network of interconnected text units but . . . an enhanced notion of text." In fact, extra information takes the form of links between one bit of text and another. Print, holographic, and oral texts all contain such indications that readers should perceive some connection between the text they are reading at the moment and some other text or texts. Devices like naming, citation of authority, allusion to other works all prompt readers to make connections between one text and another and thereby instantiate the effect of the text they are presently reading. Hypertext reifies such links, most obviously in the matter of something like InterLex, which dynamically links each word in a text to the *American Heritage Dictionary* entry for that word, but also in the matter of

WV contrast 4.6

3.19

links to the full social, literary, scientific, philosophical, and religious contexts.

Conclusion: (More) advice for hypertext designers

Now that hypermedia systems exist, designers must use those now available to gain first-hand experience of various approaches before designing new systems. Equally important, designers must gain experience not simply of hypertext systems themselves but of working with substantial bodies of hypertext materials, those with at least several thousand documents. These materials, moreover, should not be fixed or static but continually changing .

Designers of educational materials, like designers of entire hyermedia systems, have to recognize that no matter how powerful a hypertext system may be, it only provides an environment in which authors and readers have to make decisions. Authors of hypertext materials must develop and employ stylistic and rhetorical devices that extend beyond those associated with writing texts for publication as a printed book. In so doing, they must distinguish carefully between adapting printed works to hypertext and creating new ones in this new information medium.

Once instructors have access to workable hypertext systems, they have to decide for precisely what ends they wish to use them. Creating hypertext modules for a course requires that instructors also create appropriate assignments and evaluative methods. It also requires that instructors rethink their conceptions of education and their roles as teachers as well.

DJ corroboration 12.7-8

References

[1] Yankelovich, N., Haan, B., Meyrowitz, N. K., and Drucker, S. (1988). Intermedia: The concept and construction of a seamless information environment. *IEEE Computer, 21*, 81-96.

[2] Landow, G. P. (1989). Hypertext in literary education, criticism, and scholarship, *Computers and the Humanities, 23,* 173-198.

[3] Beeman,W. O., et al.(1988). *Intermedia: A Case Study of Innovation in Higher Education,* Providence, R. I.: Office of Program Analysis/IRIS

[4] Landow, G. P. (in press). Hypertext and collaborative work: The example of intermedia. In R. Kraut and J. Galegher (Eds.), *Intellectual teamwork,* (pp. 407-428). Hillsdale, N. J.: Lawrence Erlbaum.

[5] Landow, G. P. (in press). Hypertext, metatext, and the electronic canon. In Myron Tuman (Ed.), *Literacy online: The promise and peril of reading and writing with computers.*

[6] Landow, G. P. (1989). Course assignments using hypertext: The example of intermedia. *Journal of Research on Computing in Education 21,* 349-365.

[7] Putka, G. (1989). "New kid in school: Alternative exams," *The Wall Street Journal,* November 16, p. B1.

[8] Utting,K. and Yankelovich, N. (1989). "Context and Orientation in Hypermedia Networks," *ACM Transactions on Information Systems, 7,* 58-84.

[9] Landow, G. P. (1987). "Encoded relational links and the rhetoric of hypertext," *Hypertext '87 Proceedings,* 331-344, Chapel Hill, N. C.

[10] Landow, G. P. (1989). "The rhetoric of hypermedia: some rules for authors," *Journal of Computing in Higher Education, 1,* 39-64.

[11] McCluhan, M. (1964). *The Gutenberg galaxy: The making of typographic man,* Toronto: University of Toronto Press.

[12] Eisenstein. E. (1979). *The printing press as an agent of social change: Communications and cultural transformations in early-modern Europe,* 2 vols., Cambridge: Cambridge University Press.

Chapter 4
Models of Hypertext Structure and Learning

Peter Whalley
The Open University, UK

Keywords

access structure; argument structure; distance teaching; linearity; phenomenological learning; relevance assignment; representation

Contents

Introduction

The dominant conception of the hypertext form is a medium for information retrieval rather than learning, and where learning is considered, it is usually only of a fairly rudimentary form. An important question is whether the 'control' given to the hypertext user may be merely illusory, since the fragmenting effect of the non-linear text forms can make it more difficult for the reader to perceive an author's intended argument structure. The artefacts introduced by the hypertext form, in order to improve accessibility, mitigate against its use as the principal teaching medium. It is suggested that designers of hypertext materials might usefully adopt some of the supposed constraints of the linear text form, and that until various problems have been overcome, hypertext might best be used to supplement rather than supplant printed materials for many learning purposes.

JL corroboration 13.17, 15.11, example 13.1, background 19.19

PWr parallel 16.12

Issues in hypertext design

The history of the use of new technologies in education tends to reflect the search for panaceas rather than the serious attempt to solve problems. Ravetz [6] describes the confusion

NATO ASI Series, Vol. F 67
Designing Hypermedia for Learning
Edited by D. H. Jonassen and H. Mandl
© Springer-Verlag Berlin Heidelberg 1990

of 'technical' problems with 'practical' problems. Technical problems always have practical solutions, but all practical problems do not necessarily have technical solutions. Because the creation of educational materials involves practical as well as conceptual issues, its problems are often mistakenly perceived as technological, and thought to be susceptible to a technical 'fix'.

DR comment Of course, so is raw text. Forms come about through convention and use of media in practice.

One of the great strengths of hypertext, but also a potential source of weakness, is that it is essentially a formless medium. It is quite possible to reinvent the scroll, book, frame-based CAL, and even the video recorder within hypertext systems. Whether this is a wise use of resources will depend on the user's goals, and to some extent on technological developments in terms of cost and ergonomics. It is difficult, and perhaps not too useful, to attempt a formal definition of such an evolving medium. The basic features identified by Conklin [2] of machine supported links and some measure of interaction by the reader would appear adequate as a working definition. A graphic component must also be assumed in addition to natural language. Few teaching texts would be complete without some graphic element, and the hypertext medium itself seems to benefit from an additional graphic 'navigational' level. As technological developments occur, the present hypertext-hypermedia distinction is likely to blur as the graphic component of hypertext incorporates animation, simulation and video forms.

PK background 7.2

This paper attempts to relate the three issues of representation, linearity and the forms of learning which might be best supported by hypertext. The focus of the paper is the author's interest in the creation of distance teaching materials at the tertiary level of education. The assumed model of learning and considerations of the appropriateness of different roles for hypertext in education should be viewed in terms of this context.

Representation

An important issue concerning the role of hypertext in learning is the fragmenting effect of the medium, the 'nuggets of knowledge' problem. This is not just a matter of screen size but stems from the basic, and conceptually simple, pointer structures underlying hypertext systems. Whatever the screen size, the author has to make semantic decisions about the size of information nodes; the amount to be displayed at any one time. This has both pedagogic and epistemological consequences. If it turns out that the hypertext form is best suited to encyclopediac or fragmented forms of knowledge, then it is likely that hypertext will only be useful for the more technical forms of education.

A possible, but mistaken, notion concerning hypertext is that the arbitrary 'webs' of facts in hypertext systems have much semantic significance. There is not the space here to do more than sketch the problems relating to understanding the development of knowledge structures. However the essential ideas missing from the 'fact webs' of hypertext are the crucial notions of context and relevance to the individual. The simple web structures of hypertext are not of the same order of complexity as human semantic knowledge structures. Obviously 'frames' or levels of pointer structures could be employed to attempt to represent context and relevance information. However given the lack of success by the AI discipline in representing complex semantic knowledge structures, it seems unlikely that the relatively simple technology of hypertext will solve what is effectively a conceptual problem. It is worth noting that members of the AI community regularly castigate each other for the abuse of the terms 'semantic' and 'knowledge', eg McDermott [3]. A related issue is the wish expressed by some exponents of the hypertext technology to 'connect everything to everything'. It is possible to see where this idea came from in the origins of hypertext, but of course it is computer-science as epistemology and makes little sense.

SH contrast 7.16
RH contrast 4.4, 7.16, 23.13

RK contrast 1.7, DJ contrast, 7.1-7

AR parallel 19.3

A practical consequence of these issues is that the detailed hypertext web created by one individual has very little meaning for anyone else. The ability to record and play back the learner's path through a hypertext structure is obviously going to be useful to authors undertaking evaluative studies. However it is unlikely to be useful to other learners because of their individual nature. A further limitation is that the webs are almost certainly also syncronic, representing only a 'time slice' for the particular individual. It is a salutary experience to look back at the notes and pointers one has added to papers only months previously and wonder why one made them. A corollary to this effect is that it is also possible to look back at lecture notes made twenty years previously, and they can look as fresh, but meaningless, as when they were made.

Linearity

Hypertext is often described as being 'structured' and 'non-linear', presumably in contrast to conventional 'unstructured', 'linear' text. However it is a mistake to think of conventional texts, and particularly expository teaching texts, as being

WV parallel 5.8, RH parallel 5.3

purely linear. Text linguists such as Grimes [4] and de Beaug-rande [5] have shown how under a superficially linear form, authors may create rich complex relational structures. It could even be argued that the simple pointer and hierarchical structures provided in hypertext are semantically more limiting that the implicit relationships created in conventional materials. Distance teaching texts may encompass a whole academic year's worth of study. These may properly only be described in terms of Grimes' staging metaphor where cycles of ideas are repeated and overlayed upon each other. For example a central idea may be repeated within progressively more complex contexts. The skillful author may use the linear text form to weave an entirely non-linear pattern of associations in the reader's mind.

Van Dijk [6] has developed an analysis of the way that linguistic and graphical cues can be used to assign the relative relevance of parts of a text. Within this framework it is possible to identify several levels where hypertext can make an original contribution, but it is important to note that such explicit cues will never be the only, or necessarily the most significant, forms of non-linearity and argument structuring within a text. An important consequence of the fragmentation effect in hypertext is that it is likely to make it more difficult for the learner to perceive the author's intended argument structure, unless certain linearity constraints are imposed on the hypertext form. For example it may be necessary to impose a certain ordering of concepts until some critical point is reached.

SH parallel 23.16

Analysis must be made of the relative merits of linear and non-linear text forms for the various phases of reflective study. It is also necessary to relate the underlying cognitive processes involved in the different levels of study activity to the practical domain of the hypertext form. An overly narrow view of possible reading purposes will lead to a restricted consideration of possible hypertext structures. Waller [7] has developed a descriptive framework for comparing text genres. His model is based on the notion of three components within the text, the topic structure, the artifact structure, and the access structure. These are of course heuristic concepts in that they are effectively overlaid within any particular document. The usefulness of this framework is that it makes it possible to think of, and analyze, a trade-off between ease of access and increasing artefact. It is important to achieve the right balance, and this will depend on the learning purposes and skills of the reader.

Writers of distance teaching materials have to concern themselves with the problem of the 'over organized' text. When attempting to create a complete 'tutorial-in-print', there is always the danger of pushing the student into a passive role, and leaving them no room to think for themselves. I would argue that the artefacts introduced by the hypertext form, in order to improve accessibility, mitigate against its use as the principal teaching medium. The solutions to the problems of navigation and orientation within the hypertext genre will involve providing the very same high level structures that many educators would wish their students to be creating for themselves as active independent learners.

Learning

The most natural mode of study with hypertext would appear to be that of browsing. For information retrieval and certain aspects of learning this is an entirely appropriate study strategy. However many educators would consider the browsing activity to be ill-suited to the courses that they wish to create, and the forms of learning that they wish to encourage. Where an author is trying to develop ideas within a particular context or framework, or where the student is being required to develop a deeper understanding, then browsing is likely to be inappropriate. The hypertext reader might flit about between the trees with greater ease and yet still not perceive the shape of the wood any better than before.

RK parallel 12.5

PD contrast 8.5

When instruction is viewed as producing learning rather than guiding it, then it is most likely to upset the learner and interfere with their progress. It must be remembered that hypertext is merely another form of 'teaching arrangement', to use Marton's [8] term, and not the knowledge that it is wished to impart. What are the implications for hypertext if we take the phenomenological view of learning as a process of change in the way that the individual views something, rather that the mere aggregation of facts? Phenomenological studies have generally found at least five qualitatively different conceptions of academic learning among undergraduate students:

AR parallel 6.10

RK contrast 1.7

a) a quantitative increase in knowledge
b) memorizing
c) the acquisition of facts, methods, etc which can be retained and used when necessary
d) the abstraction of meaning
e) an interpretative process aimed at an understanding of reality

Reflective critical reading requires the student to alternately suspend and then make judgments concerning the author's argument, and linear texts contain 'turn-taking' cues to encourage such activities. Although it is unlikely that a simple technology such as hypertext will achieve much in terms of the higher level learning skills, it will be important to organize hypertext structures to at least not impede their growth. A difficulty will arise in devising hypertext structures suited to browsing that will also facilitate and encourage such deep processing. The idea of 'putting the rhetoric into the resource' put forward by Russell may provide a solution, as may the analysis of 'rhetorical space' proposed by Streitz. However at present, it remains an open question as to which forms of learning are aided, or perhaps least discouraged, by media forms such as hypertext.

PD contrast 8.7

SH example 23.16

It will also be necessary in the design of hypertext systems to devise structures that do not just hand over to the student a spurious form of 'control'. The most successful uses of hypertext will involve the learner and lead them to adopt the most appropriate learning strategy for their task. They must provide guidance and encouragement to students to make more than a surface level pass through the material. In this way they will allow the learner to develop higher level learning skills, rather than simply become the passive recipients of a slick new technology.

Conclusion

Given that the non-linear text forms are not going to replace the linear text form for pedagogic reasons, an important issue for learning from hypertext is as to whether hypertext should be regarded as the principle controlling/tutoring medium, or simply as an additional reference resource for conventional expository teaching materials. As an inherently formless medium, hypertext may take on a linear aspect. However, for both ergonomic and economic reasons its current use is likely to be best directed towards the provision of complementary resources. Handled properly, hypertext is potentially capable of greatly enhancing educational materials.

WV contrast 15.4

References

[1] Ravetz J.R. (1971). *Scientific knowledge and its social problems*. London: Oxford University Press.

[2] Conklin J. (1987). Hypertext: an introduction and survey. *IEEE Computer Magazine, 20*(9), (pp. 17-41).

[4] McDermott D. (1981). Artificial Intelligence Meets Natural Stupidity. In: J. Haugeland (Ed.), *Mind Design*, Cambridge: MIT Press, (pp. 143-160).

[4] Grimes J.E. (1975). *The thread of discourse*. The Hague: Mouton.

[5] Beaugrande R. de (1980). *Text, discourse and process*. Norwood, NJ: Ablex.

[6] van Dijk T.A. (1979). Relevance assignment in discourse comprehension. *Discourse Processes, 2*, (pp. 113-126).

[7] Waller R. (1987). The typographic contribution to language. PhD Thesis, Department of Typography and Graphic Communication, Reading University.

[8] Marton F. (1987). The phenomenography of learning- a qualitative approach to educational research and some of its implications for didactics. In: H. Mandl, F. de Corte, and H.F. Friedrich (Eds), *Learning and instruction in an international context*. Oxford: Pergamon.

PART II

DESIGNING THE
INFORMATION MODEL

Chapter 5
Macro-Operations for Hypertext Construction

Rainer Hammwöhner
Fachgruppe Informationswissenschaft
Universität Konstanz, FRG

Keywords

Automatic hypertext construction; text linguistics; text analysis; macro-operations; text unit; paragraph

Contents

Introduction

The use of scientific and technical journals is essential for research and tertiary level education. Because of the vast number of journals available today efficient access methods to full text information are required.

One of the major weaknesses of current full text information systems [1] is that almost the entire effort supports query formulation. The user of information retrieval systems, being in an "anomalous state of knowledge" [2], has problems expressing his/her informational needs. Therefore query formulation is supported by expert systems [3], natural language interfaces [4], and user models [6]. Having retrieved a set of relevant texts from a database the user faces the following problems:

•Based on the best match paradigm [7], most IR systems measure the relevance of a document according to the degree of similarity between document repre-

DJ parallel 12.7

sentations (eg. indexes) and query (search terms). A user interested in pieces of information scattered over several texts may therefore have to read redundant texts before she/he reaches a text which contains a new informational item.

- Additionally the presentation techniques employed in conventional retrieval systems are rather poor. In the worst case the user is confronted with a list of references.

The difficulties in obtaining information from a set of retrieved texts contribute to defeciencies in full text retrieval performance [8,9].

One way to overcome these shortcomings — the best one for users with fact oriented questions — is to complement full-text retrieval by text-based question answering systems [11]. Question answering systems and retrieval systems employ different notions of relevance, which in one case is based on informational needs and in the other on thematic overlap [12]. Relevant chunks of information are chosen according to an inference process, which additionally comprises the relevant information to a concise answer. In this paper I will deal with an alternative appproach to information retrieval and presentation.

A common feature of various recently developed information systems is the decomposition of linear document structure necessitated by conventional print media. Instead, an organization (networks or hierarchies) of information units of different forms (textual, graphical and pictorial presentation modes may be combined) is provided. Additionally, the presentation of textual information is enhanced by alternative presentation styles, like tables [13]. Documents organized in this way are called hypertexts. Hypertext systems are devoted to the exploratory paradigm [14] — reading a hypertext means traversing a network of text-units using a browsing-facility. Many hypertext systems offer string oriented retrieval functions, hierarchies of organizational text units like the tocs of Trigg's textnet [16] or predefined paths (textnet) to support hypertext navigation. Context free retrieval functions don't seem to be sufficient to the heavily content dependent navigation model of hypertext systems, therefore Frisse [16] proposes context sensitive (but still string oriented) retrieval functions.The conversion of texts into hypertext with its variety in presentation and navigation techniques is an alternative approach to improve online retrieval performance.

There are different approaches to converting texts into hypertext that are distinguished based on the answers given to the following two questions:

- What are the text units constituting a hypertext?
- What sort of links between the units will be provided?

The I3R-System [17] for instance is based on statistical clustering — hypertext-units are references to documents, and links are based on a similarity measure or on citation. Another system based on clustering is the IOTA-System [18] which allows for indexing and therefore interrelation of parts of documents (chapters etc.). An adaptation of this statistical approach to hypertext is given by Larson [19]. Frisse [20], on the other hand, proposes a semi-automatic text decomposition method. Text units of the resulting hypertext are identical with passages of the linear text. The hierarchical organization of the hypertext is based on the structural characteristics (eg. chapters or sections) of the original text. This occured in hypertext systems that originally emerged from text formatters like Superbook [21]. Non-hierarchical semantical or rhetorical links between text units may be provided by the user.

The approach we propose, the TWRM-TOPOGRAPHIC system, which was developed at the University of Konstanz from 1982-1988 [22], is based neither on statistical evidence nor on the surface structure of texts, but rather on text-linguistic regularities. Many semantic theories of text, like text grammars based on macrostructures (eg [23]) or the definition of semantic coherence through binary relations [24,25] are based on the two-dimensional structure of text [26, pp. 51-55]. Based on these text-linguistic models, texts may be converted to hypertext as follows:

- The text is fragmented to coherent text units which are mapped onto semantic representations [28].

DJ contrast 3.19

- Content oriented relations similar to the rhetorical relations mentioned above can be computed on the basis of these representations [28]. Thus, text passages taken from linear text can be rearranged as networks, such that every possible path in this network is semantically coherent.
- Macrostructures which resemble the hierarchical structures as found in conventional hypertexts (content nodes) reflect the topical structure of documents.

Macrostructures can be computed either

- •bottom up for the purpose of text analysis (the text—the leaves of the macrostructure—is given): so called macrorules are applied to text units creating a more general topical description [23], or
- •top down for the purpose of text generation (the topic—the root of the macrostructure—is given): the inverse rules are used to create more specific propositions [29].

Hypertext systems comprise both of these aspects. A hypertext may be regarded as a static network with a given hierarchical deep structure (comparable to the text-graphs as introduced by Reimer/Hahn [30] for linear texts). Navigating a hypertext implies the choice of subgraphs from the network which fit the user's (topical) interest. The application of macrorules with respect to this interest may be viewed as a user oriented reinterpretation of the hypertext (bottom up) as well as a navigation driven text construction process (top down). Macrorules implement a context oriented notion of relevance [31] fulfilling the requirements of relation and quantity [32] which deal with choice of relevant and the elimination of redundant information. This paper will give a semi-formal description of macrorules for the construction of hypertext deep structures (based on a frame-like formalism) and outline their role in hypertext navigation.

The application of macrorules is controlled by prototypical text plans, comparable to superstructures [33] or story grammars [34]. The proposed macro-structure model of hypertext is thought of not only as a text linguistic device for the description of text structure but as a cognitive model of text comprehension [35,36]. Kieras [37], for instance, shows and explains the effect of discourse cues —especially cues on correct generalizations — on the comprehension of simple technical prose according to a text model based on macrostructures. Thus macro-structuring of hypertexts is a prerequisite for the provision of semantic discourse cues as demanded by Charney [38] which will help to avoid confusion in hypertext navigation as observed by Jones [39] .

Macrostructures _____

The oldest science which deals with structuring and formulation of text is rhetoric, which has a tradition reaching back to ancient Greece. The special fields of rhetoric traditionally are:

- inventio: the discovering of the very ideas which shall be expressed in a text,
- dispositio: the ordering of these ideas and
- elucutio: the finding of adequate formulations.

Writing a text may be thought of as a interlocking process of inventio, dispositio and elucutio which leads to a stepwise refinement. A (still to be developed) rhetoric of hypertext has to reconsider the role of text disposition, which takes place in two phases. The hypertext author provides a network structure (dispositio) which contains chunked pieces of information (inventio) verbally expressed in text units (elucutio). The final ordering of these text units to more or less linear hypertext paths is done by the reader of the hypertext. In the search for hypertext disposition rules it should be helpful to consider theories of rhetorics and text linguistics about the structuring of linear text.

SH parallel 23.5, explanation 23.5

DJ reference Landow, G. (1989). The rhetoric of hypermedia: Some rules for authors. Journal of Computing in Higher Eduation, 1, 39-64.

Macrostructures of linear text

Garcia-Berrio/Mayordomo [29] point out the strong connection between the rhetorical concept of dispositio and the textlinguistic [40] notion of macrostructure as developed by van Dijk [33,23,41]. Macrostructures reaching beyond the domain of single sentences are elements of the semantic deep structure (a hierarchy) of texts. Macrostructures are sequences of propositions, which can be expressed in first order calculus. They can be derived from the microstructure of a text (surface structure) by the application of so called macrorules. These macrorules are semantic transformation rules mapping tuples of propositions to more general (macro-)propositions. Applied recursively, these transformations produce more and more general descriptions of the text. Thus, a hierarchy can be built which reaches from sentence topics over paragraph and chapter topics to the topic of the whole text. The four macrorules which are employed in this process follow.

The first macro-rule deals with the deletion of accidental information. Information which is not needed to understand the subsequent text is deleted:Attacking from behind the Tumtum tree the knight killed the Jabberwocky. $d_a \rightarrow$ The knight killed the Jabberwocky[43].

DR comment How is 'accidental information' determined? Seems difficult, despite the explanation in 5.16-17 governed by the . The user must still define 'relevant with respect to the query.' 5.16 24)

GL comment The macro-rule leaves out crucial information about both the action and the character of the actor and in some contexts could be taked to generate a major effect, eg. irony.

The application of the second macro-rule results in the deletion of constitutional information. Information which can be inferred by presupposition is deleted: He fought the Jubjub bird and didn't shun the frumious Bandersnatch. He is a brave man. $d_c \rightarrow$ He fought the Jubjub bird and didn't shun the frumious Bandersnatch.

The third macro-rule treats simple generalization: special information is replaced by more general information:Alice was having smalltalk with a tiger-lily, a rose and some daisies. $g \rightarrow$Alice was having smalltalk with some garden flowers.

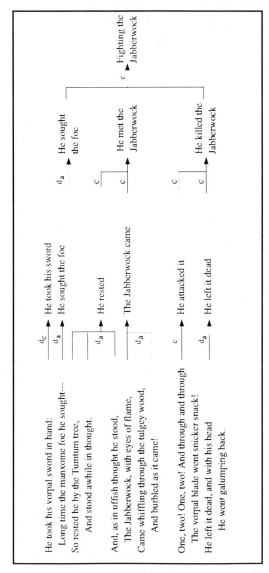

Figure 1. The (slightly simplified macrostructure of three verses taken from the poem "Jabberwocky" [43 pp. 140-142].

The fourth macro-rule is about the construction of propositions: A proposition is constructed which comprises a set of propositions from the text or macro-propositions from macrostructures:An egg with hands and feet is sitting on the wall. $c \rightarrow$ Humpty Dumpty is sitting on the wall.

Figure 1 shows a partial macrostructure of a poem by Lewis Carroll. Although the reader is furnished with a fixed set of macrorules, the derived macrostructure is not independent of the readers interests (if the reader had any interest in the "tulgey wood", it would possibly appear in a high level macrostructure) and knowledge (eg that a sword is usually taken in hand).

What is in a text unit?

The focus of global coherence in hypertext are the text units. The substructures of text units are unchangeable during dialog, whereas the position of a text unit in a hypertext path is fixed only to that extent, that its predecessor and successor must be linked to it. This uncertainty in the final positioning of a text unit demands that text units must be self sufficient with respect to the following aspects:

> •thematic unity: the boundaries of a text unit must coincide with the boundaries of a semantic theme.
> •anaphora, pronouns: all occurring anaphora and pronouns must be resolvable within the text unit itself or within the preceding hypertext path.

If we want to construct hypertexts from sets of linear text by a knowledge based text decomposition, we need to identify what text parts fulfill these conditions. This task will probably enable the modularization of hypertexts by human authors as well — a discussion which is often dominated by the idiosyncrasies of contemporary hypertext systems [45 p. 42].

The role of text units in hypertext is comparable to that of paragraphs in linguistics. Both bridge a gap between structural levels: fixed ordering — flexible ordering in the case of text units, sentence level — text level in the case of paragraphs. Both of these contrasting pairs reflect the difference between global and local coherence phenomena. Although the paragraph is not generally believed to be a canonical text segmentation unit Phillips [p. 90] refers to the frequency of erroneous paragraphing. The importance of the paragraph for text structuring is widely accepted in linguistics and psychology [48,49,50].

The paragraph is considered as semantic unit on a certain discourse topic, [29,47,51], thus a paragraph oriented decomposition of text cannot be based on syntactic evidence (eg. indentation) alone but must be based on a semantic model of text, which is capable of dealing with incorrect syntactic paragraphing. Stark [48] shows that human readers correctly distinguish semantic paragraphs in spite of erroneous paragraph markers. Furthermore there is no anaphoric reference to the paragraph topic from outside the paragraph [52]. Thus, the prerequisites for text units as mentioned above are fulfilled.

An additional property of the paragraph, which makes it a useful concept for hypertext, is the creation of paragraphs [53] according to their internal structure (linkage between sentences, local coherence), thematic progression [54] and discourse function. Narrative paragraphs with temporal linking and backward referencing can be distinguished from expository paragraphs with causal linking [55,56,57] Restricting paragraph types in a hypertext is a way to reduce the complexity of text analysis and hypertext planning. In this paper we will further deal with descriptive or expository paragraphs with a temporal linking. Typed paragraphs can be regarded as the terminal symbols of a hypertext grammar based on macro- and superstructures [33].

In addition to the types of discourse, two types of thematic bordering can be discerned [52]:
The paragraph is cut off before a new discourse topic is introduced (eg the second verse of the poem shown in Figure 1). The paragraph is cut off immediately after the new discourse topic is presented, providing a stronger link to the following paragraph (eg the first verse of the poem shown in Figure 1).

Macrostructures in hypertext
Macrostructures in hypertexts differ in several aspects from macrostructures of linear texts. In linear texts, macrostructures give a hierarchical representation of the text's topical structure on a meta-level. They reflect the process of generalization in text analysis or stepwise refinement in text generation. Both of these processes are ruled by a special notion of relevance (eg. before the application of the first macrorule it must be determined which information can be regarded as accidental and thus be deleted). Where text generation is driven by

contextual relevance determining what ideas the author wants to express, text analysis is guided primarily by textual relevance which asks if particular information is important to understand the following text (also, does it fit the reader's informational needs) [58].

Macrostructures of hypertexts as meta-level descriptions of the deep structure of the complete hypertext networks correspond to macrostructures of linear text. Hypertext navigation may be understood as the construction of texts, so called hypertext paths, which are built up from a set of given pieces, or text units. These text units fulfill the criteria of textual wellformedness and therefore have macrostructures themselves. Elements of these path-macrostructures are macro-text-units which are derived from the original text units by the application of macro-operations. These macrostructures in hypertext comprise the (contextual and textual) relevant information of a set of text units in a condensed form. These text units may stem from different linear texts, therefore macrostructures in hypertext reflect special aspect of intertextuality of document fragments [61]. Regarded as part of the hypertext derived text units can be used as navigational aids in hypertext browsing. The presentation of macro-text-units for instance, may be graphically presented as a conceptual network [22] or as a textual abstract [62] can help to choose the appropriate hypertext path to follow.

SH example 23.20

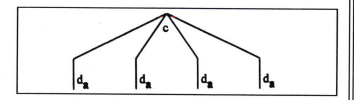

Figure 2. Several text units describe aspects of a single concept

The definition of prototypical macrostructures (textplans) helps to adapt the dialog to special informational needs and user purposes. A hypertext containing text fragments taken from computer magazines (the domain all further examples are taken from) can be traversed for instance following a path:
- which gives a description of one special device (Figure 2) or
- which compares two (or several) devices with respect to their properties (Figure 3).

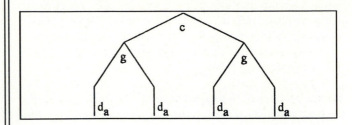

Figure 3. Instances of a generic concept are compared with respect to their properties

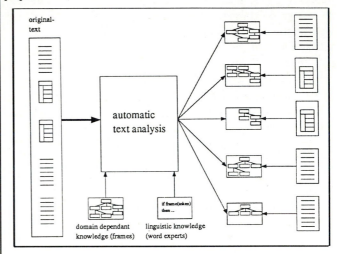

Figure 4. A text is fragmented into text units amd mapped to representation structures by automatic text analysis—eg by the TOPIC-system.[27,70].

A frame-oriented hypertext model ⸻

Recently published formal approaches to hypertext emerge from the emphasis each puts on a special aspect of hypertext. A strong stress on linking motivates the choice of semantic networks as a formal basis for hypertext in TEXTNET [16] or Thoth-II [63]. TEXTNET employs a semantic network which directly connects chunks of text by semantic and rhetorical relations. The approach of Thoth-II is better suited for automatic integration of new text segments. Thoth-II is provided with a semantic network modeling of the concepts within a given domain of discourse. The connection between text and conceptual knowledge is established by a string-oriented matching procedure, although string-oriented are an insufficient means for automatic text processing [64]. If the handling of hypertext nodes is emphasized, object oriented approaches to hypertext are preferred [65,66]. Planning hypertext dialogs requires additional features like agent models that support of an extrinsic task (eg. support of software engineering) with an agent/task driven hypertext [67,68] or constraints on the intrinsic task of planning argumentation [69] which is supported by constrain graphical objects at the presentation level. The intended hypertext model has to fit the following context:

- •The first step of hypertext construction is the automatic decomposition and analysis of texts. A mapping from text units to representation structures is computed based on linguistic knowledge and background knowledge about the domain of discourse (Figure 4).
- •Based on these representations semantic relations between text units and macrostructures of sets of text-units may be established (Figure 5).
- •The presentation of hypertext paths depends on a user formulated query [71], text plans and prototypical informational objects, which control the mapping from semantic objects to graphical objects [72] and thus form the elements of a graphical text presentation language [73].

DJ parallel 7.4-6

AR contrast 19.17

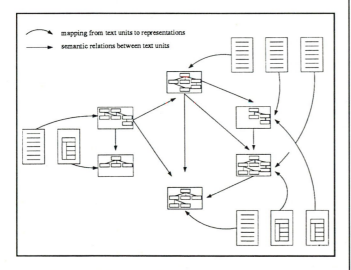

Figure 5. The network structure of the hypertext depends on semantic properties of text unit representations (eg conceptual networks)

A uniform representation formalism, which can be used for conceptual knowledge, text plans and graphical structures as well, is the frame construct, which was introduced to AI by Minsky [74]. Frame-like structures like case frames [75] or scripts [76], are widely used in linguistics and text understanding. The relationship between the constructs of frame- and object-oriented languages is a programming issue in computer graphics [77], including inheritance and perspectives [78,79].

The basic representation structures

The frame formalism we will employ in our hypertext model is an extended version of FRM, the representation language of the TOPIC-system [80,81]. The text units contained in the hypertext are mapped to sets of frames. A frame is built up by a set of slots, each of which is associated with a set of permitted and a set of actual entries. Additionally, an activation weight is assigned to frames, slots, and actual entries. This structure may be formalized as a cascade of partial mappings (Figure 6):

$$HTREP := \{f \mid f: Tu \cup \{w.q\} \rightarrow FRAMES\} \qquad (D1)$$
$$FRAMES := \{f \mid f: Names \rightarrow \{<s,w> \mid s \in SLOTS, \qquad (D2)$$
$$w \in \{rejecting, irrevelant, relevant, dominant\}\}\}$$
$$SLOTS := \{f \mid f: Names \rightarrow \{<act,.perm, w> \mid \qquad (D3)$$
$$act \in Entries, perm \in 2SDO1(Names,),$$
$$w \in \{rejecting, irrevelant, relevant, dominant\}\}\}$$
$$ENTRIES := \{f \mid f: Names \rightarrow \{irrelevant, relevant\}\} \qquad (D4)$$

Names is a non empty set of concept identifiers and *Tu* is a set of text unit identifiers.

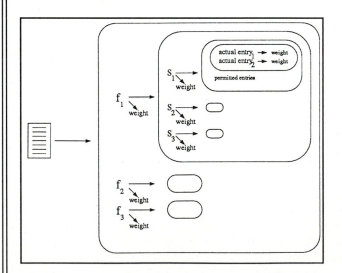

Figure 6. A hypertext representation as a cascade of mappings.

Based on the cascade of mappings as described above, the following functions may be defined, which allow access to:

- the frames of text unit (D5),
- the weight of a frame (D7),
- the slots of a frame (D8),
- the weight of a slot (D9),
- the permitted entries of a slot (D10),
- the actual entries of a slot (D12), and
- the weight of an entry (D11).

Elements of tuples are obtained using a projection function:
$$P_{n,i}(<x_1,x_2,..,x_i,..x_n>):=x_i$$

$$frames := \lambda kb.f \mid f \in dom\ kb\} \qquad (D5)$$
$$fslots := \lambda kb\ .\lambda f.p_{(2,3)}(kb\ (f)) \qquad (D6)$$
$$fweight := \lambda kb\ .\lambda f.p_{(2,2)}(kb\ (f)) \qquad (D7)$$
$$slots := \lambda kb\ .\lambda f.\{s \mid s \in dom\ fslots\ (kb)(f)\} \qquad (D8)$$
$$sweight := \lambda kb\ .\lambda f.s\ p_{(2,3)} fslots\ (kb)(f)(s) \qquad (D9)$$
$$eperm := \lambda kb\ .\lambda f.\lambda s.p_{(2,2)}(fslots\ (kb)(f)(s)) \qquad (D10)$$
$$eact := \lambda kb\ .\lambda f.\lambda s\lambda e.p_{(2,2)}(\&slots\ (kb)(f)(s))(e) \qquad (D11)$$
$$entries := \lambda kb\ .\lambda f.\lambda s\ \{e \mid e \in dom\ eac(kb)(f)(s)\} \qquad (D12)$$

These representation structures cover the aboutness [82] of text units as follows (For a deeper understanding see [27]):

- Prototype frames (frames without entries) represent the background knowledge, which is needed to understand the text unit. A set of prototypes contained in a special text unit representing the domain dependent knowledge is the basis of text analysis.

$$prototype(kb,f):\Leftrightarrow kb \in FRAMES \land f \in frames\ (kb) \land \qquad (D13)$$
$$\land \forall s \in slots\ (kb)(f):entries\ (kb)(f)(s)=\{\}$$

- Instance frames (frames containing at least one entry) represent special knowledge as learned from the text. Every instance frame has exactly one corresponding prototype which is taken from the domain dependent knowledge.

$$instance(kb,f):\Leftrightarrow kb \in FRAMES \land f \in frames\ (kb) \land$$
(D14)
$$\land \exists s \in slots\ (kb)(f):entries\ (kb)(f)(s) \neq \{\}$$

- The activation weights indicate the salient concepts of a text unit. The most salient ones are dominant, followed by relevant ones. Irrelevant frames contain only background knowledge. (Rejecting can only occur in a query: see the D22).

The frames within a knowledge base are not just isolated objects but are interrelated by a specialization hierarchy which can be inferred from the slot-structure of frames. In this context the notion of non-terminal slots is important — these are slots the names of which are identical to a frame within the knowledge base. The permitted entries of a non-terminal slot are the subordinates of the corresponding frame.

$$non\text{-}term(kb,s): \Leftrightarrow kb \in FRAMES \land s \in frames\ (kb) \qquad (D13)$$

There are two specialization relations [80,81].:

  •The is-a relation deals with concept specialization by adding new slots to a concept or by restricting the permitted entries of a given slot (Figure 7).

$$isa(kb,f,f'): \Leftrightarrow prototype(kb,f) \land prototype(kb,f') \land f \in frames$$
$$(kb) \qquad (D14)$$
$$\land \forall s\ 'vslots\ (kb)(f'): \exists s\ \in slots\ (kb)(f):$$
2
$$(s = s\ 'vnon\text{-}term(kb,s\ ) \land non\text{-}term(kb,s\ ') \land e\text{-}is\text{-}a(kb,s,s\ ')) \land$$

$$\qquad\qquad\qquad\qquad\qquad\qquad 3$$
$$\land \forall s \in slots\ (kb)(f) \cap slots\ (kb)(f'): \qquad\qquad 4$$
$$eperm(kb)(f) \leq eperm(kb)(f')(s\ ) \land \qquad\qquad 5$$
$$\land \exists s \in slots\ (kb)(f):(s \notin slots\ (kb)(f') vs \in slots\ (kb)(f') \qquad 6$$
$$\land eperm(kb)(f)(s\ ) < eperm(kb)(f')(s\ )) \qquad\qquad 7$$

  •Specialization within the *inst* (instance) relation re-quires additional slot-entries (Figure 7).

$$inst\ (kb,f,f'): \Leftrightarrow \qquad\qquad\qquad (D17)$$
$$(prototype(kb,f') vinstance(kb,f')) \land instance(kb,f) \land \qquad 2$$
$$\land (instance(kb,f') \Rightarrow \qquad\qquad 3$$
$$\Rightarrow \exists s \in slots\ (kb)(f): \qquad\qquad 4$$
$$\exists e \in entries\ (kb)(f)(s\ ):e \notin entries\ (kb)(f')(s\ )) \land \qquad 5$$
$$\land \forall s \in slots\ (kb)(f'): \forall e\ '\in entries\ (kb)(f')(s\ ): \qquad 6$$
$$(e\ '\in entries\ (kb)(f)(s\ ) vnon\text{-}term\ (kb,s) \land \qquad 7$$
$$\land \exists e \in entries\ (kb)(f)(s\ ):e\text{-}is\text{-}a\ (kb,e,e'))) \qquad 8$$
$$\land slots\ (kb)(f) = slots\ (kb)(f') \land \qquad\qquad 9$$
$$\land \forall s\ \in slots\ (kb)(f):eperm(kb)(f)(s\ ) = eperm(kb)(f')(s\ )\ \ 10$$

The *e-is-a* relation is the transitive closure of is-a and ins

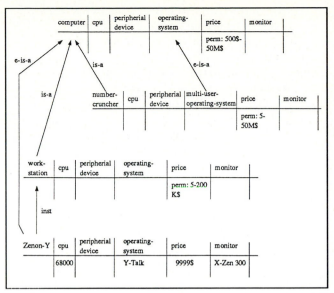

Figure 7. The *is-a* relation between computer and number-cruncher holds because of the restricted set of permitted entries in the price-slot and the specialization of the slot operating-system to multi-user-operating-system. The inst relation between workstation and Zenon-Y holds because of the actual slot entries.

$$e\text{-}is\text{-}a(kb,f,f'):\Leftrightarrow is\text{-}a(kb,f,f')\lor inst(kb,f,f')\lor$$
$$\lor \exists f'':(inst(kb,f,f'')\, is\text{-}a(kb,f'',f') \qquad\qquad \text{(D18)}$$

Macro-operations in a frame-oriented hypertext model

Based on the hypertext model defined above, macro-operations can be defined which allow for the derivation of abstract macro-text-units and the clustering of text units contained in a hypertext according to a user formulated query and a context oriented notion of relevance. In the following we will outline the formalization of the macro-operations as introduced above and give a concise formalization of the deletion of accidental information d_a).

- The *generalization* operation g ($g \in \{f \mid f\text{:}FRAMES\text{:} *2^{FRAMES}\text{:}\to FRAMES\}$) of a cluster of text units under consideration of domain dependent knowledge may be used as a test function for text unit clustering, because it maps improper clusters to the empty knowledge base. The units of a cluster must have salient concepts which are direct subordinates of a common prototype f_p. Each subordinate of f_p may occur only once within a cluster (to avoid uncontrolled redundancy). A (not empty) macro-text-unit of a cluster of text units is mapped to fulfill the following conditions:

a. The frames representing the salient concepts are copied to the macro-text-unit.

b. Additional, more general prototypes are taken from the domain dependent knowledge.

c. Activation weights are shifted to more general concepts.

d. Eventually, existing further frames are not copied.

•The major difference between *generalization* and *construction* is that the latter employs the slot-relation instead of the specialization hierarchy, thus aggregating properties (or parts) of a concept which are mentioned in different text units.

•*deletion of constitutional information:* The definition of this macro-operation requires representation structures (defaults and constraints on slots), the presentation of which would exceed the scope of this paper (but which are part of FRM).

The *deletion of accidental information* is governed by the salience of concepts within the text units on one hand and the query on the other hand. This macro-operation is a mapping from pairs of knowledge bases, including queries and text units to knowledge bases
$(d_a \in \{f \mid f{:}FRAMES{:}\ *FRAMES \rightarrow FRAMES\})$. The resulting macro-text-units are stripped of all frames which are not relevant with respect to the query, thus irrelevant text units are mapped to the empty knowledge base. A frame f_t which represents a salient concept of the text unit TU is relevant with respect to a query Q if there is a dominant frame f_q in Q and

•f_q has the same name as f_t or

•f_q is superordinate of f_t or

•f_q has the same name as a dominant slot of f_t

•and there is no frame f_r in Q which inhibits the selection of f_t.

In this case, f_t is element of $d_a(Q,TU)$ (D19) without any difference in its structure (D20). Additionally prototypes of relevant instances are mapped to the macro-text-unit (D21). The interrelation of frames which are part of different text units—eg the closure of name identity and specialization (D23) — is based on the presupposition that all representations are derived from the same domain dependant knowledge and therefore contain prototypes which are common to all text units.

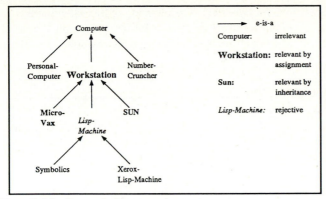

Figure 8. Inheritance of relevance assignments

The inheritance of relevance assignments may be restricted by rejective assignments (D24, Figure 8).

$\forall Q, TU, \quad f{:}f \in frames \ (d_a(Q,TU)) \Leftarrow r \ (Q,TU,f)$ (D19)

$\forall Q, TU, \quad f{:}f \in frames \ (d_a(Q,TU)) \Leftarrow prototype \ (Tu,f) \wedge$ (D20)

$\wedge \exists f_i inst(f_i,f) \wedge r \ (Q,TU,f_i)$ 2

$\forall Q, TU, \quad f{:}f \in frames \ (d_a(Q,TU)){:}TU(f)=d_a(Q,TU(f)$ (D21)

$r \ (Q,TU,f_0{:}\Leftrightarrow f) \in frames \ (TU)$ (D22)

$\qquad \wedge (fweight \ (TU)(f) \in \{dominant, \ relevant\}) \wedge$ 2

$\qquad \wedge \exists f_q(Q){:}$ 3

$(fweight \ (Q)(f_q)=dominant \wedge$ 4

$\qquad \wedge (i(TU,f_t,Q,f_q) \vee f_q \in slots(TU)(f_t) \wedge$ 6

$\qquad \wedge sweight(TU)(f_t)(s)=dominant) \wedge$ 7

$\qquad \wedge \neg \exists f_r \in Q{:} b(TU,f_t,Q,f_r))$ 8

$i(TU,f,TU',f'){:}\Leftrightarrow f \in frames \ (TU) \wedge f' \in frames \ (TU')$

(D23)

$\qquad \wedge f=f' \vee \exists f'' \in (frames \ (TU) \cap frames \ (TU')){:}$ 2

$(e\text{-}is\text{-}a(TU,f,f'') \wedge (f''=f' \vee is\text{-}a(TU',f'',f'))))$ 3

$b(TU,f,TU',f'){:}\Leftrightarrow f \in frames \ (TU) \wedge f' \in frames \ (TU') \wedge$ (D24)

$\qquad \wedge fweight(TU',f')=rejecting \wedge i(TU,f,TU',f') \wedge$ 2

$\qquad \wedge \neg \exists f'' \in frames \ (TU'){:}$ 3

$fweight(TU'')(f'')=dominant \wedge$ 4

$\wedge \ is\text{-}a(TU',f'',f') \wedge i(TU,f,TU',f'')$ 5

Concluding remarks

In this paper, we have discussed concepts of text oriented linguistics like macrostructures and paragraphs as text segmentation units which can be useful for designing hypertext. Furthermore, we have defined a frame-oriented hypertext model and used it as basis for the formalization of macro-operations for hypertext. The planning of hypertext paths based on macro-structures and script-like prototypical text plans, which additionally makes use of paragraph types, shall be dealt with in another paper.

References

[1] Belkin, N.J. and Croft, B.W. (1987). Retrieval techniques. In Martha E.Williams, (Ed.), *Annual Review of Information Science and Technology, 22*, (104-145).

[2] Belkin, N. J., Oddy, R. N. and Brooks, A. M. (1982). ASK for information retrieval. Part I: Background and Theory. *Journal of Documentation, 38,* (2), 61-71.

[3] Biswas, G., Bezdek, J. C., Marques, M., and Subramanian, V. (1987). Knowledge-assisted document retrieval: I. The natural language interface. *Journal of the American Society for Information Science, 38*, (2), 83-96.

[4] Smith, L.C. (1987). Artificial intelligence and information retrieval. In Martha E.Williams, (Ed.), *Annual Review of Information Science and Technology, 22*, (pp.41-77).

[5] Biswas, G., Bezdek, J. C., Marques, M.and Subramanian, V. (1987). Knowledge-assisted document retrieval: II. The retrieval process.*Journal of the American Society for Information Science, 38,* (2), 97-110.

[6] Brajnik, G., Guida, G., and Tasso, C. (1987). User modeling in intelligent information retrieval. *Information Processing & Management, Special Issue: Intelligent Information Retrieval, 13*, (4), 305-320.

[7] Robertson, S.E. (1980). Some recent theories and models in information retrieval. In O Harbo, ad C. Kajberg, (Eds.). *Theory and applications of information research,* (pp. 131-136). London,UK.

[8] Blair, D.C. and Maron, M.E. (1985). An evaluation of retrieval effectiveness for a full text document retrieval system. *Communication of the ACM, 28*, (3), 289-299.

[9] Tenopir, C.(1985). Full-text database retrieval performance. *Online Review, 9*, (2), 149-164.

[10] Rau, L.F. (1987). Information retrieval from never-ending stories. In *AAAI87 — Proceedings of the Sixh National. Conference. on Artificial. Intelligence, Vol. I*, 317-321,Los Altos, Ca.: Morgan Kaufman.

[11] Simmons, R.F. (1987). A text knowledge base from the AI Handbook. *Information Processing & Management, 13*, (4), 321-339.

[12] Swanson, D.R. (1977). Information retrieval as a trial-and-error process. *Library Quaterly, 47*, (2), 128-148.

[13] Stibic, V. (1985). Printed versus displayed information. *Nachrichten fur Dokumentation , 36*, (4/5), 172-178.

[14] Bates, Marcia J. (1985). An exploratory paradigm for online information retrieval. In Brookes, B. C. (Ed), *Intelligent Information Systems for the Information Society. Proceedings of the Sixth International Research Forum in Information Science*, (pp. 91-99).

[15] Trigg, R.H. and Weiser, M. (1986). TEXTNET: A network-based approach to text handling. *ACM Transactions on Office Information Systems, 4.*,(1), 1-23.

[16] Frisse, M.E. (1987). Searching for information in a hypertext medical handbook. In Proceedings. of the Hypertext '87 Conference, 57-66. University of North Carolina at Chapel Hill.

[17] Croft, W.B. and Thompson, R.H. (1987). I3R: A new approach to the design of document retrieval systems. In *Journal of the American Society for Information Science, 38*, (6), 389-404.

[18] Defude, B. and Chiamarella, Y. (1987). A prototype of an intelligent system for information retrieval: IOTA. *Information Processing & Management, 13*, (4), 284-303.

[19] Larson, R.P. (1988). Hypertext and information retrieval: Towards the next generation of information systems. *Information & Technology, Proceedings. of the 51st Meeting of the American Society for Information Science.*195-199, Atlanta, Georgia.

[20] Frisse, M.E. (1988). From text to hypertext. *Byte, 13*, (10), 247-253.

[21] Remde, J.R., Gomez, L.M.,and Landauer, T.K. (1987). SuperBook: An automatic tool for information exploration— Hypertext? In *Hypertext '87 Papers*, (pp.175-188.). University of North Carolina at Chapel Hill.

[22] Thiel, U. and Hammwohner, R. (1986). Graphical interaction with a full-text oriented information system: The retrieval component of the end user interface TOPO-GRAPHIC. In *Proceedings. of the Second International. Conference. on the Application of Micro-Computers in Information, Documentation and Libraries*. Amsterdam, NL.

[23] van Dijk, T. (1980). *Textwissenschaft*, Munchen, FRG.

[24] Hobbs, J.R. (1983). Why is discourse coherent? In Fritz Neubauer (Ed), Coherence in Natural Language Texts. *Papiere zur Textlinguistik Band 38*, (pp. 29-70). Hamburg,FRG.

[25] Mann, W.C. and Thompson, S.A. (1988). Rhetorical structure theory: Toward a functionatheory of text organization. *Text, 8,* (3), 243-281.

[26] Gulich, E. and Raible, W. (1977). *Linguistische textmodelle*. Basel.

[27] Hahn, U. and Reimer, U. (1986). TOPIC-Essentials. COLING-86. *Proceedings of the 11th International Conference on Computational Linguistics*, 497-503.

[28] Hammwohner, R. and Thiel, U. (1987). Content oriented relations between text units — A atructural model for hypertexts. In *Hypertext '87 papers*, (pp. 155-174). University of North Carolina at Chapel Hill.

[29] Garcia-Berrio, A. and Mayordomo, T.A. (1988). Compositional structure: Macrostructure. In Janos Petofi (Ed.), *Text and Discourse Constitution.*, (pp 170-211). Berlin, FRG.

[30] Reimer, U. and Hahn, U. (1988). Text condensation as knowledge base abstraction. In *Proceedings — The Fourth IEEE Conference on Artificial Intelligence Application*. Washington,D.C.: Comp. Society. of the IEEE.

[31] Tiamiyu, M. and Ajiferuke, I.Y. (1988). A total relevance and document interaction effects model for the evaluation of information retrieval processes. I*nformation Processing &*

[32] Grice, H.P. (1975). Logic and conversation. In R. Cole, and J.L. Morgan (Eds.), *Syntax and Semantics, Vol. 3, Speech Acts,* (pp. 41-58). New York.

[33] van Dijk, T. (1980). Macrostructures, Hillsdale,NJ: Lawrence Erlbaum.

[34] Rumelhart, D.E. (1975). Notes on a schema for stories. In D.G. Bobrow, and A. Collins (Eds.), *Representation and Understanding: Studies in Cognitive Science.,* (pp. 211-236). New York.

[35] Kintsch, W. (12982). Aspects of tText comprehension. In J.F. LeNy, and W. Kintsch (Eds.), *Language and Comprehension.,* (pp.301-312). Amsterdam ,NL.

[36] Ehrlich, S. (1982). Construction of text representation in semantic memory. In J.F. LeNy, and W. Kintsch (Eds.), *Language and Comprehension,* (pp. 169-177). Amsterdam, Ne.

[37] Kieras, D.E. (1982). A model of reader strategy for abstracting main ideas from simple technical prose. In *Text, 2,* (1-3), 47-81.

[38] Charney, D. (1987). Comprehending non-linear text: The role of discourse cues and reading strategies. In *Proceedings. of the Hypertext '87 Conference,* (pp. 109-120). University of North Carolina at Chapel Hill.

[39] Jones, W.P. (1987). How do we distinguish the hyper from the hype in non-linear text? In, H.J. Bullinger, B. Shackel, and. K. Kornwachs (Eds.), *Human-Computer Interaction — INTERACT 87, Proceedings of the Second IFIP Conference on Human-Computer Interaction,* U.of Stuttgart, FRG.

[40] de Beaugrande, R.-A. and Dressler, W.U. (1981). *Einfuhrung in die Textlinguistik,* Tubingen, FRG.

[41] Ballmer, T.T. (1976). Macrostructures. In: T. A.van Dijk (Ed.), *Pragmaticsof Language and Literature* (pp. 1-22). Amsterdam, NL.

[42] Petofi, J.S. (1979). Die struktur der TeSWeST. Aspekte der pragmatisch-semantischen interpretation von objektspra-

chlichen texten. In Fritz Neubauer (Ed.), *Coherence in Natural Language Texts*. Hamburg,FRG.

[43] Carroll, L. (1939). Through the looking-glas. In T*he Complete Works of Lewis Carroll*, (pp. 126—250). Glasgow, Scotland, UK.

[44] Burchfield, R.W. (1976). A Supplement to the Oxford English Dictionary, Oxford, UK.

[45] Conklin, J. (1987). *A survey on hypertext*, (MCC Technical Report No. STP-356-86, Rev. 1).

[46] Phillips, M. (1985). *Aspects of text structure — An investigation of the lexical organization of text*. Amsterdam, NL.

[47] Longacre, R. E. (1979). The paragraph as a grammatical unit. In T. Givon (Ed.), *Syntax and Semantics 12*, New York.

[48] Stark, H.A. (1988). What do paragraph markings do? *Discourse Processes*, *11*, (3), 275-303.

[49] Garnes, Sara (1987). Paragraph perception by seven groups of readers. *Ohio State University Working Papers in Linguistics, 35*, 132-141.

[50] Koen, F., Becker, A., and Young, R. (1969). The psychological reality of the paragraph. *Journal of Verbal Learning and Verbal Behaviour, 8* (1), 49-53.

[51] Pike, K.L. and Pike, E.G. (1977). *Grammatical analysis*. Dallas,Texas.

[52] Giora, R. (1983). Functional paragraph perspective. In Janos S. Petofi,.and Emel Sozer (Eds.), *Micro and macro connexity of texts*, (pp. 153-182). Hamburg,FRG.

[53] Groe, E.U. (1974). *Texttypen*, Stuttgart, FRG.

[54] Danes, F. (1978). Zur linguistischen analyse der textstruktur. In Wolfgang Dressler, (Ed.), *Textlinguistik*, (pp. 184-192).Darmstadt, FRG.

[55] Longacre, R. E. (1974). Sentence structure as a statement calculus. In Ruth M. Brend, (Ed.), *Advances in tagmemics,* (pp.251-283). Amsterdam NL.

[56] Longacre, R. E. (1976). Discourse. In Ruth M. Brend,and

Kenneth L. Pike (Ed.), *Tagmemics — Aspects of the field.* Paris, France.(1-44).

[57] Zimmermann, K. (1978). *Erkundungen zur texttypologie,* Tubingen.

[58] van Dijk, T. (1979). Relevance assignment in discourse comprehension. Discourse Processes, 2, (2), 113-126.

[59] Hutchins, J. (1987). Summarization: Some problems and methods. In K. P. Jones (Ed.), *Informatics 9: Proceedings. of a Conference....* King's College, Cambridge, 26-27 March 1987, London, 151-173.

[60] Fum, D., Guida, G.and Tasso, C. (1985). Forward and backward reasoning in automatic abstracting. In *Proceedings of the Ninth International Joint Conference on Artificial Intelligence,* 840-844.

[61] Begthol, C. (1986). Bibliographic classification theory and text linguistics: Aboutness analysis, intertextuality and cognitive act of classifying documents. In *Journal of Documentation, 42*, (2), 80-113.

[62] Sonnenberger, G. (1988). Flexible generierung von naturlichsprachigen abstracts aus textreprasentationsstrukturen. In H. Trost, (Ed.), *4.Osterreichische Artificial IntelligenceTagung, Wiener Workshop —Wissensbasierte Sprachverarbeitung,* (pp. 72-82). Berlin FRG.

[63] Collier, G.H. (1987). Thoth-II Hypertext with explicit semantics. In *Hypertext '87 papers,* (pp. 269-289) University of North Carolina at Chapel Hill .

[64] Hahn, U. (1986). Methoden der volltextverarbeitung in informationssystemen. In Rainer Kuhlen (Ed.), *Informationslinguistik.* Tubingen, FRG. (pp.195-216).

[65] Christodoulakis, S., Ho, F., and Theodoridou, M. (1986). The multimedia object presentation manager of minos: A symmetric approach. *Sigmod Record, 15* (2), 295-310.

[66] Woelk, D., Kim, W., and Luther, W. (12986). An object oriented approach to multimedia databases. *Sigmod Record, 15,* (2), 311-325.

[67] Garg, P.K.and Scacchi, W. (1987). On designing intelligent hypertext systems for information management in software engineering. In *Hypertext '87 papers*, (pp.409-432). University of North Carolina at Chapel Hill.

[68] Garg, P.K. (1987). Abstraction mechanisms in hypertext. In *Hypertext '87 papers,* (pp.375-395). University of North Carolina at Chapel Hill.

[69] Smolensky, P., Bell, B., Fox, B., King, R. and Lewis, C. (1987). Constraint-based hypertext for argumentation. In *Hypertext '87 papers* (pp. 215—245). University of North Carolina at Chapel Hill.

[70] Hahn, U. and Reimer, U. (1988). Knowledge-based text analysis in office environments: The text condensation system TOPIC. In W. Lamersdorf, (Ed.), *Office knowledge: Representation, management and utilization* (pp. 197-215). Amsterdam, Ne.

[71] Thiel, U. and Hammwohner, R. (1987). Informational zooming: An interaction model for the graphical access to text knowledge bases. In C. T. Yu, and C. J.van Rijsbergen, (Eds.), *Proceedings of the Tenth Annual International ACMSIGIR Conf.erence on Research & Development in Information Retrieval* (pp. 45—56). New Orleans, Louisiana.

[72] Thiel, U. and Hammwohner, R. (in press). Interaktion mit textwissensbasen —ein objektorientierter ansatz. In *Tagungsband der jahrestagung der gesellschaft fur informatik*

[73] Lakin, F. (1987). Visual grammars for visual languages. In *AAAI87 — Proceedings of the Sixth National Conference on Artificial Intelligence, Vol. II* (pp.683-688). Los Altos, Ca.

[74] Minsky, M. (1975). A framework for representing knowledge. In P. Winston, (Ed.), *The psychology of computer vision* (pp. 211-277). New York: McGraw Hill.

[75] Fillmore, C.J. (1968). The case for case. In E. Bach, and R.T. Harms, (Eds.), *Universals in linguistic theory* (pp. 1-88). New York.

[76] Schank, K. and Abelson, R. (1977). *Scripts, plans, goals,*

*and understanding.*Hillsdale, N.J.

[77] Hollan, J.D. (1984). Intelligent object-based graphical interfaces. In G. Salvendi (Ed.). *Human—computer interaction* (pp.293-296). Amsterdam, Ne.

[78] Stefik, M. and Bobrow, D.G. (1986). Object oriented programming: Themes and variations. *The AI-Magazine, 6,* (4) 40-62.

[79] Bobrow, D.G. and Winograd, T. (1977). An overview of KRL-0, a knowledge representation language. *Cognitive Science,1* (1), 3-46.

[80] Reimer, U. (1986). A system-controlled multi-type specialization hierarchy. In L. Kerschberg (Ed.) *Expert Database Systems. Proceedings of the First International Workshop* (pp.173-187). Menlo Park/CA: Benjamin/Cummings.

[81] Reimer, U. (1989). *FRM: Ein frame—reprasentationsmodell und seine formale semantik.* Berlin, Heidelberg, FRG.

[82] Hutchins, W.J. (1977). On the problem of 'aboutness' in document analysis. *Journal of Informatics, 1* (1), 17-35.

Chapter 6
Concepts as Hypertext Nodes: The Ability to Learn While Navigating Through Hypertext Nets

Ray McAleese
University of Aberdeen, UK

Keywords

concept maps; Gordon Pask; knowledge representation, semantic nets, constructivism

Contents

Introduction and overview ──────────

Most hypertext models assume a network metaphor consisting of information nodes with labelled or typed links to similar nodes. The nodes in hypermedia systems can be typed as *text*, *graphics*, *moving images*, or a combination of these three. The information content of such a system depends on the granularity or "chunk size" of the information units or nodes. Different nodes will have different amounts of information. The granularity of information in hypertext is not determined by the hypertext metaphor but rather by the way information is organized by the designer of the system. As such systems allow the size of nodes to vary from large chunks of text, graphics, etc. and pictures at one end of a continuum to concept labels. Such an entity is defined as "the minimum entity that signifies or denotes an understanding by a user and has meaning by itself". A singularity state for the node is repre-

DJ definition 1.3-4, parallel 2.3

sented by the concept label. In some systems a document consisting of many thousand characters will compromise nodes (eg *Intermedia*) [1,2]. In others, only a few characters can constitute a "node, for example, an explanation box in Microsoft *Guide*.

This chapter argues that a state of "singularity" exists where the concept label can constitute a node. The chapter focuses on the question, "What happens when the size of a hypertext node is a "singularity"?".

RH contrast 5.7

A system called SemNet is being evaluated in Aberdeen as a way of representing information in a web or net of labelled nodes. SemNet is a knowledge representation tool that is based on a constructivist approach to learning and knowledge acquisition. [4] Knowledge is represented by nodes with labelled links representing semantic relationships. SemNet runs on Macintosh SE/ II computers and uses the Mac's graphical interface to show graphical representations of knowledge and permits users to interact with such knowledge bases through a map or web of nodes. Bounded views of nodes and contiguous neighbors are presented to the user. Learners navigate the knowledge base from node to node by pointing at new concepts which in turn are shown as the central node with their first level labelled relationships. Experience using SemNet has shown that it is possible to facilitate learning by allowing students to navigate through such a network of concept labels. Students overlay their own understandings over existing networks. Where students browse from node to node, they can add, delete or modify the node labels or the relationship labels. There is no need to make knowledge instances fixed. Further learners and "experts" can represent in a formal way their understandings and misunderstandings using the SemNet metaphor. Browsing through the network can be monitored and replays of trails are possible.

DJ comment assumes semantic distance can be spatially represented. See Holly, C.D. & Dansereau, D.F. (Eds.), (1988). *Spatial learning strategies.* NewYork: Academic Press.

Assumptions Made About Hypertext ———

Some assumptions are made in this chapter about hypertext systems. In summary these assumptions are:

1. Hypertext systems are designed to capture, store and present information.
2. Hypertext systems can consist of labelled and or typed nodes and labelled and or typed links.
3. Hypertext nodes can vary in size from the singularity of a

concept label to many thousands of characters.

4. The size of the hypertext node, its granularity or its information content is determined by the designer of the system.

5. Concept labels, when they constitute nodes taken along with their labelled links, constitute the information content of a knowledge representation hypertext system.

6. The locus of control in a hypertext system rests with the user, not the designer.

Hypertext Granularity

An important issue in hypertext systems is the information content of the nodes. This "grain size" of the information effects the way systems are used. It is inter-dependent with the underlying network metaphor. The net metaphor permits a wide range of node size. Granularity effects the way the user navigates or browses through a system. For example, in a small grain the node could be limited to no more than 50 ASCII characters (much less than would appear on a Hyper-Card "card"). A large grain node, on the other hand, might consist of many thousand ASCII characters along with bit-mapped elements of graphics pictures and sound (something like the information that would be available from a hyperme-dia node consisting of picture, text and graphics).

Granularity

If we consider the relationship that exists between the user and the computer, some insights with regard to hypertext navigation, browsing and "grain size" can be achieved.

Four premises exist.

1. There exists a dynamic relationship between the user of the hypertext system and the information in the hypertext system.

2. This relationship exists in a closed system.

3. Users move from node to node in order to maintain a stable relationship.

4. Harmony is a stable state where the computer meets the needs of the user.

Navigational or browsing choice represents the stabilizing effect in keeping a harmony between the user and the computer. A measure of the *choice* (**C**) at each node is dependent on the information content of that node (I_n) (expressed as the number of bits of information required to represent the information at the node) *expressed as a ratio* of the information processing capacity of the user (I_{pu}) (based on a number of values such as the readability of the information, typographic characteristics of the information) multiplied by the cognitive processing capacity of the user (C_{pu}) (based on a large number of variables such as the number of new concepts in the node in relation to old or existing concepts that the user "knows" or is explicitly and implicitly aware of, the number and type of links that exist between concepts for the user, etc).

Choice $\qquad$ $C = I_n / (I_{pu} * C_{pu})$ $\qquad$ **(1)**

For this value, a continuum exists from 1 to a very large value [5].

In the *Singular* case with **C=1**, the information presented at the node *equals* the information and cognitive processing capacity of the user at the node.

Singularity $\qquad$ **In = Ipu * Cpu** $\qquad$ **(2)**

As I_n increases then unless there is a concomitant increase in I_{pu} an/or C_{pu}, then there exists a state where the Choice **C** value increases. In some cases C_{pu} can increase as familiar information is presented; however I_{pu} tends to be rather static and dependent on the nature of the human computer interface. With I_n taking on a value many times greater than $I_{pu} * C_{pu}$ then some accommodation has to exist between the ability of the user to process information at the node and the inherent information that exists.

A continuum of practice

At one extreme there is the grain size that approaches singularity, that is, minimal information content. The concept label is an example of such an information chunk. A concept label only signifies a concept; it is not the concept itself. The concept label has a very low I_n value. Characters constituting the label have a high certainty value for the user. At the other end is the very rich hypermedia node with a very large value for I_n. Unless there is an increase in I_{pu} or C_{pu} then the value of C increases and "wobble" at the node increases.

This continuum represents the real possibilities for the hypertext designer. Hypertext as non-sequential information organization does not make any explicit demands on the node size. There may be hidden expectations for grain size. For example, the HyperCard system implies a small node size given the card metaphor. Similarly, the card of the NoteCards system necessitates a relatively small grain size. In the former case there is in practice, if not in theory, a tendency to limit the amount of information at a node to the space available on the card. In theory, using scrolling fields, the amount of information may increase. Similarly with NoteCards, the 3 by 5 file card is the model. Here again the practice varies with regard to the amount of information stored. In general there is a limit placed on the information by the stereotype and the design of the screen interface. In contrast, Intermedia makes an explicit assumption that the node size is a document. Documents can be very large with many tens of thousands of words, pictures etc. Experience shows that the very large nodes in Intermedia are impractical as this decreases the *degrees of freedom* given to the user to an extent that no navigation may occur at all.

Examples of node size

In Figure 1, the user is represented as interacting with a Small Grain node system. The number of possible choices that can be made is very much larger than in the Large Grain node system shown in Figure 2. One can think of a *degree of freedom* or "wobble" that exists at each node. This wobble, is dependent on **Choice (1)** and it effects the probability of any other node being chosen.

The probability of choosing a node can be represented as:

$$\textbf{Node Probability} \quad N_p = (N_n * I_n) / (I_{pu} * C_{pu}) \quad (3)$$

With increasing node size the wobble decreases. The information content (I_n) of the node will in part determine the range of choices the user makes. Designers make implicit and explicit choices about how much information to put at a node. This choice in turn will affect the way hypertext systems are used. When using a grain size of the concept label there is a very wide range of choices open to the user when deciding where to "go" next. This would be a characteristic of a knowledge representation type of hypertext system as exemplified by SemNet. The information content of each node of the SemNet system is dependent on the number of concept labels, their relationships and the prior knowledge the user has about the implied relationships.

Granularity is important to hypertext systems as it affects the way users browse, the time on each task element and eventually the possible complexity of the system. SemNet is a system with a very low granularity that encourages browsing and necessitates an effective way of allowing the user to communicate intent to the system. In general, users express their "intent" by choosing to move from one node to another. Actions, in terms of choosing another node, imply "intentions." The "intentions" of the users indicate the way they wish to learn about new nodes and relationships.

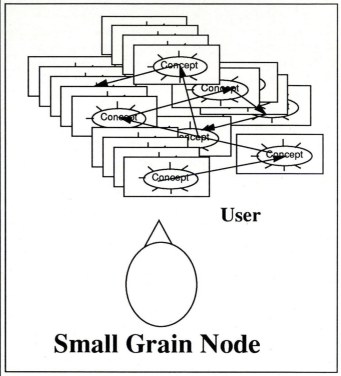

Figure 1.

Concept map metaphor ————————

AR parallel 7.6

A metaphor is often used to help describe a process which is only partly understood. The concept map or network metaphor serves this purpose. It assumes that knowledge can be represented as nodes and links in a network, with nodes representing the concept labels and links representing the relationships that exist between concepts in declarative statements. For example, suppose someone believes something like:

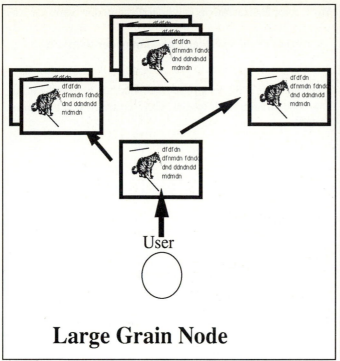

Large Grain Node

Figure 2.

A camera has a lens

This can be represented as two nodes

Camera

Lens

along with one relationship

has-a

In simple notation this is represented as:
{camera}, *has_a*, {Lens}

(Note: A suggested convention is to put all concepts into curly braces { } and represent the relationship as one text string with individual elements separated by underscores, eg _).This statement can be represented in a graphical way as can be seen in Figure 3.

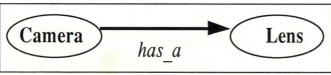

Figure 3.

More complex statements can be represented in a similar way.

Cameras require a steady hand in order to give a sharp picture.

This statement requires a little more analysis before the node-link-node structure is imposed. Three concepts can be represented:

cameras

steady_hand

sharp_picture

Two relationships exist:

requires

gives

This belief or statement is represented in the map in Figure 4:

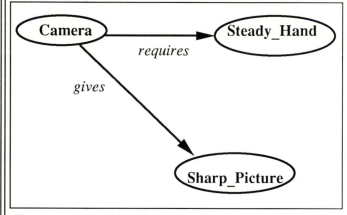

Figure 4.

It is sometimes difficult to force statements or beliefs into the net metaphor. It is possible but may require some restructuring of the belief as initially expressed. In practice this is acceptable if the restructured statement is seen as indistinguishable from the former by the person holding the belief or making the statement.

SemNet as hypertext
SemNet is a form of hypertext system, because is exibits the characteristics listed above.
a) SemNet is a store of information.
b) SemNet represents knowledge using a network metaphor

c) SemNet permits global to global linking of information units

6.9

d) the access to and control over the ordering of node access is in the control of the user, NOT the designer
e) SemNet permits the nodes to be "filled" with text, graphics and bit mapped images
f) SemNet has inbuilt tracking of the nodes visited
g) SemNet allows direct jumps from one node to another
h) SemNet can be set in browse only mode to allow students to read the content but not change content.

The idea of using a semantic net formalism is not new. At least one other system has used the name "SemNet" [6]. A number of other systems closely resemble SemNet, in particular TextVision devised by Piet Kommers and the Learning Tool devised by Bob Kozma [7]. A predecessor of SemNet, CASP, was a system built for the Apple][computer by the present author . CASP permitted the representation of concept maps [8]. The SemNet "version" used in this research is a Macintosh application designed for representing a domain of knowledge in the form of a "semantic network" - a multi-dimensional knowledge base or collection of concepts linked by relations [9]. SemNet represents information as a collection of concepts linked by relations. Concepts appear to the user in ovals or rounded boxes. A pair of nodes linked with a relationship is known in SemNet as an "instance" (See Figure 9 for a SemNet example). The "rules" of the representation system have been simplified in two assumptions [10]:

PK parallel 4.2-7

1. Concepts have word labels or names.
2. These labels are usually (but not always) nouns [11].

There are concepts that lack word labels and are difficult to represent in such a semantic network. Much domain expertise and knowledge can be represented as declarative statements consisting of nouns; some cannot. However, this does not invalidate SemNet. SemNet is not designed to be a general purpose knowledge representation system. Rather it portrays, where appropriate, such knowledge as can be represented in the formalism described by Jo Novak, Leo West and many others [12,13].

Some concept nets can be very large. Some consist of several hundred nodes with even more links. Some attempts have been made to alleviate the problem of providing a conceptually clear view of the nature and extent of such systems for users with overviews [14]. Fish-eye browsers and compass

DJ parallel 4.3

AR example7.5

browsers reduce the problem but one is left with the general hypertext problem of giving the user a sense of the detail while at the same time allowing the content to grow.

SemNet solves the viewing problem by displaying one "frame" at a time. Each frame contains one central concept (e.g., {resin}) with its closely related concepts ({**separation column**},{**reverse_phase**}, etc.) (See Figure 5). Related concepts are displayed at various points on the periphery of the screen and are connected to the central concept by labelled lines representing relations (***is_a _part_of, contain_by,*** etc.).

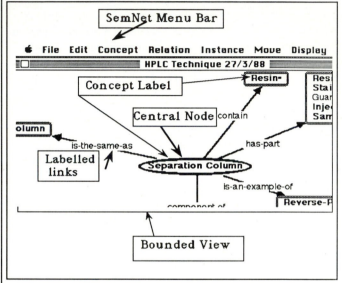

Figure 5.

Assumptions about learning

DJ corroboration 3.3
AR parallel 4.5

A convenient way of explaining learning is with reference to "learning as RE-construction" [15]. That is, learning can be shown to be a process by which existing concepts are re-ordered or re-constructed into new and stable structures. Based on the premise that knowledge is constructed of concepts, then to know something is to have a concept-based structure that embodies that "knowledge". So for example to know about (ie to know that ...) a {**computer**}, can be seen as a construction of other concepts, {**memory, keyboard, language...**}. When someone learns about a {**computer**}, then

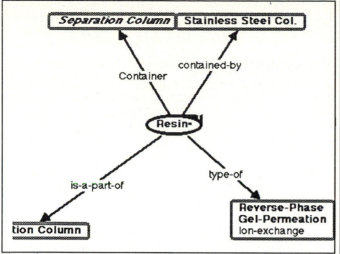

Figure 6.

the pre-existing concepts are re-ordered, or more accurately re-constructed into a complex web of interdependent concepts that taken as a whole give the understanding of {**computer**}.

This explanation of learning can be substantiated with empirical evidence and is the basis of cognitive theories of knowledge acquisition[16]. At the basis of this explanation is the premise that concepts (that is, *understandings)* can be represented by concept labels. A concept label is the minimal unit of understanding. The grain size of the information is unity. A learner may know about {**resin**}, that is using the signs **R, E, S, I, N** taken as an entity, can be communicated to mean {**resin**}. Someone can articulate the label as [*rez-in*] or write it as resin. In other words the sign **r e s i n** , stands for the understanding of {**resin**}. It is possible to denote the complex web of understandings that forms the foundation for any knowledge by drawing such relationships as concept maps [17]. Thus a simple understanding is denoted in Figure 7 is that "*Gel-Permeation is a type of Resin and at the same time an example of a type of Separation Column*". Learners construct and RE-construct tacit understanding contained in such graphical representations. There is no right or wrong way to negotiate understanding. The totality of the web gives the subtle connotations that are possible. When they navigate a hypertext system based on concept labels, learners negotiate their own specific and unique understandings based on the web.

PK comment Negotiation needs two actors. So the reader needs a more explicit representation of the author's knowledge.

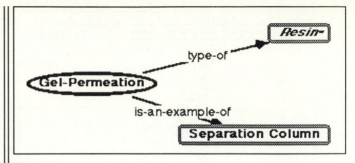

Figure 7.
To re-construct an understanding is to re-assemble the concept labels that are used to denote a unique understanding. The map or graphic representation in Figure 8 representing another understanding.

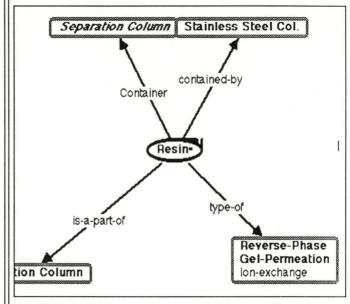

Figure 8
Learning of course is not simply the acquisition of new nodes. Coming to know something is a stable agreement that certain concepts cohere together [18]. Indeed, coming to know can be seen usefully as a negotiation of understanding between different parties. A teacher and a student negotiate a meaning of something through the medium of instruction. For example a teacher says " resin is contained by a stainless steel column". To say that a learner comes to know such a thing is to say that the learner comes to agree that " resin is contained by a stainless steel column" is true. That is, it is a valid and stable understanding. Such agreements between teachers and students take place through language. Similarly if the teacher

were to write or in some other way represent such a understanding, then by reading such signs the learner can come to
such an understanding. His or her concepts are re-ordered so
that they are the same as that of the teacher. To begin with the
student may know something as represented in Figure 9.

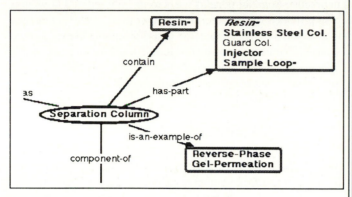

Figure 9

After instruction (navigating a hypertext net) the learner may
know something different as shown in Figure 10.

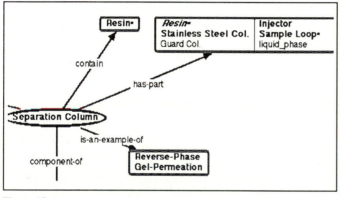

Figure 10.

In other words the learner has now added the concept label
{liquid_phase} to the list of [has-part] related concepts. The
process of coming to know new relationships is a process of
RE-constructing personal understandings in light of public
understandings. Public understandings are denoted by the
nodes and labelled links of the net. The confrontation of
private understandings with public understandings results in
a process of accommodation, reconciliation, integration and
probably differentiation [19,20]. How this instruction takes
place is not the issue under scrutiny; the ability of the learner
to acquire by "discovery" such an understanding is quite

possible. Further, such an understanding can be enhanced by use of a graphic interface.Learning is therefore "<u>a personal negotiated understanding given meaning in the representation of concepts and relationships</u> " .

In practice SemNet permits users to interact with a knowledge base provided by an expert or an other user. The user engages in a personal dialogue with the assertions made in the instances. The user negotiates meaning in interacting with the system. The understandings that are induced or the cognitive dissonances that occur are the outcomes of using such a hypertext system.

How SemNet induces learning

This section is an attempt to bring together the main ideas of a possible explanation of what happens during a session using SemNet. It is a first attempt to theorize on the process. It is therefore open to comment and critical comment. SemNet is an example of a dynamic concept map with many different maps "drawn" for the user as they browse through the system. Table 1 is the first few steps of a typical browse captured by SemNet's tracking facility.

open at.........Separation Technique
—is-used-for—>HPLC
—comprises—>Separation Column
—has-part—>Resin
—type-of—>Gel-Permeation
—type-of—>Resin
—type-of—>Ion-exchange
—type-of—>Resin
—type-of—>Reverse-Phase
—based-on—>Hydrophobic Interaction
—is-the-opposite-of—>Hydrophilic Interaction
—is-the-principle-of—>Reverse-Phase
—type-of—>Resin
—is-a-part-of—>Separation Column
—has-part—>Injector
—changes—>Switch
—changes—>Injector

Table 1.

The net was opened at {Separation Technique} and the node {Resin} was chosen with the relationship *has-part*. Next the user looked at the knowledge base from the perspective of {Gel-Permeation} and the relationship *type-of*. {Resin} was revisited then the user chose to look at the knowledge base from the perspective of {Ion-Exchange}. And so on. At each frame the user has the information shown in Table 2 on display. This Table shows the detail of the information available to the user at each selection. Each of the individual frames represents the nodes and relations that are displayed graphically.

1. **open at**.........Separation Technique
—is-used-for—>HPLC

2. **HPLC**
—comprises—>Separation Column
>High Pressure Pumps
>Detection System
>Recorder
—is-used-for—>Separation Technique

3. **Separation Column**
—is-the-same-as—>Column
—component-of—>HPLC
—is-an-example-of—>Reverse-Phase
>Gel-Permeation
—has-part—>Resin
>Stainless Steel
>Guard Column
>Injector
>Sample Loop
—contains—>Resin

4. **Resin**
—has-part—>Resin
—is-a-part-of—>Separation Column
—type-of—>Reverse-Phase
>Gel-Permeation
>Ion-Exchange
—conained-by—>Stainless Steel Column
—container—>Separation Column

5. **Gel-Permeation**
—type-of—>Gel-Permeation
—is-an-example-of—>Separation Column

6. **Resin**
—type-of—>Resin
—is-a-part-of—>Separation Column
—container—>Separation Column
—contained-by—>Stainless
Steel Column
—type-of—>Reverse Phase
>Gel-Permeation

Table 2.

For example Figure 6 in this chapter is the graphical interface to the information shown in frame 4 of Table 2. In general it seems that users of SemNet read the information as a series of statements. Take for example frame 2.

2. **HPLC**
—comprises—>Separation Column
>High Pressure Pumps
>Detection System
>Recorder
—is-used-for—>Separation Technique

This can be read as follows:

{HPLC} comprises-of {Separation Columns, High Pressure Pumps, Detection System, Recorder} is-used-for {Separation Technique}

Each of the frames can be read as a series of SemNet "instances". The node-link-node instances constitute the understanding. The user chooses an appropriate node from which to further explore the knowledge base. For example in Frame 3, the user chose {Resin}. The resulting Frame 4, shows the knowledge from the point of view of {Resin}. The browsing or navigation undertaken by the user is a process of checking out the instances. It is as if the net is being held by one node at a time, the user looking at the adjacent nodes. New nodes are selected and a new view is given. The initiative to move from one node to another is in part, dependent on the information content of the node and the cognitive processing of the user.

In terms of the assumptions about learning referred to above, the user of the system has to accommodate the external realization of the knowledge (as shown by the SemNet system) and his/her internal or private understanding. The learning process is an accommodation of the public and the private understandings. Such accommodation is an example of cognitive processing overhead. As such it effects the probability of choosing nodes.

DJ definition 1.18

In similar ways, any hypertext system allows the users to accommodate their current understanding of ideas with that presented in the hypertext nodes. With systems that have large grain size to the nodes the assimilation and accommodation of the information presented is rather more complex, but is based on the same process. The "wobble" or number of choices available at any node, referred to above, is a function of the information content of the frame being read.

Guidelines and principles

Guidelines eminating from the work are centered around the question of granularity, the nature of knowledge representation systems as forms of hypertext and the nature of learning. It is possible to make some assertions about the design of hypertext systems if some premises are acceptable. The following guidelines are based on the utility of the respective premises.

GIVEN:

- a network metaphor for a hypertext system
- a hypertext system that permits a variety of node types (text, graphics...)
- the ability to vary the amount of information collected at each node of the system

THEN *Granularity Guidelines*

1. reduce information into the minimum sized node possible in order to maximize the number of routes through the "knowledge base".

2. maximize the number of links between nodes to ensure that individual differences between users are catered for.

3. refrain from pre-determining acceptable routes through hypertext systems

PD explanation 8.7

4. use large grain nodes where information exists as a coherent entity to be communicated (eg instructions)

5. use small grain nodes where the certainty factor of the knowledge/ information is low or where there is a degree of value judgement in the validity of the knowledge/ information.

GIVEN:

- that knowledge is constituted by concepts
- that a concept label is a symbolic free form representation that signifies a concept
- that concept labels are used to represent such concepts
- that relationships between concepts can be represented

by similar labels
- that for at least one individual valid beliefs exist which can be represented as concepts and relationships in the form of one or more node-relationship-node instances
- graphical representations of these relationships can be made in two dimensional maps called concept maps

THEN *KR Guidelines*

1. decompose knowledge into concept labels
2. represent relationships between concepts by symbolic labels
3. allow a free use of concept and link labels to maximize the public representation of private (expert) understandings
4. use graphical interfaces to facilitate and help experts to make explicit their tacit or private understandings

GIVEN:
- that learning, in general, is an active reconstruction by learners of concepts and their relationships
- that a wide variety of learning styles exist
- that learning is a process by which individuals negotiate meaning through interacting with events, ideas, concepts...

THEN *Learning Guidelines* include:

1. allow leaners to overlay their own understandings on hypertext nodes and links
2. provide overviews of what is to be learned and what has been learned to enable learners to contextualize knowledge/information

References

[1] Yankelovich, N. et al. (1988). Intermedia: The concept oof a seamless information environment. *IEEE Computer, 21*(1), 81-96.

[2] Duncan, E. B. and McAleese, R. (1984). Qualified citation indexing on-line? In M. Williams (Ed.), On-line processing. New York: Learned Information.

[3] Brown, P. J. (1986). Interactive documentation. *Software-Practice and Experience, 16*(3), 291-299.

[4] Brown, P. J. (1988). Hypertext: The way forward. In J. C. van Vliet (Ed.), *Proceedings of EP 8*. Cambridge: Cambridge University Press.

[5] Fisher, K. et al. (1989). *SemNet manual, version 1.0*. University of California at Davis.

[6] Fairchild, K., Poltrock, S., and Furnas, G. (1988). SemNet: Three dimensional graphic representation of large knowledge bases. In R. Guideon (Ed.), *Cognitive science and its application for human computer interaction.* Hinsdale, NJ: Lawrence Erlbaum Associates.

[7] Kozma, R. B. (1987). The implications of cognitive psychology for computer based learning tools. *Educational Technology, 28* (11), 20-25.

[8] McAleese, R. (1986). The representation of knowledge in authoring environments. In N. Rushby and A. Howe (Eds.), *Aspects of educational technology XIX, educational, training, and information technologies—Economics and other realities,* (pp. 104-113). London: Kogan Page.

[9] Novak, J. and Gowin, D. (1984). *Learning to learn.* Cambridge: Cambridge University Press.

[10] West, L. and Pines, J. (1985). *Cognitive structure and conceptual change.* New York: Academic Press.

[11] McAleese, R. (1989). Navigation and browsing. In R. Mc Aleese (Ed.), *Hypertext: Theory into Practice.* London: Blackwell.

[12] Ausubel, D. P. and Robinson, F. G. (1969). *School learning: An ontroduction to educational psychology.* New York: Holt, Rinehart, and Winston Inc..

[13] Cohen, G. (1983). *The psychology of cognition.* London: Academic Press.

[14] Pask, G. (1984). conversation theory: A review. *Educational Communications and Technology Review, 15,* 78-104.

[15] Arzi, H. J. and West, L. H. T. (198 6). *Ausubel revisited: More insights from a seemingly exhausted source.* Paper presented at the Annual meeting of the American Educational Research Association, San Francisco, 1986.

Chapter 7
Graph Computation as an Orientation Device in Extended and Cyclic Hypertext Networks

Piet Kommers
Twente University, NL

Keywords

Concept map; graph computation; Gordon Pask; Kees Hoede; digression; centrality index; network editor

Contents

Introduction

Hypertext techniques have evolved from the concept of *virtual information*, which states: you may see the information where you need it without actually copying and replacing the information. This position is supported by those who promote *cognitive support* for the user, such as adapting the information to be presented to the *cognitive need* of an individual. The same is true for the phase of text creation: Inserting text, *merging different perspectives, parsing semantic clusters, pruning* etc. They are all principles of virtuality and the flexibility to combine nodes to information. Hypertext can stand alone in *educational settings* . The best of our interactive systems are or will be equipped with browsers, digressive tools, sound and even video.

The project I shall describe analyzes the essential structure within information and the need for computational power to organize in the enormous networks of more than several thousands of nodes. The basic problem that we have explored in the project, "Conceptual Graphs and the Elicitation of Knowledge," is:

"How can we support teachers and students in navigation through cyclic networks?"

We have addressed this problem in the context of study skills, specifically the phase of 'schematizing'. A well known method to stimulate *meta-learning* is "Becoming aware of conceptual structures" ie. the cognitive effects of *schematizing*: It is accomplished by directing the learner to: "Mention the most important concepts you remember from the text, place them in a figure,and connect them if there is a clear relation between them." A bottom-up way of creating such a network is by highlighting words in the text as it is read and placing them in an overall structure afterwards. Our project team investigated the information processing which occurred while the person configures such a network. Many learners immediately asked for a blank sheet and started from scratch (*top-down*) by retrieving the most *salient concepts* from his/ her mind at that moment. This is referred to as *conceptual mapping*. It concerns a *spatial (visual) representation* of the relations between concepts as they exist in our mind.

DJ definition 6.6-10

DJ parallel 8.2-3

Hypertext as an example of *text digression*, can be seen as a procedure to create implicit *conceptual structures*. Every *link* that arises from a paragraph *entails* to one or more other concepts. For instance, in explaining the essential meaning of hypertext, I use new words in order to describe the concept under concern. Each of these words again can start a new description field, again introducing new words, and so on. Long chains of *entailments* may arise, especially if many authors *collaborate* and if the *domain of explanation* is large. The structures that evolve during *digression* certainly are not as clear and balanced as we would like. They tend to be *cyclic*. Concepts refer to their own as people start their explanation. Authors are surprised when they perceive *recursion in their explanations*. One way of solving the tension between *mental transparency* and *implicit recursion* is *conceptual mapping*. Mapping in the spatial sense can be an adequate intermediate between *personal knowledge* and structure in the *chains of descriptions*. This led us to explore the utility of a *network editor*, which enables the author (and finally also the reader) to construct a *spatial structure* according his/her conception of the subject.

7.3

DJ implication 6.6-10

In order to support conceptual mapping by authors and learners. we developed Textvision in a 2- and a 3-dimensional version. It has been used by teachers, domain experts, and students. Though it only accepts one type of relation (*associative*), it elicits from the user relationships between concepts. It asks:

1. 'Is there' a relation?
2. Is it clear and important enough to be mentioned here?
3. Are there more *dominant concepts* to be mentioned?
4. How are they related to concepts mentioned just before?
5. How should then be placed in my concept space (two dimensional plane)?
6. Can I reconfigure the positions of nodes so that there are fewer *crossings of the links?*
7. Can I *prune the nodes* or *prune the links* while retaining the essence?
8. Are there *cliques* or *clusters* to be *subsumed* in a *super concept*?

Experimental study of these sessions show iterative procedures that occur until there is a certain *level of saturation*. This means not only that the network is extended enough, but it also concerns the question: "Does this configuration really reflect what I mean?" In other words, "Does it legitimate what I mean?" or "Is it representative of the domain I am trying to cover?" As soon as the network contains *cycles* and the number of nodes goes beyond 5 or 6, we say that the user becomes interested in *structural entities* like:

PK background 6.3

- The center of the graph
- The longest cycle
- The direction of the links: Undirected, directed or bidirectional
- Concept replacement: The same links but a better spatial position
- Merging 'bundles' of relations

These practical questions motivated us to explore *graph*

analyses for *user assistance*. It became clear that the *network tools* should express the direction of a relation, and it should prompt the user where the *center of the information* was found. These needs proved to be quite diffuse in the beginning, but soon became clear as we presented prototypes to the users. The main group of experimental users were in the field of primary education. The network *schematizing* approach fitted in study-programs very well and motivated teachers to think aloud and to give emotional feed back.

In order to analyze the scientific background of conceptual mapping and how it can be applied to *hypermedia* and *knowledge elicitation tools*, I will now concentrate on graph computation, *3-dimensional network editors,* and *network browsers* for very large encyclopedias.

Hypertext, conceptual entailment and the implicit need for graph computation _____

Virtual conceptual relations as defined in hypertext systems may foster *mental flexibility*, but at the same time, they can easily lead to *digression*, *entropy* and *losing one's way*. The power of hypertext *resource manipulation* is in the flexibility of the user options like *multi-windowing, stack-oriented backtracking* and *dynamic network display*.

DJ explanation 1.13-18

Two hypertext systems have been constructed in order to *mock-up* real-life learning and entertainment sessions.*Textvision* has been built for a MacIntosh coomputers using MS-Windows. It enables the user to construct *concept networks* with textual explanations of each node. The network editor has been developed in a 2-and a 3-dimensional version. Hypernet runs on MS-DOS computers and covers a 4000 concept Medical Encyclopedia. The user (author and consumer) is invited to *zoom in* on the complexity of interrelations. The display of networks can be *pruned* by means of *graph computation*. Two pruning criteria are used: *hierarchy* and *reference*. The first reflects the level of description while the second can be compared with the *citation-index*. The assumptions of the Hypernet metaphors include

AR parallel 8.8

- concept-object relations
- associations as links in a network of items

Both Textvision and Hypernet are precursors to CD-ROM(XA) based user interfaces and can demonstrate the trade-off between *expressiveness* and *tractability* in order to match cognitive needs to the computational power of current information systems.

Mapping the implicit hypertext relations

Without seeing the network of nodes and the relations between them, browsing unstructured hypertext is quite similar to *tours in a maze*. Users visit a set of adjoining concepts en route to a desired item in a database, rather than retrieving the item directly, such as through keyword lookup. Passing through intermediate items can give an orientation in the total structure of references and confronts the reader with the leading concepts before arriving at the target concept. Digression in browsing can destroy the original goal of the user, as he/she perceives that the points of interest are not explained in the current database. If the user has a purposeful question, digression is negative consequence. Digression, if the user has a more global interest in a topic area, can be seen positively as "Finding what one was looking for ," which is inherent to *exploratory learning*, or more popularly as serendipity.

Two types of user attitudes are allowed in hypertext systems. The most salient role that the user can take is to be a consumer of text information. In this case, the relational network can act as an orientation device like seeing a map on your way through a foreign town. If the actual visualization of the map cannot be presented, we may presume that the reader has to build up one or another kind of representation in order to return to a previously visited place or in order to be aware which part of the total "space" still has to be explored.

The second role of the user might be one of creator of conceptual networks. In this case, the user needs to have some spatial orientation of the entire structure. Beyond that, the mapping technique will be useful to check if the *elaborated concepts* still match the main ideas he or she wants to express. Constructing networks in the last sense often acts as *mental pruning* which can also be used as a *retrieval schema.* Both consumption and construction of ideas by means of network representation are strongly acknowledged by cognitive psychologists as *cognitive structure* and *schema-theory*" [1,2,3]. It is this synergism between "*cognitive schema*" as a mental device for human knowledge acquisition and the *network display by computers* that suggests the potential of hypertext for learning situations. Theorizing about the function of schemas in human thinking and memory began in the early thirties [4] and is still a central core in cognitive research [5]. Besides the assumption that schemas are present as structural entities in the human mind, they have been used as a metaphor for designing learning tools and tools for representation of knowledge in computers. This metaphorical function, broadens the meaning of concept entailment and digression which is the leading principle in hypertext systems.

AR parallel 6.6

Entailment structure: Knowledge maps for learning

The link between hypertext links and Pask's notion of entailment structures might be strange for those who are unfamiliar with conversational strategies and the need to identify prerequisites and subsume mental concepts [1,2] (those who see learning as eating information). Pask, who developed *Conversation Theory*, started with the idea that the fundamental unit for investigating complex human learning is a conversation involving communication between two participants who commonly occupy the roles of learner and teacher. Conversational learning is both a procedure to maintain *cybernetic learning* in an individual student and a procedure to identify a *relational network* which can act as a guidance for learning conversations. The first premise of *Conversation Methods* is that the control of the learning situation should be based on an *external representation* of the *subject-matter domain*. The second premise is that teacher to pupil conversation should consist of demonstration and explanation. Demonstration occurs when one partner shows an application of a concept. Explanation occurs when one describes the meaning of a concept in words and explains the relations with other concepts in the topic area. The third premise is the need to meet the requirements of strict conversation.

- All conversational topics are part of the predetermined *Conversational Domain*, which has been established by subject matter analysis.
- The conversation has been partitioned into *occasions*. Each of them must beterminated by *understanding*. Understanding arises if both partners mutually agree with the interpretation of the current topic of discourse.

Learning is seen as taking place through interpreted formal relationship. Formal relations in Pask's sense can be:
- is a part of -
- next -
- dual -
- precedes -
Formal relations are applied to a subject matter domain like physics, social science, justice etc. Embedded in the domain knowledge, a formal relation becomes a set of propositions, expressing a law, formula or mechanism and is called a topic. Understanding a topic means satisfying the relationship embodied in the topic, rather than simply giving a description of it's concepts and their attributes. To ensure that the demonstration of understanding is unambiguous, Pask uses a visual representation of the knowables, acting as a map for guiding the route of learning, called the entailment structure. Before going into details of entailment structures, and the function they have during strict conversation, I would like to describe Pask's approach to learning by man- machine interaction. Pask [6] states that, "... a human being in contact with a machine, is 'self-organizing' insofar as the ratio of its actual variability to its potential variability is always greater than zero." This criterion, in combination with the approaches of Piaget, Vygotsky, or Papert, requires *conversational methods* for exteriorising normally hidden events. *Conversational theory* rests on our notion of human to human conversation. Pask's teaching devices do make a strong appeal to the teacher participant of the conversation Self-organizing will occur only if both student and teacher can reconstruct each other's mental ideas within a *strict conversation*. While the student has to grasp the relatively stable concepts within the subject-matter domain, the teacher has to interpret the variety of possible misconceptions in the student. The teacher is both conversational partner and observer. In order to trace misconceptions in the learner, the teacher should be a researcher as well. In the research Pask reports, the mental processes used by the learner are exteriorized by providing apparatus which controls his/her learning and also allows records to be made of the steps taken. An essential part in it is the subject-matter representation is a diagram of the relationships between concepts which needs to be grasped before the topic as a whole can be understood. Since the experimenter needs to provide appropriate corrective assistance, he/she needs a mental "map" of the subject matter against which to compare the student's responses.

7.7

SH parallel 23.10

In order to elicit an entailment structure from a subject-matter specialist, Pask recommends that we ask which topics should be engaged in the domain to be taught. Secondly, the teacher should explain how each topic should be derived from the other topics. Each derivation is only accepted if the explanation can also be made backwards. The *cyclicity criterion* saturates the evolving graph, and will finally result in an *entailment mesh*. Pask recommends completing the cycles because experts often recognize the *true head node* fairly late in the process. Pruning the entailment mesh means that some arcs are removed. By removing the subordinate relations, a hierarchy arises. Pask forces the expert to remove the entailment cycles so that it can act as "a conversational domain". As *Textvision-3D* and *Hypernet* have illustrated [9,10,11,12,13], *graph theory* enables us to compute centrality indexes in cyclic graphs as well. This facility can be used to postpone or even to prevent pruning Hypertext relations before displaying them in a visual network on a computer screen.

Content vs context

It is essential for hypertext to *decontextualize elements of information*, so that they can be interpreted in a meaningful way, independently from other items. *Linear text* originally stems from *episodic description*. The text reflects the order of the events as they happened or as the author conveys to the reader. Many application fields have specified their own needs for text designs. Both implicit and explicit structures in text have been stressed in text research of the last two decades, especially texts for information retrieval and texts for instruction [14]. The most prominent model for sequencing information in text is *schema theory* [3]. New information in text must be reconciled with the schematic or *prototypic knowledge* in the reader. The weakness of this theory is its lack of prescriptions for the designing *linear text*. The variability of prior knowledge in the reader precludes a single optimal text. *Interactive text* enables the reader to adapt the text to his/her actual *cognitive need*.

Explicit techniques for structuring text have been researched by psychologists in order to signal the attention of the reader. Signalling, punctuation, diagraming and outlining can contribute to processing of information in the text. However, the problem remains if the presentation medium is passive: Different readers ask for *differential prompting*. The medium should at least enable the reader to adapt the presentation sequence to the actual state of knowledge and momentary interests.

A third relevant outcome of research is the notion that learning from text should be approached as a process of active construction, rather than a "match" between old and new information. This leads us to search for new *interaction metaphors* for text consultation. Computer based systems challenge the designer to develop new models for the interaction between the learner and the system. Hypertext starts with the assumption that text can be separated into items, and that reading means tracing the relations between concepts which link the items. Designing implicit and explicit text structures for single items are the same, except that a computer system can individualize the prompting, depending on the actual sequence of presentation.

SH parallel 23.8

AR parallel 4.5, 6.10

7.9

Most hypertext techniques today have focused on the *context* of text items. The user interface supports the traversal from one item to another. The *readability* of the item itself, and the validity of the outgoing relations has not been researched so far. Most of the effort in the design of hypertext browsers has focused on a *direct manipulation-style* interface. The physical entities in the *WYSIWYG metaphor* facilitate quick and easy-to-learn actions, but they can prevent the user from describing more abstract relations and concepts. The same is true for hypertext authoring systems. On the level of operations, it is quite simple to digress on a certain item by installing new sub-concepts and relating new concepts to existing ones. The problem is the same at the level of semantics.

> How crucial is this concept within the overall subject area? Is it central enough to act as a root for further digression?
> Do I forget to relate words in this item to existing concepts, so that they stay unreachable?
> Did I use a synonym for that concept elsewhere?
> Did I use this word for another concept before?

The quality of hypertext facilities is heavily dependent on the relations between the information elements. The way the user arrives at certain information influences the search process by providing this item as the answer to the interest that arose in a former item or providing the users with a more precise indication of where they can find the actual information they are looking for. If the answer on the first question is "yes", then the user either wants to go backwards to the item where the question originated and continue the original line of interest or the user wants to elaborate upon a point of interest in the current or intermediate items. If the answer on the first question is "no", then the user returns to the former item and tries to find the fact of interest via another link, backtracks even further than the former item in order to find a more substantial direction to meet his/her points of interest, or is caught by one of the elements in the intermediate items and shifts his/her attention to another point of interest.

Content and context of an item of hypertext information are spheres of motivation that are interwoven. The ease of branching to related text *distracts* attention to the context instead of the content of an item. One of the reasons to study hypertext relations is to distinguish between some global notions of *centrality*, as mentioned previously in the literature. If there is a computational rationale for centrality, apart from the semantical arguments in the text itself, then it could be of importance for the design of the user-interface. One of the first tasks to be performed by the user interface is to provide an orientation to the user- showing the position of the user in the network of nodes and links. In order to hide redundancy, the network level presentation needs information about which concepts are in the center of the connections, and which concepts can be pruned without blocking the view of related contexts. Before discussing the problem of synergy between tool and method, I will analyze hypertext structures by means of graph computation.

Hypertext links, connectivity, and the feedback to the users

Hypertext for text consultation lies somewhere between traditional linear text and text retrieval by key word search in a database. Traditional text on paper enables the reader to jump between distinct locations in the text but is typically read in the physical order as it is printed. Databases, on the other hand, enable the reader to retrieve fragments of text by means of keywords, like the key-word search mode in the *Grolier Encyclopedia* on CD-ROM. The problem for the reader is to chose the right *discriminatory terms*. Hypertext prompts the reader, helping them find the next node. The reader can neglect this advice and simply jump to any concept in the text base. Many hypertext systems enable the reader to trace backward chronologically (backtracking) to find a previous node. The central objective in designing hypertext nodes is to define and validate the relationship between:

> • The structural position of the nodes in a hypertext graph and the centrality of the nodes assigned by the author.

- Structural position of nodes in the graph and the way they are addressed by the users during Hypertext sessions. If a clear relation exists, graph computation can be used as a global predictor for user behaviour in advance.

Hypertext relations and the need for cyclicity. Frisse [15] discussed the problem of hypertext indexing, in order to assist the user in browsing and retrieving a requested piece of information. In this discussion, he introduces the terms intrinsic and extrinsic weight. Intrinsic weight reflects the correspondence between concepts within the item and the query concepts stipulated by the user. Intrinsic weight can be derived from Salton's algorithm, which assigns concept weights to items as a function both of the frequency of occurrence of the concept in the entire search space and of the number of items containing the concept. The algorithm assigns a higher weight to items containing infrequently-used concepts and to items containing several occurrences of a concept that are not found in many other items.

```
weight_ij = k x freq_ij x (log(n) -
log(docfreq_j)+1)
```

Weight(i,j) is the weight component of item i due to concept j; k is a constant ; freq(i,j) is the number of occurrences of concept j in item i; n is the number of items in the hypertext base; and docfreq(j) is the number of items containing concept(j). For a second determinant for a item's utility, Frisse mixes the intrinsic weight component with the relationship of the item with its context. The extrinsic weight describes the component of a card's total weight contributed by the *propagation* from neighboring cards. In other words: An item's *extrinsic-weight component* depends on the weights of its immediate *descendant items*.

$$\text{totalweight}_i = \sum_j \text{weight}_{ij} \ (1/y) \sum_d \text{totalweight}_d$$

in which y is the number of immediate descendants of item(i), and d is an immediate descendant of item(i).

Frisse proposes to start the propagation function recursively upwards from the leaf items up to the root. The extrinsic-weight component can only be computed for uncyclic graphs. Frisse proposes to prune down cycles in what he calls "aberrant" cases. The experience of a current study show that cycles in concept references show up quite often especially if the hypertext base has been created bottom-up (declaring concepts while composing the text in the items). Much confusion would result if the system would force the author to avoid reference cycles. Frisse's notion of intrinsic and extrinsic weight is useful, however, in order to complete the more primitive computations derived from the so-called citation-index by Garfield. He proved that the relevance researchers assign to a publication correlates positively with the number of citations to the same work. Garfield's citation index does not include a weight factor for the status of the person who's citing. It would be useful to explore the surplus of power for the relevance prediction if we correct Garfield's outcomes for the citator-status. The trade-off between content versus context is quite related to the notion of intrinsic versus extrinsic weight as introduced by Frisse. However, neither Frisse nor Garfield solve the problem of cyclicity.

Graph structures as a lean representation of conceptual relations. In the case of conceptual relations as in hypertext, graphs offer the possibility to process cyclicity in an efficient way. This is the major advantage of the graph formalization beyond *dynamic-indexing*, *path algebra* and *Petri* networks so far. Traditional graph analyses have been performed for directed and undirected graphs. The most elementary representation of the relations in a hypertext structure is a *directed graph*. The *nodes* in the graph represent the items, and the *arcs* represent the references from one concept to another. *Graph computations* as we know them from sociometric research, use *unlabelled and unconditional graphs*. The computational possibilities with graphs enable hypertext systems to recompute the consequences for structural changes during network editing. In order to tackle the problem of recursion in cyclic structures, we need the most advanced algorithms from graph theory and *matrix algebra*. As most of the problems in graph computation are *N-P complete,* it is good to be aware that current computer power is only able to process small networks within acceptable limits of time. Concept networks as they can be derived from full-size encyclopedias contain about 20,000 to 50,000 nodes, and should be parsed into subgraphs. The key-concept to be explored is *centrality*. Tree structures as they can occur in hypertext structures are the most elegant situation for the definition of centrality. Tree structures enable us to perform a strict top-down or bottom-up strategy without intensive computations. If the tree is unbalanced then the extrinsic-weight computation of Frisse can give a better estimation of centrality. The nodes with a larger domain of subreferences can be be raised in status. This produces the situations that, on the same level of distance from the root concept, there is a differentiation in status, due to number of subordinate concepts.

If we disregard the actual content of the concepts, graph computation can offer some indication of its role in the configuration of relations. In the case of hypertext relations, we should be aware of the extent to which the graph representation reduces the actual information. It would be presumptuous however to abandon associative links and jump into a sea of typed relations.

Graph structures share the following features. The order of creation has been omitted. If we take into account that some of the concepts were created initially and some of them were created as an appendix, then it would be easier to generalize the conclusions. The different types of relations in hypertext links are omitted. Traditional graphs are restricted to one type of relation. The recent work of Bakker and Hoede go into the potential of *knowledge graphs*, which express the types of relations, in order to extract formalized knowledge from scientific documents. The strength of the relations between concepts in hypertext is disregarded. In most cases it would be good to ask the author how strong the relation is between nodes. If the domain of knowledge has been formalized before, it is reasonable to constrain the relation by adding a rule or precondition that has to be satisfied before the link is executed. The choice whether computer power should be used to produce a lean representation or a more expressive one raises the trade-off between *tractability* and *expressiveness* [16]. They argue that this dimension is important for choosing symbolic structures and for the selection of appropriate processing algorithms. Nevertheless, it clearly illustrates the power of reduction (non-expressiveness) while increasing the tractability (computation) by computers. In fact, the *unbounded search* for *reasoning by computation* neglects the power of *man-machine symbiosis,* where the primary problem is one of cooperation and task division. The discussion about the ultimate *representation formalism* for hypertext systems can be clarified by the reference to the article of Levesque and Brachman.

GL corroboration 3.18

Structural centrality. In order to get an idea of the structural centers in a directed graph hypertext, we can make use of a rich tradition in applied graph analysis. The basic notions

about structural centrality, point centrality, and graph centrality have been presented by Hoivik and Gleditsch [17]. In
relation to the analysis of graphs in hypertext systems, centrality supplies the necessary ingredients for *importancy-match-
ing* by the author and browsing behavior by the user. Freeman's distinction between *adjacency, betweenness* and
distance had to do with *undirected graphs*. They represent the
three major parameters for labelling concepts in a hypertext
graph. *Adjacency* defines *centrality of a node* as the number
of relations with another node. The application of this measure
was to define the position of a person within a communication
network. Persons with many direct (undirected) relations with
other members of the group were able to exchange ideas. The
transfer of this notion to hypertext differentiates between in-
and outgoing relations of a certain item. An outgoing item
embedding many concepts enables the user to browse away
according to his/her point of interest. An ingoing item *em-
bodying the explanation* of a concept which has been mentioned in many other explanations has a high chance to be
visited by the user.

Betweenness defines the number of times the node will be
visited on the way between two other nodes. One should ask
which nodes have an important *gate function*? In terms of
hypertext, which nodes are extremely important in order to
connect separate *clusters* in the text base? If a node connects
two separate *clusters*, it is important to know how big the
clusters are and if the connection has been made with the
essential nodes of the clusters. Betweenness in its graph
computational meaning is not the same as *distance*. Betweenness reflects the *dynamics of transitions* in a *directed graph,*
while distance simply denotes the number of intermediate
nodes. Distance reflects the sum of the distances to every
other node. Some hypertext systems provide a *directory-item*
listing all the names of the nodes in the text base. Differentiat-
ing between in- and outgoing relations again comes down to
centrality versus *attainability*. Freeman's classification of the
three aspects of *structural centrality* does not cover analyses
of *influence*, which says that the position of a node cannot
exhaustively be characterized by taking into account the first
order relations. When designing hypertext , the position of a
item can only be qualified if we regard all the possible routes
that finally lead to this particular item. Also the indirect and
redundant routes should be taken into account. The work of
Hoede [18], Katz [19] and Taylor [20] contributed to this
problem of *n-sequency*. This means that in computing the

centrality of a point, it is not sufficient to state how many relations are 'going to' or 'coming from' a specific node, but an *attenuation factor* should be included in order to reflect the importance of the neighbor concept. Hoede [18] adopted the idea of Katz [19] to compute the relational status of elements in a network as the sum of all direct and indirect influences via all possible sequences.

$$s(i) = \sum_{j=1}^{n} [w(i,j)] + \sum_{j=1}^{n} [w^2(i,j)] + \sum_{j=1}^{n} [w^3(i,j)] + ..$$

An element $[W ** k](i,j)$ represents all sequences of length k from point i to point j, weighted by a factor that is the product of the weights attached to the lines in the sequence [18].

$$s(i) = d(i) + \sum_{j=1}^{n} w(i,j).s(k) \quad [20]$$

From graph computation back to hypertext navigation

Traffic behavior in the one-way streets of a big city can partly be predicted by studying the *connective patterns*. Squares where many one-way roads are coming in and fewer one-way roads are going out will be crowded. The few roads that are going out will be quite busy. The reverse is true for squares with many outgoing roads and only few ingoing ones. The pure graph representation as it has been used to describe centrality in hypertext structures comes from the fact that human users choose their routes on basis of local interest, or because they expect to find information somewhere 'behind' in a specific direction. This means that for the more inert users of hypertext , the graph representation will be a better predictor of *browsing routes* than for the more involved users who are obsessed with the content elements of the text base. For those users, even the paths of conceptual references as predefined by the hypertext author are too narrow. They will create by-passes by directly referring to unpredictable concepts and will even extend the subject area by adding new concepts and new texts. Though hypertext linkages (and their graph equivalents) may be useful to examine the potential *highways* in browsing behavior, we should be aware that it is a weak determinant of the psychological space of the user. If the user of hypertext gets absorbed by the content of the text

AR contrast 6.14
PWh parallel 4.3

base, the characteristic of the route becomes less important than the adventure of being caught by the meaning of the information itself.

Concluding remarks

Graph theory enables a computer-performed pre-assessment of the patterns of connections in hypertext networks. The *cyclicity of conceptual references* complicates the user's orientation in hypertext graphs and system support as well. Based on a review of the various graph computations for *centrality*, Hoede's Status Score has been selected as a promising candidate for determining relevant areas in complex hypertext networks.

The educational use of hypertext is based upon the promise of ease of use, richness in presentation, and flexibility. These are laudable goals, but they have a price. Hypertext enables both teachers and students to produce many relations between concepts in the text and at the same time elicits subtle opions and feelings about the semantics in the domain. As learning targets become more obvious in the phase of examinations, teachers become nervous: Did we coach the students enough? Are they aware what to know instead of *how to know?* In hypertext, both teachers and students are able to digress, instead of focussing on the core of the subject matter. It is important to explicate the mental effects of knowledge elicitation and knowledge acquisition by hypertext . One of the methods that I have described in this chapter is to supply mental tools that guide the user to the central passages of the Hypertaxt base. The tool I recommend is based upon a mathematical rationale, however, I expect that it is far from cognitively valid. Still, I hope it will provide an alternative and some assistance as a method for computer-based cognitive support in learning resources.

References

[1] Ausubel, D.P. (1963). *The psychology of meaningful verbal learning: An introduction to school learning*. New York: Grune and Stratton .

[2] Ausubel, D.P. (1966). *Educational Psychology: A cognitive view*. New York: Holt, Rinehart & Winston.

[3] Rumelhart, D.E. & A. Ortony. (1977.). The representation of knowledge in memory. In R.C. Anderson, R.J. Spiro & W.E. Montague (Eds.), *Schooling and the acquisition of knowledge*. Hillsdale, New Jersey: Lawrence Erlbaum Associates.

[4] Bartlett, F.C. (1932). *Remembering: A study in experimental and social psychology*. New York: Cambridge University Press.

[5] Anderson, J.R. (1983). *The Architecture of cognition* . Cambridge, MA: Harvard University Press.

[6] Pask, G. (1976). Conversational techniques in the study and practice of education. *British journal of educational psychology, 46*, 12-25.

[7] Pask, G. (1975) *Conversation, cognition and learning: A cybernetic theory and methodology*. Elsevier, Amsterdam.

[8]   Pask, G. (1978). Conversational techniques in the study and practice of education. *British Journal of Educational Psychology, 46,* 12-25.

[9] Kommers, P.A.M. (1984). Web teaching as a design consideration for the adaptive presentation of textual information. In *Readings on cognitive ergonomics, mind and computers*. Berlin, FRG: Springer Verlag.

[10] Kommers, P.A.M. (1985). Adaptieve tekstpresentatie: Multiwindowing en netwerkafbeelding t.b.v. Kennisgroei. Bijdrage voor de bundel en voordracht voor het NGI-symposium "Programmatuur naar menselijke maat" *TH Delft,* November 05.

[11] Kommers, P.A.M. (1986). Adaptive presentation of text: Multi-windowing and network display for the acquisition of knowledge. *Proceedings of the Programs up to Human Measure Conference ,* Ed. by G.C. v.d. Veer. Bussum, The Netherlands.

[12]   Kommers, P.A.M. (1988a). Textvision: elicitation and acquisition of conceptual knowledge by graphic representation and multiwindowing. In van der Veer G.C. and Mulder G.(Eds.), *Human-Computer Interaction: psychonomic aspects,* (pp. 237-249) Berlin FRG: Springer-Verlag.

[13] Kommers P.A.M. (1988). TEXTVISION, conceptual representation beyond the HYPERTEXT metaphor. *European Journal of Psychology of Education*, September.

[14] Jonassen, D.H.(1986). *The technology of text, principles for structuring, designing and displaying text*. Englewood Cliffs, New Jersey: Educational Technology Publications

[15] Frisse, M. (1988). From text to hypertext. *Byte* (October), 247-255.

[16] Levesque, H.J. & Brachman, R.J.(1977). A Fundamental tradeoff in knowledge representation and reasoning. In Brachman & Levesque (Eds.) *Readings and knowledge representation* Los Altos, Ca.: Morgan Kaufmann.

[17] Hoivik, T., and N.P. Gleditsch, (1970). Structural parameters of graphs; a theoretical investigation, *Quality and Quantity, 4,* (pp.195-209).

[18]Hoede, C. (1978) *A new status score for actors in a social network*. Twente University of Technology, Dept. of Applied Mathematics.

[19] Katz, L. (1953). A new status index derived from sociometric data analysis. *Psychometrica, 18,* 39-43.

[20] Stokman, & Veen, V.D. (1981). *GRADAP user manual* Amsterdam.

Chapter 8
Discussion: Formal and Informal Learning with Hypermedia

Philippe C. Duchastel
LearnTech, Colorado, USA

Keywords

Change; interest-driven access to information; information-rich context; effin factor; flexibility; expliciteness

Contents

Introduction

Hypermedia (which includes hypertext as a subset) is an emerging technology which has the potential to radically enhance our interaction with the information world we live in. George Landow expresses this view best when he states "Hypertext ... changes the way texts exist and the way we read them." His comment does not imply that texts as we traditionally know them will disappear, but rather that new forms of text will appear (and are already appearing!). Hypermedia is an additive technology in this respect, just as the computer was (despite early predictions of the paperless society). As such, it is an enhancing technology, and while the field of information technology is still very much in the early stages of its involvement with hypermedia, it is already useful to examine how such enhancement can be best realized, particularly in the area of learning and instruction.

DJ explanation 3.2

What I will be expressing in this chapter is a bold adaptation of George Landow's phrase above; to read *Hypermedia may well change the way instruction exists and the way we learn from it*. In particular, I will be arguing that hypermedia is

DJ corroboration 4.3

better suited to informal learning than to formal instruction, and as a corollary to that view, that we should beware of overly structuring the information contained in a hypermedia net.

The character of hypermedia

Hypermedia characterizes the begining of what I call the Age of Information Access. Hypermedia is defined not by the wealth of information made available - although that is one aspect of it - nor by mapping that information or collaborating with others in the production of information, but rather by the capability to quickly access additional information related to the information currently under consideration. Information organized in a network that makes quick and easy access possible is what constitutes the essence of hypermedia. Other features often associated with hypermedia, such as concept maps, collaborative arrangements, etc., are structures which are overlaid upon hypermedia to further enhance it. In terms of basic interactive processes, it is primarily a *skip and jump* approach to information acquisition that is made possible by hypermedia.

DJ example 6.1-17

I will illustrate this view not by reference to current hypermedia systems (many of which are represented in this book), but instead by looking forward a few years (how many is a moot point) to a more fully developed hypermedia technology.

Figure 1 graphically portrays this future technology.

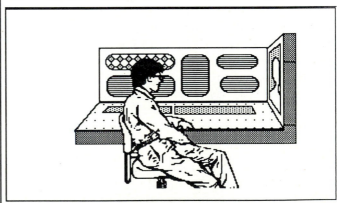

Figure 1. Future hypermedia workstation

You are viewing the evening news on your large screen high definition television and your curiosity about Chinese imperial dynasties is sparked by a news item concerning a recent archeological find in Kiangsu province. You interupt your viewing of the newscast and request a textual view of the speaker's last one minute of news presentation. By touching your screen on the words 'Chinese' and 'dynasties', you branch to an overview graphical representation of the information elements available in the network's hypermedia banks, as well as summary indications of the extent of other information on this topic available in other accessible hypermedia banks. You may now access any of this information.

By navigating through the information presented, some of which is detailed, some in the form of information maps, some of which is graphical, some textual, some video, you intellectually involve yourself in exploring this topic of interest, doing so for its own sake and on your own terms.

AR background 19.17

When your curiosity is satisfied, or your interest in this topic dissipates itself, you resume your viewing of the evening news (now a video-recording) where you left off.

While this scenario is futuristic, it is currently possible in technological terms. It involves a merging of television and computing technologies, something which is already underway, as well as a slight infusion of artificial intelligence (AI). In reality, a larger reliance on AI may very well substantially upgrade the functionality and adaptiveness of the system for individual users. Even without this, however, the core functionality of hypermedia as illustrated here centers on *interest-*driven access to information elements in a rich network of multi-media information.

DJ contrast 4.3

Learning while interacting with hypermedia

This notion of an information-rich learning context will greatly affect forms of learning and instruction. To imagine something of the impact that such a context can have on the way we do things, we need only consider in a relativistic manner our own current situation. Most of what I learn derives from interacting with books and other printed sources. But consider a time quite some while ago when such resources were simply not very available. Much greater recourse was then made to learning directly from other people — and that was of course the only way to learn prior to the invention of the printed resource itself in the late 15th century.

An information-rich context means not only one in which a rich store of information exists, but more importantly, one in which there is easy access to that information. The reason that print is so common today as a learning resource is quite simply that it is very readily available. It is well recognized today that Guttenberg's invention had a revolutionary impact on the potential for education within society. In effect, knowledge became much more accessible than it had ever been before.

It is useful to ponder this notion of an ever increasing information rich learning milieu, for there is something at once fascinating and suspicious about the possibility that the mere increase in information accessibility will lead to more or better learning.

Consider the current situation. Today's student may not have instant access to all desired information, yet there is a tremendous wealth of information which is available both in a home's encyclopedia and in the local public library. However, despite this relatively vast wealth of information available to the student, there seems to be little use made of it (certainly much less use than has been predicted). Why is this? The answer would seem to lie in the relationship existing between effort and interest, what I would call the *effin factor*.

PWr comment definition DJ reference   Salomon, G. (1984). "Television is 'easy' and print is 'tough': The differences in investment of mental effort in learning as a function of perceptions and attributions". *Journal of Educational Psychology 76*, (4), 647-58.

The effin factor (<u>eff</u>ort to <u>in</u>terest trade-off) concerns the appeal (or lack of appeal) of some activity or resource. It involves the effort a learner is willing to invest in an activity or in accessing a resource in relation to the learner's current intrinsic interest in the topic. The effin factor characterizes the intrinsic motivation of the learner, otherwise known as epistemic curiosity.

I believe that vast quantities of information will be readily accessible in the future in a variety of compelling forms, and that such an information-rich context will dramatically affect how we go about learning. The major consequence of the emergence of hypermedia will be an increase in informal opportunities for learning (as pointed out in the illustrative scenario presented in the previous section).

What information access means in terms of learner initiative is that I can drop the study of a topic at any time and still just as readily pick it up later on when I want to come back to it. There will be no penalty for doing that (in sharp contrast to today's largely group-based and instructor-initiated learning context).

Information access also means that compelling forms of relevant information are available. This, as we have seen, implies interest-generating information which can *pull* a student into a curriculum rather than having to *push* her through it [1].

Thus, the fact that I can easily come and go in my learning tasks and that the resources available are interesting and fun make me want to engage in learning experiences. As with television and other forms of entertainment, I come to enjoy learning. We can now begin to commonly speak of 'whim learning' or of 'leisure learning', something that in the past was reserved for personal hobbies or for the type of learning often found beyond formal schooling.

The conclusion that must be derived from this view of hypermedia and of the type of learning that it encourages is that hypermedia systems should be viewed not principally as teaching tools, but rather as learning tools. Currently, this conclusion is controversial. For instance, Peter Whalley, emphasizing the relativity of knowledge and the structural aspects of argumentation, concurs that hypermedia may be inappropriate as an instructional vehicle. But he still focuses on the centrality of teaching (through other means, such as textual ones) in the area of knowledge acquisition.

DJ corroboration 13.3
AR contrast 19.16

Many of the researchers in this book, frame their views of hypermedia within a formal learning context, essentially because that is where many hypermedia developments are currently taking place. John Leggett in Texas, George Landow at Brown University, Oliveira and Pereira in Portugal, Bruillard in Paris, Mays in Scotland, Verreck and Lkoundi in Holland, all explore hypermedia in a goal-directed, hence formal educational context. This involves overlaying the basic hypermedia environment with various sorts of instructional tasks which orient the student's use of the system. However, any structure imposed upon the situation in order to enhance the learning experience to be derived from it is really extrinsic to hypermedia itself. Hypermedia proper is the underlying system used as a tool to obtain information, in the very same sense that the card catalog in the library was used (and still is used) to access information for the completion of school projects.

Formal learning and hypermedia are conceptually distant from one another, even though the first may at times make use of the latter. By contrast, hypermedia and informal learning seem more synergistic: through the effin factor, one very much makes possible the other. The hypermedia projects presented in this book that seem to reflect a more informal learning philosophy are those of Dan Russell in California, Tom Duffy in Indiana, and in certain respects George Landow at Brown University. It should be noted that these projects involve, or expect to involve, very large hypermedia information banks. While instruction focuses attention and orients the student's interaction with highly-selected information, interest-based informal learning will be successful only in as much as very diversified information (and hence large amounts of information) is made readily available to the user.

Structuring Hypermedia ───────────

Jonassen and Grabinger introduce two areas of concern within hypermedia which relate to *structural aspects of information: the information model and the intellectual interface.* The first relates to the network of relations created between the information elements, while the latter concerns how that network of relations can be represented to the user so as to facilitate browsing and minimize the cognitive overhead associated with juggling multi-faceted perspectives of a topic. The principles which I believe should guide design in this area are the following: keep the network flexible, and make it explicit to the user.

Flexibility is important in that the user should feel comfortable in coming and going through the network, and indeed eventually between networks, the world of information available to a user being in effect a vast hypermedia network. If we agree that hypermedia is particularly appropriate for informal learning, that leads us to the view that what drives exploration and learning is user interest, that is, the level of epistemic curiosity generated by the information elements encountered by the user as she travels in the network. Attempts to *structure the information elements in particular ways,* even if these attempts are meant to assist the user in understanding the information encountered, may instead do violence in some way to the user's particular interest at that moment in time in the topic being explored. One should therefore be cautious of structure.

8.7

Based on this argument, we may conclude that hypermedia is not very appropriate for highly structured learning tasks, for which more directive instructional forms such as computer-based instruction and some forms of intelligent tutoring are more particularly suited. Structural learning, which involves overcoming misconceptions or the comprehension of tightly interrelated knowledge, does not seem to fit well with the open-ended nature of hypermedia exploration. By contrast, associational learning not based on the structural framework of our world seems particularly well suited to hypermedia browsing.

SH contrast 23.10

SH contrast 20.3

PWr contrast 20.3

The stage of development of hypermedia for learning is still very early. Furthermore, our conceptions of learning itself are once again in transition, making it difficult to generalize in this area. For instance, Tom Duffy points to the rationale of *situated learning* for providing a hypermedia information base of concrete situations which can serve to anchor abstract concepts in experience, thus increasing their comprehensibility. Hypermedia information may also be combined with more directive forms of cognitive intervention in what become hybrid systems aimed at direct instruction in a given field, as in the OpticLab ITS/Hypermedia system designed at Laval University in Quebec [2].

DJ explanation 12.1-25

AR example 19.26

Another aspect of hypermedia structure concerns *how that structure is represented to the user*. This representation, in effect *an important interface issue*, will very directly affect the ease with which the user will be able to navigate and situate herself within the hypermedia network.

At a conceptual level, a few general principles seem to apply to the design of this representation. For one, it is important to clarify the nature of the information elements the system contains, as well as situate the user to the manner in which the elements are related. This may result in a need for multiple overviews representing different perspectives of a topic so that access to the informational elements themselves can proceed along different lines according to the user's particular interests at the moment.

SH explanation 23.20
AR parallel 7.4

For another, it is important that easy access-level tools be made available which permit the user to quickly situate herself within a hypermedia network. In effect, the user must be able to zoom in and out of information webs with ease. An example of this capability from the field of instructional design is elaboration theory [3], much of which would seem to apply to the field of hypermedia.

At a technical level, one should not be overly concerned with the current constraints involved with the use of today's computer technology, nor with the difficulties engendered by them. For instance, *getting lost in hyperspace*, as some have called it, may well turn out to be a consequence of the constraints (for example, the small screen) of today's computers, constraints which will disappear as the technology evolves. In this particular case, very large screens (as in Fig. 1), along

DJ explanation 7.2
AR explanation 7.4

with *3-D conceptual mapping of structure* (already being researched by Piet Kommers) might contribute a lot to keeping the user situated in the information space being browsed. The field of computer technology in general and of user interface design in particular is rapidly evolving and will continue to offer enhancements to hypermedia.

Conclusion

The researchers presenting their experiences and ideas in this book collectively demonstrate that the interest hypermedia has generated in the field of instruction and learning is vibrant. This interest will likely blossom into a multitude of research efforts aimed at further exploring the capabilities of hypermedia and at furthering our understanding of this technology and of learning itself.

In this chapter, I have advanced two points of view. One, that hypermedia is not instructional, but rather appropriate for informal learning. Two, that one should be cautious when structuring hypermedia, and that, whatever structure there is, it should be made clear to the user.

Both of these points of view are likely to prove controversial, and that is an excellent result of the interchange that has occured.

References ———————————

[1] Brown, J.S. (1983). Learning by doing revisited for electronic learning environments. In M. A. White (Ed.), *The Future of Electronic Learning*. Hillsdale, NJ : Erlbaum.

[2] Duchastel, P., Imbeau, J. and the STI Group (1989) On Interacting with Information: OPTICLAB. *International Journal of Educational Research* (in press).

[3] Reigeluth, C. and Stein, F. (1983). The elaboration theory of instruction. In C. Reigeluth (Ed.), *Instructional Design Theories and Models: An Overview of their Current Status*. Hillsdale, NJ : Erlbaum.

PART III

DESIGNING THE
USER INTERFACE

Chapter 9
Evaluating Hypertext Usability

Jakob Nielsen
Technical University of Denmark

Keywords

Evaluation; measurement; usability

Contents

System Acceptability ────────

The overall acceptability of a computer system is a combination of its *social acceptability* and practical acceptability. As an example of social acceptability of hypertext systems,

NATO ASI Series, Vol. F 67
Designing Hypermedia for Learning
Edited by D. H. Jonassen and H. Mandl
© Springer-Verlag Berlin Heidelberg 1990

consider the French LYRE system [1] for teaching poetry. LYRE allows the students to see the poem from various "viewpoints", each highlighting certain parts of the poem as hypertext anchors to relevant annotations and allowing the student to add new annotations. LYRE does not, however, allow the student to add *new* viewpoints since that capability is reserved for the teacher. The premise is that students should work within the framework set up by the teacher and not construct completely new ways to analyze the poem. This is obviously socially acceptable in the Southern European tradition in France, and indeed an alternative design might well have been deemed socially *un*acceptable in that country because it would have undermined the teacher's authority. On the other hand, many people in Denmark, where Scandinavian attitudes are more prevalent, would view the current design of LYRE as socially unacceptable because it limits the students' potential for independent discovery.

Given that a system is socially acceptable, we can further analyze its practical acceptability into various categories, including the traditional categories such as cost, support, reliability, compatibility with existing systems, and the category of *usefulness* which is of special interest to us in this paper. Usefulness is the issue of whether the system can be used to achieve some desired goal. It can again be broken down into the two categories of *utility* and *usability*, where utility is the question of whether the functionality of the system in principle can do what is needed. Usability is the

DJ contrast 18.2

PWr parallel 10.2

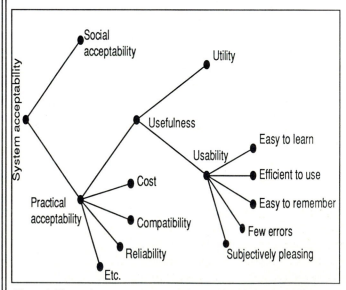

Figure 1. The various parameters associated with system acceptability.

question of how well users can use that functionality. Figure 1 shows the simple model of system acceptability outlined here.

Most of the parameters associated with practical acceptability are studied within traditional computer science. For example, the reliability of a system means that it must have few bugs and follow its specification correctly. The usefulness of the system is then determined by whether or not that specification is what the users need. In real life, however, <u>no computer system will completely without bugs and those bugs will certainly have a human factors impact on the users.</u> I am unaware of any studies on this human factors impact, however, anecdotal evidence suggests that users acquire certain strategies for dealing with buggy software such as saving their work more frequently when using programs which are likely to bomb.

For distributed hypertext systems, such as the Xanadu system, reliability becomes not just a question of avoiding software bugs but also a question of being able to survive hardware problems in various parts of the network of front end and back end machines. The ideal is a system showing graceful degradation in the sense that users can continue to use it as long as their own computer is up without experiencing any other impact other than a slight performance degradation as the system has to route information through less optimal paths through the network. Achieving such graceful degradation requires redundancy in both the hardware part of the network and in the storage of the hypertext information, but again we can refer to ongoing research in traditional fields of computer science for information on how to do this. In Figure 1, I also mention cost and compatibility as parameters for the practical acceptability of systems. Cost is an obvious factor, since only cheap systems will get a chance in most environments. Cost is related not only to the price of the software but also to the computing and staff resources necessary to run the software. For example, Peper et al. [2] found that the same information base took 90 K storage space when stored in a hypertext format and 250 K when stored as an expert system knowledge base. Furthermore, the size of hypertext engine was 300 K while the expert system shell was 1800 K, meaning that the total storage requirements for the hypertext were only 19% of the storage requirements for the expert system. The main reason for the disparity in storage requirements is that the hypertext representation relies on the user's natural intelligence for an interpretation of the meaning of the information. In the case studied by Peper et al. this was no problem since users actually performed more effectively when using the hypertext than when using the expert system, but in general, we might need more sophisticated computer representations to increase the usefulness of the information.

From a theoretical economic viewpoint [3], of course, we ought to calculate the net present value (NPV) of the cash flow resulting from an investment in the system. But the positive part of the net value results from the *benefits* of using the system and such benefits are often difficult to quantify. For example, it is likely that using a graphical system instead of a text-only system will result in significant improvements in learnability and working efficiency. But the company will only realize such savings slowly over the lifetime of the system so many managers may be blinded by the short term added cost required by the more modern graphical computers. For educational use of hypertext we have the added problem that the time students may have to waste on a poor system is often calculated as having a value of zero. Actually, the students' time does have some value, of course, even if they do not receive any direct hourly wages and that value must be larger than the tuition or other cost per student in a viable educational system.

Another factor which is holding back the introduction of modern user interface is the practical need for *compatibility* with existing systems. Most companies already have a large investment in place in the form of systems running on mainframes which they have no desire to make obsolete by changing to modern computers. In theory it should be possible to run new systems on modern graphical personal computers and use these computers for cooperative processing with mainframe systems running various forms of databases and management information systems. In practice, we find very few such systems and there are hardly any of the current hypertext systems which can be integrated with existing information systems running on other computers. Certainly, there is no reason why hypertext should not be used from terminals connected to mainframes or from text-only personal computers and several successful examples of such systems do exist. But to achieve full benefit from the more advanced aspect of hypertext such as overview diagrams it is probably necessary to have a graphical user interface.

Assuming that practical problems like the ones outlined here can be solved, there remains the issue of the *usefulness* of the system. The functionality of the system needs to have a high *utility* and do something which we need, since "nothing can have value without being an object of utility" [4] (utility can include having fun, as in the case of entertainment software). For hypertext systems, utility is very much related to the quality of the information in the hypertext nodes. A special advantage of hypertext compared to alternative representations is that many hypertexts allow the users to easily annotate the hypertext and add new information to customize the information base to more closely match their specific needs. The utility of hypertext is also related to having links which allow users to navigate in ways matching their tasks. Again, many hypertext systems allow users to add their own links and thus increase the utility of the system for their specific tasks. It is very likely that hypertext system will only achieve their full potential utility when they can interlink truly large information bases. We don't know very much about this since almost all the practical experience with hypertext to date has been with small (hundreds of nodes), medium (thousands of nodes) or medium-large (tens of thousands of nodes) information bases. The scale problems of having hundreds of thousands or millions of nodes are currently unsolved.

Usability is traditionally associated with five usability parameters:

1) *Easy to learn:* The user can quickly get some work done with the system.

2) *Efficient to use:* Once the user has learnt the system, a high level of productivity is possible.

3) *Easy to remember:* The casual user is able to return to using the system after some period of not having used it, without having to learn everything all over.

4) *Few errors:* Users do not make many errors during the use of the system, or if they do make errors they can easily recover from them. Also, no catastrophic errors must occur.

5) *Pleasant to use:* Users are subjectively satisfied by using the system; they like it.

We should note that the "few errors" usability parameter is related to the errors committed by the user: This is when the system correctly does as it is told, but when the user has actually told it to do something wrong. Cases when the system does something other than what it has been told would come under the classification of reliability as discussed above.

DJ comment Not so in a print environment as this book has shown.

DJ corroboration 10.13

System response time is an issue which often is treated as having to do with practical acceptability. We will tend to view it as a usability problem, however, since it actually does not matter how fast or slow the system is in performing its tasks. The only interesting issue is the effects the system's speed has on the user's ability to perform tasks fast and to be satisfied with the system. Of course, we do know that slow system response times tend to also slow down users and that users are normally dissatisfied with slow systems, so speeding up the system is one way to improve some of its usability characteristics.

There are typically *tradeoffs* involved in a user interface design with respect to the five usability parameters. The most classic is the relation between ease of learning and efficiency of use where certain design choices tend to improve one but decrease the other. For any given interface design, one has to prioritize the usability parameters in order to determine which will be the most important to optimize. For example, some systems require extreme ease of learning in the form of "walk-up-and-use" usability. This is for example true for trade show or museum information systems [5] where users cannot be expected to want to spend time learning the system itself. On the other hand, there are also many applications where usage over periods of weeks, months, or even years has a dominating influence making the learning period pale in comparison.

Since most hypertext systems are not used for such critical applications, as e.g. process control, medical applications, or financial asset management, the subcriterion of preventing catastrophic errors is of less importance. To the extent that hypertext is used for authoring, we would still like users to be prevented from easily wiping out their entire work, however. Except for this qualifcation it seems that usability of hypertext systems really fits the general definition of computer system usability quite well, so it will also be used in this article.

Usability parameters for hypertext ———

For a discussion of the usability of specific hypertext systems, we can refine the primary usability parameters somewhat. The first point is that the usability of a hypertext system is determined by a combination of the usability of the underlying hypertext system *engine* (i.e. the basic presentation and navigation support available), the usability of the *contents* and *structure* of the hypertext information base, and by how well these two elements fit together. From the user's perspective, all of this is of course seen as one single interface, and the user will not care whose "fault" it is if something is not usable. But from an analytical perspective, this distinction between the underlying system and the information base is probably an advantage. Furthermore, the relevant secondary parameters will be different for readers and for authors in many cases. Normally, the "easy to learn" parameter will be of less importance for a hypertext author who will spend a lot of time with the system.

Easy to learn

For users. The hypertext engine itself is easy to learn. Users are quickly able to understand the most basic commands and navigation options and use them to locate wanted information.When users enter an information base for the first time, they are immediately able to understand the first screen and to browse from it. Users are quickly able to learn the basic structure of the hypertext network and where or how to look for specific information. Users of educational or entertainment hypertexts can learn something/enjoy the session without having to familiarize themselves with the entire hypertext structure.The contents of the hypertext information base is easy to understand: Each node contains text (or other information) which is easy to read.
For authors. Authors who are editing an information base constructed by somebody else can easily understand the basic structure of this hypertext and are able to modify it without knowing the entire contents of the information base.

Efficient to use

For users. Given that users want to find a certain piece of information, they either get to it quickly or soon discover that it is not in the information base. When users arrive at a node, they are quickly able to orient themselves and understand the meaning of the node in relation to their point of departure.

DJ parallel 10.8

For educational hypertext. Users learn the facts or concepts which are most relevant for their purpose without having to learn or go through more than necessary irrelevant material or material they already know.
For authors. Authors can quickly construct a hypertext structure to reflect their understanding of the domain. It is easy to modify and maintain this structure.

Easy to remember

For users. After a period of not having used the hypertext engine, users have no problems in remembering how to use and navigate in the hypertext. After a period of not having used an information base, users can remember its general structure and are still able to find their way around the hypertext network and to recognize landmark nodes. Users can remember any special conventions or notations for special anchors, links, and nodes. Users can transfer their knowledge of the use and navigation of one information base to the use of another information base with the same engine.

For authors. When a hypertext structure needs revision after some time, it is easy for the author to return to the information base and update it. The author can remember or is reminded about the basic structure of the information and does not need to remember details in order to update it.

DJ corroboration 10.8

Few errors

For users. Users will rarely follow a link only to discover that they really did not want to go to wherever the link leads. In case users have erroneously followed a link, it is easy for them to return to their previous location. Users can in general easily return to locations where they have been, in case they decide that some lengthy digression should be abandoned.

For authors. The hypertext has very few links that erroneously lead nowhere or somewhere else than where they are supposed to go. The information contained in the nodes is correct.

Pleasant to use

For users. Users prefer using the hypertext system to existing alternative solutions such as paper or other, non-hypertext computer systems. Users are rarely frustrated with using the hypertext engine or disappointed about the result of following links. Users feel that they are in control with respect to the hypertext and that they can move about freely rather than feeling constrained by the system.

For non-work related hypertext such as interactive fiction, users find using the hypertext an entertaining and/or moving and/or enriching experience.

Guillemette [6] asked users to evaluate traditional (non-hypertext) documentation and found that their replies could be characterized by the following seven factors which explained 65% of the variance:

• *Credibility* (correct-incorrect, reliable-unreliable, believable-unbelievable)
• *Demonstrative* (precise-vague, conclusive-inconclusive, strong-weak, complete-incomplete)
• *Fitness* (relevant-extraneous, meaningful-meaningless, appropriate-inappropriate)
• *Personal affect* (varied-monotonous, interesting-boring, active-passive)
• *Systematic arrangement* (organized-unorganized, orderly-chaotic, structured-unstructured)
• *Task relevance* (useful-useless, informative-uninformative, valuable-worthless)
• *Understandability* (clear-confusing, understandable-mysterious, readable-unreadable)

The terms in parentheses after each factor are the semantic-differential scales associated with each factor. These seven factors are of course somewhat related to the five usability parameters but can also be viewed as a new set of dimensions according to which one could evaluate hypertext. They have the advantage that they match the way users view documentation but the disadvantage that hypertext can be used for many other applications than online documentation. It is not clear whether the factors will cover other application areas too.

Measuring hypertext usability

In the previous section, I developed a fairly detailed understanding of the parameters of hypertext usability. In order to apply certain usability engineering methods, we also need to be able to *measure* those usability parameters, so we develop such measurement strategies in this section.

Several methods exist for evaluating how well a given user interface scores on each of the primary usability parameters and for refining them to even more precisely measurable secondary parameters. See e.g.Gould [7], Whiteside et al. [8], and Landauer [9] for lists of such methods and for issues to study in an evaluation process.

Most discussions of hypertext usability are not founded on measurements of the usability parameters but are more in the nature of conjectures based on personal experience. Nielsen [10,11] surveyed the few existing studies. There are several possible reasons for the relative lack of hypertext usability measurement results, but the most important reason is probably that hypertext systems have not been all that much *used* in real life yet. Most of the research effort in hypertext has been on the development of the technology in the first place and we are only now reaching the point where sufficiently well-designed systems exist to make usability measurements imperative for any further progress.

The test plan

Before starting any test, it is necessary to have a test plan with at least the following items:

• Purpose of test (e.g. to iteratively refine a design or to choose between two alternatives).
• Who are the test subjects; how can we get hold of them?
• How many subjects should be tested?
• Description of the task subjects are asked to perform.
• Definition of when we will consider the task as having been solved.
• What kind of help is available to the subjects (none, manual, online help, ...).
• What kind of assistance from the experimenter may be given (normally none).
• Plan in advance what to data analysis to perform (that will impact what data we collect).
• Criteria for "test OK" in case we are doing a quality assurance test.

This type of test plan is the same as we would need for any usability experiment, no matter what kind of system was being tested. There are a few special considerations, however.

For the testing of educational or entertainment software, the end users may be small children, and because of the general need for always having representative users as test subjects, we would have to run our test with children. This is no insurmountable problem but certainly has an impact on the kind of testing we can do. For example it will probably not be possible to use questionnaires to collect subjective data. It may also be advantageous to replace the traditional thinking aloud method with the constructive interaction method of having two users use the system in collaboration.

GM example 13.14

The second special consideration leads to more serious difficulties: Some future hypertext structures may be extremely large with millions of nodes. Even the hypertexts being constructed today often contain tens of thousands of nodes [12]. Hypertexts basically have no regular structure, so usability problems may crop up in any individual node or link. Therefore the user interface design of a large hypertext is distributed over potentially millions of locations in the information space. Certainly one can never hope to be perfect in a user interface design, so maybe we should be willing to settle for the removal of the most glaring usability problems in the individual links and nodes. Since it will be impossible to test the usability of all the nodes and links empirically in large hypertexts, we need to rely on heuristic methods in the development process. Detailed empirical evidence will have to come from field use of the hypertext where we might use methods like navigation logging and user relevance feedback (e.g. have buttons where users can click to indicate that *"this link is **useless**"*).

Measuring learnability

Learnability is defined as the ability of the user to quickly get some useful work done with the system. It is typically measured by taking a group of novice users and have them learn the system from scratch. One measures the time until each user has reached a certain level of skill with the system. This usability parameter is usually the easiest to measure since it does not require the use of experienced users as subjects. "Anybody" can be taken off the street and function as test users with the only requirement being that they are representative in some way of the intended final user population. Probably because ease of learning is the easiest parameter to measure, it has been measured relatively extensively for most types of computer system. Actually, we do not have all that many measurements of hypertext learnability, probably because the most natural comparison would be between learning to use paper books and learning to use a hypertext system. In our current culture, it is impossible to find people who know how to read but are not already expert users of paper books.

WV example 15.9

For individual hypertext systems, learnability has been assessed in many cases but normally with different tasks given to the users of different systems. Therefore it does not make sense to compare the measurement results. One study [13] of hypertext usability did use a single method to compare the learnability of several hypertext systems (the Symbolics Document Examiner/Concordia, Guide, HyperCard, Hyperties, KMS, and NoteCards). In all cases, subjects were taught to use a given hypertext system by a coach who measured the time until the subjects "understood how to use the system". Using this somewhat poorly defined metric, Hyperties came out as the easiest system to learn with a coaching time of 15 minutes while NoteCards was the hardest to learn with a coaching time of 40 min. This result should not be surprising considering that learnability was one of the most important considerations in the design of Hyperties which was intended for use by for example museum curators, while NoteCards was designed as a "power tool" for knowledge workers. The coaching method used in this study is rather unusual but has the advantage of quickly producing a set of experienced users who can then be used in tests of efficiency of use (which was the real goal of Boyle et al.). Just to give an example of the measurement of learnability for an individual hypertext system, Shneiderman et al. [5] found that their original design of Hyperties did not fulfill their requirements for walk-up-and-use learnability (essentially that a user should be able to use the system immediately without any training). Their revised design did pass the test.

Measuring efficiency of use

The most classic examples of measurements of efficiency of use are probably the various studies of the reading speed from paper and computer screens [14,15]. Subjects were asked to read the same text in one of two conditions: Either from a piece of paper or from a computer screen. For most of the computer screens tested, the reading speed was about 25-30% slower than from paper. It was only possible to achieve the same reading speed when the computer screen was both high-resolution and used anti-aliased proportional fonts.

A similar experiment was conducted by Kreitzberg and Shneiderman [16] who compared the use of many small nodes versus a few large nodes in Hyperties. Subjects read one of the two versions and were asked to answer a set of questions about the information contained in the hypertext. The time taken to answer each question was measured and used as an indicator of the efficiency of the organization of the hypertext information. Results showed that users answered the questions faster when the information was structured in many small nodes (125 sec. vs. 178 sec.). In general, "time-to-answer-questions" seems to be a very popular metric for hypertext efficiency in many other studies.

Gordon et al. [17] tested users' ability to recall as many concepts as possible from articles they had read on a hypertext system. First users read the hypertext, and they were then asked to list the concepts discussed in it. This method is a way to measure how much users have actually learned of the information in the hypertext, even though it of course does not measure users' *understanding* of that information. Even though the measurement technique uses a memory test, it can be viewed as a measurement technique for efficiency of use and not of ease of remembering. The recall technique used here does not measure users' ability to remember the system or the structure of the hypertext after some time, which is what we mean by ease of remembering. When recall tests are used immediately after users have finished using the system, they seem to measure how much information users have assimilated from using the system, and that is a question of the efficiency of the hypertext. Actually, the experiment conducted by Gordon et al. is not a good example of the measurement of efficiency of use since they tested novice users. But the same measurement technique could be used to test users who were experienced in the use of a particular hypertext engine and were using it to read about a new area. Since "efficiency" with respect to hypertext should often be defined in relation to the amount of understanding a reader gleans from the information base, one might also consider the measurement technique used by Egan et al. [18,19] to assess their SuperBook system. They had users read a text in either the SuperBook hypertext format or in a printed format and then write an essay based on the information contained in the text. These essays were scored by an impartial judge with the result that the readers of the hypertext version were seen to have written significantly better essays with an average score of 5.8 on a 1-7 scale compared to only 3.6 for the readers of the printed book.

Measuring ease of remembering

The ability of casual users to return to using the system without having to learn everything all over is of course extremely relevant for the usability of hypertext. Just consider how often you return to a printed book you read some time ago to check some fact. It is very likely that users of hypertexts would also want to return to specific hypertext documents some time after the initial reading. And there might also be hypertext systems offering facilities which one would only need in rare circumstances and which one would therefore always use as a casual user.

In spite of this need for good usability characteristics on the "ease of remembering" parameter, it is the one which has received the least attention in current studies of hypertext usability. We therefore know very little about this usability parameter in the context of hypertext user interfaces. From usability studies in general, we do have methods to measure subjects returning to using a system. Typically one will first have subjects use the system for a specified period of time and then let them do something else for a week or a month. The subjects are then asked to return to the laboratory and are given a performance test of a similar nature to those used to test efficiency of use. The better performance, the easier the system must have been to return to. One can also measure users' error frequency when they return to the system, or one could give them an exam to test how much of their knowledge of the system they had retained. Measurement techniques which actually look at subjects using the system are probably more valid than those which question users away from the system, since studies [20] have shown that there are some systems where users find it difficult to recall the details when they are away from the system even though they have no problems recognizing and using them when they actually sit in front of the computer.

Measuring error frequency

A typical example of a study of error frequencies is the test by Wilkinson and Robinshaw [21] of proofreading from screens and paper. During the first ten minutes of the experiment, subjects had about the same error rates in the two conditions (25% vs. 22%) but after they had been proofreading for 50 minutes, the subjects using computer screens did significantly worse with an error rate of 39% vs. only 25% for paper. So this experiment showed that users get fatigued fairly quickly when reading from the current generation of computer screens.

The normal way to measure error frequencies is just to count the number of errors committed by users while they perform some standard task. Certainly the term "error" is not always completely well defined, but one simple definition would be to count actions leading to an error message or to system states from which the user immediately backs out. The real serious errors, however, are those which would not be caught by such simple means and one will therefore also have to measure errors in the user's work product.

Measuring subjective satisfaction

It is almost impossible to directly measure users' satisfaction with a system. A few studies have been conducted where users' level of stress during system use is assessed through measurement of skin conductivity and similar methods from the field of medicine. We have not found any such studies of hypertext usability, however. The standard method of measuring user satisfaction is by *asking* the users themselves to report their satisfaction. Usually this is done by questionnaires asking users to state their level of agreement with statements such as "the system was pleasant to use" on a 1-5 scale.

Nielsen [22] asked a group of computer science students to judge whether they would prefer having their manuals, their textbooks, and fiction available in an online form instead of in a printed form. The question was asked both for online systems including the possibility for user annotations (a form of hypertext) and for plain online text without an annotation feature. Users were asked to rate their agreement with the statement that the online system would be an advantage on a scale from 0 to 4 (disagree much, disagree a little, neutral, agree a little, agree much). For the questions assuming a facility for user annotations, results showed that the students viewed online manuals as a big advantage and online textbook as a small disadvantage, while online fiction was viewed as an very big disadvantage. Comparing the responses for questions about systems with and without an annotation facility, shows that that users found annotations to be a small advantage for online manuals and a big advantage for online textbooks but not to be any advantage for online fiction.

Users' preconceived opinions about hypertext are of interest since they will determine the speed with which the new technology can penetrate the market. Unless the purpose is that of assessing users' attitudes towards a proposed new technology, we would normally recommend that one does *not* use the method of asking people how they would like a proposed design which they have not used. Experience shows [23] that there is very little relation between what users say about a design before they have tried it and after they have tried it. And normally the parameter of most interest to us will be users' subjective satisfaction *after* having used the system.

PWr parallel 10.13

In another study, Marchionini [24] had high school students use the *Grolier's Academic American Encyclopedia*a in both print form and electronic form. The subjects were then asked to compare the print and electronic encyclopedias. Half said that the electronic version was faster, three said that it contained more information than the printed version, and one said that it was more up to date. This was in spite of the fact that the two versions of the encyclopedia actually contained the *same* text and that the subjects were measurably slower with the electronic version. This indicates another problem with subjective evaluations and the seductive qualities of novel technology in that the subjective satisfaction usability parameter will not always be positively correlated with the other usability parameters. This is actually only a special case of the general need for making tradeoffs between the various usability parameters since a given design cannot always score high on all parameters. In some cases such as when a system is to be used by highly discretionary users, subjective satisfaction is the most important and one might have to design systems with poorer actual performance than could have been achieved with a less pleasant interface.

PWr comment Important point.

Wright and Lickorish [25] used an interesting metric to measure users' subjective impression of two systems. Instead of asking people to state their satisfaction with the system, they asked them to rate the suitability of various kinds of information for display in hypothetical future electronic books. Users rated ten kinds of information (e.g. tourist information for overseas visitors and car part identification numbers for mechanics repairing cars) on a 1-10 scale, and Wright and Lickorish counted the proportion of hypothetical electronic books getting a "highly suitable" rating of 9 or 10. Even though all users were asked to rate the same kinds of information, this proportion was 58% on the average for ratings from subjects who had used one of the user interface designs tested by Wright and Lickorish, while it was only 24% for ratings from subjects having used the second design. On the basis of this result, we can conclude that users of the first design had the most positive experience since they were more positive towards hypothetical future systems.

Hypertext usability engineering _____

Current practice in usability engineering [8, 26] is to refine user interfaces iteratively since one cannot design them exactly right the first time around. One example of a usability study which can be used for such a purpose is Hardman's [27] evaluation of the understandability of the icons used in Glasgow Online to denote various services at hotels in a manner similar to many guidebooks. When test subjects went through the hypertext in the study discussed above, Hardman stopped them when they first reached a screen showing information about a particular hotel (where the hotel service icons were found) and asked them to tell her how they would interpret each of the icons. For each subject she then made a list of the icons guessed correctly as well as the icons the subject could not guess or guessed wrongly. For example, one user thought that an icon showing a globe of the Earth meant that the hotel offered facilities for exchanging foreign currency whereas it actually was intended to mean that the hotel had conference facilities (presumably the idea was to induce an association with international meetings). Several other users believed that an icon showing a pineapple meant that the hotel had fresh fruit in the rooms or that it served fresh fruit, while the intention was to indicate that the hotel catered to special diets (such as vegetarians).

This information about wrong guesses can be very useful when it comes to redesigning icons to reduce the probability for mistakes. One would especially want to redesign icons where some users make disastrously wrong guesses. Hardman also accumulated the number of correct and wrong guesses for each icon to a list indicating their overall understandability. One would also want to redesign those icons where many subjects made wrong guesses, even if none of the guesses were disastrous.

Iterative design is indeed one of the recommendations in a report on guidelines recently published by Apple [28] with advice for the construction of *HyperCard* user interfaces. The report also contains broad guidelines for the use of sound and graphic design and more detailed guidelines for the use of specific HyperCard interface elements such as buttons, icons, and animated visual effects. Especially with regard to the latter issues, an evaluation technique would be to check whether a given HyperCard user interface followed the guidelines. This method is called *heuristic evaluation* and can also be conducted with respect to general heuristics for the properties of usable interfaces [29]. As an example of heuristic evaluation of hypertext user interfaces, Nielsen [12] discusses various CD-ROM hypertexts with respect to heuristics for navigational dimensions, backtrack facilities, and other concepts. By using heuristics for user interfaces in general or hypertext in particular, it is often possible to identify issues in a hypertext interface design without extensive testing. Empirical testing is still necessary, however, to supplement the heuristic evaluation and to probe details of the design.

Furthermore, field studies [30] are also needed to supplement laboratory studies for the evaluation of hypertext user interfaces. The usability of hypertext is extremely dependent on individual user characteristics and the users' tasks [10] in their everyday environment. This is true for all interfaces, and field studies are of course always a good idea. But hypertext systems are similar to integrated software for business professionals [31] in having their usability determined by situated use in environments where users interpret the information in the hypertext relative to their own knowledge and tasks. Laboratory studies giving users artificial tasks where they cannot use their embedded skills will often not predict the true usability of a hypertext.

Conclusions

The main practical advice which follows from this paper is that:

- It *is* possible to evaluate the usability of hypertexts.
- We *do* have established techniques which can be used for the measurements.
- Iterative design on the basis of usability evaluations *have* improved many hypertexts.
- Therefore you *must* perform a usability evaluation if you develop a hypertext.

We also have to conclude that hypertext usability has not yet been studied in sufficient detail to provide us with detailed knowledge about all the relevant usability parameters. This should not keep practitioners from performing their own usability evaluations — on the contrary, the lack of data in the literature just increases the need for empirical tests.

Acknowledgements

Ray McAleese, Terry Mayes, and Norbert A. Streitz provided useful comments on a previous version.

References ————————————

[1] Bruillard, E. &Weidenfeld, G.(1989, July). Some examples of hypertext's applications, this volume.

[2.] Peper, G., Williams, D., Macintyre, C., and Vandall, M.(1989). *Comparing a hypertext document to an expert system..* Manuscript submitted for publication IBM Dept. 77K, Bldg. 026, 5600 N 63rd St., Boulder, CO 80314.

[3] Copeland, T.E. and Weston, J.F.(1979). *Financial Theory and Corporate Policy.* Reading, MA: Addison-Wesley.

[4] Marx, Karl (1867.). *Das Kapital: Kritik der politischen Ökonomie.*

[5] Shneiderman, B., Brethauer, D., Plaisant, C., and Potter, R. (1989). The Hyperties electronic encyclopedia: An evaluation based on three museum installations. *Journal of the American Society for Information Science.*

[6] Guillemette, R.A. (1989). Development and validation of a reader-based documentation measure, *International Journal of Man-Machine Studies 30*(5), 551-574.

[7] Gould, J.D.(1988). How to design usable systems. In Helander, M. (Ed.), *Handbook of Human-Computer Interaction* (pp. 757-789). Elsevier Science Publishers.

[8] Whiteside, J., Bennett, J., and Holtzblatt, K.(1988). Usability engineering: Our experience and evolution, In Helander. M. (Ed.), *Handbook of Human-Computer Interaction* (pp. 757-789).Elsevier Science Publishers.

[9] Landauer, T.K.(1988). Research methods in human-computer interaction. In Helander, M. (Ed.): *Handbook of Human-Computer Interaction* (pp. 905-928). Elsevier Science Publishers, 1988.

[10] Nielsen, J.(1989,November). The matters that really matter for hypertext usability, *Proceedingsof the ACM Hypertext' 89 Conference* (pp. 239-248. New York: ACM.

[11] Nielsen, J. (1990). Survey of hypertext usability. in J. Nielsen. *Hypertext and Hypermedia.* Boston: Academic Press.

[12] Nielsen, J. (1990). Three medium sized hypertexts on CD-ROM. *ACM SIGIR Forum , 24,* 1.

[13] Boyle, C., Williams, C., and Teh, S.H. (1989). *An empirical analysis of hypertext interfaces.* Technical Report, Hypertext Research Lab., Dept. of Computer Science, College Station, TX: Texas A&M University, 77840.

[14] Gould, J.D. and Grischkowsky, N. (1984). Doing the same work with hard copy and with cathode ray tube (CRT) computer terminals. *Human Factors 26 ,* 323-337.

[15] Gould, J.D., Alfaro, L., Fonn, R., Haupt, B., Minuto, A., and Salaun, J.(1987). Why reading was slower from CRT displays than from paper, *Proceedings of the ACM CHI+GI'87* (pp. 7-11). Toronto, Canada.

[16] Kreitzberg, C.B. and Shneiderman, B. (1987). Restructuring knowledge for an electronic encyclopedia. *Proceedings of the Intl. Ergonomics Association 10th Congress .* Sydney, Australia.

[17] Gordon, S., Gustavel, J., Moore, J., and Hankey, J. (1988). The effects of hypertext on reader knowledge representation. *Proceedings.of the 32nd Annual Meeting,of the Human Factors Society* (pp. 296-300).

[18] Egan, D.E., Remde, J.R., Landauer, T.K., Lochbaum, C.C., and Gomez, L.M. (1989). Acquiring information in books and SuperBooks. *Proceedings.of the Annual Meeting American Educational Research Assoc.* (pp. 27-30). San Francisco, CA.

[19] Egan, D.E., Remde, J.R., Landauer, T.K., Lochbaum, C.C., and Gomez, L.M. (1989). Behavioral evaluation and analysis of a hypertext browser. *Procceedings of the ACM CHI'89 Conference of Human Factors in Computing Systems* (pp. 205-210). Austin, TX .

[20] Mayes, J.T., Draper, S.W., McGregor, A.M., and Oatley, K .(1988). Information flow in a user interface: The effect of experience and context on the recall of MacWrite screens, in Jones, D.M. and Winder, R. (Eds.), *People and Computers IV*. (pp. 275-289). Cambridge, UK: Cambridge University Press.

[21] Wilkinson, R.T. and Robinshaw, H.M. (1987). Proof-reading: VDU and paper text compared for speed, accuracy and fatigue. *Behaviour and Information Technology 6(2)*, 125-133.

[22] Nielsen, J. (1986). Online documentation and reader annotation. *Proceedings of the 1st Conferemce on. Work With Display Units* (pp. 526-529). Stockholm, Sweden.

[23] Root, R.W., and Draper, S. (1983). Questionnaires as a software evaluation tool. *Procceedings of the ACM CHI' 83* (pp. 83-87). Boston, MA.

[24] Marchionini, G. (1989). Making the transition from print to electronic encyclopedia: Adaptation of mental models. *Int.Journal of Man-Machine Studies 30(6)*, 591-618.

[25] Wright, P. and Lickorish, A. (1989). An empirical comparison of two navigation systems for two hypertexts. *Prococeedings of the Hypertext II Conference*. York, UK.

[26] Nielsen, J. (1989). Usability engineering at a discount. *Proceedings of the Third Conference of.Human-Computer Interaction, HCI-Intl.' 89*. Boston, MA.

[27] Hardman, L. (1989). Transcripts of observations of readers using the Glasgow Online hypertext. *Technical Report AMU8835/01H*, Scottish HCI Centre, Edinburgh, Scotland.

[28] Apple Computer (1989). *HyperCard Stack Design Guidelines*. Addison-Wesley .

[29] Molich, R. and Nielsen, J. (1990). Improving a human-computer dialogue: What designers know about traditional interface design. *Communications of the ACM, 33* (3).

9.22

[30] Nielsen, J. and Lyngbæk, U. (1989). Two field studies of hypermedia usability. *Proceedings of the Hypertext 2 Conference.* York, UK.

[31] Nielsen, J., Mack. R.L., Bergendorff, K.H., and Grischkowsky, N.L. (1986). Integrated software usage in the professional work environment: Evidence from questionnaires and interviews. *Proceedings of the. ACM CHI' 86 .* (pp. 162-167). Boston, MA.

Chapter 10
Hypertexts as an Interface for Learners:
Some Human Factors Issues

Patricia Wright
MRC Applied Psychology Unit, UK

Keywords

Advice; design; functionality; human factors; interface; reading

Contents

Introduction

There are several book-length reviews concerned with interface design [1,2,3]. The general aspects of good practice in screen design and dialogue construction will apply to hypertexts just as surely as they apply to other instances of human computer interaction. Hypertexts do raise additional issues relating to ways in which readers can be helped to move within the information resource and to exploit novel information handling techniques (e.g. creating their own personal links within the material).

NATO ASI Series, Vol. F 67
Designing Hypermedia for Learning
Edited by D. H. Jonassen and H. Mandl
© Springer-Verlag Berlin Heidelberg 1990

There is also every reason to expect the principles expounded in books and journals on instructional design to have relevance to learning from hypertexts. However, the conjunction of hypertexts and learning provides an opportunity for examining the kind of advice that hypertext authors need and the form in which that advice can be made available so that it is easy to use. The results of such an examination may have broad relevance to the application of human factors knowledge to information design, and so to the creation of learning support environments that do not involve hypertexts.

Political factors

The following discussion will focus on issues relating to interface design for hypertexts, but it is worth reminding ourselves at the outset that there are many considerations outside the scope of human factors which will have a powerful impact on the use of hypertexts for learning. For example, political decisions will determine content and curricula in schools. This has implications for the kinds of hypertexts that will appear to be successful within the prevailing educational climate. Suppose it is the case that hypertexts are particularly good at developing learners' problem solving skills (e.g. through encouraging them to learn by interacting with some dynamic domain); and further suppose that educational attainment continues to be assessed by examinations placing considerable emphasis on the recall of information. Given this scenario, it is conceivable that the use of certain kinds of hypertexts may appear to impair rather than enhance educational attainment. The design of hypertexts will therefore be driven by political and social factors as much as by research which points out the potential of the domain.

PWr parallel 9.2

Technological factors

Another powerful factor influencing hypertext design is of course the technology. Marketing factors will influence the direction of technological advances and so constrain what is available for the delivery of hypertext materials (i.e. what storage media, what display media, etc). Organizational and economic factors will determine who has access to which kinds of learning resources. These are not factors which educational researchers can do much about, but at the end of the day they may be the factors which determine the role that hypertexts come to play as a learning resource. These are the factors alongside which the significance of the human factors questions must be assessed.

Hypertexts and learning ───────────

Hypertext applications to learning are diverse. They span not only the educational range from primary school to university but they also include commercial and industrial training, as well as learning in informal settings such as museums. In many of these contexts, traditional teaching procedures already offer learners optional routes through explanatory or other parallel materials. So the novelty of hypertexts, particularly as extended to hypermedia with its inclusion of video and audio information, may be limited to the routing being computer-assisted and available to the learner at a single 'learning station', to paraphrase the terminology currently prevalent in the domain of microcomputers. Given the broadening of affordable computer capabilities, the term hypertext will be used throughout the following discussion to include hypermedia.

Architectures for hypertexts

It would obviously be helpful to know which learning tasks, or which components of learning tasks, are most suitably dealt with as hypertexts. This needs to be seen as a human factors issue in the sense that selecting an appropriate communication vehicle is the first interface decision that must be made by those creating the learning environment. Consequently the author's interface decisions will need to include choices about sensory modality (vision, hearing) and about the forms of representation to use within that modality. There are unlikely to be quick and simple recipes for making such decisions. This becomes evident if we respond to Jakob Nielsen's plea for closer consideration of the question, "What really matters?" when it comes to designing hypertexts [4]. The answer will nearly always depend upon the task that the learner is engaged in. This task will determine the functionality required by the learner (e.g. language learning benefits from an audio channel, learning to use a spreadsheet may not but might make good use of animated displays). For these particular examples the point about different functionality requirements may seem obvious; but how will the hypertext author know in general, for any learning task, what the functionality requirements are going to be? Books are used in many ways and for many purposes. The same is likely to be true of hypertexts. So how can hypertext designers cater to divergent usage?

DR contrast 24.2

One important aspect of the conjunction of functionality and interface design concerns the choice of platform (i.e. combination of hardware and software) to be used as the means of creating and transmitting the hypertext. As this workshop showed, there exist a wide range of platforms (e.g. Guide, gIBIS, HyperCard, HyperCardPlus, HyperTIES, Intermedia, KMS, NoteCards, SuperCard). It has been pointed out that the interface will always be architecture dependent [5]. So choosing an appropriate architecture may be the second critical interface decision that hypertext authors must make - deciding to use hypertext at all was the first. Before an architecture can be chosen, hypertext authors have to decide whether functionality such as multiple windows, facilities for annotating and sorting will be provided. In order to be able to do this they will need to be able to analyze the constituents of learning tasks at a much finer grain than the major categories of learning which have sometimes sufficed for other purposes.

Which design factors really matter?

The learning task determines the functionality requirements and also influences the way that functionality is most helpfully *instantiated* for learners. Most computer functions can be made available in a wide variety of ways. For example, search functions may be provided either through a command line interface (e.g. "grep" in UNIX™) or, at the other extreme, entirely by clickable options presented in a constrained dialogue. Nielsen mistakenly assumed that the significance of instantiation options can be determined by counting the differences in the magnitude of treatment effects reported by researchers. However, for any given learning task it is often the case that neither the issues of functionality nor the broader questions about instantiation have been addressed by researchers (e.g. there may be no point in exploring how to give learners the functionality to perform actions such as saving their work when the software could do this for them automatically). Scientific concern with advancing theoretical understanding of how learning takes place may require studying learning in contexts which distinguish among current theories. As a consequence researchers may not have explored issues of instantiation across a diversity of complex learning tasks which might seem to be a prerequisite for developing a technology of learning environments. As Nielsen's review of the literature shows, much research is done on things that do not necessarily matter much to educators.

Educational research has repeatedly demonstrated that there is a broad bandwidth where the "interface" decisions make little difference to teachers or learners. In his paper at Hypertext II, Dan Russell eloquently listed why educational theory is unlikely to get better. In short there are just too many components [6]. Among the potential troublespots that could cause difficulties when creating an 'Information Design Environment' were:

- the domain knowledge may be incomplete
- the knowledge structure may be unhelpful
- the task analysis may be faulty
- the sequence progression (storyboarding) may be askew
- the language or graphics may be ambiguous
- the model of the student may be wrong

In any single evaluation it is difficult to pinpoint where things may have gone wrong and where combinations of decisions may be cancelling each others effects. So there can be no answer to the question, "What really matters?" because the question is seriously underspecified. This is as true when the question is applied to hypertexts as when it is applied to learning more generally. Some educational researchers have argued that it is desirable to specify at least three learning parameters: the learning of what, by whom, for what purpose(s). If human factors information is going to be useful to hypertext designers it has to be given with respect to at least these three factors.

Cumulating case history information

We have yet to determine where hypertexts have a valuable contribution to make within the learning space defined by these parameters. The optimist might hope that as a wide variety of hypertexts are tried out in different parts of the learning space, the resulting "case histories" will provide tentative answers to this question. Unfortunately two factors may undermine the cumulative effect of such efforts. Readers may need to acquire new information-handling skills if they are to exploit fully the new technologies. For example, in order to do an effective string search readers need to grasp the desirability of searching not on a word but on its root morpheme (i.e. WRIT will find write, writer(s), writing(s), written). Such skills may well be easy to teach but they are seldom obvious to the untutored searcher. In some studies of hypertexts used in school and college contexts the combination of the requirement for new skills and the reliance on well-

10.5

DR comment ... and they interact in far too many ways...

DJ parallel 8.5

173

developed reading abilities have resulted in the more able students benefitting most from having electronic access to reference materials [7]. So in the short term, it is likely that the case-history data will underestimate the potential of hypertexts as learning support environments, simply because learners have not yet acquired the relevant new skills.

The second factor that undermines the accumulation of case history data about hypertexts used for learning is that some of the computer-based products may not be well designed, either lacking in necessary functionality or having some of that functionality provided in a way which makes it difficult for learners to access. This appears to take us full circle. We need to know about the interface characteristics of good hypertexts, but we can only meaningfully explore these in appropriate parts of the learning domain. It might help us find out where such regions were if we could decompose learning activities to a level where it is possible to articulate the commonalities and differences in these cognitive processes across tasks. One starting point is the decomposition of 'reading' itself.

WV example 16.5

Hypertexts and reading

 As the Glasgow On-line hypertext has shown, the information within hypertexts can sometimes be predominantly graphic rather than verbal [8]. Nevertheless, in order to pursue the discussion of the level of analysis of the learners' behaviour at which it becomes viable to think of offering hypertext authors design advice, let us focus just for the moment on learning from written texts. Reading for learning can take many forms, but let us start with an approach to reading that has been shown to have relevance to the design of written technical information [9]. Readers' activities can be divided into three broad bands which correspond roughly to sets of cognitive activities that take place before, during and after the process which the layman would think of as 'reading'.

Constituents of reading
In many hypertexts, before readers find the information they want to read they will need to search. Later more will be said about the different kinds of search tasks readers can engage in, but a common component of many search tasks is that readers' need to filter out material that is not relevant to their current task. The interface options for helping learners do this may range from computer assisted dialogues that enable

readers to skip or hide information not currently wanted, to a highlighting facility that increases the visual salience of relevant information either 'automatically' or 'manually'. While searching through printed media readers may often find things that are useful for other tasks, although completely irrelevant to the current search objective. That is to say, readers find things that they were not currently looking for. It may be a serious problem for any form of electronic document retrieval, hypertexts included, to know how to provide this kind of adventitious retrieval. The more successful the interface is at supporting filtering, the less likely it is that serendipitous findings will occur.

Once the reader decides that relevant material has been located then a range of cognitive activities take place. Comprehension processes may well be influenced by display factors such as the amount of text that can be viewed simultaneously. In addition to understanding the current text, readers have to decide whether their information needs are now adequately met or whether they should search elsewhere in the material. If they decide they should look elsewhere they may need to plan both where and how to look in order to search efficiently. Undoubtedly such cognitive decision making occurs with printed texts. Its special relevance to hypertexts is that the interface could support readers by helping them create and carry out such plans. Few hypertexts currently offer such functionality, perhaps because few have been designed from a perspective where the need for such functionality could be seen.

After readers consider that adequate information has been found they may still need to remember what they have read in order to make further use of the information. Indeed such usage may require manipulation of the material found (e.g. knowing the dates of a war may be only part way to determining how long a particular group or individual was involved in the conflict). Again this points to the potential functionality that learners need and that hypertexts could make available even though other teaching materials (e.g. books, videos) cannot.

TD parallel 12.12

The present thesis is that human factors issues of functionality and its instantiation become visible and tractable when the tasks being performed at the interface are decomposed to a level where the constituent cognitive activities are characterised in detail. Even though the level of decomposition just outlined has implications for the interface, this will be too high a level of analysis for many purposes. To illustrate this let us consider some of the varieties of search tasks that readers engage in, together with the implications that these have for the functionality required of the interface.

Constituents of search tasks

Search target simple and fully known. In the simplest instances of searching the searcher knows precisely what information is sought and can specify the target without resorting to complex qualifications. Examples of such search tasks include wanting to know the date of the French Revolution, the capital of Chile or the boiling point of parrafin. The functionality required for such tasks includes the ability to carry out string searches. This means that the software must be intelligent enough to cope with mis-spellings and morphemic variations of the specified string. In a learning environment there may be several such targets (e.g. relating historical dates with economic indices). Therefore learners may need assistance both in keeping track of the targets already searched for and the answers found.

Search target simple but only partially known. There are many occasions where searchers may be uncertain about the string which will correspond to the search target even though the concept sought is very precisely defined. Sometimes the uncertainty may be due to linguistic factors (e.g. being unsure of the German word for Town Hall). At other times the uncertainty arises from the absence of precise labels - e.g. wanting to contact the school on the corner of the High Street but not knowing the name of the school. Here the interface may be able to help by offering aliasing functions, and perhaps suggesting to searchers that they "see also" (this is the solution often offered by publications such as Yellow Pages). Sometimes the gaps in the searcher's knowledge can only be met by recasting the target in a way that increases its complexity.

Search target complex and fully known. Perhaps the kinds of searches for which computers most excel over printed media occur when searchers are seeking information which is complex and fully known (e.g. What is the time of the first direct flight from Amsterdam to Stutgart on Monday? Who has written books on 18th century diet in urban and rural France?). Here the searcher must build up a definition of the target by combining a range of logical operators (and, but not,

---

DR comment I find this analysis of search tasks compelling and useful.

DJ parallel 9.7

DJ corroboration 9.8

GM illustration 2.9

etc). Although readers need to be trained to conduct boolean searches, this kind of functionality can be instantiated in relatively painless ways that do not involve knowing that all the parentheses have been correctly set in an algebraic formulation.

Search target computed from online trade-offs and feedback from the computer. In many real life search tasks readers find that the target they originally defined does not exist and so they need to modify their search in the light of what they find is available. For example, a student may wish to choose a course that has requirements both in terms of the amount of work it is likely to demand (e.g. no lab courses), the time and location of the lectures, and their own broad interests. Here the functionality required of the interface includes offering searchers note making facilities, and giving them feedback on the closeness of the near misses to the target sought. If the search process culminates in a message saying 'Match not found' the searcher is no further forward in trying to find the information needed.

Search target simple but unspecifiable to a computer. Searchers do not always know exactly what it is that they are looking for. There are probably a number of search activities which relate to what the layman calls "browsing". One example is the potential student who simply wants to know whether there are any classes at the local college that they might want to join. Here the needed functionality would seem to include rich cross referencing, that helps readers go quickly to other parts of the information that may be of interest. Searchers also need "footprints" so that they can keep track of where they have already been as an aid to deciding where to go. When readers are taking criss-cross paths through the information in hypertexts they may also need to be forewarned about jumps that take them to locations previously visited. Without such forewarning readers can become surprised or confused to discover that they have inadvertently retraced their steps.

JL comment "history, breadcrumbs"
GL example 3.11

Search target unrecognizable for the purposes of terminating the search. For learners trying to pursue all the ramifications of a topic such as the discovery of radium, or penicillin, it may be very difficult to know when all the potentially relevant parts of the data base have been explored. Here the functionality required by searchers may include not only very full cross-referencing but also help in specifying the search target in a variety of information-rich ways so that alternative avenues can be explored during the search.

This discussion of six types of search activity demonstrates how serious a mistake it can be to suppose that a single word in the English language corresponds to a single learning activity, far less a single cognitive process. Words like search, read and plan are umbrella terms which cover a diversity of cognitive activities. As the above examples illustrate, hypertext authors will find it useful to analyze these labels for more detail about their constituents because these lower level activities can often differ in their functionality requirements.

Reading for learning

While the above discussion has explored 'reading and hypertexts' we must not forget that in the domain of learning the generic action of 'reading' can be undertaken for a diversity of purposes many of which will generate their own requirements for cognitive support. The following brief sketch of three kinds of reading for learning will illustrate how these different reading purposes result in learning activities which differ in the skills they require from readers and in the functionality that they demand from the interface.

Reading for writing

Reading for writing is a common educational task, particularly at secondary and tertiary levels. Readers may need skills in extracting or highlighting and annotating the information they have found. This might suggest that printed materials will be a more suitable medium than an unmodifiable text on a computer screen. But a hypertext environment could offer these facilities. In addition, hypertexts can provide readers with various means of collecting and organizing their information before they start writing, thereby offering more powerful learning environments than traditional materials.

Reading for comparison

Reading for comparison purposes is another common educational task. Obviously the interface requirements of some comparisons will differ from those of others. Comparing the water resources in Quebec and California makes many different demands from comparing the use of irony in two 19th century novels. Nevertheless, there are common activities that readers engage in with these different materials. For example, the information to be compared not only has to be found but may need to be assembled in some form that has privileged accessibility. To achieve this the interface may need to offer readers a range of windows and views of the information of interest. Therefore readers may need to have skills in manipulating the interface. Sometimes the hypertext environment can offer considerable support for such manipulation. There is software that links texts and their commentaries in a way that readers can not only see each in separate windows but which keeps the two in unison as readers choose to move through either text.

Reading for reference

Reading for reference purposes has been dealt with earlier in the discussion of search activities. Although this might seem to be one of the simplest of learning activities, and may involve minimal changes in the learner's knowledge representation (witness how often learners may look up the same information again and again) - yet even for this simple task readers need to know how to formulate queries. "Why did my plant die?" needs to be recast into targets that can be searched for. Without adequate knowledge of the domain (in this case potential causes of plant failure) formulating appropriate questions may be difficult for learners to do. As was mentioned earlier, the interface can offer assistance in a variety of ways, including "see also" hints on where to look.

This brief sketch of three reading purposes serves to illustrate the dependence of interface functionality on readers' activities when they are reading for learning. Throughout this discussion of hypertexts and reading the focus has been on the question of functionality rather than on how that functionality might be implemented in the design of particular hypertext interfaces. This emphasis has been deliberate, since human factors issues are sometimes thought of as being only the questions of instantiation. Arguably the inconvenience to readers and learners is greater when they are unable to do something at all, than when they are able to do it only by some cumbersome means.

Human factors advice _____

Given that there already exists advice on creating interfaces and on the design of instruction, it might seem surprising that some hypertexts have been less than ideally constructed. We have suggested that sometimes the analysis necessary for specifying the functionality learners will require may not have been carried out in enough detail. Another potential contributor to infelicitous instantiations may be the form of advice that is available to hypertext authors. It is common for human factors advice to approximate a list of principles. These can be given at a high level, such as "Try to engage the learner's interest", or at a low level such as "Try to have fewer than 10 buttons simultaneously visible on screen".

Such lists have shortcomings. It is difficult for researchers to see where design issues have been overlooked (e.g. some browsing activities require "footprints" but these are seldom mentioned in guidelines for interface design). It is also extremely difficult for hypertext authors to know how to compute tradeoffs when there appears to be a conflict among the principles (e.g. 'remove screen clutter' versus 'provide readers with as much information as possible on screen'). So let us consider other ways in which human factors advice about hypertext design might be given.

There are several alternative models of ways of giving advice. Guidelines in various forms are a familiar solution, but among the alternatives are some which do not carry the overtones of 'the expert knows best'. Many decisions about information design have to be taken with reference to local knowledge. The teacher responsible for putting together a particular course is always likely to know more than any distant expert about the learner characteristics, the topic or the organizational constraints (e.g. the hours allotted for tuition or the specific attainment targets for the course or the availability of hardware). So the sort of advice that such a teacher, or hypertext designer, will find useful is very unlikely to be in the form of recipes to do this and do that. What alternative forms are there for giving advice? Let us consider what milage there might be in the metaphor of maps as alternatives to guidelines.

Guidance from maps

Seldom does a map tell its user the only way to get between A and B, but it does indicate the hazards of going in certain directions. Maps as advice resources are "constructional" rather than "instructional" in Philippe Duchastel's terms. That is to say they leave the onus on the user to select among the alternatives (here the hypertext design options). Of course advice on interface design for hypertexts will not have the physical appearance of a map. The important similarity is functional. Hypertext designers are invited to use the advice in much the same way as they would use information from a map, that is, they assess what options they have available and then compute the tradeoffs among subsets of these options.

Designing an interface with respect to *subsets* of features is vitally important because what may work well in isolation (e.g. an arrow enabling movement to a new display screen) may become less desirable if the content of the material being taught is itself the representation of a dynamic system that incorporates arrows showing flows within the system. For this reason interface design requires a problem-solving approach. Simplistic caveats such as "Use an arrow to indicate this" do not help the hypertext designer know what to do when the caveat is clearly inappropriate in a given context.

Another characteristic of maps is that they are *task specific*. Consider the following examples from three very different domains: road maps, rail maps, mountaineering maps. A road map (e.g. of the city of York) designed for a motorist and for a pedestrian is likely to include different information and indeed will probably be drawn to a different scale. Similarly the rail maps used by commuters or tourists differ in many ways from the representations used by those involved in managing the railway system. It is this characteristic of maps that makes them such excellent resources of help and advice.

Criteria for interface design

Since problem-solvers need to start by finding the right maps, this suggests that hypertext designers will similarly need to start by finding advice of an appropriate kind. So 'task functionality' might be what distinguishes among maps (i.e. one map may deal with supporting search tasks, another with supporting comparison tasks). Each map then seeks to give human factors information about the effects of instantiating that functionality in various ways. We have shown that by decomposing the learning task to the level of constituent cognitive activities, hypertext designers can more easily see what task functionality they need to consider. Therefore maps would give advice by relating this level of functionality to performance characteristics associated with different interface decisions available to hypertext authors.

It may sound straightforward to assemble the information, or carry out the research, that would form the basis of a map. However, in practice there can arise a number of thorny problems. There can be alternative criteria for evaluating design options. Jakob Nielsen raised the issue of whether the appropriate measure of a well-designed hypertext was the reader's happiness or their attainment [10]. Piet Kommers has suggested that the learning environment needs to be engross-

PWr parallel 9.15, 7.16

ing or entertaining [11]. Similar claims have been made in other contexts involving human-computer interaction [12]. But it is still not obvious that having fun is an essential feature of learning support environments, although it probably always helps. Other researchers have drawn a useful distinction between the learner being active, in the sense of pressing buttons on the screen and navigating hither and thither, and the learner being "engaged" in a motivated sense and so learning from the material encountered. Engagement may be far more critical that entertainment, but it is not a well re-searched topic among those who study reading for learning. For example, few studies have explored why it is that readers so often choose not to read some of the information which is right in front of them at the moment [13]. In the context of hypertexts, where readers have so many options about what they read, it may become vital to have a better understanding of the factors which influence readers' strategic choices about what and how they read. There can be little point in providing information in a form which enhances the reader's learning if for some reason most learners choose not to read it. Principles such as 'engagement' are obviously not specific to learning from hypertexts, and we have already mentioned that the general principles of learning and instruction design would be expected to apply to hypertexts. Detailed analyses of how interface design influences engagement are not yet available.

Returning to the issue of whether the criterion for evaluating hypertexts is more appropriately happiness or attainment, there is surely a need to discover the cognitive causes of this discrepancy when it occurs. Understanding these causes might generate insights into viable compromise designs. Meanwhile what criteria does one use to decide which is the 'better' interface?

Perhaps here too there is need for deviation from the conven-tional human factors approach. Knowing what is 'better' may not the most important question for hypertext designers to ask. It could be that authors only really need to know what will NOT work well. This assymetry between good and bad features has been well illustrated in the domain of Desk Top Publishing. DTP does not inevitably lead to better communi-cations, but it is possible to advise users about some of the hazards which may seriously detract from the success of their communication. Indeed it has been suggested that just as early DTP products suffered from 'fontitis' so early hypertext products may suffer from 'linkitis' [14]. If the design questions are approached by means of the kind of task analysis described earlier, then it may be easier for hypertext authors to appreciate which links are vital, which are optional extras and which are totally unnecessary.

Functionality is central

In summary, it is being suggested that we need to provide hypertext authors with human factors advice based on task functionality, where the cognitive constituents of learning tasks are fully articulated. The advice can be used by hypertext authors much as a map is used and will give two important categories of information. It will help hypertext designers appreciate the range of ways any required functionality can be instantiated, and it will point out that dangerous territory is being entered when that functionality is instantiated in particular ways. For most of the design options which work adequately, an author's choice may well need to be governed by logistic factors such as available space on screen or memory. Such factors can become major items when the design options include presentation modality (sight or sound) and form of representation (e.g. pictures / words). The most important feature of the approach being suggested here is that the human factors advice is topicalized on functionality, not on physical or structural properties of the interface such as the use of colour or the nature of the input device.

The current absence of a comprehensive analysis of the *functionality* requirements of learning tasks, or even of reading-to-learn tasks, hampers the generation of 'maps' showing where communication catastrophes occur at the interface. But if research on hypertexts can produce such information then, whether or not hypertexts result in better learning than books or other conventional approaches, this may contribute to the formulation of better questions about learning support environments in both computer-based and traditional domains.

References ⎯⎯⎯⎯⎯⎯⎯⎯⎯

[1] Galitz,W.O. (1985) *Handbook of screen format design.* (second edition) Wellesley Hills, MA: QED Information Sciences.

[2] Heaton, N. and Sinclair, M. (Eds). (1985). *Designing end user interfaces*. Berkshire, UK: Pergamon Infotech Ltd. 1988

[3] Helander, M. (Ed.) *(1988).Handbook of human-computer interaction.* Amsterdam: North Holland.

[4] Nielsen J. (1989). The matters that really matter for hypertext usability. *Proceedings of the ACM Hypertext '89* (pp 239-248). New York: ACM.

[5] Leggett, J.J., Schase, J.L. and Kacmar, C.J. (1990). Practical experience with hypertext for learning. This volume, Chapter 2.

[6] Russell, D. (1989). Hypertext in design. *Proceedings of Hypertext II,* York, UK.

[7] Marchionini, G. (1989). paper to AERA meeting in San Francisco, April.

[8] Baird, P. and Percival, M. (1989). Glasgow on-line: database development using Apple's HyperCard. In R. McAleese (Ed), *Hypertext: theory into practice.* Oxford, UK: Intellect Ltd.

[9] Wright, P. (1987). Writing technical information. *Review of Research in Education, 14*, 327-385.

10] Nielsen, J. Evaluating hypertext usability. This volume, Chapter 9.

[11] Kommers, P. (1990). *Conceptual mapping for knowledge exchange by hypertext.* This volume, Chapter 7.

[12] Carroll, J.M. and Thomas, J.C. (1988). Fun. *SIGCHI Bulletin, 19*, 21-23.

[13] Wright, P. (1988). The need for theories of NOT reading: some psychological aspects of the human-computer interface. In B.A.G. Elsendoorn and H. Bouma (Eds), *Working Models of Human Perception,*(pp. 319-340). London: Academic Press.

[14] Van Dam, A. (1988). Hypertext '87 keynote address. *Communications of the ACM, 31*, 887-895.

Chapter 11
Designing the Human-Computer Interface to Hypermedia Applications

Andrew Dillon
Loughborough University of Technology, UK

Keywords

Interface design; group discussion; human-computer interaction; users as learners; learning tasks

Contents

Introduction

In this chapter, I will discuss the human-computer interface as it pertains to hypermedia systems and outline the issues that emerged in the discussion group on this subject that was held at Rottenberg. In order to represent the many diverse views expressed, I will describe the general dichotomies of opinion which divided participants and try to draw them together into a cohesive view. The notions of the interface as multi-levelled, adaptable and conventional are discussed. Coherence is best obtained by viewing learning as consisting of multiple tasks for which no one interface will prove optimal. In order to develop a usable interface the designer must therefore understand the end-users in terms of the learning tasks they will be performing with the system.

DJ corroboration 10.3

Definition of the interface _____

The role of the interface in human-computer interaction has gained importance over the last decade, and it is generally understood that despite functionality, a system will often stand or fall on the strength of its user interface. The recent excitement about hypermedia systems and their potential for restructuring information in previously impossible ways has led some researchers to forget or overlook the fact that even with such systems, *a user (learner, reader, information seeker,)* still ultimately interacts with a machine. This fact alone necessitates careful consideration of the interface issues.

The key notion behind interface design is that a user and a computer engage in a communicative dialogue whose purpose is to complete a task. The interface is therefore the communication channel afforded by the computer, allowing transfer of modality independent information between machine and user. As a communication channel, the interface is both physical (keyboard, mouse, display) and representational (iconic, metaphoric) i.e., it offers the means of control as well as providing a model of its operations, whether this model is made explicit (e.g. the Macintosh desktop) or not (e.g. the MS-DOS operating system). The physical aspects are becoming reasonably standard across systems, the representational ones can vary at the application level.

PD parallel 8.8

With respect to hypermedia systems the physical interface usually consists of a the standard triumvirate of screen, keyboard and mouse, but there is still some debate about the value of such features as large screens [1], mice versus function keys [2], and the use of color [3]. Furthermore, many of the published findings on such interface issues were obtained using non-hypertext tasks, so there is no guarantee that they transfer readily to this domain.

At the representational level there are issues pertaining to document models, manipulation facilities — should the document be paged (like a book), scrolled, windowed, jumped through or a combination of these?— icon design [4] and navigation facilities [5] to name but a few .

In fact, many of these issues, both physical and representational, are interrelated, e.g., input device suitability may interact with manipulation facilities and so forth. There is no ideal interface waiting to be discovered (or designed) that will suit all hypermedia applications. Rather, certain combinations of interface attributes will prove suitable for some tasks but not for others. For example, when reading an academic article, a hypermedia system incorporating a large screen and a mouse which retains the paper model of the document structure is likely to be more usable than a system incorporating a small screen, function keys and an alternative document structure. The latter design however might prove suitable in other domains (cf. the design criteria for the HyperTIES system, [6]). Thus it is important to understand the task domain of the application before drawing any conclusions about interface design.

User as learner

In the present context we are discussing learning and the design of interfaces to support the learner. This may appear to place major constraints on the range of interfaces we are concerned with, but such limitations are more illusory than real. Learners perform a diverse range of activities on an equally diverse range of information sources. They may browse, search, study, annotate, copy and store any of a number of books, magazines, journals, articles, textbooks, newspapers, manuals, notes and encyclopædias (and then some!). If we choose to be more specific we can limit our definition of learners to school-children, undergraduates, postgraduates or more specific subsets thereof, e.g. undergraduate students of English studying a course in Romantic poetry. Obviously this is what some researchers do, but there is always the danger that others assume that what holds true for such learners must be so for all learners (and by extension all users).

One solution is to increase specificity at the level of the learning task i.e., investigate the relevant interface issues for particular activities that learners may perform. This is the approach manifest explicitly in the McKnight et al chapter, but it is also present to varying degrees in other chapters such as Streitz, who considers authoring of learning materials and Marchionini, who argues for evaluation methods suitable to the learning task. In this sense, we cease to talk about the pros and cons of learning in hypermedia environments but consider instead the value of using hypermedia to support specific learning tasks such as essay writing, literature searching, code generation, or fault diagnosis and so forth. We may find that interfaces which help learners to locate relevant material in a

SH example 23.11
DJ parallel 10.15

large database are not optimized for reading and digesting that material. This approach avoids the confusion inherent in lumping such behaviours together, discussing them as one generic activity called "learning" which hypermedia may or may not support and encourages more accurate trade-offs to be assessed in situations where task boundaries merge.

Conflicting conceptions of the interface ───

A problem inherent in discussing user issues with designers is that many feel they understand the user very well and invoke their own experiences as evidence and justification for designs. This is a well-documented phenomenon in system design generally [6]. With the advent of hypertext packages, like HyperCard, there is the added danger that as educators master it to develop applications they begin to lose sight of how casual users of their output may respond and dismiss all discussion of interface issues with statements such as "anyone can use this" or "it's so easy to learn". A particularly insidious Hawthorne effect occurs where educators generalize their assessment of hypermedia's worth on the basis of their own students' performances (the latter ever sensitive to what it takes to reinforce the teacher!)

Within the group discussion at the conference, it was clear that no one position suited everyone. The wider view of the interface expounded above seemed novel to many of the participants who, I feel, view it literally as the mouse, screen and shape of the buttons! This is probably due to the mix of professionals present: psychologists, computer scientists, educationalists etc. and accounts for the distinction that emerged between participants in terms of the importance they attributed the interface. This distinction manifested itself in various ways through comments and points of view which I shall now outline.

The "thin" interface

JL comment conceptually thin

The descriptor "thin" was coined by John Leggett to suggest how a good interface should look. The implication is (I think) that very little should separate the user from the machine's functionality. It is reminiscent of the notion of transparency [7] and was juxtaposed with the idea of the interface as intrusive and (dare I say it) "fat"! In principle, there was no disagreement here except that some people took "thin" or noninvasive to equate to sufficient and "fat" to superfluous. Those of us who view the interface as the essential aspect of any system were held to be over-emphasizing its importance. In reality, everyone agrees that a good interface should be non-invasive (if we take this to mean that it doesn't intrude on task performance and consume the limited attentional resources of the user). Far from relegating the interface in importance such a perspective poses the question, how do you design something so well that, physically and representationally, users "see through" it?

Adaptable interfaces: All things to all users or a failure to design properly?

Two opposing views were put forward on how interfaces should be designed. One school of thought was that the interface should be adaptable, i.e., the users should have the facility to change the interface to suit their needs and preferences. This would manifest itself in the ability to design one's own icons, buttons, fonts, window sizes etc. This approach presumed a default interface style that the end users could work with if they did not want to design their own.

This seemed to be a popular point of view, especially among the more computer-oriented members of the group but was opposed vociferously by many (the humanists?). The major objections can be summed up as follows. First, such a design philosophy is superficial and solves nothing. Masquerading as a solution, it actually requires the designer to develop a default interface anyway as well as suitable facilities for any user to alter it. In other words, interfaces must still be designed for the end user. Bad design will prevent the user either utilizing such facilities or working effectively with the default interface. Second, it was remarked that such adaptable interfaces had been the goal of more traditional HCI research over the last decade and were not very effective even in comparatively limited task domains. As Jacob Nielsen remarked: "users are not necessarily good designers".

A counter-attack from the protagonists of adaptation was that users develop over time and as they do, they will learn to exploit the advanced features of a system. Therefore it was enough to give them the basics and let them get on with it! This was dismissed by others who argued that the history of research on users interacting with computers had shown that in such instances most users will learn just enough to get things done and will then stick rigidly to less-than-optimal strategies that work for them [8]. It's worth adding that if the interface is poor to start with, some users will just give up!

Obviously users develop, and it is worth considering the range of facilities that a more experienced user may want. Designing a system that is in some sense adaptable is desirable but brings with it a range of problems that need to be addressed. Designing adaptable interfaces necessitates <u>more</u> careful consideration of the interface not <u>less</u> and should not be seen as the cure for all interface ailments.

Interface as convention

A second area of discussion covered the extent to which readers' established patterns of interaction with paper should be supported by hypermedia systems. This stemmed from a comment that a number of conventions exist in paper texts that aid the reader in navigating through the material e.g., textbooks have a contents list at the front and an index at the back. This does not hold for existing hypertext documents where various implementations often provide unique access structures.

It was generally felt by all participants that the interface should reflect the conventions of the paper equivalents. There was no reason why hypermedia documents should not have indices and contents lists if relevant. However, the key word here is relevance. It is clear that the new medium affords interactions with the document that paper could never support and it would be foolish to accept the latter's limiting conventions wholesale. Furthermore, hypermedia will support document types which are unique to the medium, for which conventions, except in the very broadest sense, do not exist (yet).

GL corroboration 3.14

This was an interesting discussion. <u>The temptation to transfer the paper version to computer with its inherent paper qualities intact is hard to resist and is seen by some as a panacea to many interface problems.</u> The opportunity to provide "added-value" with the hypermedia version in the form of rapid searching facilities and so on is a user-ignorant designer's dream solution. Unfortunately, when such systems are implemented users find that they lack so much of the tangible qualities of paper texts that the similarities are more apparent than real. Furthermore, as noted elsewhere, such implementations do not seem to make optimal use of the technology.

Multi-level interface

The question of how far the interface extends in the hypermedia environment was raised several times in this discussion. A
way of making sense of the various perspectives was proposed
by George Landow who spoke of the "levels" of interface that
needed to be addressed. For example, the typography (font
and layout etc.) of the text was one level while the linking
facilities available to the user was another. To talk about the
interface as if it existed on just one level was bound to confuse. Indeed it certainly did confuse those participants who
felt, as remarked above, that consideration of the interface
began and ended with the input and display devices.

By taking a wider or multi-levelled approach we can arrive at
a perspective that sees the hypermedia application as the
interface between a learner and an information source. It
raises questions about how information should be organized
so as to promote better learning, just as much as questions to
do with system response rate or button size. In so doing, it
draws on the literature across a range of disciplines from
information design to ergonomics. However, few researchers
are capable of dealing with such a wide range of issues and it
behooves them to make explicit their level of concern in
designing better hypermedia, such as the distinction between
the user and the intellectual interface.

Continuum of interfaces

It was obvious from the comments of the participants that
agreement on how hypermedia interfaces should look was not
going to occur in the short term. In attempting to draw the
various viewpoints together, Dave Jonassen proposed a
continuum of interface styles:

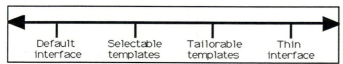

Figure1. A proposed continuum of interfaces from the group discussion

This is closer to a "tailorability" dimension with extremes of
none and total tailorability of the user interface separated by
templates that the user either selects or can tailor (though of
course, a "thin" interface need not be tailorable at all) than a
continuum. The templates were seen as the most reasonable
options in that they required the document author to take responsibility for placing a certain structure on the information
while affording the end-user or learner some flexibility in
deciding how to use it.

While the continuum is a reasonable summary of the issues covered in the discussion, I am not sure that if reflects a consensus within the group. The issue of how to design suitable templates was never directly addressed and seems to me another way of asking how we design suitable interfaces. Just answering "we use templates" is a restatement of the problem, not a solution. Offering tailorability is all well and good, but it must be employed usefully, not as an easy option.

Summary of positions

Participants were divided primarily on the importance they attributed the interface. Those who felt it was largely irrelevant in hypermedia applications argued for adaptable user interfaces that employed conventions from paper texts where necessary but afforded the functionality for the user to perform more complex activities as they acquire interactive skills. Opponents of this view argued that the interface consisted of all software and hardware between the user and the information contained in the system and was thus extremely important. They felt that just calling for adaptability and non-intrusion on the part of the interface was simplistic and side-stepped the real issues. In reality few participants adopted the extreme positions wholeheartedly, most tending one way rather than the other but appreciating the merits of some of the other views.

Advice to designers

What advice then can be offered to interface designers of hypermedia systems? First and foremost, know the users. Who are they, what skills and abilities will they have and most importantly, what tasks are they going to perform with the system? It may seem obvious, but there is little point in designing a powerful, adaptable interface for users who will never interact with it for longer than a few minutes to extract simple information. Similarly, but less obvious, there is no point placing all one's emphasis on ease of learning if, after becoming proficient the user finds the system incapable of satisfying his/her information needs. There will be occasions when it is impossible to identify the users' tasks accurately or when the hypermedia system will significantly alter the tasks of the users. However, even limited knowledge of this type can prove valuable in making accurate design decisions at the system specification stage.

It is impossible to gain total knowledge about end-users in advance so consider interface design as a process. Use prototypes if possible and evaluate the interface with real users as early as possible. The unwritten law is that users know best. Gain feedback and re-design accordingly. If you do not do this, the system starts to take form and, either through designer intransigence or for reasons of economics, it becomes too late to change the interface.

Don't assume that any system will or should solve all the problems. No one system or interface could ever do that (not even Ted Nelson's Xanalogical structures!) A usable system that lets a user perform some of their tasks is better than an unusable one that theoretically does everything they want but in practice they can't operate.

I have avoided formal guidelines here as I don't believe they are appropriate in this instance and because, taken on face value and/or out of context, they can be more harmful than helpful. However, guidelines pertaining to interface design for hypermedia applications are emerging [9] and the HCI literature in general is awash with them [10]. As with all guidelines they should be taken with a pinch of salt and are no replacement for informed design and early evaluation.

In conclusion, I must say that I am cautiously optimistic. The quality of user interfaces that abound today are orders of magnitude better than those of 10 or even 5 years ago. However, those who would dismiss the interface as an issue in these WIMPy times would do well to review the experimental literature on comparisons between hypertext and paper which, so far, has shown that most of the time (not always) users perform better with paper, however "better" is measured. This may change eventually, but is likely to remain the case if we ignore the interface issues.

Acknowledgements

This chapter takes the form it does because of the issues covered and comments made by the participants in the group discussion. I have tried to be faithful to the original speakers' viewpoints but it is likely that my recollections are limited, subjective and reflect my biases on what is important. As author, I take all the blame! The discussion was lively and good humored, and I have tried to retain that spirit in this description.

References

[1] Richardson, J., Dillon, A. and McKnight, C. (1989). The effect of window size on reading and manipulating electronic text. In E. Megaw (Ed.), *Contemporary Ergonomics 1989*. London: Taylor and Francis.

[2] Ewing, J., Mehrabanzad, S. Sheck, S., Ostroff, D. and Shneiderman, B. (1986). An experimental comparison of a mouse and arrow-jump keys for an interactive encyclopedia. *International Journal of Man-Machine Studies, 24*, (1), 29-45.

[3] Wright, P. and Lickorish, A. (1988). Colour cues as location aids in lengthy texts on screen and paper. *Behaviour and Information Technology, 7 ,*(1), 11-30.

[4] Lansdale, M. (1988). On the memorability of icons in an information retrieval task. *Behaviour and Information Technology, 7* (2), 131-151.

[5] Hammond, N. and Allinson, L. (1987). The travel metaphor as design principle and training aid for navigating around complex systems, in: D.Diaper and R.Winder (Eds.), *People and Computers III,* Cambridge: Cambridge University Press.

[6] Shneiderman, B. (1987). User interface design for the Hyperties electronic encyclopedia. In *Proceedings of Hypertext '87*, TextLab Report TR88-013, Dept. of Computer Science, University of North Carolina.

[7] Dehning, W, Essig, H. and Maass, S. (1981). *The adaptation of virtual man-computer interfaces to user-requirements in dialogs*. Lecture Notes in Computer Science Series, Berlin: Springer Verlag .

[8] Dillon, A. (1987). Knowledge acquisition and conceptual models: a cognitive analysis of the interface. In D.Diaper and R.Winder (Eds.), *People and Computers III*, Cambridge: Cambridge University Press.

[9] Hardman, L. and Sharratt, B. (1989). *User-centred hypertext design: the application of HCI design principles and guidelines*. Paper presented at Hypertext II, the 2nd Annual UK Conference on Hypertext, University of York.

[10] Smith, S., and Mosier,J. (1986). *Guidelines for Designing User-Interface Software*. Report 7 MTR-10090, Esd-Tr-86-278, Mitre Corp., Bedford, MA.

11.11

PART IV

HYPERMEDIA
AND INSTRUCTION

Chapter 12
Hypermedia and Instruction:
Where is the Match?

Thomas M. Duffy and Randy A. Knuth
Indiana University

Keywords

Hypermedia systems; databases; hypertext technology; learning environments; collaborative systems; semantic retrievals; pedagogy; computer assisted learning

Contents

Introduction

We have recently begun a major project to design, develop, and implement an enriched learning environment (ELE) for undergraduate education. Our initial thinking was very technology oriented. A hypermedia environment would allow

NATO ASI Series, Vol. F 67
Designing Hypermedia for Learning
Edited by D. H. Jonassen and H. Mandl
© Springer-Verlag Berlin Heidelberg 1990

students to explore a knowledge domain and see the relations between ideas; it would allow students and instructors to create new links and new units of information reflecting their interests and needs; it would permit faculty to catalogue and organize their instructional materials and permit them to create high quality text, graphics, and even animation in the comfort of their office; and finally, it would permit students and faculty to communicate and debate. We were attempting to define a technology that would be all things for all students and instructors. It would be a tool that would serve any use of a database and any communication in the learning process. Those rather naive notions have long since passed. .

In reflection, our early thinking simply was an avoidance of instructional theory. We were going to provide an atheoretical tool that would aid a professor in developing and delivering instruction regardless of his or her instructional theory or strategy. As we reflect on much of the writing about hypertext and hypermedia, we have come to recognize that in fact most of the thinking on hypermedia is instructionally atheoretical and technology based.

In this paper we want to look at the link between the uses of hypermedia and pedagogy. We will critically evaluate the features and the uses of hypermedia from an educational perspective. In the final section of the paper, we will describe the current conceptualization of ELE.

Uses of hypermedia

Hypertext or hypermedia systems have three characteristics: a database of information, referred to as nodes or frames; machine supported links between these nodes that allow for rapid movement through the information; and a consistent user interface for interacting with the hypertext [1]. Furthermore, the linking is not arbitrary, but rather is based on the semantic relationships between nodes. In addition to these basic characteristics, a hypertext designed for educational purposes must allow the user to easily author (create) new nodes as well as establish links between that new information and nodes that already exist [2]. Thus the content and the semantic structure reflected in the linking may be generated by the teacher, the student, some third party author, or any combination of these three.

Basically, then, we have a database that can be rapidly accessed, modified, and reconfigured and that presents information in some organized manner. How might we use such a system in an educational environment? Looking at the current and proposed applications of hypertext, we see four basic types of use. We do not mean to suggest a one-to-one match between each category of use and a particular application. Indeed, most applications will employ more than one. Our purpose in identifying these categories is to aid us in evaluating the linkages to pedagogy.

Exploring a large database

The emphasis here is on the joint occurrence of a large database and a user activity of "exploration". The use is to <u>give the learner access to more information and to help the learner, through link traversal, acquire the important relations and the structure in that body of information.</u> Hypertext environments are designed to "store and retrieve large amounts of [information]...presented in a fairly unstructured environment where the students could pursue their own individual interest..." [3, pp. 2-3]. Since the link traversal is fast and easy, large amounts of information can be provided for a user to "explore" or reference.

The goal is to assist students in exploring relations—in reaching out. It is one of providing a rich array of information. While we want the student to be able to move through the database efficiently (i.e., navigation through the information is easy), there is not an emphasis on efficiency of learning but rather on the richness of learning.

Accessing elaborations on core information

SH parallel 23.9

The emphasis here, in contrast to the first application, is on efficiency. The goal is the comprehension or use of some core body of information by the selection of elaborating information. The strategy is to allow <u>the student to select elaborations on that core body of information as is necessary for comprehension.</u> This application is very much in tune with the traditional instructional goal of efficiency of learning and hence the approach is common in many CBT packages. The usefulness of the approach grows with the diversity in the amount or type of knowledge of the user population. Thus, the approach would be very useful in presenting human computer interface design theory/guidelines for use by experts and novices in computer science, English, and Psychology. In this use, hypermedia simply permits a richer and larger database of support information than would be available in CBT. The

PD implication 8.4

issue here is efficiency of learning in the sense that the student can get at the appropriate information (no more, no less) in a relatively short period of time. Of course, efficiency in movement between nodes, i.e., efficiency in navigation, is also important in the use just as it is in any information access task. Indeed, *efficiency in navigation* is a primary consideration in the first use of hypermedia that we discussed. However, the "efficiency issue" particular to this second use of hypermedia is information specific: the user sees only what is required for comprehension.

Operating on a database

Here we are emphasizing the situations where *tools* are made available to operate on the database. The hypermedia system provides the opportunity for making tools available on an "as needed" basis that can be used to manipulate the information in the database. The tools are ones that will permit us to go beyond exploring the database. These may include tools for compiling or pulling together relevant information, analyzing or computing, and comparing or contrasting. The goal here is to make sense of the data by reorganizing it in some fashion. However, the data remains unchanged In fact, the operation on the data is at the level of the user, i.e., it becomes a personalized view of that data.

Building a database

SH parallel 23.10

The emphasis here is on *authoring information* in contrast to the previous uses which all involved working with a database that already exists. As we noted at the outset, these uses may all be present in a single application. Thus the user may be able to add nodes of information to an existing database. However, there are also important applications in which the *management of information* as it is generated is central, e.g., in collaborative writing, problem solving, issue analysis, etc. One could imagine this use resulting in hypertexts of many sizes and functions. For example there would be those that are constructed by an individual for personal use as well as those jointly constructed by many individuals for community use.

While we have categorized the functions of hypertext into these four uses, we recognize there is a rich diversity within each category. In part, however, this diversity represents a diversity of the goals in that particular use. In the next section we would like to consider the variety of pedagogical goals that each type of use might serve.

Pedagogical assumptions for hypermedia use

Exploring a large database

This is the most widely cited use of hypermedia. It is the basis of the original writings on hypermedia by Vannavar Bush [4] and a significant component of Ted Nelson's [5] literary environment. We agree with this use as a reference tool, where the user is searching for particular information. However, this is *goal directed searching* and the function of the hypertext system is encyclopedic. We also agree with the potential value of this application for graduate work and for professional work, i.e., for users who are attempting to "foster the creation of information webs" [6, p. 16]. These users presumably have a strong grounding in the knowledge domain. However, we have some question as to the pedagogy that would support this use for elementary, secondary, or even undergraduate education. These learners are apprentices, attempting to gain user skills in the basics of the knowledge domain.

What are the pedagogical arguments for this use of hypermedia? Perhaps the most basic argument is that it opens up the knowledge domain and permits the learner to explore and search out issues of interest to him. This has a motivational impact since it is *learner directed*. More importantly, however, will be the transfer of features of the knowledge domain being explored. Both specific and general transfer have been hypothesized. The specific transfer is of the semantic network of the knowledge domain. That is, it has been suggested that we can use hypermedia to represent the knowledge structure of the expert. Then, as the student explores the knowledge domain he will learn the experts structure. It has even been suggested that we look at the semantic network of the student using card sort methodology [7] or semantic network software (e.g., Semnet) to examine the change in the user's structure.

Transfer of a semantic network is quite specific. It has also been argued that exploring the database leads to more *general transfer of a nonlinear way of thinking* [8]. It is argued that books promote a linear mode of thinking and as a consequence the learner thinks in terms of simplistic cause and effect. However, as the learner explores a hypermedia database he/she will see that there is no simple cause. Eventually, he/she will also see that school subject matter is an artificial categorization of events, i.e., art, literature, social sciences, sciences, etc. all have mutually interdependent effects and can all be linked in a historical timeline.

We think there needs to be some serious questioning of all of these assumptions of the educational benefits of exploring a large database. We suspect that this use of hypermedia might be useful, but we would argue that the usefulness is very limited. In particular we would like to discuss two issues related to this application: the value of a large database and the learner's activity in the database. We would like to frame our concerns for this approach and the associated "theory" by appealing to educational practice and educational theory. In essence we want to ask why this approach is educationally sound.

Learner activity. Let us begin with the learning activity of the user: *exploring the database*. This is more than simply retrieving facts or references as one might do in a reference database. The goal is the transfer of semantic structures and hence the user must pass through the links, attending to the semantic relations. The instructions given to literature students using Intermedia best illustrates the goal of the student activity. As it is most frequently used in these discussions, *browsing is goal free* — the student wanders, fancy free, through the database. For example, consider this inclusion in the course syllabus for the literature course taught using Intermedia:

> How will the computer work, or, how is it supposed to work? It should function like an adventure game, permitting you to wander through a world of facts and ideas, jumping from one to another or linking them when you wish to do so. We have envisioned the entire program and its visual and verbal contents as one enormous web of interrelated facts and ideas that you can enter and leave at any place" [9, appendix A]

The statement likens the use to that of playing an adventure game. Indeed, players of adventure games do move through a domain and learn a lot about that domain in the process of playing. However, that learning is all organized around, and related to, the goal of the game. Thus, the player learns where to jump to get extra power, or how to check on a path to see if danger lurks, or to remember a path so backtracking will be possible if a blind alley is encountered.

GL comment Misleading. That hypertext supported a new pedagogy cannot prove it had no major effect on that pedagogy.

The important point is that <u>we learn what is required or related to achieving our goal.</u> But what is the goal in exploring? What is the student to achieve? Hypermedia systems have too often been defined in terms of the technology (indeed, arguments as to what is or is not a hypermedia are typically based on the technology). The use of hypermedia systems has too often been described in terms of what "could" happen. It is time for a little reality testing; time to ask just how or why a learner might explore the knowledge domain and to seriously consider the effects of that exploration.

What might be the *goals for exploring*? We can think of many: preparing for a debate, writing a paper; attempting to find linkages, for example, between historical periods, etc. Note that these tasks all involve an *active student searching for relationships* that will support a point of view. We expect that virtually every educational use of a hypermedia system involves specific assignments like these. Students are seldom told to simply explore without any sense of a goal. The learning goal will arise out of course requirements and those requirements are an important component in any consideration of educational uses of hypermedia technology. Effective assignments will place responsibility on the student to discover relationships and build arguments. That is, the assignment will require her to "explore" the database searching for links relevant to the specific issue. If we are to understand the effective use of hypermedia as a database to explore, <u>we simply must give more attention to the nature of the assignments</u> that accompany that exploration.

AR background 19.4

GL parallel 3.5-6
DJ corroboration 3.19

AR parallel 13.12

What is learned? The goals in exploring the hypermedia database are to learn the specific semantic relations so one thinks like an expert and to develop nonlinear thinking habits. At least these are the anticipated for effects. Let's examine the goal of transferring the semantic network first. Why might we want to do this? Do we presume some ultimate reality in the particular network that is developed? Is there THE expert's network? Certainly there are many expert points of view. We might hope that our students will look at these multiple points of view and be able to contrast the differences.

The issue of expert representation is a particularly important consideration in the design of some hypermedia systems. For example, the Intermedia applications that have been developed are based on the organization and thinking of the particular professors [10]. There are not multiple points of view, as one might get at a library, but rather "a" point of view. Even if conflicting viewpoints are included in the database, there is still the censor determining which alternatives are relevant. Indeed, rather than aiding discovery, we can imagine the hypermedia system limiting discovery.

Let us presume for the moment that we do indeed want the students to think like the professor who created the hypermedia database. How would that be accomplished? Clearly, the student would have to work in the domain doing the same kinds of tasks as the professor did. The student would have to have experiences like those of the professor [11]. Simply learning the links in the database is certainly not going to result in someone thinking like the professor. Rather, it would be a rote enumeration, much like list or paired associate learning.

What is learned in using the database will depend on how it is used. We have already discussed the kinds of tasks that might be given to encourage exploration of the database. The student will develop understandings based on the evidence she gathers to complete those tasks. It won't be a replication of the database (certainly that sounds like a very limiting learning task), but rather it will be an abstracting, reorganizing, and adding to some subset of the database. The particular subset abstracted will be the information the student deems relevant to her argument. The reorganization will be based on building an argument relevant to that issue (presumably it is not an argument literally addressed in the database — again, this would be a mundane assignment). Finally, the information added would be new linking arguments and information suggested from the learner's internal knowledge base. Hence, we are looking for new organizations rather than acquiring THE organization.

Now let us turn to the issue of nonlinear thinking, the second hypothesized benefit of hypermedia. Once again, the designers of the Intermedia applications present the best example of this application to education. The instructors using Intermedia believe that it will "suggest a [nonlineal] way of thinking, a more effective means [for students] to understand their world." [9, p. 106][1] .

---

[1] We are still focusing on exploring a database or using it as an information resource. While we expect authoring in a hypermedia system (using it to organize ones thinking) may affect the process of argumentation or analysis, we do not think that simply working in a database will promote new strategies simply because of the organization of that database.

Does exploring Intermedia, or hypermedia systems in general, promote nonlinear thinking? We think not, at least not to any meaningful degree. In part, we are once again back to the issue of the user activity of "exploring". Simply seeing nonlinear relationships — having them pointed out to you — does not promote nonlinear thinking. Indeed, one of the problems with hypermedia systems is maintaining the big picture — maintaining a sense of the complexity of relationships. This orienting information is generally provided in *overview frames*. The Intermedia system also uses graphic techniques, such as *timelines*, to show multiple causality. If anything, we suspect it is these overviews and time graphics, not the linkages, that support the recognition of multiple causality. Furthermore, this graphic approach to illustrating multiple causality is not even dependent on a hypermedia environment. Jones and her colleagues [12] have done extensive work on developing graphic and text presentation techniques to represent multiple causality in the design of a history textbook. This has included the use of timelines and interaction graphs.

GL comment Inaccurate. Concept maps (overviews) are not timelines used in this way. The instructor downplayed timelines for technical and pedagogical reasons.
GL comment   Illogical. Evidence something is not the only factor does not indicate it is not a factor.

The professors goals and instructional strategies, quite aside from Intermedia, also play a significant role in promoting nonlinear thinking. For example, in the original literature course that was eventually supported by Intermedia, the instructor tended to be lecture oriented and focused on discussing literary works individually. In a revision of the course that did not involve using Intermedia, the instructor began to think in terms of the students interrelating the different literary pieces to each other and to the activities of the period. While he chose a core text that he felt should be the focus of thinking about relations, he was never explicit about this to the students. A second change in the course was his decision that the students should drive the class discussion more than they had in the past. An interesting sidelight to the improvement of instruction in Professor Landow's class is that a great deal of the change in methodology was due to the creation of the materials for the Intermedia project. In fact, the course was taught for one semester after the materials had been produced but were not used in the class for technical reasons. The class was significantly better even without the computer technology [13].

In the second revision of the course, these two goals were made even more explicit. While Intermedia was a part of this implementation, the changes in instructional goals and strate-

12.10

gies were not dependent upon Intermedia. Thus, the instructor now "began students thinking right from the start in terms of piecing together interrelationships as a means to understanding English" [9, p. 83]. Also in this iteration, the instructor would stand quietly in the class until the students initiated discussion — again, increasing the emphasis on student directed discussion.

Finally, we might note that the availability of Intermedia did not necessarily lead to this nonlinear, student directed learning. A graduate student took over for the professor one class during the time Intermedia was in use. The class requested that the assistant begin with a brief lecture — in contrast to the pattern the professor had established. The assistant obliged and then maintained a teacher centered class for the whole period.

These examples demonstrate that the pedagogy that emphasizes attending to relationships and demands it of students is the key element. That pedagogical goal can be realized in the design of a textbook, in the design of the classroom requirements, or in the demands for the use of a hypermedia system. The question to ask is how the use of the technology can best contribute to the realization of that pedagogy.

Role of Hypermedia. Thus far we have argued that exploration of a hypermedia database is really the use of the database to build an argument or an understanding of some specific topic. What is learned are the relationships that come from abstracting and reorganizing a segment of that database. It is unrealistic and even undesirable to presume that the semantic network will be transferred to the learners head — regardless of the nature of the tasks. Furthermore, we have argued that the promotion of nonlinear thinking rests primarily in the pedagogy of the professor rather than in the database.

Then what is the use of hypermedia for exploring or accessing information? There are two related uses that have been promoted. First, hypermedia can make more and different types of information available to the learner -- he can have a huge database, employing a variety of media, at his fingertips [14]. Second, he can *traverse that database easily*, readily searching for possible relationships. Thus it is the speed with which the learner can access volumes of related information.

Speed is obviously important. If there is a large database, then it will only be usable to the extent that traversal is fast and easy. However, what is the pedagogical value of a large database? Do we really need a large database? We think that it can promote a diversity of viewpoints on an issue and that is indeed valuable. However, we want to emphasize that bigger is not always better. It is how the student works with the information, not the amount of information accessed, that is important. Access to large databases , e.g., Perseus [15], is very important for professional work or graduate study when the user is attempting to advance the state of understanding. However, our focus is on the learner at the early stages of knowledge and skill development.

It might be argued that the large database will permit students to write better papers by having access to more information and being able to explore more relations. Frankly, before we go to the expense of building the large database we need to seriously question the degree to which the difficulty of accessing material is limiting the quality of papers. We would suggest that <u>students easily locate more than enough relevant material, rhetorical skills, motivation, and the demands (or lack thereof) made by the instructor are certainly vastly more important than access.</u>

If an instructionally based rationale for a large database cannot be provided then this type of application — searching through or exploring a large database — is obviously not appropriate for hypermedia. <u>The relationships and structure for small databases can easily be presented in a book [12] and a learner can easily explore a book in a nonlinear fashion</u> (in spite of much of the rhetoric on the benefits of hypermedia). We are arguing that there needs to be more realistic thinking of just how exploring a large database will advance instructional effectiveness for undergraduates and for K-12 learners.

We have spent a considerable amount of time discussing the use of hypermedia for exploring information. This is because it is the use most often discussed and promoted. While we have a number of questions as to the utility of this use, we do not question the potential utility of hypermedia systems. Indeed, we see the potential for significant improvements in instruction and learning with each of the other three uses of hypermedia systems. We will now consider the use of hypermedia to elaborate on, to operate on, and to create information.

12.11

DR contrast 5.9

GM comment This is an important limitation in the discussion.

Accessing elaborations on core information

This application has direct instructional implications; it is tied very closely to current instructional design practices. There is some core information that the student is to acquire or understand. If the basic presentation is adequate, the student can go on. However, if it is not adequate, the student can ask for a variety of elaborations. This may include examples, entering a microworld, obtaining more explanation, etc. In essence the *goal is one of individualizing instruction or explanation.* Hammond [2] describes an instructional system where hypermedia is used in this way. The approach is also very common in presenting text. That is, the text is compressed into a series of headings. More and more detailed information under a heading is revealed upon the users request. Jakob Nielsen's trip reports[2] are a good example of this use.

In virtually all instruction there will be a subdomain in which the student will be required to develop some competency. Furthermore, there will most certainly be individual differences in the ability of students to understand and use the concepts and principles in that subdomain. The hypermedia systems may be especially useful in providing that information or instructional support — again, regardless of the pedagogy. Thus, the primary instruction might be didactic and a microworld or simulation may be the hypermedia support for understanding the relations between concepts and the use of those concepts. Alternatively, the primary instruction may be less didactic and employ the microworld. The hypermedia support would provide elaborations on the concepts used in the microworld. The strength is in the efficiency. That is, only that information the student needs is presented and then only when it is requested.

JL corroboration 15.11, 17.3, 21.3, explanation 10.6

Finally, in defining this support role in the use of hypermedia, we might note that the information being elaborated upon need not be part of the computer based hypermedia system. Depending on the size of this core database and how it will be used, it may make more sense to keep it in hardcopy with a computer based hypermedia support system.

SH parallel 23.20

Operating on a database

This is perhaps one of the key features of computer applications in general. Spread sheets, word processors and databases all permit a variety of operations to be performed in the text or data stored in the program. In essence a variety of computing tools or application programs can be made available to assist the individual in her work with the database. If we presume that students learn by working with information, then providing effective work tools is critical. Of course it is critical that the tools are appropriate to the application, i.e., to the way in which students should be working on the data. Let us look briefly at two examples.

Intermedia provides at least three tools that may aid the learner: the ability to juxtapose frames of information; the ability to annotate the database; and the ability to create personalized links. First the learner can juxtapose any two nodes providing for ease of comparison and contrast. This was a capability that was particularly useful in studying Biology, though the data suggest, and we might assume, that it was not particularly important for literature. Second, there is a tool for attaching annotations to the nodes in the database. There is very little if any suggestion that this tool was used. Indeed, an examination of the assignments did not suggest any use. Finally, there was a tool for manipulating links in the systems, basically allowing the student to configure her own hypermedia network. We might suspect that a tool which allows the student to personalize the information in a hypertext would be useful. However, rather than configuring their own semantic network of the database, we see the tool as most useful for abstracting information from the database and organizing it to achieve a particular goal, e.g., writing a paper.

GL comment Inaccurate. Students annotated material in later courses.

One of the best hypertext applications that we have seen, one that represents a substantial amount of information and which embodies many analysis tools is the Hyperbible by Beacon Technology, Inc. The information is accessed by interacting through a nicely defined interface and tools are provided that individuals would find very helpful in studying the Bible either formally or informally. The tools include interactive maps, measurement conversion tables, a concordance, digitized pronunciations, a variety of indexes, and many more. Since much of Bible study involves locating, comparing, and analyzing what is said at different places on different issues, these tools are ideal instructional aids. It must be re-emphasized, however, that although the Hyperbible is a model hypertext, its capabilities are realized in the learning goals that the learner brings to the system.

12.14

Authoring environment

Hypermedia systems offer tremendous potential for supporting the authoring of complex documents and the processing of ideas, especially in a group or collaborative environment. We would imagine that authoring will be a critical component of any hypermedia application. Learners require the capability to annotate information frames for themselves, and they need to be able to collaborate with other students and with the teacher over specific units of information. Most importantly, they must be able to build their own knowledge system, either from scratch or by abstracting, rearranging and adding to an existing database.

SH parallel 23.22

There is sufficient research to indicate that learning must be an active process; that the learner must work with the information and come to see it as relevant to his context. Hypermedia systems, with active authoring facilities, are ideally suited to support this active learning. We must emphasize, however, that if the authoring is with an existing database, the authoring must support the meaningful use of the information. This is going to be determined, of course, by both the technological capability and the assignment given. If the system only permits annotation cards that stay attached to a single node and if the assignment is simply to note important points while browsing, then we suspect that the authoring system is ill-used. Authoring should support the learner in extending the ideas in the database and creating his own, personalized information.

SH example 23.14

Even more important than individual authoring, hypermedia systems provide great potential in the support of *collaborative work*. We are increasingly coming to realize that collaboration is a very important component in the learning process. Collaboration may be with either the teacher or other students. As Collins et al, [16] discuss, the teacher based collaboration can provide expert modeling and expert guidance in learning (or, more aptly, in the use of information). The teacher may serve as the master in the master-apprentice relation.

GM comment Collaboration can also take place with the computer.

SH contrast 20.3

While collaboration with the teacher is important, the collaboration with other students may be even more important. In working with other students, the learner must confront other points of view and must be able to argue and explain their understanding. This is one of the prime benefits to the tutor in a peer tutoring context. However, the idea extends well beyond the learner-student relationship to the collaborative development of understanding of any issue.

Both KMS [17] and Concordia [18] were developed to support collaborative writing and information development. Both systems have been used in developing large technical documentation databases. The extension to collaborative writing is straight forward, though there are many other options for collaborating in these environments . A third system developed specifically to support collaboration is gIBIS [1]. Instead of collaborative writing, this system supports collaboration in the management of argument development. The educational implications are obvious.

Enriched learning environment

The discussion in the last section concerning our conceptualization of the uses of hypermedia systems, grew out of our initial struggle as to the way in which hypermedia might best be used in education. The student use that dominated our thinking was that of "browsing the large database". Thus we envisioned creating (and working with the teacher in creating) a knowledge structure in which students could explore and learn. The students would be able to annotate and send mail, but the major emphasis was on *exploring the network*. The teacher would have the *authoring responsibility*. In essence, she would maintain the network of information and pull material from the network to use in her classroom presentation. The students' benefit was that they would have access, in the hypermedia system, to the information the instructor used in class.

We were supporting a traditional approach to instruction — the transfer (or pouring) of expert knowledge structures into the head of the learner. There were two factors that moved us from this position. First, there were practical issues. The primary effort would involve building the knowledge domain. This would entail defining knowledge chunks in terms of both size and semantic classification. We did not see it as a simple chunking of the textbook as, for example, occurs with Superbook [19] or as Leggett, et al. did in two of their studies. First off, it is not "simple" to decide on meaningful chunks. Second, we wanted to go beyond the textbook. If acquiring the knowledge structure is the goal, then we must be extremely confident that we have a good knowledge representation.

While building this system would have been a great intellectual exercise, the approach simply was not practical. Our goal was to build a system that had some generality. However, the amount of expertise and the amount of labor required to build the database placed tremendous limitations on the generality. The analysis of the knowledge domain and the definition of information units would have to be performed anew for each knowledge domain. While we could export the technology, if we truly believed that the network was the critical factor, then the tool by itself is not useful.

The second factor in moving us from the "browsing of a large database" use evolved from our concern of pedagogical issues. These issues were discussed in the previous section. Briefly, the development of the hypermedia network (of the knowledge domain) makes some presumption that there is "an" accurate representation of the semantic network. Whose semantic network were we to use? Is the project specific to a particular instructor's viewpoint? Would other faculty be willing to use this individual's representation? In essence, in undertaking the approach, we would have to buy into a particular construction of knowledge. And, if we wanted a generalizable product, then we would have to be sure that other instructors in the domain would buy into that construction as well.

We also began wondering how the student would browse in the database. What are the assignments the instructor would be giving the students? It is with this consideration, that we began to recognize two important points. First, the critical instructional issue is the assignment the teacher gives to the student. Thus, we should be focusing our attention on the kind of assignments or uses to be made of our Enriched Learning Environment. Second, we were reminded that learning is an active process. If students are to learn, they must work with information, manipulate it, and use it. Thus, rather than focusing on browsing, we needed to focus on supporting the student in operating on, as well as in producing, information.

GL corroboration 3.5-6

In sum, the rethinking of the project is very much in terms of pedagogical issues. The planning is now for the design of an enriched learning environment from the view of effective learning. Of course, the technology also has a significant influence on our thinking. The technology opens real instructional opportunities which, in turn, direct our attention toward ways of capitalizing on those opportunities. Finally, the development of instructional theory cannot occur context free. The relevant theory and instantiation of the concepts will depend on the particular type of course being supported. Important factors of a course include its instructional goals, class size, level of instruction, etc. ELE will evolve over the course of the next year as a function of the analysis of these three components: technology, pedagogical theory, and the learning environment. The remainder of our discussion will address the pedagogy and the learning environment. Since the system is in the early stages, it is premature to discuss the technology.

Pedagogy of the Enriched Learning Environment

The focus of Enriched Learning Environment is on facilitating the transfer of what is learned in the classroom to its application in everyday life. The goal is to create an enriched learning environment in which the student can and is required to use the concepts and principles "learned" in the classroom. The emphasis will be on "information uses" that reflect the complexities of the real world. There are two key conceptual underpinnings to the design of ELE: the belief that the understanding of a concept grows out of (or, is indexed by) the use of that concept and the belief that collaboration is a critical component of effective learning. In the next section we will briefly describe some of the key research and thinking underlying these two components of our pedagogy.

Experience as an index of understanding. This thinking is perhaps best grounded in the philosophy of Ludwig Wittgenstein [20]. Early in his career he was one of the leading logical positivists, strongly contending that a concept had a single true meaning and that we could arrive at that meaning through linguistic analysis. However, he eventually rejected the logical positivist position to argue that the meaning of a word is not fixed, but rather is dependent on the context in which it occurs. Additionally, its meaning is equally dependent on the goals of the person using the word in that specific context.

The implications of the shift from logical positivism is well illustrated in the consideration of the concept "game". In the logical positivist approach, "game" would be seen as having a fixed, true meaning. In essence, it would be possible to identify the criterial attributes of "game" that could be used to categorize all possible objects or events into games and nongames. The context or experiential view, in contrast, argues that "game" cannot be defined in terms of critical attributes . No set of features can be identified that will permit us to distinguish all games from nongames: a game may be individual or group, competitive or cooperative, have an end goal or simply an activity, be physical or mental, etc. Furthermore, and most importantly, from our perspective, an individual's understanding of the concept "game" will grow as she experiences more events considered to be games, i.e., the meaning of "game" is indexed by her experience with games.

Traditional instruction has most often reflected the logical positivist position. A subject matter domain is neatly pre-scribed and defined. The concepts and principles in that domain are defined in terms of critical attributes and students are taught those critical attributes. In the last several years there have been three specific criticisms of this approach to instruction that are particularly relevant to the ELE project. The criticisms are all based on the failure of this approach to provide a context relevant to the use of the knowledge. That is, each criticism espouses the view that meaning (and hence usability) is indexed by the experience one has with the concepts. (Let us note that while we are focusing on three current arguments, the importance of embedding instruction in a functional context has a long history in instructional re-search and theory [21, 22]).

Bransford [23] and his colleagues have argued that much of school learning remains inert. The information is "learned" in that the student can recall it and even apply it if instructed to do so. However, the student isn't taught when or for what purpose to use what is learned. He isn't taught to notice when the information might be usefully applied. Simon [24] has made this same argument with specific reference to mathemat-ics instruction.

There are three key components to Bransford's strategy for providing context. First, the knowledge development is contextualized in a problem solving framework. The student learns about concepts in order to solve problems. Hence, rather than being inert, the information, from the beginning, is identified as usable. Second, Bransford emphasizes the use of *macrocontexts*, i.e., the problem is placed in a larger context than simply word problems. Too often in instruction, problem solving is used as an activity in and of itself. Hence the learner works on a series of independent problems, each designed only to have the student use the particular concept. In providing a macrocontext, the student sees the use of the concept (solving the problem) not as an end in and of itself, but rather as a step along the way to some larger goal. These first two points are critical to the development of usable knowledge. The third component of his approach involves *giving the students more responsibility in developing their own issues*. In Bransford's terms, the students become "producers of knowledge" rather than "consumers of knowledge."

An interesting feature of Bransford's work is the use of videodisk technology in virtually all approaches to instruction. There are many movies that provide exciting events that can be used to teach science and math and many movies that accurately portray history, geography, and social issues. Thus the movies provide both motivation and a realistic representation of the subject matter. Furthermore, on a videodisk, the students can readily access and use parts of the movie in creating instruction or solving problems.

The second line of research that is critical of traditional instruction is that by Spiro and his colleagues [25]. They argue that students have a difficult time transferring from school based learning because schooling presents the concepts and principles in an oversimplified framework. In essence, once the student enters the complexity of the real world, she typically won't even be able to recognize the concepts she learned about because of the complex surround. If she does recognize it, she probably won't be able to respond appropriately because she has never encountered the range and complexity of constraints on possible responses.

In essence, Spiro argues that schools simplify the representation of knowledge in order to help the student see the main point. However, the context in which the main point occurs is critical to its understanding: the simplified concept is a different concept. Removing the context does not merely simplify the concept but rather it teaches a different one altogether. To return to our early example of the concept "game", it is much like teaching "game" as a well defined concept with fixed attributes. That simplified understanding will handicap the student in the use of the concept in the real world.

Spiro has argued for *case-based learning* in which the cases capture and represent the complexity of real experiences. A student works through several cases, moving back and forth between them, examining the use of a concept in different contexts. Thus, the student comes to see the multiple contexts in which a concept occurs and can begin to index its meaning in real contexts. It is important to note that Spiro's approach is not simply a matter of using realistic (complex and rich) cases. It is also the strategy for moving through those cases. The instruction is focused on developing an understanding for a concept and that understanding must arise through working with the concept in the different environments or cases. Thus, the strategy for crisscrossing the terrain in which the concept occurs is critical.

Spiro has suggested that his case based approach to learning is most appropriate for ill structured domains and for advanced study. His work has been primarily in the areas of economics and medical training. We would argue, however, that the approach is fully appropriate to learners at all levels. If we are to promote transfer or real world use of school learning, we cannot wait until students reach advanced study. We must begin in the early grades. The context of use will be different since it will represent the context of their use of the concepts, but it will nonetheless represent real world cases of the concept and those cases will be rich and complex. The experiences indexed by the cases (or the functional contexts) must be relevant to the learner's world of use.

The final line of research is that reflected in the writing of John Seeley Brown, Collins and their colleagues [11, 16]. They argue that learning is making sense of some experience, thought, or phenomenon. That is, people in everyday life, be they engaged in daily activities or in professional work, make sense of concepts (learn) through engaging in activities that circumscribe those concepts. The basic hypothesis advanced by Brown et al [11] is that our representation or understanding of a concept is not abstract and self sufficient but rather is constructed from those contexts, social and physical, in which the concept is found and used. That is, our understanding of a concept is indexed by our experience with that concept.

Given the Brown et al [11] argument, if our goal is for students to use what they learn, then it is essential that we provide students with "authentic experiences" with the concept, i.e., we must provide them with experiences that capture the process of using knowledge in ways that it is actually used in the world outside the classroom. Schooling fails when it teaches abstractions devoid of connections to the real world. The absence of such connections will result in "school learning" that does not index real use and hence is not easily transferred to the nonschool environment.

The work of Sticht and Hickey [26] nicely illustrates the authentic and not so authentic experiences that can be provided in a learning situation. Their goal was to design a basic electricity and electronics course for training Navy personnel. This material was to be learned in a foundation course that all sailors took before they went on to their advanced electronics course. It was to provide the fundamentals. In the existing course, students learned the basic theory of electronics: ohms law was taught and the students practiced analyzing circuit diagrams. It was generally felt that if one understood the theory, then that theory could be used in any specific application. This, of course, is the traditional approach to instruction in which the concepts are abstracted from their use in the real world.

In contrast to this traditional approach to instruction, Sticht and Hickey [26] used what they called a functional context approach. Basically their goal was to *ground the instruction in familiar, real world problems*. Thus their course began with familiar objects like a hair dryer and flashlight and a real problem: the object didn't work. The students were encouraged to formulate hypotheses as to why it didn't work and then their hypotheses were related to the functional components of the circuits. More complex and more abstract representations evolved from these more familiar groundings. Note that the critical components of the approach included both the physical context and the problem solving context.

Collins et.al [16] argue for *cognitive apprenticeship* as another important strategy for providing authentic experiences. The cognitive apprenticeship approach provides the learner with models of the real use of knowledge. The learner can observe real uses of the knowledge, which includes not only the concepts but, perhaps more importantly, the heuristic, control, and learning strategies. This observing provides the first step in an apprenticeship. Given the model of authentic activities, the student can then attempt her own work, with coaching from the expert. As the student masters the more basic components of the work, there is increasing complexity and increasing independence. Collins et.al [16] describe three examples of apprenticeship applications: Palincsar and Brown's [27] *reciprocal teaching,* Schoenfeld's [28] method for teaching mathematical problem solving, and Scardemelia and Bereiter's [29] approach to teaching writing.

In summary, the goal of thetransfer of school learning to use outside of the classroom, requires that the student engage in real world uses of the knowledge to be learned. This engagement must emphasize the *use of the information in a problem solving* context. A problem solving context exists anytime the learner has a goal and there is uncertainty how or whether the goal is achieved. It must also capture the complexity of the real world relationships and constraints. Finally, there must be <u>multiple real world experience, and a system for aiding the student in his apprenticeship in the use of that knowledge.</u>

DJ explanation 18.1-7

Collaboration in learning and work.   Many of the issues discussed above suggest the importance of collaboration in learning. Most clearly, the apprenticeship model calls for collaboration between expert and novice: the expert and novice taking turns at a task, observing and commenting on each other's strategies. However, collaboration with fellow students is also critical. If understanding a concept is indexed by ones experience with that concept, then we can expect a student to have a far richer understanding to the extent she encounters alternative understandings of a concept or alternative strategies for achieving a goal and must resolve those differences with her own understanding or strategy. Thus, we see collaboration as a means of engaging the student in the *negotiation of meaning* with both the expert and with fellow students.

There are additional reasons for emphasizing collaboration in our environment. Collaboration is an integral part of most work environments. In some instances, it is a group with divided responsibilities for a single task and the collaboration permits sharing of information. In other cases, collaborators hold different positions or roles and have different priorities. While there is a common goal, the individual responsibilities lead to different interpretations of those goals. Thus the collaboration is one of negotiating meaning and strategies. Finally, there is *collaboration in the form of consultation*. Individuals with different perspectives and access to different information are called upon to provide advice and assistance. While we have been referencing the world of work, these same kinds of collaboration occur in virtually all aspects of our experience — except school.

In contrast to this rich world of collaboration, schooling traditionally discourages collaboration. Students are expected to work individually. Indeed, collaboration is frequently synonymous with cheating. If we are to aid students in adapting to the work environment, then it is simply essential that they develop the collaborative skills required in that work environment. Indeed, as the discussion in the previous paragraph suggests, collaboration is an important component of many authentic experiences in a knowledge domain. Thus, it is a component of the process of the use of knowledge that is to be learned.

Finally, the research literature on cooperative and collaborative learning has rather consistently indicated that it is an effective instructional strategy even when used in traditional approaches to instruction. Students tend to learn more and are more highly motivated in the collaborative environment. Thus, it is an approach we would choose for its effectiveness quite independently of its integral role in our pedagogy.

Learning environment

The first application of ELE — the grounding of the prototype development — will be a specific course in the School of Education. Since the School is engaged in professional training, the pedagogy discussed above, with its emphasis on transfer to the real world, is very consistent with the explicit instructional goals in the school (though we certainly hope all instruction has the goal of providing usable knowledge and skills.)

We see a hypermedia system as central to meeting the pedagogical goals just discussed. However, the system is not a large data base of information that the student can explore to see semantic relations. Indeed, the explanatory material is not a part of the hypermedia environment. Rather it is a database that provides experiences in the use of concepts and principles applied in the course. It is a database of instances or contexts in which the student can work. The student navigates to instances that will involve her in the use of the concepts under discussion in class. The materials in the database will include case studies, raw materials that provide the contexts in which the knowledge domain can be seen, microworlds, simulations, and, in general, materials that contribute to a work environment in which the student use the concepts discussed in class. A *visual environment* is essential to providing a rich context for the use of the concepts. Thus, we may use videodisks of movies that focus on instruction, e.g., "Stand Up and Be Counted". We may also have videos of interviews with students, teachers, and parents. Finally, we may have videos of actual classroom activity. Students will attempt to analyze these real world materials, applying the concepts learned in class. Since this is not idealized material, it is likely that there will be no "right" answer. Thus, the context will support rich student dialogue on the interpretation of the material. This may be contrasted to traditional approaches where brief instances, usually idealized, are presented for the student to judge.

In the first half of this paper we discussed four uses of hypermedia systems. We see the ELE system as heavily based on two of those uses: tools for operating on the knowledge base (or instances) and authoring. The tools will be used by the students to analyze the instances and perhaps to construct their own instructional sequence on a topic by assembling relevant material from the database. An authoring system to support the collaboration and the debate is essential to our goals. Non-idealized instances (real world occurrences) will clearly lead to alternative interpretations. Providing a forum to support the debate over those alternatives is key.

Acknowledgements

We would like to thank John Leggett for his assistance in moving us forward during this early stage.

References

[1] Conklin, J. (1987). Hypertext: A survey and introduction. *IEEE Computer, 20*(9). (pp. 17-41).

[2] Hammond, N. (1989). Hypermedia and learning: who guides whom? *ICCAL Proceedings '89,* (pp. 167-181).

[3] Yankelovich, N., Landow, G. & Cody, D. (1987). Creating hypermedia material for English students. *Sigcue - Outlook, 20,* (pp. 1-11).

[4] Bush, V. (1945). As we may think. *The Atlantic Monthly, 176*(1), (pp. 101-108).

[5] Nelson, T. H., (1981). *Literary Machines.* Swathmore, PA: Nelson.

[6] Yankelovich, N. &Meyrowitz, N. (1985). Reading and writing the electronic book. *Computer, (10)*,15-30.

[7] Palmer, J., Duffy T., and Mehlenbacher, B. (In press). A System for Aiding Designers of Online Help. *Lotus:acm SIGCHI*.

[8] Beeman, W., Anderson, K., Bader, G., Larkin, J., McClard, A., McQuillan, P., and Shields, M. (1987). Hypertext and pluralism: From lineal to nonlineal thinking. *Hypertext'87 Papers*, (pp. 1-20).

[9] Beeman, W., Anderson, K., Bader, G., Larkin, J., McClard, A., McQuillan, P., and Shields, M. (1988). *Intermedia: A case study of innovation in higher education*. (A final report to the Annenberg/CPB project). Providence, RI: Brown University, IRIS.

[10] Yankelovich, N., Landow, G., and Heywood, P. (1987). Designing hypermedia Ideabases-The Intermedia Experience. (IRIS Technical Report 87-4). Providence, RI: Brown University, IRIS.

[11] Brown, J. S., Collins, A., &Duguid, P. (1989). Situated cognition and the culture of learning. *Educational Researcher 18* (1), 32-42.

[12] Jones, B. F., Pierce, J., &Hunter, B. (1988). Teaching students to construct graphic representations. *Educational Leadership,* (pp. 20-25).

[13] McQuillan, P. (1987). *Computers and pedagogy: The invisible presence*, Technical Report, Brown University, IRIS, Providence, RI.

[14] Franklin, C. (1988). The hypermedia library. *Database, 11*(3), (pp. 43-48).

[15] Crane, G., & Mylonas, E. (1988). The Perseus project: An interactive curriculum on classical Greek civilization. *Educational Technology 28*(11), (pp. 25-32).

[16] Collins, A., Brown, J. S., &Newman, S. E. (1988). Cognitive apprenticeship: Teaching the craft of reading, writing, and mathematics. In L B. Resnick (Ed.), *Cognition and instruction: Issues and agendas*. Hillsdale, NJ: Erlbaum.

[17] Akscyn, R. M., McCracken, D.L., and Yoder, E.A. (1988). KMS: A distributed hypermedia system for managing knowledge in organizations. *Communications of the ACM, 31*, (pp. 820-835).

[18]. Walker, J., H., (1989). Authoring tools for complex document sets. In E. Barrett (Ed.), *The society of text*. MIT Press.

[19] Egan, D. E., Remde, J. R., Landauer, T. K., Lochbaum, C. C., & Gomez, L. M. (1989). Behavioral Evaluation and analysis of a hypertext browser. *CHI' 89 Proceedings,* (pp. 205-210).

[20] Wittgenstein, L. (1953) *Philosophical investigations*. New York, NY: Macmillan.

[21] Shoemaker, H. (1967). The functional context method of instruction. HumRRO Professional Paper No. 35-67, Alexandria, VA: Human Resources Research Organization.

[22] Sticht, T. G. (1975). *Reading for working: A functional literacy anthology*. Alexandria VA: Human Resources Research Organization.

[23] Bransford, J. D., Sherwood, R .D., Hasselbring, T. S., Kinzer, C. K., and Williams, S. M. (in press). Anchored instruction: Why we need it and how technology can help. To appear in a volume edited by D. Nix & R. Spiro. Hillsdale, NJ: Erlbaum.

[24] Simon, H. A. (1980). Problem solving and education. In D. T. Tuma & R. Reif (Eds.), *Problem solving and education: Issues in teaching and research*. Hillsdale, NJ: Erlbaum.

[25] Spiro, R. J., Poulson, R. L., Feltovich, P. J., & Anderson, D. K. (1988). Cognitive flexilbility theory: Advanced knowledge acquisition in ill-structured domains. In *Proceedings of the Tenth Annual Conference of the Cognitive Science Society*, 375-383. Hillsdale, NJ: Lawrence Erlbaum.

[26] Sticht, T. G. and Hickey, D. T. (1988). Functional context theory, literacy, and electronics training. In R. Dillon & J. Pellegrino (Eds.), *Instruction: Theoretical and Applied Perspectives*. NY: Praeger Publishers.

[27] Palincsar, A. S., and Brown, A. L. (1984). Reciprocal teaching of comprehension fostering and comprehension monitoring activities. *Cognition and Instruction, 1*(2), (pp. 117-175).

[28] Schoenfeld, A. H. (1985). *Mathematical problem solving.* New York: Academic Press.

[29] Scardamalia, M., and Bereiter, C. (1985). Fostering the development of self-regulation in children's knowledge processing. In S. F. Chipman, J. W. Segal, & R. Glaser (Eds.), *Thinking and learning skills: Research and open questions.* Hillsdale, NJ: Erlbaum.

Chapter 13
Learning About Learning From Hypertext

Terry Mayes, Mike Kibby and Tony Anderson
Scottish HCI Centre
University of Strathclyde, UK

Keywords

Hypertext; interactive learning;learning support environments;
Information science; Query; cognitive overhead; navigation;
disorientation; protocol analysis; constructive interaction

Contents

Introduction

Hypertext is a term now applied so widely that it is no longer
clear that it means anything other than the ability to retrieve
information rapidly and relevantly by direct selection. In fact,
the differences between hypertext systems for, say, information management, specialist writing environments, design or
learning systems, so outweigh their similarities that it no

longer seems sensible to talk about hypertext as though it is a generic technology with features, such as browsers, that are intrinsically desirable. Instead, it is more important to consider hypertext within the context of specific applications, each with its own task demands. In this paper we attempt first to illustrate this specificity by considering some of the features of hypertext from the point of view of learning requirements. Secondly, we ask how we can actually discover what the optimal features of a hypertext learning system might be.

Hypertext learning systems

We start with the assumption that, of course, learning will occur from the use of any hypertext (or, for that matter, any information presentation system), without any tools or other features being designed explicitly to support and facilitate learning *per se*. Indeed, an issue that should lie at the heart of understanding interactive learning systems is the question of how deliberate, explicit learning differs from implicit, incidental learning [1]. Explicit learning involves the conscious evaluation of hypotheses and the application of rules. Implicit learning is more mysterious: it seems almost like a process of osmosis and becomes increasingly important as tasks or material to be mastered becomes more complex. Much of the learning that occurs with computer systems seems implicit. It would not be disputed that we now know a lot about making systems easy to learn how to use [2]. What is at issue here is whether we know how to design systems that are easy to *learn from*, in particular, whether we can design systems for the *explicit* learning of curriculum materials in education, or of more skill-based knowledge in training.

AR parallel 12.7
DJ explanation 20.11-14

To make clear when we are referring to systems designed in the CAL or CBT tradition, to 'deliver' learning to a target group in the field of education and training, we will call their users "learners". Mere "users" on the other hand, will refer to people who acquire knowledge or skills as a byproduct of using a computer for the achievement of some other task, such as retrieving information for a particular goal.

Assumptions about learning

DJ contrast 10.3

At first sight, there seems something almost contradictory about the idea of a hypertext system posing as CAL. After all, the essence of hypertext is that users are entirely free to follow links wherever they please. The basic assumption upon which most of the CAL tradition has been based is that the principles of programmed instruction or generative CAL provide an automation of the most essential step of giving the learner, at an appropriate moment, the next piece of information to learn or the next problem to try. Underlying the way in which learning materials are sequenced will be a principled pedagogical strategy. Hypertext-based instruction, on the other hand, seems to offer the learner almost complete control over learning activities, particularly over the choice of a route through the learning material, and thereby seems to relinquish fundamental responsibility for the learning process. There is even more of a contrast with intelligent tutoring methods [3]. Most of the difficulties of that enterprise, such as the problem of developing a suitable representation both for the domain knowledge and for the student model, to say nothing of the problem of developing pedagogical techniques to ensure that the individual learner is provided with the right material at the right time, are simply bypassed by handing responsibility for almost all decision making to the learner. Thus, CAL systems based on hypertext are rightly called *learning systems*, rather than *teaching systems*. Nevertheless, they do embody a theory of, or at least an approach to, instruction. They provide an environment in which *exploratory or discovery learning* may flourish. By requiring learners to move towards nonlineal thinking, they may also stimulate processes of integration and contextualization in a way not achievable by linear presentation techniques [4]

JL example 13.8, 21.3, 24.5, 7.5, corroboration 6.13, contrast 19.4
PD explanation 8.5
DJ corroboration 8.5
AR corroboration 19.4

AR contrast 19.4

Nevertheless, what distinguishes the appearance of a hypertext learning system from that of any other structured browsing and retrieval system is that the former usually provides a range of tools which considerably extend the basic navigation facilities. The most extensive attempt to develop hypertext in this direction is Brown University's *Intermedia* project [4,5]. In fact, even here, when learners simply follow the links offered in a passive way there is little reason to suppose that learning is any more effective than that from an old-fashioned branching programme in the programmed instruction tradition. Certainly, *Intermedia* seems to have demonstrated that a rich and extensive use of hypertext, with a carefully designed interface for the author as well as for the learner, is capable of providing a successful environment for various kinds of learning activities. A reasonable interpretation of the evaluations, however, might be that such a system promotes effective learning only in so far as the users are engaged in actively making their own connections and integrations at the conceptual level. One might point out that, thirty years ago, the authors of programmed texts probably benefited in a similar way from engaging their subject matter at the level of detailed structure. There is no evidence here that simply navigating around the fixed links in *Intermedia* provides effective learning.

Perhaps the system that best exemplifies this class of CAL based on the provision of specific guidance tools built on top of a hypertext network is *HitchHikers' Guide* [6,7]. The principle espoused here is that of extending and tailoring basic hypertext facilities, not only with the fairly standard aids to access, such as browsers, but also with tools that help the user to explore the material conceptually, such as guided tours, indexes, and quizzes. Hammond & Allinson [8] have referred to such a system as a Learning Support Environment (LSE). The success of this system may also be due in no small measure to the care that has gone into the design of the interface. The learner is offered the consistent metaphor of a travel holiday to guide the exploration of the underlying instructional material.

Interactive learning systems with hypertext features

A number of other LSE systems, while not being traditional hypertext, have features closely enough related to the systems described above to demand attention. What is actually necessary? Is a network of nodes and fixed links a basic requirement for an effective LSE?

Mayes *et al* [9] have described the influences that led to the development of *StrathTutor*. This system was primarily conceived as a small-scale exemplar of one kind of approach to the problem of specifying links in large and potentially extensible hypertext networks. In *StrathTutor* links are computed on the basis of attribute coding, from a set of up to 60 attributes predefined by the author for the particular domain. Each designated 'hotspot' of text and/or graphics is so coded. The system computes the 'relatedness' of all remaining unseen frames to the current frame ('frame' is arbitrarily set at the size of a single screen) or hotspot. Each frame can be represented as a profile of attributes, summed across all hotspots in that frame.

JL parallel 17.7, 21.9, 22.14, 24.9

StrathTutor demonstrates that fixed links between objects such as individual graphics or fragments of text are not necessary to generate a hypertext system, if by hypertext we mean the provision of such links at run time. Moreover, we contend

that removing explicit links provides a more flexible environment. During the development of our software, it became
clear that as further ideas evolved for tools to support exploration by the learner, so they could be incorporated without
drastic recoding, merely by reference to the knowledge base.
We do not suggest that all fixed links should be avoided. On
the contrary, *StrathTutor* has such links as part of its overall
learning support environment. However, much useful structure will be implicit, and many links may be generated using
this approach that will be unanticipated by the author of a
conventional hypertext.

A further potential advantage of this kind of knowledge
separation is that it becomes possible to have *dynamic hypertext*. In our system each frame is separate, united with its
underlying knowledge but independent of all other frames
until a link is formed at run time. A frame may be deleted and
the system will still operate without the need to remove links
now undefined. Similarly, a frame together with its attributes
may be added and the system automatically takes it into
account when links are generated.

 The learner can choose to navigate by accepting the 'related'
frames offered by the system, or can proceed to access named
frames. Details of the way in which *StrathTutor* achieves this
computation are given in [10]. *StrathTutor* is a fairly uncom-
promising learning-by-browsing system but the browsing is
encouraged to take place in *conceptual space* , rather than in
the spatially organized network of conventional hypertext,
with fixed links. There is, however, a traditional hypertext
feature whereby some hotspots are explicitly linked to windows presenting explanatory material. Nevertheless, a much
more important feature of this system is the opportunity it
offers learners to try out hypotheses about the meaning of
attributes and the relationships between them. A learner can
'interrogate' the system by designating a combination of
attributes that may be beginning to seem meaningful and the
system will respond by giving the learner a 'guided tour' of
all frames that are coded with that particular subset of attributes. This may be regarded as more closely related to information science techniques for query-based access than to
hypertext, but the combination of the two seems to offer
powerful systems for learning [11].

The distinction between a browsing environment and an
information retrieval system is made more easily in terms of
the user's goals than of the functionality of the system. Frisse

[12] has discussed how the way in which a hypertext system is conceptualized affects its design. If a hypertext node is seen as relatively autonomous then retrieving its information will involve the 'small-document' approach. If on the other hand the semantic links between nodes are emphasized then retrieving information will be seen as similar to traversing a directed graph. The small-document approach emphasizes pattern matching; the graph-traversal approach emphasizes browsing. When the number of nodes is small and the semantics of links is understood then the limited information retrieval capabilities of conventional hypertext systems (a combination of simple pattern matching and graphical browsing) is quite effective. For the kind of large-scale systems now being developed, however, these capabilities are simply inadequate.

Remde, Gomez & Landauer [13] have implemented a range of sophisticated facilities for structuring, viewing and searching texts which, unlike conventional keyword or synonym searching, attempt to make use of the full statistical structure of a text. The facilities are integrated in a system, *SuperBook ,* which shares many of the goals of hypertext presentation systems, although it does not support an explicit static hypertext network. Indeed, the statistical search method used in SuperBook, 'latent semantic analysis' [14], has points in common with the algorithms used in *StrathTutor*. The "latent semantic indexing" approach takes advantage of implicit higher-order structure in the association of terms with text objects by using a technique called "singular-value decomposition". The application of such information science techniques to the 'vocabulary problem in HCI' [15] is an area that holds considerable potential in the development of hypertext.

Storrs [16] has proposed a scheme for a hypertext-based training system, built in HyperCard. The material to be learned is produced as a stack, for browsing. On a separate stack the author represents the underlying concepts, with one concept on each card and the relationships as labelled links between them. The author may tag each of the cards containing the course materials to show which of the concepts are covered by the material on that card. Storrs describes how such a simple system for linking different levels of knowledge could be used to present the material to the learner in several different pedagogical styles. Unconstrained browsing through the 'lower' stack would constitute the simplest level. More directed browsing could be achieved by using clustering algorithms on the concept tags to calculate which cards are most closely related. The concept stack could also be used to control the sequence of presentation entirely. This notion of two separate 'stacks' or databases, one of which contains the control rules for the other is similar to an idea currently being used to develop *StrathTutor*.

Do the problems with using hypertext constrain learning?

Disorientation

In his penetrating review, Conklin [17] identifies a number of problems in the use of hypertext. Some of these are simply problems with current implementations, such as a lack of interesting or powerful specialized 'views' of networks. Others are fundamental to hypertext and may, argues Conklin, ultimately limit its usefulness. The first of these is the *disorientation problem*. This is the problem of 'getting lost in hyperspace', of not being sure where you are in relation to other parts of the network, or of not being able to find other information that you know is somewhere in the system. This tendency is bound to increase as the size and complexity of the hypertext increases. There are two aspects to this. One, rooted in the nature of hypertext, is (simply) a navigational problem. The geography of the network may be too complex to grasp, even with a map. However, an important strand of current research into hypertext concerns the attempt to develop more powerful tools for the visualization of structure. As far as browsers are concerned, work on graphical approaches to database management and software engineering has developed systems to display data within large and complex databases using multiple views and different display representations [18]. There is also related work in the emerging area of program visualisation [19]. Most of this work has confined the display to two dimensions using multiple display windows, or separate screens, to cope with additional dimensions. However, significant advances in the understanding of molecular chemistry were made with the advent of computer graphic systems capable of displaying complex molecular structures in three dimensions, using colour to show grouping, etc. [20]. Using these techniques, networks can be displayed in a sophisticated way in two- or three-dimensional space so that a 'virtual spatial environment' is created. Nevertheless, if a hypertext network is on the scale of, say, the *Engineering Data Compendium* [21], then the sheer number of nodes and links create a problem of scale that make it almost impossible to maintain an acceptable virtuality with a spatial metaphor

RK contrast 3.12
PD contrast 8.8

unless some kind of filtering is also involved. But there is a more fundamental objection to the pursuit of visual metaphors for dealing with the disorientation problem. What these visualisation techniques do is give the user a better way of *locating* information in space: they give ways of accessing information, of knowing where it is. They don't in any sense help us navigate in *conceptual* space: they don't tell us *about* anything, only where it is. For learning systems a far more important aspect of disorientation is conceptual.

GL implication 3.12-13

Conklin [17] points out that 'information space' has no natural topology. It is true that there is a "high level/low level" view that can often be mapped onto a hierarchy but this is relevant for probably only a small minority of knowledge domains. Are there as many structures as there are domains? Or can all knowledge be organized along a few relatively straightforward dimensions? For the building of intelligent tutoring systems, where the system must in some sense 'know' about the subject matter to be taught, then it is crucial to have an answer. In the context of exploratory learning, however, we can make a virtue out of giving the learner no 'view' at all of overall structure. The learner's essential task is to *discover* , or even to *create,* the structure underlying the instructional material.

The StrathTutor approach to navigation

Under certain conditions (not all), disorientation in conceptual space is a necessary prerequisite for depth of learning. In discovery learning systems like *StrathTutor*, it is a design goal that learners decide where to go next in their exploration of the knowledge, not only guided by system information but also by serendipity. Since the point of discovery learning is that the learner is continually engaged in a process of trying to map the information being discovered on the system onto her own developing framework of understanding, then making 'wrong turns' is a *necessary* part of the process of learning.

We must be clear about how this differs from disorientation in a spatial network of links and nodes. There is a fundamental difference between network-based hypertext systems for direct navigation, such as *HitchHiker's Guide* , and an attribute based system, such as *StrathTutor*, relying mainly on search and query techniques. An advantage of the latter is the facility it gives for the learners to "navigate with concepts". *StrathTutor* turns normal hypertext on its head by requiring the learner to 'make sense' of the link between two nodes. The learner may click on a hotspot, meaning "tell me more about this" and the system will simply provide a new frame. The learner now has to solve a problem: what is the connection between the previous material and this? In fact *StrathTutor* provides a menu choice of *Why show this frame?* which will, when chosen, display a list of the attributes in common between the two frames, or the hotspot and the new frame. Often the links will remain obscure; only as the learner becomes immersed more deeply in the content and the nature of the relationships between nodes, by 'second guessing' the system, will any understanding of some links be possible at all.

In a system of this kind, it is important for the learner to be able to engage in a kind of dialogue with the system. This is done in two ways in *StrathTutor*: first, by allowing the learner to interrogate the system with combinations of attributes which are beginning to make sense. In this manner the learner is probing the system with hypothetical 'links' and asking the system to confirm the nodes, by presenting just those frames having that particular subset of attributes. The set of links and their nodes produced in this way can be regarded as a filtered view. A 'conceptual slice' is taken through the information space. Secondly, the *StrathTutor* 'quiz' invites the learner to play a kind of game, in which he or she tries to identify the areas across the two frames which have maximum overlap in attributes. Here the learner is pitting herself against the author who created the attribute tags on each hotspot. In each case the learner is expected to create for herself a view of the underlying conceptual space.

Navigating through space and navigating with concepts.
A fundamental issue for hypertext research is to discover effective methods of elision [17]. The user needs to be given a level of complexity that is compatible with the limits of his or her visual cognition, and to be given the ability to shift the view or the detail suppression while navigating through the network. It is easier to see how to do this for the visuo-spatial dimension than for the conceptual. It is, however, not necessarily the case that spatial representations are more suitable for telling the learner where something is rather than what it is. Much conceptual structure can undoubtedly be effectively represented by graphic display, and conceptual disorientation, as well as spatial disorientation, can also be corrected by having some form of map. Conversely, it is possible to imagine navigating in a hypertext network through the use of queries rather than with a browser. Apart from *content* search

13.9

PD corroboration 8.2

DJ parallel 6.1-18

there is also *structure* search which operates at the level of a hypertext network and looks for particular network patterns. Halasz [11] gives an example of a query based on both content and structure: "all sub-networks containing two cards connected by a 'supports' link where the target card contains the word 'hypertext'".

A query system approach gives an interesting contrast to the normal way of approaching the problem of gaining a particular view of the network. Instead of regarding each node as a unit of presented information, a screen-sized frame of text and graphics, the *attributes* in the implicit network of *StrathTutor* can be regarded as the nodes and the links can be regarded as the particular tagging of these attributes to individual frames. A particular combination of attributes can then be pursued through the knowledge base, giving what in *StrathTutor* is rather misleadingly called a 'guided tour'. The degree of initial disorientation that is generated by this approach, however, may be undesirable for some domains and for some learners. The point to make here, however, is that disorientation is not *a priori* an undesirable state for learning.

We believe that the most effective learning systems we are capable of designing today would have the advantages both of hypertext and of query-based exploratory environments. The particular balance of features is a question best settled empirically. There are unlikely to be general solutions that are optimal for all learners in all domains.

Cognitive task scheduling

The second of Conklin's inherent disadvantages of hypertext he refers to as *cognitive overhead* or the cognitive task scheduling problem. The requirement to keep track of links imposes an additional cognitive load which may mean that some information processing capacity which would otherwise be allocated to thinking about the material in question is diverted to the meta-level decision making task that is the essence of working with hypertext. This cognitive overhead applies even to the process of simply reading hypertext. The reader or learner is presented with a large number of choices about which links to traverse. There is no escaping this requirement for extra processing; it is one of the claimed advantages for hypertext systems that users are liberated from an imposed linearity of thought. At the heart of the idea of hypertext is the assumption that the user can take immediate advantage of associations, tentative thoughts or fleeting images in a way that 'flat' text will simply not allow. As Conklin has put it:

These problems are not new with hypertext, nor are they a spurious artifact of computer-based thinking. People who think for a living -writers, scientists, artists, designers, etc- must contend with the fact that the brain can create ideas faster than the hand can write them or the mouth can speak them. There is always a balance between refining the current idea, returning to a previous idea to refine it, and attending to any of the vague "proto-ideas" which are hovering at the edge of consciousness. Hypertext simply offers a sufficiently sophisticated "pencil" to begin to engage with the richness, variety, and interrelatedness of creative thought. This has advantages when this richness is needed and drawbacks when it is not.

For learning systems, the question is whether the cognitive overhead of using hypertext tools is a significant factor. At present we have no evidence about this. As with most systems, the process of coming to grips with the system itself, its initial *usability,* is likely to be critical for new or intermittent users. So, the cognitive overhead of actually learning to use a hypertext system will certainly be important. But this is not the issue Conklin has raised. The issue is whether the inherent choice offered to the learner by such a system, the degree of *learner control*, can actually detract from the cognitive resources devoted to the task of understanding and remembering the material? It seems at least arguable that in most learning situations the choice offered to a learner for considering what to do next will enrich the process of learning rather than detract from it. Is it not the continuing process of looking for alternatives, for new viewpoints and new connections, that is the essence of gaining understanding? Certainly the fleeting thought or idea must be nurtured, and a learner continually 'fighting' a system will not be attending fully to the proto-ideas that will so easily be lost. But in learning it is perhaps more important that such proto-ideas are continually being generated than that each one should be protected from interference. At any rate the issue of which features of a LSE are necessary or desirable will only be pinned down by carrying out an more fine-grained analysis of learning with these systems than has so far been attempted.

Learning from watching people learning from hypertext

How can we proceed from simply speculating about how effectively hypertext can support the needs of learners and start to build a theory? In a real sense our task of trying to understand these issues mirrors the task of a learner in a hypertext system. Just as the learner will use a variety of strategies, both explicit and implicit, in order to build a framework of understanding, so should we. We believe our own efforts to evaluate *StrathTutor* are instructive in this context, and we will illustrate some of the issues involved using some examples from our own research.

Empirical comparisons

Our first approach was to carry out a conventional test of the effectiveness of this kind of learning by matching two groups of school pupils on their prior knowledge and instructing one group with a conventional illustrated lecture and the other with a session on *StrathTutor* using exactly the same set of materials. Post-test performance was compared across the two groups. The results revealed that the group receiving conventional instruction had learned marginally more, although the difference was not significant. This was not at all the result we wanted to see, so we rejected this approach to evaluation altogether! With hindsight, of course, it is easy to see that such pre/post test comparisons are impossible to interpret with any confidence. Too many potentially important variables are simply uncontrolled. In this case some of the students took much of the learning time exploring the novel features of the system, a strategy which would have paid off had the learning session been extended. Even worse, from the point of view of weighing the potential of *StrathTutor* against that of 'conventional' instruction, the 'lecturer' delivering the latter was unusually effective in revealing the underlying structure of the material. In addition, we came to realize that most of the interest for the kind of cognitive analysis we were aiming at was obscured by looking solely at overall performance.

We therefore turned to a much more detailed analysis of performance on the system, by concentrating on the trace files. Part of the *StrathTutor* system is a trace facility, called *ST Viewer* , which records not only a complete trace of each interaction but also a statistical summary, with such measures as *number-of-frames-seen*, *mean-time-per-frame*, *total-attrib-*

DJ methodology 20.14

utes-seen, total-time-on-tutorial ,%use-of-quiz, gold-points
(first attempt) and silver-points (second attempt), pre-test-
score, post-test/pre-test-difference and several other measures.
The subjects for this experiment were two groups of 'novices',
one of which had prior experience with the Macintosh interface and one which had not. The to-be-learned material was
on the topic of glaciation, using extensive graphics of land-
scapes and glacier cross-sections. StrathTutor records eleven
types of interaction with the frame or menus for each frame
visited. This information was aggregated together with
descriptors of gender, group, and test results to provide 21
variables (n=17) describing each subject and their interaction
with the tutorial. High post-test/pre-test differences or high
scoring of 'game points' were taken as being indicative of
successful interaction with the discovery learning environment, and significant associations were sought between these
metrics and various aspects of usage of the interface. A clear
association between certain sets of variables was apparent. A
large set included number-of-frames-seen, mean-time-per-
frame, total-attributes-seen, and total-time-on-tutorial (some
subjects halted voluntarily before others). When these more
obvious factors were taken out several significant correlations
were still present. What could be deduced from these? Actually, disappointingly little. We did conclude that those subjects who learned most were those who most often successfully used the quiz option. Did this mean that students who
learned most did so because they were able to make most
intelligent and appropriate use of the StrathTutor facilities for
exploration? Unfortunately, we can't draw that conclusion
since other aspects of what one might assume was a flexible
use of StrathTutor tools, such as search by title, showed no
particular relationship with amount learned. Similarly, it is
just as plausible that subjects who had already gained a good
understanding of the material would choose more often to take
the quiz option. Thus, success with the quiz would simply
reflect learning rather than cause it. Even if such conclusions
were possible from these data we still have the difficulty of
knowing what was actually being evaluated. Was the extent
of the students' increased understanding of the tutorial domain
a measure of the effectiveness of the learning environment, or
of the effectiveness of the tutorial material?

Verbal protocols

We have turned more recently to methods of protocol analysis,
involving a focus on qualitative aspects of the interaction.
One method involves the use of retrospective protocol genera-

tion by subjects who have recently used the system. Individual subjects are shown the sequence of frames they went through frame-by-frame using *STviewer*, and are asked to explain and elaborate on their moment-to-moment choices. This method has proved to be slow and inefficient at generating relevant data because our subjects have had difficulty in recalling their thoughts approximately one hour after the session. In fact, the problems with such verbal protocols are now well-known [22, 23]. The basic objection is that forcing the subject to talk out loud in a situation that would normally be silent is likely to cause subtle, but possibly serious, changes to the way in which the task is performed. This is particularly a problem with observations of learning, when much of the process may be implicit. Asking subjects to report on their awareness of implicit learning is a contradiction in terms. As Reber & Lewis [24] point out: "... the very introspective act transmutes the cognitive process and we lose the implicit element, the very thing we wish to study." Since the process of implicit learning will be largely unavailable to conscious inspection no method which involves the elicitation of verbal reports from the learners is likely to furnish new insights about this kind of learning. However, since we have no way of knowing in advance about the balance between implicit and explicit processes in a particular learning session it is prudent to try to capture data which will reveal something about the nature of both. Only the most painstaking observations of the learning events are likely to reveal the nature of implicit learning. Having *one learner talking to another*, however, when they are performing the task jointly, may well be a fruitful technique for circumventing most of the problems associated with getting subjects to talk about their explicit stategies.

Constructive interactions

The method we have adopted, therefore, is to have pairs of subjects use the system together, making collaborative decisions concerning how to proceed through the hypertext. The resulting dialogue is transcribed and annotated as carefully as possible with information about the interaction itself, and the resulting protocol is subjected to microanalysis. This general method of using pairs of subjects to work together on a problem and analysing the resulting dialogue to infer subjects' hypotheses and reasoning as they proceed through the task has been called *constructive interaction* by Miyake [25], and it has been used in several studies. For example, Miyake examined subjects' understanding of the mechanisms of sewing machine operation using this method, and O'Malley, Draper and Riley [26] have used it to study human-computer interaction. O'Malley [27] points out several advantages of using constructive interaction as a method for eliciting protocols. These include the fact that the dialogue is intrinsic to the task rather than extraneous to it, as is the case with think-aloud protocols. Furthermore, having two individuals work together making decisions jointly about strategies forces them to articulate and justify their hypotheses or proposals to one another. This in turn results in the subjects articulating both what they think and why they think it, making a usually invisible process visible.

There is evidence that constructive interaction can itself prove efficacious in promoting learning in a variety of learning situations as compared with individual performance. For example, research in developmental psychology by Doise and his colleagues has shown that group performance of children on Piagetian conservation and spatial transformation tasks is superior to the performance of any of the individuals working alone [28]. In the work reported here, however, constructive interaction has so far been used merely as a method for eliciting natural protocols in an attempt to reveal some insight into the strengths and weaknesses of learning from a hypertext system.

Constructive Interaction using StrathTutor. We have recorded a number of interactions in which same-sex pairs of subjects used *StrathTutor* to learn about glaciation together. All sessions have been a minimum of twenty minutes long, and have been videotaped with the students sitting one at each of two adjacent sides of a square table with the computer placed between them. The video camera has been located in such a way that the sides of both students' faces and the computer screen are simultaneously visible on the recording; this greatly aids transcription.

Even without considering what the dialogues can reveal, we have seen that the use of the system is very inefficient. Of eight possible methods of navigation, three methods together accounted for nearly sixty-five percent of all selections made. These three were: selecting the *next frame* offered in the frame menu (nineteen percent of the total), selecting the *previous frame* from the same menu (eleven percent), selecting through the hotspot mechanism (thirty-five percent). Overall, therefore, selecting the next frame offered by the system (whether from the frame menu or via a hotspot) accounted for some fifty-four percent of all selections made. Selections of frames on the basis of their titles or on the basis of the attributes they possessed accounted for a small minority of selections overall (nine percent); indeed, these two strategies were employed by only one dyad.

The protocols of dialogue generated while the subjects used *StrathTutor* have first been examined to attempt to gain some insight into why the options available in the system were being seriously underused. The dialogues clarify the issue. There is considerable support here for the idea that 'cognitive overhead' is indeed just as critical a variable in learning systems as it is in the kind of hypertext uses discussed by Conklin [17]. With few exceptions our subjects adopted the 'next frame' options by default. The dialogues reveal that the subjects are by no means adopting a passive strategy in their exploration of conceptual space by doing this. It also confirms the view expressed above that active exploration of the hyperspace is by no means the same thing as active exploration at the conceptual level. In several cases, it seems clear that the subjects are quite absorbed in the task of learning the material presented in the tutorial, and as a result fail to adequately learn or use the full range of exploration options available. This was illustrated by one dyad in particular, who spent the greatest average amount of time on each frame, engaging in detailed discussions concerning the conceptual content of the frames they viewed (and incidentally showed one of the greatest average pre- to post-test gains in score on a multiple choice test on glaciation). This dyad rarely used the *frame* menu at all; most transitions between frames occurred as a consequence of clicking on hotspots. One gets the impression of two eager learners who are keen to follow up what they are reading but who lose track of how this is best achieved within the system. Lengthy discussions of the material to be learned embed minimal discussion on how navigation should proceed. Consider the following extract, part of a lengthy exchange on how it is that ice flow can be rotational:

P.   ...I mean rotational: How can it be rotational ice flow?

R.   Does it -: no. I was going to say does it depend on the kind of surface structure it's meeting, but I don't think so. I wondered about that as well, and I thought it sounds a bit strange. I've never thought of ice: flow as rotating. Let's get the next frame.
(R clicks infobox option; new frame shown).

> P.   Right, we've had that one, haven't we?

Two utterances later, the following comment occurs:

> R.   Right, will we go to utilities? What were utilities again?

And again, later in the dialogue:

> R.   What are utilities, I can't remember what utilities are.

A final interesting exchange occurs at the end of a lengthy discussion of the contents of an infobox on glacial plucking, a concept which the subjects had found difficult to distinguish from that of glacial erosion:

> P.   Because it's frozen: it'll: pluck the whole block out: and that's how you get this: right? Press next frame?
>
> R.   Yeah.
>
>   (Frame change occurs; new frame, glacial plucking, shown).
> P.   Oh, that's the one that we saw: that's how it causes that.

This dyad appear to be so absorbed with the task of learning that they simply forget how to navigate within the system. This exchange occurred well into the dialogue at the selection of the thirteenth frame.

A careful perusal of the dialogues leaves the strong impression that subjects either learn to navigate or they learn the instructional material but, at least during the initial stages of use of *StrathTutor* that we have so far studied, they cannot do both together. There is also evidence that learners will exhibit a tendency to 'regress' to an earlier stage in their use of the system as their attention becomes more focused on the learning domain. Nevertheless, one can observe an increasingly flexible use of the system paying dividends. One particular pair of subjects had, during the earlier stages of the session, mainly used two frame selection methods, namely, the *next* option from the *Frame* menu, and the *next* option in an infobox. Having accessed the 'alpine erosion' frame using the *next* option from the *Frame* menu, they used hotspot clicks to access infoboxes for further information, but twice called up entire frames by this method, and then decided that they wished to view the 'alpine erosion' frame again (although by this point they had forgotten its title). They used the *previous* option from the *Frame* menu, but found that it took them back to the last frame (which had been accessed by a mouse click on a hotspot) and that the 'alpine erosion' frame was, at this point, rather further back in the sequence than they had realised. They then obtained the *Frame* menu and the following exchange occurs:

> K.   Select by: what was it we were looking at? We were looking:
>
> M.   Frost shattering - no, it was after frost shattering. Glaciation:
>
> K.   Will we try select by title?
>
> (This option is taken).
>
> M.   Ehm: it was alpine erosion, wasn't it?
>
> K.   (Clicks repeatedly on the title among the list, not on the 'open' option).
>   Oh: sorry: Open: (The frame is then displayed). It <u>was</u> that!
>
> M.   Right: (They both read the frame contents). Aretes:

In this extract, the subjects initially try to remember the relevant frame title but forget what it is. At this point subject K, who is at this point perusing the frame menu, suggests using the 'select by title' option, since this option's list of titles is likely to lead to recognition. On re-reading the frame, they then decide to seek further information on another item within the frame, namely aretes. The segment of dialogue of which the above extract is a part clearly indicates the subjects' increasing flexibility of use of the system: trying one selection strategy to obtain what they want, failing, and then opting to try a completely different strategy which they had never used before, which succeeds. This contrasts strongly with their previous extensive (indeed almost exclusive) use of 'next' options.

Some conclusions and advice for designers

Let us attempt a summary of our main points:

1. <u>There is little available evidence about the benefits of hypertext learning systems.</u>
Despite the widespread assumption that hypertext-based learning systems provide an effective alternative to programmed instruction or intelligent tutoring systems, there is actually little evidence to support this. Even *Intermedia*

RK parallel 12.14

seems to have been successful mainly when learners were
acting as authors.

2. Information science techniques should be combined with
those of hypertext.
We discussed various possibilities for adding the power of
search and query techniques to hypertext. This is our main
design recommendation.

3. Disorientation can be a good thing for learning.
We then examined the two main problems with the use of
hypertext, identified as *disorientation* and *cognitive overhead*,
from the point of view of designing effective learning systems. While conventional aids to navigation in hypertext are
necessary for learners to find their way around hyperspace, we
concluded that they were of little value in the more fundamental navigation for learning, that of *conceptual* space. However, getting lost in the latter sense may not be a disadvantage
at all. In exploratory learning the important thing may not be
whether a map can be found but whether one can be created
by the learner.

4. The cognitive overhead of providing choice will have to be
tolerated, but perhaps not in the earliest stages of learning to
use the system.
We also wondered about cognitive overhead. Is it not more
important that learners should be challenged by the availability of a powerful set of tools, rather than protecting them from
the interference inevitably caused by choice? But how important is the initial usability of the system? A design principle to
consider is to build systems that provide full functionality
only after the user has mastered the basic operations.

5. Evaluate LSE's by listening to learners talking to each
other.
Having concluded that such questions can only properly be
resolved by empirical work, we then offered a brief account of
our attempts to evaluate *StrathTutor* . The main lesson drawn
so far is that the dialogues produced by the constructive
interaction methodology represent a rich data set for evaluation.

6. Learners are users too.
Several aspects of the use of *StrathTutor* have been revealed
by the requirement for learners to externalize their learning
processes. The dialogues clearly reveal that the effective use

13.19

DJ comment How true:
Knowledge is construction!

245

of the system requires skill. It is an old story in human computer interactions: greater functionality being traded off for initial usability. Only when sufficient overlearning of the navigational options in *StrathTutor* has resulted in their selection involving automatic, rather than controlled, processing [29] can we expect to find learners using the system efficiently when all available cognitive resources are focused on the learning of the instructional material.

Final thoughts

While it may be regarded as a mark of successful design that attentional resources should be focused on the application and not on the interface, the *StrathTutor* example reveals that some attention must be devoted to choosing the appropriate tool at a particular moment in the learning process. If the system becomes cognitively invisible [30] before the learners have become skillful in their use of the full functionality of the system, then much of its interactive power of providing several alternative ways of 'interrogating' a knowledge domain is simply not used. Many learners will proceed by default and will choose to use *StrathTutor* in its least interesting way, as a provider of *next* frames. This is not because learners are inherently idle or unadventurous but rather because the initial usability of the system allows learners to allocate most of their cognitive resources to grappling with the to-be-learned material, and the features of the system that would actually make this easier are simply neglected. Our primary goal is for learners effortlessly to use the right option for exploring the learning domain at precisely the moment when it becomes appropriate. It is not possible to design such a system in advance. The HCI features must, of course, evolve through an iterative cycle of design and evaluation. What has never been very clear with interactive learning systems is how to proceed with the evaluation part of this cycle.

Evaluations of the pre-test, post-test variety will only provide evidence about the quality of the working system as a whole, or at least about features of the design that have been systematically varied. Another approach is that exemplified by our analysis of information from each trace file in an attempt to uncover distinctive patterns of use that we then correlated with individual performance. In contrast with the constructive interaction methodology, however, this seemed to reveal little. Why were we so impressed with the dialogues of constructive interaction?

The conventional approach to experimentation is to pursue data-reduction methods. The argument is that we are swamped with the complexity of real-world tasks and in order to see anything at all we look for simple relationships between variables. The problem is that we don't know in advance what aspects to measure and what to discard. The constructive interaction methodology is a way of making visible as much of the underlying cognition as possible. By recording the interaction on video we allow a number of 'experiments' to be conducted as passes through the dialogue. These can proceed for as many times as the evaluators have hypotheses. As little as possible of the complexity is discarded, although it may still be obscure and classification techniques must be developed for the dialogue analysis. Perhaps the main advantage is that the users tell each other what is going on, as an intrinsic feature of the task. By listening to what they say, we learn too.

References

[1] Berry, D.C. & Broadbent, D.E. (1988) Interactive tasks and the implicit-explicit distinction. *British Journal of Psychology, 79,* 251-272.

[2] Norman, D.A. & Draper, S.W.(Eds.), (1986) *User Centered System Design: New perspectives on Human-Computer Interaction.* Hillsdale, New Jersey: Lawrence Erlbaum

[3] Wenger, E. (1987) *Artificial Intelligence and Tutoring Systems: Computational and cognitive approaches to the communication of knowledge.* Los Altos, Calif.: Morgan Kaufmann.

[4] Beeman W. O., Anderson K. T., Bader G., Larking J., McClard A. P., McQuillan P., and Shields M.(1987) Hypertext and pluralism: from lineal to non-lineal thinking. In J. B. Smith, F. Halasz, N. Yankelovich, M. Schwartz, and F. Weiss (Eds.), *Hypertext '87* . Chapel Hill: University of North Carolina, (pp. 67-81).

[5] Meyrowitz,N. (1986). Intermedia: the architecture and construction of an object-oriented hypertext/hypermedia system and applications framework. *OOPSLA '86 Proceedings*: Portland, Oregon.

[6] Hammond N.V. and Allinson L..J. (1988c). Development and evaluation of a CAL system for non-formal domains: the hitch-hiker's guide to cognition. *Computers and Education, 12*, 215-220.

[7] Allinson,L.J. and Hammond,N.V. (1989). A learning support environment: The hitch-hiker's guide. In R. McAleese (Ed.), *Hypertext: theory into practice*. Ablex: Norwood, NJ.

[8] Hammond,N.V. & Allinson,L.J. (1988b). Travels around a learning support environment: Rambling, orienteering or touring? In E. Soloway , D. Frye, and S.B. Sheppard (Eds.), *CHI' 88 Conference Proceedings: Human Factors in Computing Systems*. ACM: Washington DC, (pp. 269-273).

[9] Mayes J.T., Kibby M.R., and Watson H. (1988a) StrathTutor: the development and evaluation of a learning-by-browsing system on the Macintosh. *Computers and Education, 12*, 221-229.

[10] Kibby M.R. and Mayes J.T. (1989). Towards intelligent hypertext. In R. McAleese (Ed.), *Hypertext: from theory to practice*. Norwood, New Jersey: Ablex.

[11] Halasz, F. (1987). Reflections in NoteCards: seven issues for the next generation of hypermedia systems. In J. B. Smith, F. Halasz, N. Yankelovich, M. Schwartz, and F. Weiss (Eds.). *Hypertext '87* . Chapel Hill: University of North Carolina, (pp. 345-365).

[12] Frisse M.E. (1987). Searching for information in a hypertext medical handbook. In J. B. Smith, F. Halasz, N. Yankelovich, M. Schwartz, and F. Weiss (Eds.), *Hypertext '87* . Chapel Hill: University of North Carolina, (pp. 345-365).

[13] Remde,J.R., Gomez,L.M. & Landauer,T.K. (1987). SuperBook: An automatic tool for information exploration - hypertext? In J. B. Smith, F. Halasz, N. Yankelovich, M. Schwartz, and F. Weiss (Eds.), *Hypertext '87* . Chapel Hill: University of North Carolina, (pp. 175-188).

[14] Deerwester,S., Dumais,S.T., Furnas,G.W., Landauer,T.K. & Harshman,R. (1989). Indexing by latent semantic analysis. Journal of American Society for Information Science, in press.

[15] Furnas, G.W., Landaur T.K., Gomez L.M., and Dumais,S.T. (1987). The vocabulary problem in human-system communication. *Communications of the ACM*, 1987, *30*(11), (pp. 964-971).

[16] Storrs, G. (1988). An intelligent hypertext-based training system. In P.Duffin (Ed.), *KBS in Government: Proceedings of the Second European Conference*. Blenheim, London.

[17] Conklin J. (1987). A Survey of Hypertext. *MCC Technical Report, No. STP-356-86, Rev.2.*

[18] Herot C. F., Carling R. T., Friedell, M. and Kramlich D. (1980). A prototype spatial data management system. *SIGGRAPH'80 Conference Proceedings* (pp. 63-70).

[19] Myers, B.A. (1986). Visual programming, programming by example, and program visualisation: a taxonomy. In *Human Factors in Computing Systems : Proceedings of CHI'86,* Boston.

[20] Reid P. (1987). *Dynamic Interactive Display of Complex Data Structures.* Unpublished Report. Scottish HCI Centre, UK.

[21] Glushko, R.J., Weaver, M.D., Coonan, T.A., and Lincoln, J.E. (1988). "Hypertext Engineering": Practical methods for creating a compact disc encyclopedia. *ACM Conference on Document Processing Systems,* Santa Fe, New Mexico.

[22] Nisbett, R.E. and Wilson, T.D. (1977). Telling more than we can know: Verbal reports on mental processes. *Psychological Review, 84,* 231-259 .

[23] Ericsson, K.A. and Simon, H.A. (1984). *Protocol analysis: Verbal reports as data*. Cambridge, MA: MIT Press.

[24] Reber, A.S. and Lewis, S. (1977). Towards a theory of implicit learning: the analysis of the form and structure of a body of tacit knowledge. *Cognition, 5 ,* 333-361.

[25] Miyake, N.(1986). Constructive interaction and the iterative process of understanding. *Cognitive Science, 10, ,* 151-177.

[26] O'Malley C.E., Draper S.W. and Riley M.S. (1985). Constructive interaction: a method for studying human-computer interaction. In B. Shackel (Ed.), *Human-Computer Interaction*. North-Holland, Amsterdam.

[27] O'Malley C.E. (1987). Understanding explanation. Paper presented to the Ergonomics Unit, University College, London, May 1987.

[28] Doise W. and Mugny G. (1984). *The social development of the intellect*. Oxford, UK: Pergamon.

[29] Shiffrin, R.M. and Schneider, W. (1977). Controlled and automatic human information processing: II. Perceptual learning, automatic attending, and a general theory. *Psychological Review, 84,* 127-190.

[30] Mayes, J. T. , Draper, S., McGregor, A., and Oatley, K (1988b). Information flow in a user interface: the effect of experience and context on the recall of MacWrite screens. In D. M. Jones and R. Fisher, (Eds.), *People and computers IV* . Cambridg, UK: Cambridge University Press.

Chapter 14
Psychopedagogic Aspects
of Hypermedia Courseware

Armando J. Oliveira
University of Aveiro, Portugal
Duarte Costa Pereira
University of Porto, Portugal

Keywords

Audio-visual media language; cognitive model of the user; communication structure; didactic module; hypermedia grammar; intelligent help; logical code for visual communication; shape and location of working areas; structure of the screen image

Contents

Introduction

One of the most promising technological advances for education is represented by the text and image driven, non-linear techniques of information handling and searching of the hypermedia architectures. We will not be arguing in favor of the important role these techniques will play in CAL [1], because we think everybody agrees on that point. It also seems inappropriate to theoretically explain, using currently accepted learning theories, the reasons for the purported efficiency. Instead, based on an example that we are developing, we will suggest some research lines that will help to improve the pedagogical uses of hypertext. Nevertheless many questions arise about the efficient use of these techniques. The answers to these questions are vital, but we are not able to tackle all of them. We shall attempt to answer the following: What are the hypermedia characteristics that deserve to be studied in order to improve the efficiency of courseware? Theoretically there are three types of hypermedia: non-struc-

NATO ASI Series, Vol. F 67
Designing Hypermedia for Learning
Edited by D. H. Jonassen and H. Mandl
© Springer-Verlag Berlin Heidelberg 1990

tured, semantically structured, and hierarchically structured. In the case of educational programs, all these types occur together in every program, except perhaps non-structured hypermedia environments, which we very much doubt exists.

The problem of hypermedia is fundamentally one of communication, and as we all know, every communication theory possesses at least a minimal structure, consisting of receiver and transmitter. In our view the real issue is the adequacy of these two structures, for defining a language (which is a communication structure) for hypermedia. This is not easy. Therefore, our current research only contributes to our final objective of building a formal hypermedia grammar.We are analyzing, in terms of observation and experiment, the adequacy of hypermedia for reflecting the cognitive structure and behavior of the user. This leads to another question: <u>Is there (and what is it) a natural structure (or several) of the user or even of the author of hypermedia?</u> We admit that there is neither a universal learning behavior, nor that all individual behaviors are crucially different. We think from what we know from studies of learning[2] that there are a limited number of user models, covering the great majority of cases (would this be the same for authoring?). We seek to identify these in the authoring and user structures in hypermedia. Therefore the most important question for us is: <u>What branches of psychopedagogical knowledge should be thoroughly studied in order to provide goals for the optimization of the educational use of these new media?</u> In terms of authoring, the structure cannot be based only on knowledge (both content and pedagogical knowledge) but must also fufill two additional objectives:

 • To suit the natural way of use
 • To help the learning of hypermedia use.

Learning with hypermedia tools _____

The example that we will be presenting (on the Portuguese "Descobrimentos", whose 500th anniversary is currently being commemorated) is being implemented in HyperCard (and new similar programs) which not only possesses an object oriented programming language (HyperTalk) but is also, among all the software packages available, the best for satisfactorily implementing interactive situations[3].

HyperCard is best described as an authoring language whose aim is to allow the conception, handling and managing of information under the form of screen images. The interactivity that exists between the user and the system, is contained in the working space, ie. the screen image, through interactivity operators (typically buttons). The program enables the creation of data bases on information and services within which the users browse (or navigate), searching for information. HyperCard permits a navigation based on the successive production of screen images composed of text and graphics, occasionally accompanied by sound. It is a non-linear writing/reading system that follows the natural associative nature of human thought, abandoning the sequential restrictions of text and also its hierarchical signalling structure. It is important to stress that the computer, thanks to the immateriality of the objects it manipulates and visualizes, is an ideal support for that type of non-linear writing/reading processes that printed media support very badly. This non-linear access to information may influence the development of a pluralist cognitive style[4] that is a primary interest for the cognitive based research on hypertext products. This type of structure is also at the center of current investigations on video disc and CD-ROM, whose capacities, in order to be fully exploited, demand information searching strategies based on associative power and intuition.

14.3

DJ definition 1.4

Iconographic aspects of the screen image __

The interactivity and visualization are essential aspects of HyperCard.

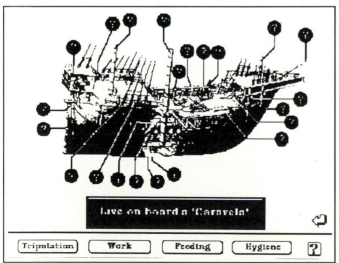

Figure.1: Examples of screen of the program "Descobrimentos Portugueses"

We have been studying the educational implications of the interrelations between graphics and iconography in representation and understanding activities[5]. This work is aimed at answering questions like: are there image decoding invariants? is the image built up of discrete elements? are there central and peripheric elements? is the information carried by the image redundant? is it accessory? is it complementary?

The problems associated with hypermedia use of the screen image as a working space raise new questions: What is the influence of the degree of realism of the image (from the symbol to the digitized photographic image) on the activity of the user (comprehension, interpretation, representation and action) ? What is the influence on the preceding cognitive operations of the item location within the screen image? What is the importance of animation within this context?

On top of these questions and the typical questions raised by the visual or textual presentation of an object or situation in CAL, HyperCard raises new questions about to the possibility of using sound as pedagogical support for the visual content, as well as essential support for interactivity. A research program to develop a syntax of an audio-visual language adapted to HyperCard is necessary.

GL corroboration 3.12-13

As we have already stated, the screen image supports the textual-propositional or visual-analogic information, with or without movement and accompanied or not by sound or voice effects. This screen image is simultaneously a representation space (when the visual form is realistic) and a simulation space (when the visual form is imaginary). In HyperCard this simulation space is usually divided in specific working areas, the decision zones (normally for interactive use). We think that it is important to study the influence on the user of the size of the zones and particularly their shape and location in order to optimize screen design. Should we use horizontal or vertical bands? to the left or to the right of the screen? on the top or on the bottom of the screen? disrupting or not the normal lateralization sequence and other culturally imposed habits? Based on research and intuition, we have adopted (experimentally) the following structure for the screen image (shown in Figure 2), which is common to all thematic cards in the program.

The use of HyperCard involves switching from one screen image to the other, using special visual effects based on the video technology to control this passage (eg. zooms, wipes,

Figure 2. Structure of the thematic card of the program "Descobrimentos Portugueses"

fades,barndoors). We also think that the type of visual effect used should be researched in order to find the psychologically and culturally most effective.

The interactive zone of the program "Descobrimentos Portugueses", which permits the user to go from a thematic treatment to other treatments of the same content, uses several buttons as shown in Figure 3.

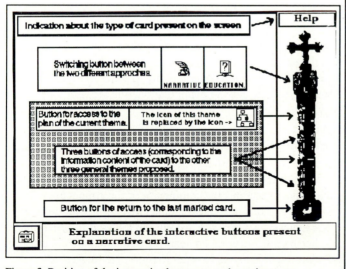

Figure 3. Position of the interactive buttons on a thematic screen

This passage from one screen image to the other is done according to precise rules and using pictograms (icons, buttons), key words, text fields or even image segments. Defined in each screen image, representing the work space, there are sensitive zones (buttons) that if acted on by the cursor, fire an action. This action might be simple or complex.

In HyperCard the chief means for communicating is the icon, which supports interactivity[6]. These interactive operators may represent objects (pictograms) or symbolize ideas (ideograms). Much research is needed on the problems of their efficient educational use. They have been used for a long time in CAL as instruments of visual communication (e.g. PLATO since the 1970's). Their role in HyperCard is exceedingly important, requiring research to define a rigorous logical code; establish the rules of grammar for their conception and use, along with associated semantic value; identify cultural problems associated with their decoding; and develop audiovisual grammatical rules for their animation and juxtaposition. Within the information zone other icons may appear with specific meanings related to the action they start.

Additional help given in the present program consists of changing the shape of the cursor according to the type of zone in which it enters or stays.

The above mentioned describes one of the issues in our multidisciplinary research work on "Iconographic study of the screen image"[6]. We think that the results of this research will help to improve the hypermedia technology that adapts the document to the user, contrary to what happens in traditional data bases. Its primary aim is to use scientific data to improve the user interface ergonomy in order to improve the transparency, the ease of manipulation, and the user autonomy.

Help in browsing

The ease of HyperCard for conceiving and creating interactive situations exaggerates the complexity of the connections. The complexity of this non-linear architecture may result in two risks: that the user fails ot cover all the relevant information or that he/she follows complex learning paths that are contrary to the learning objectives. In order to minimize these risks, several technical solutions exist in hypertext: introduce tools that allow the automatic description of the structure and the

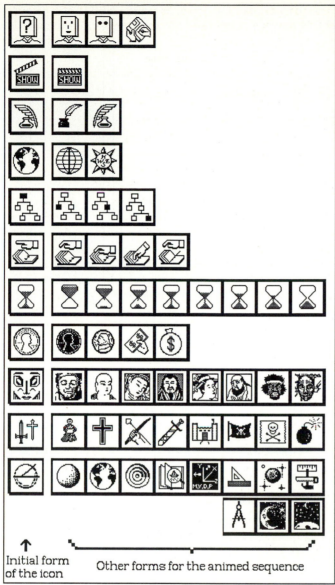

↑
Initial form of the icon   Other forms for the animed sequence

Figure 4. Examples of animated buttons in the program

content of the documents (eg. indexes, key words) and assistance in the search for information. This assistance may consist of a description of the nature of the searched for information, an analysis of formulations, a query to the user in order to guess his/her intentions and to propose other options, or the elimination of less useful connections ("junk links"). In our opinion, these solutions are limited and insufficient, and it is necessary to investigate new ones.

Although HyperCard may be considered an effective tool for

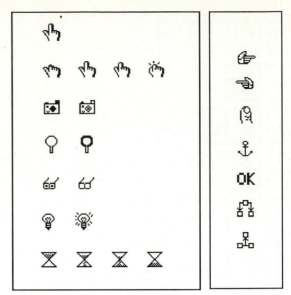

Figure 5. Types of cursors existing in the program

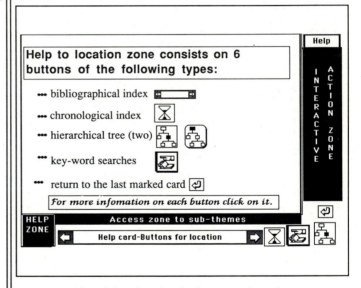

Figure 6. Position of the help to location buttons on thematic screen.

structuring data in hypermedia bases and allowing the handling and managing of an enormous amount of heterogeneous documents (texts, 2D or 3D graphics, animation, video, audio, data bases, external applications), it raises some new problems. In our example, four types of help are always offered to the user. Figure 6 shows the location and size of these help zones on a typical card.

Such help, in addition to their primary aim as being "repères" in the complexity of the existing interactive connections, are important for their future use as supports for a system of intelligent help in the pedagogical use of the program. It is important to recognize that although there may be advantages to accessing information through different routes not previously foreseen, any didactic module relies on a structure based on planning and pedagogical objectives.

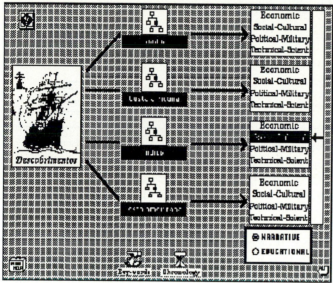

Figure 7. Example of help showing the global planning tree.

Perspectives from A.I.

We think that the integration of knowledge bases and other tools from artificial intelligence can improve both the model of the user and the user interface in order to improve its transparency, ease of handling, and the user autonomy. The application of methods and concepts of cognitive psychology and artificial intelligence is likely to represent the most important means for optimizing of the interface ergonomy, particularly in learning situations.

Three research lines seem very promising regarding this search. First designers should attempt to build a cognitive model of the user, which is related to the activity of exploring hypermedia documents. This is a fundamental step if one really wants to create adequate programs for users. The depth of information exploration in hypermedia seems to be directly related to the initial representation of the task and to the

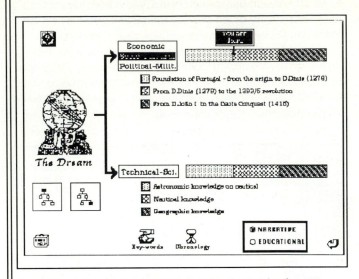

Figure 8. Example of locating help by showing chapter planning tree

cognitive capacities for using the existing relational systems and abstracting the general rules associated with their mental representation. These are two fundamental processes in browsing.

Second, in order to adapt educational hypermedia documents to the users, it is important to discover the set of intellectual activities characterizing the cognitive functioning in any learning situation. <u>Any teaching system should be based on the student model</u>. It is from the diagnosis of the student that the system determines what he or she must learn and how to act in order to improve the learning process. In addition to determining the knowledge state of the student, the hyperme-dia <u>diagnostic module must be able to describe and interpret the global strategy of the user during the knowledge acquisi-tion process</u>: the activated knowledge, the representations of the problems under consideration, the planning processes used, the criteria for the choice of the learning paths. Analyz-ing the preferences and search strategies of each user as well as the nature and level of the information processed, the program will have to run an automatic diagnostic of the user in real time in order to guess his/her intentions and interests and to help him/her propose the best path to achieve his/her instruction. This means that, in hypermedia, the user diagnos-tic module must itself be intelligent or, in other words, be capable of learning.

The last of the three research lines is directed at enabling the system to determine preferential paths for learning in order to direct the student users. Any didactic module implies planning and evaluation. Consequently, if the program is able to correlate the user's path with the learning result, it may provide such a help. Both the learning from examples (and the characterization of examples by counter-examples) and the continuous incremental learning (based on the building of a dynamic memory rooted in local parallel processes, needing the information flux from outside the system in order to maintain its own structure) seem to be the two current paradigms in artificial intelligence likely to provide adequate answers to this problem.

Advice for designing hypertext

Summing up our position, we contend that the characteristics of HyperCard provide considerable advantages in educational programming that deserve to be thoroughly studied. This advanced workshop abundantly showed that there still is a lot of work to be done.

From the discussion of our presentation, we would like to add a few comments that may be of some value for people implementing hypermedia courseware.

•The use of animated icons may not only be of motivational interest, but above all, allows a better representation of the theme it presents. For example, in our program, to indicate the access to the technical, scientific part, we could not find a single icon capable of illustrating the various points involved.

> JD comment Animation was very problematic to interface designers at the workshop. The function of animation is not clear.

•The existence of several types of cursors or changing the shape of the cursor following the zone it enters may be a possible source of adaptation problems for the user, although it may be a real help for browsing in complex hypermedia environments. Above all, it allows the author to increase the complexity and interactivity of the screen image without causing many problems to the user.

•The attempt to impose an intelligent help to the program has been delayed because it implies an extremely rich and rigid structure in order to be efficiently implemented, which is a fundamental advantage in the building of hypermedia courseware. It is exactly this rigor and complexity of the structure that allows the

14.12

conception of truly open interactivity and real free navigation. Like political systems, the more democratic and free users are, the more rigid and complex the legislation they need.

References

[1] Gomes A., Oliveira A., Costa Pereira D., O Hypercard e o Ensino Assistido por Computador, Personal Computer World, 29, 3, 86-92, 1989 (ed. port.)

[2] Bastien C., Schème et Stratégie dans l'Activité Cognitive de l'Enfant, PUF, Paris, 1987

[3] Rinaldi,F., HyperCard: la programmation en HyperTalk, Cedic/ /Nathan, Ed. P.S.I., Paris, 1988

[4] Beeman W. O. et al, Hypertext and Pluralism: From Lineal to Non-lineal Thinking, Hypertext'87 Papers, 1987

[5] Paivio,A., Imagery of mental process, New York: Holt, Reinehart and Winston, 1971

[6] Denis M., Valeur de imagerie et analyse en traits de termes generaux et spécifiques, Université de Paris VIII, Doc.du Lab. de Psychologie, 1979

Chapter 15
From Instructional Text to Instructional Hypertext: An Experiment

Wil A. Verreck and Anja Lkoundi
Open University, NL

Keywords

Hypertext; instructional design; distance education; learning experiment; instructional hypertext

Contents

Introduction

Hypertext and hypermedia systems may lead to the development of new educational products, integrating several aspects of information technology and instructional science. We conducted an experiment with a hypertext program in an existing distance education course. The experiences should provide principles for educational hypermedia design. We start by examining hypertext and learning and the possible implications of hypertext for higher distance education. We then report on our experiment and conclude with some recommendations for educational hypermedia.

Hypertext and learning _____

Characteristics of hypertext

The literature on hypertext/hypermedia is growing rapidly [1,2]. We refer to a few of these publications in order to explain our assumptions about hypertext. Conklin [2] distinguishes between hypertext systems: macro literary systems, problem exploration tools, browsing systems, and the general hypertext technology. To him hypertext is a medium for thinking and communication. We agree, but we prefer to see hypertext systems in the context of learning only as tools for *problem exploration* or a *general technology*.

Halasz [3] presents another classification of systems along three dimensions: scope of the user target (single user, work group, corporate division, whole world), browsing versus authoring (focus on information presentation or on creation and manipulation of networks), and task specificity (general, some task inclination, task specific). For learning purposes, the aspects single user, information presentation with some authoring possibilities, and task specificity are the most critical. Perhaps the best characterization of hypertext/hypermedia is by Gaines and Vickes, who defined hypermedia as "knowledge support systems that integrate existing human knowledge transfer processes with information technology, instrumentation and control technology, and the full range of media." This definition points to the integration of technologies from several disciplines that are involved in the development of these systems. The most characteristic feature of hypertext is, in our opinion, the linking of information blocks in semantic and pragmatic ways that is made available and accessible to users in a computer setting. It distinguishes hypertext from related applications, like information retrieval systems and database systems that are designed to be consulted in other ways.

Learning, education and hypertext

Experiences with hypertext systems in education are still scarce, especially large scale integrations. Beeman [5] has generated empirical observations on the effects of hypertext systems in education. Perhaps the best known application is the Intermedia system. Based upon experiences with a course on English literature within the Intermedia system, Landow [6] has developed a set of organizational rules or stylistic principles for hypertext systems.

DJ explanation 3.1

Beeman's [7] reflections about educational hypertext relate it to educational and psychological theory. He emphasizes the variety of thinking styles, especially in post-secondary education, and the development of pluralistic, integrated thinking that is promoted by Western education. He relates these to the nonlineal thinking resulting from the Intermedia system. A theory of hypertext/hypermedia systems in education will have to be developed on the basis of experiments with hypertext/hypermedia systems containing realistic educational materials, and done, if possible in a realistic educational setting.

GL implication 3.19

One of the most useful overviews relating hypertext and learning is Jonassen [8], who presents *cognitive principles based on learning theories* that may make hypertext designs valid for instruction. These are a presentation of subject matter in networks or schemas; modeling the structure of knowledge as webs of information and integrating new information into prior knowledge by web structures; instructional principles derived from web learning principles; and generative learning principles that model learning as an active process of constructing knowledge. According to these principles, acquisition of meaning from text is learner-controlled rather than text-controlled. These active processes of knowledge acquisition are important for hypertext. By structuring hypertext knowledge bases according to multiple perspectives, meaning can be generated by the user who is searching for it.

DJ explanation 1.7-8

Doland [9] claims that meaning arises as a function of structure. Links create assertions to users, and in this way, hypertext presents *interpretations* to users. Because of this, hypertext is more likely to effect conceptual fixing in the learners than textbooks that are never hermeneutically neutral.

Hypertext in higher distance education ⎯

Hypertext/hypermedia offer particular opportunities for innovation in higher distance education. The characteristics and goals of distance higher education include:

- Independent or self-regulated study by home-sent study materials
- Limited opportunity for students to visit libraries or

other information sources
- •Courseware programs and video discs are sometimes available, in regional study centers only because of the special equipment required for its use
- •Students are adults with more world knowledge and work experience that may be relevant for the study, but suggest different uses of the same databases
- •Students may select parts of the courses and programs. The opportunity for choice is expressed in the concept "open."

SH contrast 4.6

Hypertext and hypermedia materials may enable a better integration and use of various study materials [5,6,7]. Distance universities usually have their course materials available in electronic form and could readily develop these into hypertext applications. This may also be useful because of the large number of students, which provides incentives for establishing an installed base of hypertext courses and the electronic equipment to run the applications. Research projects at the Dutch Open University on hypertext are conducted by the Educational Technology Innovation Centre. We are investigating, for example, the *prior knowledge in students*, the way it can be assessed and accomodated in the development of *electronic courses*, the development of large knowledge bases in fields of study, and tools for students to use these for their learning goals. The experiment reported in this paper focuses on the development of knowledge bases to support instructional goals in environmental law and adminstrative law. The research focus was on the way students *interact with databases,* which is related to research approaches like intelligent information retrieval systems [e.g. 10], *intelligent tutoring systems* [e.g. 11, 12], *human-computer interaction* [e.g. 13]. Recent developments in hypertext and hypermedia are the most promising approach for exploring the project's purposes.

An experiment with hypertext _____

The study we report on in this chapter used an existing course at our institute on adminsitrative law. It seemed to be an interesting field for the construction of a hypertext environment. The experiment would provide experience in converting and redesigning existing course materials, which may be a useful goal by itself. The resulting course in hypertext was used for experiments with students.

Our main goal was to record observations on the way students would use the hypertext course in an ecologically valid learning situation. How would they use the content structures and the instructional features that were available in the written material? Another question concerned the time and effort to get acquainted with the new environment so that it wouldn't interfere too much with the study task. How much time is required to arrive at a stable behavior? This experiment is only preliminary because of the small sample size and limited exposure to hypertext. Longer periods of time are needed for students to integrate hypertext and computer use into normal study behavior, and much better instruments for observing behaviors and measuring effects are also required.

15.5

DJ results 15.10

Design of the printed course

The printed course on which the hypertext is based is a part of the curriculum in law. It consists of four components. We describe these parts in detail to clarify why the content structure was suited for a hypertext application. Central concepts in the instructional design model for this and many other courses at our institute are 'teaching unit' and 'block'.

A teaching unit usually consists of three components:
- an introduction to the contents of the unit, containing a list of learning goals;
- the subject matter content, also called learning kernel, which contains pedagogical features that are meant to help the student process the contents including; questions to test one's understanding of the content (with feedback) notes in the margin point to important concepts or give definitions; exercises without feedback;
- feedback to each question in the learning kernel and an explanation of the correct answer.

A major design characteristic of each teaching unit is a complete lesson that can be studied in about four hours. Teaching units sometimes are used for other parts of a course, especially a final examination or self-test that takes about the same time.

A course consists of blocks, that are designed according to subject matter criteria, and usually contains:
- study advice about the relevant chapters to be read in a textbook before continuing with the teaching-units in a workbook;
- several teaching-units;
- a final unit review of the content of the block that

consists of questions to test knowledge and under-standing with feedback and answers.

The components of the course on adminsitrative law include:
- •Textbook of about 100 pages, that contains part of the mandatory learning materials. It consists of an intro-duction to the field and is written by one professor, more or less independent of the workbook, so there are no references to it.
- •Workbook that is designed according to the instruc-tional model of teaching-units. Each contains four blocks. The block structure is part of the workbook. This means that the workbook is of central importance in the design of the course. Study may start from the textbook, but a view of the structure of the course, as well as references to learning kernels that are some-times in the textbook, are found in the workbook. The workbook is mandatory learning material.
- •Reader that consists of documents that students need in order to answer the questions in the workbook. There are references to the documents in the workbook.
- •Collection of laws, that has to be consulted in studying the course. All the sources mentioned refer to these laws.

We decided that the course structure was appropriate for experimenting with hypertext. There is a detailed and rather complex structure, a variety of information sources, and a lot of cross-references within content as well as to instructional features in the sources.

Design of the course in hypertext

The hypertext program we choose for developing the hy-pertext course was Guide [13] which runs in the MS-Windows environment. Kahn and Meyrowitz [15] compare Guide with other hypertext systems, HyperCard and Intermedia, on twelve criteria for the design of hypertext: document model, document contents, linking model, link visualization, linking user interface, directionality/nexting/multiplicity of links, extent of links, screen model, backtracking support, web visualization, single/multi-user support, extensibility.
Guide. Documents or files in Guide are called guidelines. They may consist of text, or graphics, or commands to execute external programs access and control video disk players and

modems. Guidelines (maximum 32K) are organized in networks, hierarchical and non-hierarchical. The first allows you
to traverse the network by replacement buttons, links between
visible text/graphics and hidden text or graphics in the same
file. They follow embedded menus. A replacement itself may
contain other replacements, which goes on up to 30 internal
locations and any number of end nodes in a directed tree
structure. Another link structure is the inquiry, which really is
a set of replacements presented at one time. Choosing one of
them excludes the other replacements in the inquiry. Reference buttons present the non-hierarchical approach. They
represent the links between visible text/graphic in the same or
a different file. A new window is opened or popped to the top
of all open windows, if the referenced file is already open. A
fourth button/link is the note or definition button. It is a link
between a visible text/graphic and a hidden portion of the
same file or guideline. It presents short complementary
information in a small window in the corner of the screen and
disappears again when the mouse button is no longer held
down. Buttons/links are visualized in the guidelines. Guidelines can be read as well as authored, since the tools for the
latter are available in Guide.

Design of the course in Guide. The first step was to convert
the existing course to a Guide hypertext structure, using the
sytem of text structure codes (TSC) that was in use at our
university for design and printing of texts. TSC's are similar
to SGML, which is described by others [16, 17]. Unfortunately, the TSC's could not be imported into the Guide program by converting existing codes in the text to links/buttons.
So, part of the course was retyped and scanned. The part that
was converted reflected the structure of the course. It would
take a student several hours to study it. This would give us
ample opportunity to observe not only the very first reactions,
probably showing confusion and navigation problems, but
also some stable study behavior after the students became accustomed to using hypertext.

The relevant course material of block 1 of the printed course
was selected. The hypertext course consists of the following
components:
- Textbook: a part of chapter one, about 8 pages long,
  organized into 10 paragraphs. The main references
  were to articles of law each of which could be opened
  by reference links/buttons. There were also note links
  for definitions.

•Workbook: block 1 consists of 5 teaching-units, of which three present content, one is a review, and one is the post-test. There are reference links to the other components and to questions/exercises, replacement links with units, and note links for texts in the margin. The material consists of 33 pages of text to study, three with exercises and reviews, and three with the post-test.

•Reader: a selection of 8 texts, supplementary to textbook and workbook, e.g. related cases explained in the text or contained in exercises. The reader consisted of 12 pages of text.

•Collection of laws: the complete texts of nine laws, except one for which only a few of the relevant articles were included, altogether about 115 pages of text. There were only references to and not from the laws. The division of each law into chapters, paragraphs and articles was presented in the replacement menus.

To these components were added:

•A start screen with reference links to four support files/ guidelines:

•*managing windows*; a reference to it pops up a screen with explanations and examples of window functions;

•*buttons*; a reference presents a guideline with text from Guide itself on the relevant buttons;

•*introduction to the course*; an introductory screen with a text from the printed course with a reference to three topics: introduction to administrative law, the structure of the course, and the educational features used;

•*study suggestions*; an overview screen with some study suggestions and a structured list of the files in the application; laws, educational options, suggestions for study.

•A file, 'block 1', that could be reached by a reference from the start screen or opened directly. It presented the top level menu of the course material; choices to go to textbook, workbook, reader, and laws, and an advice to start with the workbook.

•An overview screen/file of the laws included and an opportunity to open them by replacements in a hierarchical way. This option was supplementary to the direct reference to articles from texts.

•A screen containing all the questions in all teaching-units, the reviews and the post-test.

•A file containing all the answers to teaching-units and reviews.

The hypertext consisted of several layers of overview screens, especially in the start screen and block 1 file, which functioned as helps.

The experiment

The experiment consisted of five students studying the course in the hypertext form (experimental or hypertext group) and five students (control group) studying the equivalent course in printed form. Both groups took a pretest as well as a post-test and completed a questionnaire at the end of the session. Student interactions in the experimental group were recorded on video, the camera being placed in a fixed position to the screen with no operator present during study-time. The experiment took one complete day per student in both groups.

Subjects were students recruited from the State University Limbourg. Their ages varied from 18 to 28. They studied law and were in the first few years of the program, which means that they already had knowledge of basic law, which was a prerequisite to studying administrative law. The students were paid for taking part in the experiment, and in order to simulate serious study during the session, the rate of payment depended on the results of the final test. None of the students had any significant experience with computers, aside from text-processing.

Procedure

On arrival, students were given a short introduction to the experiment — the conditions (experimental or control) for study, plan of the day, the pretest and the computer, followed by the pretest. The test assessed prior knowledge of the topics in the course and took a maximum of 45 minutes to answer. Next, an introduction to the course was presented which included a short introduction to hypertext and the user environment (mouse, windows, Guide) in the experimental group. It was followed by a study period of about two hours in which students were left alone in the room. At least one of the staff members was available for assistance with the equipment and the system. After a break for lunch, the study period continued for two or three hours at a maximum (most students told that they were ready before that time). The post-test consisted of the same questions as the pretest and was designed to assess learning effects. Students in the control group then had a short introduction to the hypertext system and 30 minutes to use it in order to get a feeling for the system and to be able to answer some questions on it. Finally, students completed a questionnaire on the hypertext experience.

The complete experiment, all activities included, took seven to eight hours for each student. Two staff members (one in reserve) usually were available for running the experiment and assisting the student. The equipment was located in an office where students could study without any interruption from ongoing activities.

Results of the experiment ───────────

Test results
Both the hypertext and the control group scored higher on the post-test than the pretest to the same order of magnitude. Learning effects were equivalent for both conditions. The control group showed slightly more progress on the items in the post-test that were not directly related to the content . It seems that some incidental learning might have taken place in this group. Fatigue may have adversely affected the hypertext group's performance (see the results of the questionnaire). Incidental learning is more likely to result in hypertext because of the browsing activities involved. Our experimental period might be too short for it to show up.

Use of the hypertext course
Space will not permit the presentation of detailed analyses of the video protocols and the answers to the questionnaire. Instead we summarize comment on them. Following this we summarize the effects of the short experience of the control gorup with hypertext.

- Few of the students needed any time to begin study activities using a hypertext system. Fifteen to thirty minutes for exploring the system appeared to be sufficient. Active exploration of the learning environment was preferred by the students. Some difficulties existed, but they were probably due to the short adjustment period.
- Some students did not succeed in making an acceptable start. They proceeded in an unsystematic way, didn't pay attention to the introductions, and/or disliked working with the computer. Not every student will come to appreciate hypertext systems in education. It will not be a complete substitute for all educational materials and courses.
- Students tended to work systematically through the course, following to some extent the advised paths.

Many students developed a strategy that they persisted in using. For example, working through all paragraphs of a component (textbook e.g.), not paying attention to any references; following the menu hierarchy to consult a reference (an article of law e.g.); closing files/windows after having read them even if it wasn't necessary or useful. We are inclined to think that these behaviors result from the uncertainty students have about the hypertext environment. It is understandable that they continue to use successful behavior.

•Time on task for each file appeared to be rather short. Reading times of three to five minutes were common. This seems insufficient for learning. The possible effect of hypertext on superficial processing of information is also described by Doland [9].

•Students used the pedagogical features in a variety of ways. These differences are to be expected; they are quite normal in research on study behaviors. It indicates that user tests of these design features are necessary. An example is the way exercises and answers are used. Some students directly consulted the answers. We know that this also happens with printed texts. Hypertext offers an opportunity to observe these behaviors by following the trace of the content and pedagogical elements used. It provides a venue for pedagogical experiments, such as, building student models and testing them [18]. Learning models may also consider variables like 'time on task' related to information item, that is the time students need to read or study particular items.

•A feature that students needed was the ability to make notes, underline text, etc. [19], which is consistent with the way they study from books. The system we used offers to some limited capability to do so. However, we did not provide annotation capabilities. We think it is very important to provide better study tools to students in hypertext systems.

The control group had a very short experience with the hypertext system, after having studied the printed course. Four of the five students on the questionnaire noted that learning would go faster after some practice. One remarked that it would be much more difficult to estimate the amount of learning materials needed or to get an overview of the materials, but that concentration would be higher. Study behavior in hypertext varies. Study suggestions are not always followed.

Some users start at the beginning and others seek their own way. In using the hypertext, there is an inclination to deviate and to follow the jumps. The reactions to the hypertext environment were also varied. Some experienced few problems in getting accustomed to hypertext, and one didn't understand it at all. Most learned to use it quickly. Suggestions for improvement concerned opportunities to make notes in the text, underline text, keep a notebook, making schemes, a better overview, and better explanations.

Conclusions and guidelines for the design of hypertext for learning

We refrain from discussing general design guidelines, such as utilities for navigation, overviews, taking notes, etc. They are dealt with in other chapters. We will make a few remarks on the goal of our experiment: to use the functionality of content and pedagogical elements in existing learning materials to develop hypertext for learning purposes. Design characteristics of printed instructional texts may be generalized to the development of instructional hypertext, as we did. It would help the development of a base of hypertext applications, if we could map instructional features and content structures in hypertext structures. Problems occur in the effectiveness and use of most instructional features and to a lesser degree in the use of content structures as we learned in our experiment. They are not used in the ways that they were designed. This may result from different expectations students have about a hypertext environment [6], or it may be the usual study behavior, which can be observed explicitly in a hypertext environment. We think both aspects are operative.

The main guideline for the design of hypertext for learning that we have derived from our research is to look more closely into the functions one wants to incorporate in a hypertext database, expecially the informational and motivational functions that have to be present in educational settings. Feedback, for example, is a central function in any learning process as are the various informing and reinforcing properties of it. If an element is directed at giving feedback, what kind of feedback action or learning feedback, artificial or intrinsic feedback, the informative and affective attributional effects? There is obvious need to develop prototype systems that are aimed at these functions and to test them in real study situations [6].

[1] Nielsen, J. (1989). Hypertext bibliography. *Hypermedia, 1*, 74-91.

[2] Conklin, J. (1987). A survey of hypertext. MCC Technical Report STP-356-86, Rev. 1. Austin: Microelectronics & Computer Technology Corporation.

[3] Halasz, F.G. (1988). Reflections on Notecards: Seven issues for the next generation of hypermedia systems. *Communications of the ACM, 31*, 836-852.

[4] Gaines, B.R., and Vickers, J.N. (1988). Hypermedia design. In: Proceedings RIAO 88 *Conference on User-oriented Content-based Text and Image-handling*, March, M.I.T., Cambridge, MA.

[5] Beeman, W.O., Anderson, K.T., Bader, G., Larkin, J., Mclard, A.P., McQuillan, P., Shields, M. (1988). *Intermedia: A case study of innovation in higher education*. Final Report to the Annenberg/CPB Project. Institute for Research in Information and Scholarship, Brown University.

[6] Landow, G.P. (1988). *Hypertext in literary education, criticism, and scholarship*. IRIS Technical Report, Brown University. Also to appear in: Computers and the humanities, 1989.

[7] Beeman, W.O., Anderson, K.T., Bader, G., Larkin, J., Mclard, A.P., McQuilan, P.,Shields, M. (1987) . Hypertext and pluralism: From lineal to non-lineal thinking.In: Proceedings *Hypertext '87*, Chapel Hill, North Carolina.

[8] Jonassen, D. H. (1986). Hypertext principles for text and courseware design. *Educational Pyschologist, 2*, 269-292.

[9] Doland, V.M. (1989). Hypermedia as an interpretive act. *Hypermedia, 1*, 6-19.

[10] Croft, B. (1987). Approaches to intelligent information retrieval. *Information processing & Management . 23*(4), 249-254.

[11] Clancey (1986). Qualitative student models. In *Annual Review of Computer Sciences, 1*, 381-450.

[12]Fischer, P.M., and Mandl, H., (1988). Improvement of the acquisition of knowledge by informing feedback. In: Mandl, H., and Lesgold, A. (Eds.), *Learning issues for intelligent tutoring systems*, 187-241.

[13] Hartson, H.R., and Hix, (1989). Human-computer interface developments: Concepts and systems. *ACM Computing Surveys, 21*, 5-92.

[14] Guide. (1987, 1988). (manuals). *Guide: Hypertext for the PC; Guide 2: Professional hypertext system,* update manual.

[15] Kahn, P., and Meyrowitz, N. (1988). Guide, *HyperCard, and Intermedia: A comparison of hypertext/hypermedia systems.* IRIS Technical Report Number 88-8. Institute for Research in Information and Scholarship, Brown University.

[16] Niblett, T., and Hoff, A. van, (1989). Structured hypertext documents via SGML. *Proceedings Hypertext II,* University of York.

[17] Rahtz, S., Carr, L., and Hall, W., (1989). Creating multimedia documents: Hypertext-processing. *Proceedings Hypertext II,* University of York.

[18] Anderson, J.R. (1987). Methodologies for studying human knowledge. *Behavioral and Brain Sciences, 10,* 467-505.

[19] Leggett, J.L., Schnase, J.L., and Kacmar, C.J. (1989). Practical experiences with hypermedia for learning. *Proceedings of Designing hypertext/hypermedia for learning*, NATO Advanced Research Workshop, Deutsches Institute fur Fernstudien, Tubingen.

Chapter 16
Journal Articles as Learning Resource:
What Can Hypertext Offer?

Cliff McKnight, John Richardson, and Andrew Dillon
HUSAT Research Centre
Loughborough University of Technology, UK

Keywords
Journal usage; readers' models; information access and retrieval; database design

Contents

Introduction

Although paper has reigned unchallenged for hundreds of years as the only viable publishing medium, recent advances in computer-based technology have demonstrated that electronic storage and retrieval have several advantages such as speed of access and cost-effectiveness. Furthermore, these advances have also led to the development of alternative publishing media. In particular, the optical disk based systems such as CD-ROM have been shown to be viable both technically and commercially for a variety of publishing ventures ranging from music to encyclopædias. Conceptually at least, the age of the electronic book is upon us.

One intuitively appealing approach to the development of the electronic book is that typified by the work of Ian Benest and co-workers at York University [1,2]. Here the approach has been to implement as exact a copy as possible of the paper

NATO ASI Series, Vol. F 67
Designing Hypermedia for Learning
Edited by D. H. Jonassen and H. Mandl
© Springer-Verlag Berlin Heidelberg 1990

book on a computer. Thus, the reader selects a book from a shelf using a pointing device and is presented with a two-page display in which the pages can be turned, bookmarks can be used, text can be highlighted and so forth. The advantage of implementing such a system rests largely on the assumption that minimal learning is required by the user — the average user's many years of experience with paper should remain relevant. However, while the conceptual model of the document has been faithfully preserved, the reader's interaction with the virtual screen-displayed book is totally different to any interaction with a paper text. None of the reader's manipulative skills will be of any use and the interface will provide none of the kinesthetic feedback that is expected. Even the visual feedback is restricted. <u>Furthermore, if a new technology is to be accepted, it needs to provide even more than the system it replaces in terms of functionality, and it is not clear that the addition of, say, search facilities to an electronic copy of a book is sufficient to ensure its acceptance in place of paper based technology.</u>

The book has developed to its present form largely as a result of developments in the paper-making and printing industries. There is no logical reason for assuming that the decisions taken during the development of the paper medium will be relevant or transferable to the electronic medium and even less reason for believing that they will be optimal. If we accept this argument, then the availability of electronic publishing media provides an opportunity to 're-think' the design of information traditionally held on paper.

While the issues raised by the potential of electronic books are important, in tertiary education the journal article is probably the most commonly used 'unit of information'. It is the primary means by which the results of scholarly research and thinking are communicated to the academic community at large. Consequently, students in all disciplines are expected to familiarize themselves with the journal system. This will involve not only coming to grips with the idiosyncratic language and structure of journal articles but also learning how to follow up references to cited literature. If they are students in an experiment-based discipline, it is likely that they will not only be referred to the journals by their teachers but that they will also be required to write their own reports of experiments in a style drawn directly from the journal article style. To the students, therefore, the corpus of journals in their discipline represents an important learning resource in terms of both content and format.

DJ parallel 10.15

JL corroboration 2.10

DJ corroboration 10.4

The possibility of an electronic journal raises questions about how the information in such a journal should be structured. One of the common claims for electronic documents is that they free the reader from the confines of the linear paper document, allowing non-linear 'thought-like' documents to be produced [3]. Such claims are common in the hypertext field though one should perhaps add the caveat that people do in fact think serially for much of the time even if they do not read in this manner. Would hypertext structuring techniques offer any advantages to the electronic journal article?

While thought (or perhaps ideas) may be non-linear at times, it could be argued that the structure of a journal article ought to be linear and independent of the medium on which it is presented. This argument is based on the observation that, for the experimental disciplines at least, journal articles reporting research results follow the traditionally taught process by which science is conducted. That is, they begin with an introduction in which some section of the field is surveyed and a question isolated; a method of investigating the question is designed; results of using the method are described; and the implications of the results are discussed and related to existing knowledge.

Although this argument has merit in terms of the 'structural components' of journal articles, it does not answer the question of alternative structures built out of the same components. That is, if we accept that articles should still comprise these units, is it necessary to present the units in the same linear format? The answer to this question ought to be based on the way in which people use journal articles. An electronic journal article should allow *at least* the same tasks to be performed by the reader as the paper version. Furthermore, it should allow them to be carried out using similar strategies and skills acquired using paper texts. It is important then to understand the tasks and strategies of journal readers.

The present paper describes work carried out by the authors in designing and developing a hypertext database of journal articles. A series of studies of how people access and view paper journals was carried out during the early development of the database and their results incorporated into the design. These studies and the system are described in the following sections.

16.3

DJ contrast 16.2

How Are journals used? ————————

A study of journal usage by Dillon et al. [4] looked at 15 regular journal readers interacting with a variety of articles. The results indicated that readers develop strategies for scanning an issue of a journal in order to look for salient articles. Furthermore, journals articles are subjected to relatively consistent forms of use by readers. When an article of interest is identified, then the reader opens the journal at the start of the relevant paper and adopts one of three reading strategies.

In the first case, the abstract is usually attended to and a decision made about the suitability of the article for the reader's purposes. At this point most subjects reported also browsing the start of the introduction before flicking through the article to get a better impression of the contents. Here subjects reported attending to the section headings, the diagrams and tables, noting both the level of mathematical content and the length of the article. Browsing the conclusions also seems to be a common method of extracting central ideas from the article and deciding on its worth.

The second strategy involves reading the article in a non-serial fashion to rapidly extract relevant information. This will involve reading some sections fully and only skimming or even skipping others. Typically the method and results sections of experimental papers are skim read while the introduction or introductory sections and the discussion/conclusions are read fully.

The final strategy is a serial, detailed read from start to finish. This was seen as "studying" the article's contents and though not carried out for each article that is selected, most subjects reported that they usually read selected articles at this level of detail eventually.

While individual preferences for a strategy were reported most readers seem to use both the second and third strategies depending on the task or purpose for reading the article, time available and the content of the article. Original and interesting work is more likely to be read fully than dull or routine papers. Reading to keep up with the literature requires less "studying" of articles than attempting to understand a new area. However, even when reading at the third level some subjects still reported skimming particular sections that were not intrinsically relevant to their particular needs at that time.

Thus, readers perform a variety of tasks with journal articles from scanning for specific information to studying the contents in depth and these tasks require interactions with the text lasting a few seconds to an hour or more. Manipulations of the paper may be simple (e.g., turning a page) or complex (jumping to a particular section while keeping a marker in another). Electronic documents are likely to offer some improvements for particular task scenarios but none in others. For example, electronic storage and retrieval should make access to material easier and faster, thus offering a distinct advantage over paper. However, at the article level, merely reproducing the linear format of the text on screen is unlikely to encourage use and paper will certainly be preferred. Structuring the presentation on screen in ways not available on paper may be the answer, which brings us to the consideration of readers' models.

Readers' models of text structure _____

It was clear from comments made by subjects in the previous study that as readers, they are very aware of how an article is typically structured, how the argument is built up and where they are likely to find certain types of information. This concurs with work on memory for, and comprehension of, text [5,6] which suggests that readers develop a model of text organization or structure that facilitates manipulation and comprehension of the contents. Presumably this model develops with experience of certain text types and is more sophisticated for people who read a lot than those who do not. The extent to which this concept is important in the domain of hypertext is difficult to assess, but if one accepts that lessons learned from other areas of HCI such as user navigation of databases and menu hierarchies are relevant (i.e., users get lost in a maze of electronic information very easily), then it is likely that such models have a very real application.

DJ explanation 10.10-11

Two studies by one of the present authors [7] investigated this concept. In the first of these, subjects were presented with cut-up paper versions of two journal articles, and their task was to assemble each article into a cohesive whole. To avoid referential continuity cues, every second paragraph was removed and in one condition only the basic level headings were provided (Introduction, Method, Results and Discussion). Subjects found little difficulty in piecing the articles together in a general sense, i.e., mean accuracy rates were higher than 80% for correct placement of a paragraph in a major section. The main difficulty involved deciding where to place the secondary headings and the specific ordering of paragraphs within a section. This suggests that experienced journal readers are capable of distinguishing isolated paragraphs of text according to their likely location within a complete article. Interestingly this could be done without resorting to reading every word or attempting to understand the subject matter of the paper.

In the second study, eight subjects read a selection of paragraphs from two articles on both paper and screen and had to place each one in the general section to which they thought it belonged (Introduction, Method, Results or Discussion). Again subjects showed a high degree of accuracy (over 80%) with the only advantage to paper being speed (subjects were significantly faster at the 5 per cent level in the paper condition) which is probably explicable in terms of image quality. Taken together, these results suggest that readers do have a model of the typical journal article that allows them to gauge accurately where certain information is located. This model holds for information presented on paper and on screen.

These findings have direct relevance to the development of hypertext articles in that they suggest that drastically altering the structure of the text would not aid the reader. Rather this model should be enhanced by the hypertext version as a way of aiding navigation and manipulation of the text. In conjunction with the findings from the earlier study on how articles are used, these results suggest that hypertext articles may support several of the tasks readers perform and greatly enhance the rate of access to stored material.

The hypertext database

In order to evaluate the possibilities of a journal in hypertext format it was decided to create an electronic version of the journal Behavior and Information Technology (BIT). This journal publishes papers concerning the human factors issues associated with the introduction of information technology and its readership is typically composed of psychologists, ergonomists and computer scientists. The academic subdiscipline of human-computer factors is relatively recent and the majority of relevant papers are published in only a handful of journals. Thus by creating an electronic version of just one of the journals an appreciable proportion of the literature could be made available for experimental investigation using actual readers and realistic tasks.

Following the granting of limited copyright permission from
the publishers, all the back issues of BIT were scanned and the
resulting computer files subjected to OCR processing. Thus
the full text and graphics for all the articles were made available for presentation as a hypertext database.

The database is composed of two distinct hypertext modules:
a 'front-end' structured in HyperCard™ and the body of
journal articles which are formatted as individual Guide™
documents. The database architecture reflects the two distinct
components of reading identified in the journal usage study:
an initial period of searching or browsing at the title and
author level which typically results in a decision to read a
piece of text (perhaps only briefly). The text is then sampled
repeatedly until a higher order decision can be made with a
degree of confidence concerning its suitability for a particular
information requirement ("this text does/does not contain the
information that I want"). At this stage a more continuous
style of reading is likely to be adopted for particular sections
of the text, or the article will be abandoned and the reader will
return to the top level, possibly to repeat the process.

WV definition 15.7

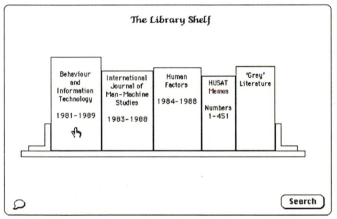

Figure 1. Initial selection point: the range of available journals, plus access
to a search facility.

Database front-end

The initial view of the database consists of a graphical representation of a library shelf with the spines of various selectable volumes visible (see Figure 1) and owes much to
Benest's earlier implementation. Such a representation has the
advantage that it draws on a wealth of experience which users
already have — everyone understands a library shelf at a local

level. However, the categorization of books often seems arbitrary to non-librarians and can result in semantically related books being distributed across widely separated shelves. Thus, this simple visual metaphor is not necessarily the optimum form of representation and would not be appropriate for a much larger database. For this reason, alternatives such as concept maps or semantic nets should be experimentally evaluated. Access to a search option is offered at the top level, which allows a string search of the author and title fields and the full text of the journal articles (see Figure 2).

Selecting a volume from the shelf leads to the display of a schematic browser for the complete contents of the journal in terms of the various volumes and parts (see Figure 3). Two means of accessing the individual articles are offered at this stage: a series of volume indices which alphabetically list the authors and titles or issue/part contents lists which present the

Enter Search Parameters then press GO

GO

Restrict search to journal ...

☒ Behaviour and Information Technology
☒ International Journal of Man-Machine Studies
☐ Human Factors
☐ HUSAT Memos
☐ 'Grey' Literature

Search for author   Wright

⦿ and / or ◯

Search in title   Colour

⦿ and / or ◯

Search articles for

Library Shelf

Figure 2. The search facilties.

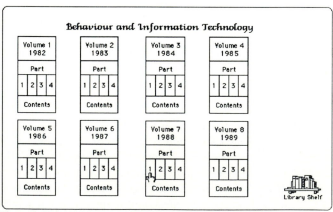

Behaviour and Information Technology

Volume 1 1982	Volume 2 1983	Volume 3 1984	Volume 4 1985
Part	Part	Part	Part
1 2 3 4	1 2 3 4	1 2 3 4	1 2 3 4
Contents	Contents	Contents	Contents
Volume 5 1986	Volume 6 1987	Volume 7 1988	Volume 8 1989
Part	Part	Part	Part
1 2 3 4	1 2 3 4	1 2 3 4	1 2 3 4
Contents	Contents	Contents	Contents

Library Shelf

Figure 3. Volumes, parts and contents selection for one journal.

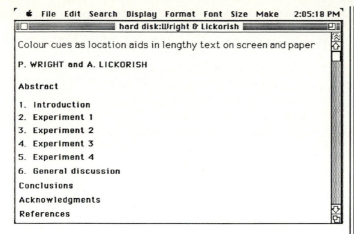

Figure 4. Top level presentation of one article. All headings are buttons.

author and title details in the same order as the paper original. Selecting an article from either display results in the 'launch' of the Guide software and the presentation of the top level of the chosen article.

Structure of the articles

The individual articles are organized hierarchically and the top level consists fo the title page details plus the major headings of the article(see Figure 4). With the exception of the title, all these items are selectable. Choosing an item with the mouse causes the text 'folded' underneath to be displayed at that point and the length of the document increases proportionally. The text that is unfolded may itself contain further 'buttons' (subheadings, figures, and tables) and this process can therefore be repeated until the full text of the article has been unfolded and is displayed on screen as a linear, scrollable document. A second type of embedding is used to display the equivalent of electronic footnotes. Selecting and of the references in the text causes a window to temporarily appear on the screen with the full bibliographic details of the reference displayed (see figure 5). If a reference is made to another article in the database then selecting it results in a separate window being opened and the display of the article as a new Guide document. If the reader quits from Guide then all the documents are closed and the reader is returned to the top level HyperCard browser.

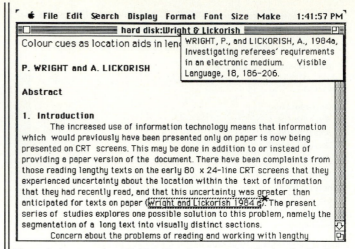

Figure 5. An example of Guide's Note button used to display details of a reference.

The interface for accessing the documents and the structure of the individual articles are designed to support and enhance the reading strategies identified in the paper journal usage study. Readers can rapidly scan the contents lists in the same way as they do with paper journals but they also have the ability to search the complete set of authors and titles to find, for example, a specific article when only a few details of the title or authors are known; all the papers by a given author or all the papers with a specific keyword in the title and, finally, any article which includes a given term in its text. The first strategy is simple but laborious using the paper version but the last strategy is totally impractical without an electronic version.

Similarly, the hierarchical structure of the journal articles is designed to support the reader whilst 'manipulating' the document. It is not true that readers access most text in serial order except at the obvious sentence level. The journal usage study indicated that readers very rarely read articles serially, preferring to 'jump about' from section to section, typically from the Introduction to the References or Discussion.

The Guide format allows readers to access directly the sections of the document that are of particular interest without the possible distraction of having to search through the entire text. Thus a reader can select and the skim-read the abstract, conclusion or even only the references. If more detailed reading is warranted then not only is the full text available but it is also possible to follow up references to other papers immediately to check on the author's interpretation of the results or even the experimental details themselves.

Can and will people use it? _____

Pilot evaluations indicate that the design is easy to learn and to use for individuals with some experience of Macintosh-style WIMP interfaces. The ability to access instantly the total contents of a journal from one's desk is seen as a major advantage. However, as we have noted elsewhere [8], individuals have difficulties with search facilities and this limits their use of such a system. Jumping to other articles is an issue that requires investigation because it is not always the case that readers want the full contents of another article; an abstract or relevant section of the selected text may be sufficient. Also, the current implementation of the database is weak in terms of the navigation information required to support jumping between articles.

Obviously further evaluations must be carried out before we can be confident that this system is viable. Offering the database as a resource in the HUSAT library is one way of field testing it though ultimately, we hope to offer readers access to it on the computer network. An iterative design process is needed, adjusting the database in the light of comments from users.

Implications for Learning from Hypertext

The present work has emphasized the role of information access and manipulation over what may be described as the more traditional learning concepts of comprehension and recall. This springs from our conviction that, for the time being at least, people prefer to study texts using paper rather than screens. This is supported by the literature on screen reading even though few studies have shown any comprehension effect for presentation medium. Developments in screen technology may go some way to overcoming this, but for the present it seems that people will limit their use of such applications to exclude full reading on screen.

Nevertheless, even if hypertext versions of standard texts are limited to these areas, we feel that they can make a significant contribution to the learning environment by acting as informa-

SH parallel 23.19

tion stores and access mechanisms *par excellence*. This aspect should not be under-rated since the identification, accessing and evaluation of source material is a major component in the work required to write an essay, lecture or journal article. Any innovation which improves the efficiency of this process will inevitably have a beneficial effect.

However, the claims that hypertext offers significant advantages for the learning process over and above its contribution as a retrieval/access mechanism involve a range of assumptions, many of which seem difficult to justify. While it is usual for a new field to be replete with assumptions, hypertext has matured to the point where such assumptions need to be supported by empirical work. Many claims have been made for the potential of hypertext, in the same way that claims were made for computer-assisted learning, but such claims now require validation.

How might we validate such claims and demonstrate a positive advantage for hypertext in learning? It is relatively easy to construct experiments which use simple, performance-based measures to compare paper and hypertext. Measures such as time taken to complete some experimenter-provided task, or accuracy of answers to a set of questions, are easy to use. However, while such measures have an obvious relationship to, say, the efficiency with which an interface may be used, they have less obvious relevance to the process of learning. Similarly, various measures of comprehension have been developed which can be applied in restricted experimental settings but which prove not viable in realistic learning environments. Of course, an additional problem with evaluating hypertext in a realistic setting is that educators who are positively disposed towards hypertext may induce performance effects in their students.

Many supporters of hypertext in learning environments stress the importance of learning by discovery, of learner-controlled instruction. However, a very small proportion of learners in the average undergraduate educational institution could be

DJ description 1.1-5

categorized as *self-organized*. To be self-organized implies the ability to set one's own goals and to evaluate one's performance in relation to those goals, yet the education system usually expects learners to adopt the educational goals of the institution — typically evaluated by the passing of exams.

If hypertext-based materials are to be used in learning environments, it is important that authors take seriously the responsibility to provide structure. In documents like journal articles, many of the decisions regarding structure do not have to be made by the author since there are structures and conventions already established by the particular journal. However, many forms of hypertext allow great flexibility of structure and it is here where care needs to be taken. The situation seems analogous to the debate over choice of programming languages, with structured languages like Pascal being recommended because they constrain the author, and languages like BASIC being vilified because — although easy to use — they allow the author to write 'spaghetti'. If hypertext is to gain more respect as an information medium than BASIC has as a programming language, authors must avoid the temptation to link everything to everything else. The role of the author is to provide structure and thereby simplify material. In 1971, Hansen [9] gave the advice "Know the user" and such advice is still valid for the designer of hypertext documents today.

SH parallel 23.9   16.13

PWh parallel 16.12

Conclusion

It is clear that educational material can be represented in hypertext. There are similarities between certain hypertext structures and certain hypothetical cognitive structures, sufficient to encourage some to suggest that hypertext is somehow 'natural' and that its use would facilitate learning. Such suggestions require empirical confirmation. Furthermore, authoring in hypertext requires increased responsibility on the part of the author. At present, hypertext can play a role as an extremely flexible storage and efficient access mechanism, and the importance of this role should not be underestimated. Claims for its use as anything other than this require substantiation.

Acknowledgements

This work was supported by the British Library Research and Development Department as part of Project Quartet. We also gratefully acknowledge Taylor & Francis for permission to use the contents of Behaviour and Information Technology.

References

[1] Benest, I.D. and Morgan, G. (1985). A humanised model for the electronic library. IEE Colloquium Digest Nº 1985/80, October, 2/1-2/9.

[2] Benest, I. D., Morgan, G., and Smithhurst, M. D. (1987). A humanized interface to an electronic library. In H. J. Bullinger and B. Shackel (Eds.), *Human-Computer Interaction— Interact' 87*. North-Holland: Elsevier.

[3] Beeman, W.O., Anderson, K.T., Bader. G., Larkin, J., McClard, P.A., McQuillan, P. and Shields, M. (1987). Hypertext and pluralism: from lineal to non-lineal thinking. *Proceedings of Hypertext '87*, University of North Carolina at Chapel Hill.

[4] Dillon, A., Richardson, J. and McKnight, C. (1989). The human factors of journal usage and the design of electronic text. *Interacting with Computers*, *1*(2), 183–189.

[5] van Dijk, T.A. (1980). *Macrostructures*. Hillsdale, NJ: Lawrence Erlbaum Associates.

[6] Johnson-Laird, P. (1983). *Mental Models*. Cambridge: Cambridge University Press.

[7] Dillon, A. (1989). Readers' models of text structures: some experimental findings. HUSAT report, HUSAT Research Centre, Loughborough University, UK.

[8] Richardson, J., Dillon, A., McKnight, C. and Saadat-Sarmadi, M. (1988). The manipulation of screen-presented text: experimental investigation of an interface incorporating a 'movement grammar'. HUSAT Memo Nº 431, HUSAT Research Centre, Loughborough University, UK.

[9] Hansen, W.J. (1971). User engineering principles for interactive systems. *Proceedings of the Fall Joint Computer Conference*, 39, 523–532.

Chapter 17
Hypertext/hypermedia-like
Environments and Language Learning

Othmar Foelsche
Darthmouth College, USA

Keywords

Language learning; hypertext; hypermedia; language work-station; learning environments.

Contents

Assumptions about language learning ____

In this paper I am using the term "language learning" for language acquisition, language instruction, and language production. Traditionally language learning is divided into five areas which I shall label "dimensions" in this paper:

- •reading
- •listening
- •writing
- •speaking
- •semiotics

A single dimension cannot satisfactorily be mastered in isolation. However, specific skills need to be mastered in each dimension in conjunction with skills in other dimensions, before mastery in one dimension or competency in the lan-

NATO ASI Series, Vol. F 67
Designing Hypermedia for Learning
Edited by D. H. Jonassen and H. Mandl
© Springer-Verlag Berlin Heidelberg 1990

guage as a whole can be achieved. A student cannot write, unless he/she can read. A student cannot converse, unless he/she has listening skills and reading skills.

Natural language learning is a constant, life-long activity of exposure to multiple dimensions of images, objects, movements, sounds, and symbols, of participation, interaction, imitation and synthesis on part of the learner.

Traditional classroom language learning means mastering analysis and synthesis of a language, speaking, translation, and reading. Recent approaches stress mastering oral/aural (direct communicative) capabilities in favor of the more traditional "translation" approaches.

During the last decades, several "methods" have been propagated by various schools and individuals, almost all of which have disappeared fairly rapidly as the novelty has worn off. Among these methods are the so-called audio-visual approaches, which have produced breakthroughs in oral/aural areas, but which have had a strongly negative impact on general writing and reading skills. Most creators of these "methods" for improving language learning attempt to address one problem area and focus on the oral/aural (communicative) aspects of language learning so exclusively that students will encounter serious problems in the other skill areas of the language.

Most of the "methods" are also personality based, that is, the success of the method really depends on the creator's presence in the classroom. Both Capretz [1] and Rassias [2], for example, have created "methods" that are highly personalized and highly successful within the immediate circle. But these "methods" are not easily transferable to other institutions unless a mentor goes along. In many instances, the "method" will be changed and adjusted for different personalities in different environments.

All of the "methods" will become superfluous at the point where the learner will design his/her own strategy and continue learning on his/her own with less supervision, but in a highly individualistic and probably a more efficient way. Conventional technology (paper, pencil, book, language lab, video) is useful for the individual learner. One major drawback of any technology is its limited ability to interact intelligently with the user; another is its often miscalculated or misunderstood role in language learning. A language lab does not really *teach* pronunciation, it only *provides* correct pronunciation. A book does not really *teach* reading, it *provides* materials to be read. Obviously, there are some exceptions to this analogy, but my point is that technology, to a large extent, has only addressed single dimensions, hardly ever multiple dimensions (i.e., combining text, sound, animation, realistic activities, and feedback, etc) in its implementation in language learning.

Computer assisted language learning

Computer-assisted instruction as implemented by Duncan [3] on the Dartmouth College Time Sharing System in the late 1970's, as well as Pusack's [4] *Dasher/Dancer* on the IBM PC and Apple II platforms in the early 1980's, represented first steps in exploiting the computing medium for the purpose of teaching single-dimensional skills with hints and help on-line. Students could solve problems and could receive feedback and help in the area of grammatical skills. In retrospect, these programs look primitive. From the students' point of view they still serve a very useful, albeit severely limited, purpose in language learning.

But language learning, instruction, and production are best supplemented or enhanced by multiple dimensions of experience and activity. So far, the multiple dimensions have been provided by experienced instructors who "made the book come to life" or who could produce an instant drill to provide a path to remediate a pronunciation problem. Technology won't replace such instructors – or any other instructors, for that matter – for a long time to come. But today's technology, in the hands of an experienced instructor, is capable of providing access to materials, reference works, and interactive work – in short, "multiple dimensions" – in ways we could only dream of just five years ago. Faster computers, more internal memory, larger storage devices, and faster networks have made all this possible.

Since Dartmouth's model of language instruction is primarily based upon the "Rassias Approach" to language teaching (an approach concentrating on freeing students from inhibitions in oral second language production, developed by John Rassias), any research on the part of Humanities Computing and the Language Resource Center had to begin with a reconsideration of the strengths and weaknesses of this approach and a focus on finding ways to supplement it usefully and efficiently. Our task, in other words, was to make a successful "method" even more successful through the enhancements technology makes possible.

Hypertext/hypermedia approaches seemed most closely to simulate the activities being pursued in language learning. Hypertext/hypermedia goes beyond one-dimensional activities, however useful, to provide the user with the ability to explore multiple dimensions of multi-layered text, reference works, sound, animation, and video in a "user-friendly environment." We do not yet have any precise data on our assumption that users do, in fact, take advantage of these dimensions. Judging by the initial interest in and success of some of our projects, however, we may have discovered a useful approach.

Language workstation project

Bantz and Foelsche, in their original proposal, had provided a futuristic vision of a language workstation based on a combination of interactive video with hypermedia/hypertext concepts in a windowed environment. Their vision specified a workstation environment fully capable of executing a large number of tasks identified in language instruction as essential but not necessarily instructor-dependent. The modular concept was proposed to allow users with smaller machines access via existing networks to various modules in the workstation for specific tasks, tutorials, readings, or reference works. Hypertext/hypermedia capabilities were proposed to provide the highest possible level of integration among texts, reference works, and video at the workstation level. A fully integrated windowed environment providing tools, materials, and activities and allowing free navigation and editing from each area to all other areas has been envisioned.

DR parallel 24.17

The environment was to consist of four parts:
- a tutorial environment
- a reference environment
- a production environment
- an authoring environment

Obviously, such a workstation concept is not limited to language learning, nor can it deny its origins. Judith Frommer's *MacLang* [5] and Stephen Clausing's *Private Tutor* [6] lead the way towards single- and multi-dimensional useful exercises. Brown's *Intermedia* [7] concept demonstrates the usefulness of hypertext, graphics, and reference materials in a single language. It could easily become an integrated part of this station, providing ready-made hypertext environments with the additional support of a large selection of additional multiple language reference works. And it could also very well be used for general-purpose work in all areas of the humanities. Jim Noblitt's *Système D* [8] points the way to painless "on screen" language production. Apple's *HyperTV* [9] and IBM's *InfoWindow* [10] as well as programs like *MacVideo* [11] and *Icon Author* [12] point in the direction of capable interactive video. *MacRecorder* [13] (for the Macintosh) and *Audio F/X* [14] (for the IBM) can provide lowcost digitized sound to be incorporated into the tutorial environment. A few years hence, speech analysis may produce usable feedback to the student. Sophisticated parsing of sentences can providelinguistic feedback on syntactical, morphological, and lexical aspects in conjunction with *all* work performed on the station. Stephen Clausing's *Otfried* program (under development) is a first linguistic tool having the capability of generating all verb forms in Indo-European languages. Apple's proposed operating System 7 will have solved the ever-present keyboard, font, direction, searching, and sorting problems in a multilingual environment of such a workstation. At that point it should be possible to write in Greek, Russian, Hebrew, Chinese, and Arabic on a single line in a single window.

Characteristics of hypertext/hypermedia workstations ⎯⎯⎯⎯⎯⎯

Over the last year, Dartmouth has used very limited funds from the Consortium for Language Teaching and Learning to explore some high priority aspects of the language workstation, in particular hypertext/hypermedia applications in modular concepts. Because of the lack of funding for full-time programmers and the more or less haphazard involvement, at certain points, of faculty members, we proceeded on the assumption that it would be more cost-efficient and productive to explore various well-defined areas than to get involved in a huge programming effort and opted for a piecemeal approach to various functionalities of the language workstation. Apple's *HyperCard* was selected as the development medium because of its flexibility, superior foreign character handling, and ease of use. Care was taken to keep accumulated data in formats that would allow easy transfer at a later date into more sophisticated environments and to other vendors.

The exploration is an ongoing process with successes and failures. Its successes were almost instantly transferred into instruction at Dartmouth College and some other institutions. Our intent is eventually to integrate the modules and create an environment with true hypertext/hypermedia capabilities. The existing and planned modules are described in the following sections.

Text and glossary/dictionary

We recognized "hypertext" as a concept that might possess new potential for developing environments in which texts, dictionaries and reference works were combined. If we could bring a foreign language text onto the screen and simultaneously provide the student with an on-line bilingual dictionary or glossary, we could reduce the well-known drudgery of reading foreign language texts. We could also motivate students to read earlier and tackle more difficult texts, because any unknown word could readily be found. We therefore reduced the concept of hypertext to a combination of text and glossary/dictionary with no direct links, considering this functionality satisfactory for beginning language instruction.

Accustomed as we were to the consistent and intuitive quality of a graphics interface, we felt that the only acceptable solution would be a dual window screen, with one window containing the dictionary and the other containing the text.

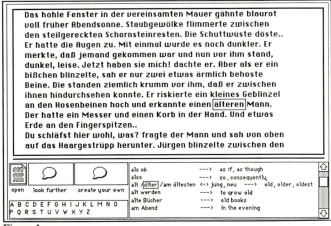

Figure 1.

What we wanted was to make available to students one of the distinctive qualities of hypertext environments, the ability to click on a word and get more information: in this case, the English translation of a German word.

Being pragmatists and also quite naive about relationships between texts and dictionaries, their structures and underlying principles, we managed to run a prototype of our program in March 1988. One major factor that enabled us to get the prototype running was probably that we were not linguists and therefore tended to worry more about speed and functionality than about linguistic appropriateness and possible consequences. Our prototype contained only a few lines of text and a 200-word glossary. For the purpose of demonstrating the functionality, this was entirely sufficient, but for actual student use, it was good for only about 35 seconds of activity.

This prototype generated a fair amount of interest at many conferences in the US and in Europe. But it was apparent to us immediately that much more work was required. Also, when observers started talking about our prototype as a translation program, it became clear to us that that we had to stop referring to our glossary as a dictionary: we needed to make sure that observers understood the glossary not as a translation program but rather as an environment in which one could read text more efficiently than just with a dictionary.

At this point we had to deal seriously with a major problem that arises when text and reference works are connected in a hypertext/hypermedia environment. The issue is that of free links vs. defined links. If we establish a free link, we select a word and search for the word in the dictionary. This is the same procedure which we use when looking up a word in a dictionary. If we establish a defined link, we select a word and build a link to a specific, i.e., text-related glossary. Ideally, of course, both links should be available, the last being the easier to implement.

In our prototype construction we concentrated on the free link and experimented with several primitive versions utilizing a glossary of approximately 5000 German high frequency entries and their 5000 English equivalents. Just as the combination of text, human brain, and printed dictionary produces results in understanding of a foreign language text, so does the combination of text on the screen, mouseclick, and display of several "hits" in the glossary. We designed the program in such a way that all occurrences of the word in the glossary would be displayed over and over again so that the user would definitely see all available equivalents and return, as if she were following a circular path to the first "hit." If the word could not be found, a primitive but extremely effective "strip and search" procedure would remove endings (one at a time) in combination with renewed searches. Inflected adjectives and nouns could almost always be found this way; as long as we included the different stem forms in the glossary, verbs could be found as well. We could also use the glossary to read English texts and find the German equivalents. Obviously, any German or English text can be read with this glossary/dictionary.

By using the human model (and assuming a fast and competent computer), we could parse the sentence in which the word occurs and deal with its syntax, morphology, and lexicology. We then could search the glossary with this additional information (for example: "mauern" is a verb and not a dative plural of a noun). This way the number of possible correct translations will be even smaller. On the other hand, the human brain will still have to make many additional decisions: it will need to decide, for example, whether the text section is idiomatic or general usage. Clicking on the word in the dictionary should bring all other related information about "mauern" to the screen. Once again, we are using the computer's selection tool, the mouseclick, to dig deeper into a hierarchy of data, in true hypertext/hypermedia fashion. Figure 2 shows the result of searching further on the first dictionary entry "Mauer." Figure 2 is a purely experimental function of our existing dictionary.

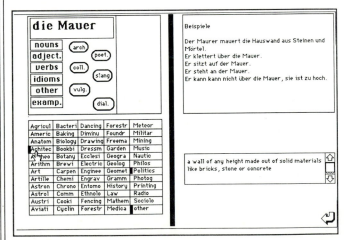

Figure 2.

We have been experimenting with several designs of dictionary interfaces. Users are telling us that 1) the way in which the material in the electronic dictionary is presented is crucial in making it superior to a printed dictionary, and that 2) entry to the dictionary should be by clicking and selecting, never by typing. We are convinced that a superior dictionary interface will evolve in the process of designing the language workstation as a result of computing and AI capabilities.

Eventually, text and dictionary should contain an invisible markup language - something similar to SGML, which would carry general linguistic information with each word and match that information with each word in the dictionary. This would also make it easier to produce "text specific" glossaries, in which users could search first, before continuing the search in a general dictionary. Eventually we would like to see a combination of highly automatic markup languages for processing the text in combination with AI, producing "text specific" glossaries through assemblage from two monolingual dictionaries.

Text, glossary/dictionary, and sound

To make a glossary/dictionary with texts a true hypertext/ hypermedia product which provides the multi-dimensional characteristics explained above, it should be possible to have the individual words in the glossary pronounced and to have the text read aloud to the user. Production of sound is easily achieved on computers of the current generation. Low-quality sound can be produced through speech synthesis, high-quality sound through digitization. Input of sound into applications is normally accomplished through a small electronic device operated like a cassette recorder, while output from an application involves executing a "sound file."

Individual words, phrases, complete texts, and even drama can be recorded, digitized, and integrated into a hypertext/hypermedia environment. Our intent is to let the student select words, phrases, or complete speeches on the computer screen and listen to them as many times as appropriate, while having the full text on the screen and all reference works and linguistic tools at her disposal. Our first implementation provides a simple and direct interface. The student selects the text, clicks on the speaker icon, and can now listen to it.

This capability allows fairly sophisticated instruction in basic reading skills with pictures, text, and sound. Our example in Figure 3 is a very academic one. Hypertext/hypermedia sound features of this type offer amazing perspectives in all areas of instruction. We foresee many applications in special education

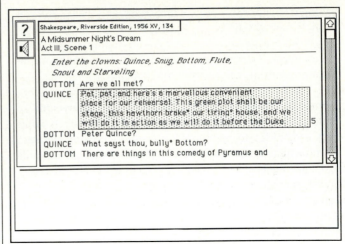

Figure 3.

at the primary and secondary level. We have already seen a broad range of programs, from one designed to supplement basic reading instruction at the kindergarten level by teaching the names and sounds of animals to one for use in higher education to teach the Russian alphabet.

Sound - especially in its high-quality, digitized form - requires very large amounts of memory. Implementations of larger blocks of texts, poetry, or complete drama take up so much memory space that only late-generation storage devices (with high up-front production costs) such as CD's, WORMs, and optical/erasable drives can satisfy the storage requirement. However, recent developments in compression algorithms for sound files seem to indicate that sound files are getting much smaller without losing any quality. Synthesized sound, on the other hand, may be the choice in the future, once quality of output is acceptable to language learners and instructors. At this time (1989), synthesized sound does not fulfill this basic requirement.

Text, glossary/dictionary, sound, and animation

Simple animation can add a tremendous dimension to the language activities described in the preceding paragraphs. Animation in a hypertext/hypermedia environment is the component which brings across those points which cannot be explained in single dimensions as they are in a book. Such language-learning tasks as mastering German prepositions requiring dative or accusative case depending on the direction or "non-direction" of motion or correctly using Chinese verbs concerning dressing and undressing can be made much easier using the computer. Dartmouth College has built two environments which demonstrate the capabilities of this combination. One is called *Mr. Wang* [15] the other *Hanzi Assistant* . *Mr. Wang* (see Figure 4) provides Pinyin, hanzi (Chinese characters), Chinese sound, and animation, in other words, an environment in which students can look around and learn by taking a path through various activities. Clicking on the button "see action" will cause the animation to run: Mr. Wang will take off a piece of clothing. Meanwhile, the learner can hear the sentence describing the animation and can read the Pinyin and the hanzi. Having four dimensions available makes it much easier to master this particularly difficult area in Chinese language instruction.

Figure 4.

The application *Hanzi Assistant* (Figure 5) started out as a collection of flashcards with animation of the brush strokes. Later on, sound, Pinyin, and translation were added. In its present form, the Hanzi Assistant has grown into a true hypermedia reference work providing thousands of simplified and traditional "hanzi," or Chinese characters, with stroke animation, disambiguation of homonyms, and pronunciation by male and female speakers. Hypertext/hypermedia features have been applied here to two entirely different languages - one western, the other non-western.

Searching for the character bin with a specific tone will bring up a list of homonyms (see Figure 6) which can be disambiguated by simply selecting (i.e., clicking on) one of the individual hanzi. The application will then bring the specific character onto the screen as in Figure 5.

Applications containing the integration of several dimensions may, upon first examination, seem dedicated to achieving very limited purposes. In the context of the language workstation, these applications do, indeed, fall into specific slots of the tutorial environment (as is the case with *Mr. Wang*) as well as into the reference environment (as with the *Hanzi Assistant*). Both should become integral parts of the Chinese areas of the language workstation. The level of integration, i.e., the users' capability of picking out one character in *Mr. Wang* and looking up all the information about it in the *Hanzi Assistant*, would make the difference between fairly simple and unsophisticated individual environments and a truly complex hypertext/hypermedia environment allowing a variety of activities with simultaneous access to all other areas.

Animation can basically be produced by flipping through a number of cards with slightly altered images to provide the sensation of movement. Professional tools can automate the process of the production of altered images somewhat. What is needed are extremely flexible and easy-to-learn tools for the production of animation. Since animation can be superior to a video image because of the lack of distracting materials, some thought should be given to the automated alteration (possibly simplification) of video images for the purpose of providing clear and simple animations.

Graphics

One of the first really impressive hypermedia/graphics presentations was the Dartmouth Atlas project. In this project, a student would see a map of Europe on the screen. If she clicked on Spain, the map would change to a map of Spain, filling the whole screen. If she then clicked on southern Spain, a map of southern Spain would appear. This process could be continued all the way down to a courtyard in a Spanish town, with some children playing soccer.

Applications of this type require immense amounts of programming and data input to make them truly useful in the study of geography. In the case of beginning language instruction, the number of layers of graphics can be very small. One layer of graphics connected with text and sound seems to be sufficient to provide the needed functionality of clicking on a visible object, seeing the word in print, and listening to the word. In language instruction the process can be reversed, of course. The student can listen to the word and drill herself either by typing in the word or clicking on it, or on the visible activity satisfies only specific segments of language instruction: listening comprehension, writing, and semiotics.

As the *Hanzi Assistant* is evolving into a truly useful database of Chinese characters, second and third generation versions of this program are being contemplated, allowing the direct connection to Chinese text (very difficult!), dictionary functions, and so on. As time goes on and as development proceeds, the Hanzi Assistant will become part of the Chinese area of the proposed language workstation.

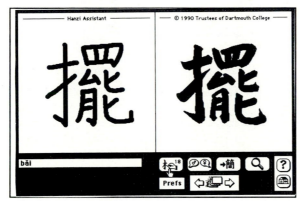

Figure 5.

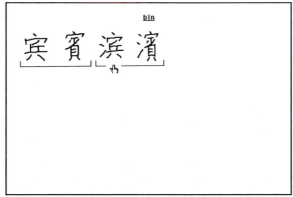

Figure 6.

Hanzi Assistant is also a generic tool which happens to be Chinese. Its modules can be used for the input and display of any other language which provides similar levels of challenge as Chinese: Japanese, Korean, and other non-western languages.

object, or by doing both. At this point we have another activity which truly expands the flat dimension of rigid conventional technologyinto a very technology into a very flexible hypermedia environment. Of course, this type of activity satisfies only specific segments of language instruction: listening comprehension, writing, and semiotics, for example. But as

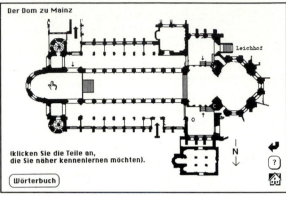

Figure 7

we have pointed out before, this tool, once integrated into the language workstation, will be extremely valuable in connection with other language learning activities.

Dartmouth College has developed a tool [16] which allows opening a color graphics window, clicking on it, and transferring the coordinates of the selected point (or area) into a hypermedia program (in this case, *HyperCard*). Figure 7 shows the layout of the cathedral of Mainz, Germany. Users can click on certain areas and will be provided with additional graphics, texts, and vocabulary.

Transfer routines can now be written that assign specific ranges of "x/y" coordinates to paths within an application. In other words, the problem of the "irregularly shaped hot area" has been solved.

There are no limits to improvements in graphics. Hypertext/ hypermedia should have full-color, high-resolution graphics in a fully interchangeable format for all major operating systems. Input via color scanners, video cameras, or so-called "paint programs" produces a huge variety of different types of files with very different editing capabilities and transfer capabilities into hypertext/hypermedia programs. Storing high resolution color images requires huge amount of space on disk or other media. Using analog pictures from laservision disks may be a compromise for some time; using other media like CD ROM or optical erasable disks is another possible choice. Two clear needs emerge: a standard, and higher compression for color graphics files.

Video

Interactive video is superior to video alone in that the user has the choice of either being controlled by the application or controlling the application herself. She can have video with sound - a euphemism for watching television - or engage in many sophisticated activities involving all dimensions of language learning except (at least for now) direct spoken communication. Interactive video in combination with hypertext/hypermedia is at the center of the proposed language workstation.

The technical issues which the use of interactive video raises are immense: they involve, among other things, the combining of a computer with combined or separate video displays, laser disk players, sound output, keyboard input, possible network connections, standard converters. The financial investment in a station consisting of a computer, two displays, and a laser disk drive is about $5000 at 1989 prices. Overlay capabilities and full color in both displays will drive up the price significantly.

The production issues involved are also immense. Whereas the technical tools are available, the pedagogical materials are almost completely absent. Only the military academies in the US have, in 1989, complete courses in full use on their machines. To my knowledge, there are no complete language courses for this medium being marketed by any publisher worldwide, despite the fact that industry has for some time been using interactive video successfully for training in many areas. Funding problems have made it difficult - even for major institutions - to get involved in the production of materials for purely academic purposes. On the other hand, many institutions are exploring low-cost, specific, and immediately useful applications. In the case of Dartmouth College, exploration of the interactive medium began with supporting the teaching of "culture" in language instruction by making pictorial databases on laservision disks available through a hypermedia interface. David Bantz' group designed Mnemo syne, a sophisticated database allowing "thumbnail" display of images in black and white on the computer screen in conjunction with large screen color NTSC display on a separate monitor.

DJ background 1.5

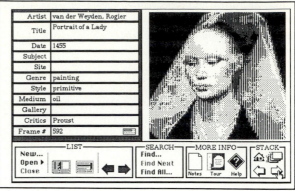

Figure 8.

Mnemosyne allows access to still pictures, guided tour segments with full-motion video and sound, creation of lists, and sophisticated searches by author, title, genre, location, critical reviews, date of creation, and so on. The program is a tool which can be used with any collection of images on any type of disk medium. *Mnemosyne* is currently being used in instruction at Dartmouth College for lectures on 19th century French painting. Figure 8 shows the "thumbnail" b/w image. The next version of the application will have the full color image in this position, and the normally required separate color monitor will be unnecessary.

Applications of this type could drastically change teaching situations in the future, particularly when integrated into the language workstation. One could imagine the language instructor going into a classroom containing a laservision disk and video projection under computer control and calling up specific dialogues, demonstrations of word usage, animations, objects, and so on. One could also imagine the art history professor and his students using a database of approximately 110,000 still images (one complete laservision disk) in this classroom to call up paintings from an obscure or famous artist to stress a point.

Video's success in the future will depend on the solution of the following problems. 1. There is a clear need for suitable materials for integration into instruction. 2. There are major problems regarding copyright for still collections as well as full-motion video collections. 3. "Repurposing" existing useful materials requires skills and a huge investment of time. 4. Production of video is beyond the financial capabilities of almost all but a few industrial training programs.

Integrating video, sound, text, and glossaries / dictionaries into a language workstation

Central to the investigation into the language workstation project is to experiment with interfaces combining texts, reference works, sound, animation, still pictures, and live video, in an integrated environment. We want to accomplish this by combining the functionalities of several of our developed applications. The result, at the moment, is a functioning application which allows us to do almost everything except full motion video on the screen – and even this would be easy to include, if appropriate funding were available.

Our original intention was to design an elegant interface which would allow the user to have access to glossaries and dictionaries in combination with the Shakespeare text. We also wanted the user to be able to select a section of text and ask for the audio part. And, last but not least, we wanted the user to select the same text and request the full motion video. We left out the full motion video in our prototype and replaced it with still pictures.

When dealing with short sections of text, such functioning prototypes are easy to build. With large sections of text, we would have to solve the text mark-up problem. Our next version will deal with larger sections of text and will incorporate a mark-up scheme that will allow us to access plain audio, video, reference works, graphics and, of course, all the other areas of the environment. This would include the capability of running two performances simultaneously on the screen, or displaying two or more texts on the screen with complete access to the accompanying critical apparatus. It would also include the capability for the student to write a paper which could include video excerpts (or grabbed frames) with which she might demonstrate her points. The whole text could be selected and exposed to a rich variety of linguistic tools, from word frequency counts to parsing occurrences of syntactic patterns and possibly even more. Such functions for the serious researcher will also be incorporated in future versions.

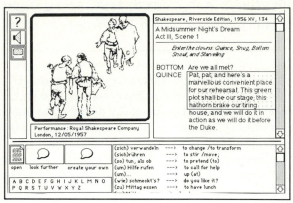

Figure 9.

Hypertext/hypermedia: Summary and a look ahead _____

The area of hypertext/hypermedia in language instruction is truly at a threshold in 1989. To date we have seen much investigation and development, albeit in narrow areas. Some of these investigations have produced immensely useful - but limited - applications, which have made their way into the classroom and into individual students' hands. Hypertext and hypermedia are exciting concepts for any language learner or instructor. They are so exciting that even the very limited availability of completed materials cannot dampen the enthusiasm for this medium.

Technological advances in computing power have made possible the combination of hypertext and and hypermedia. Further advances will make the high integration and the effortless move from hypertext into hypermedia with all their possibilities clearly a reality in the near future. Language instruction needs the high integration of hypertext, hypermedia, and reference works to allow the learner to concentrate on the essential aspects rather than wasting time with poorly organized dictionaries, handouts, and so on.

Decisions on building specific modules in particular languages are based upon input from the academic departments of the three major participants in the Workstation Project. Research and development during the next years will concentrate on the following areas:

•Building applications, interfaces, and tools which can stand-alone as well as serving as integrated modules of the language workstation. This will include transfer of existing "single dimensional" activities from other operating systems as well as the production of new activities. It will also include research in two areas: on the usefulness of mark-up languages like SGML for the purpose of combining sound and video with text and on the advisability of using video servers. Finally, it will include a number of very specific projects designed to satisfy immediate needs in instruction but ultimately destined to be integrated into the language workstation.

•Production of bilingual dictionaries in English/French, English/German, English/Spanish, English/Russian, English/Chinese.
•Production of useful electronic text from all sources - literary, technical, legal, news, etc.
•Production of speaking dictionaries.
•Determination or creation of standards, links, and file structures for text, database, sound, video, and animation.
•Determination of a platform for the optimal language workstation.

References

[1] Pierre Carpretz, Director of the Yale Language Laboratory and author of the Annenberg <u>French in Action</u> series.

[2]John Rassias, "William R. Kenan Professor" of French at Dartmouth College and author of the CBS <u>Contact French</u> series.

[3] Bruce Duncan, Professor of German at Dartmouth College.

[4] James Pusack, Profesor of German at Iowa State University and author of the <u>Dasher/Dancer</u> program.

[5] <u>MacLang</u> -an authoring system for language exercises developed by Judith Frommer at Harvard University.

[6] <u>Private Tutor</u> - an authoring system for language exercises, developed by Stephen Clausing at Yale University.

[7] Intermedia - a UNIX-based hypertext/hypermedia system developed at Project IRIS at Brown University.

[8] Système D - a word processor with access to dictionary, grammatical tables and other functions, developed by James Noblitt, Donald Solá, and Willem Pet at Cornell University.

[9] HyperTV - an experimental hardware/software combination for the purpose of putting full motion video on a Macintosh II screen, first demonstrated at MacWorld 1989 in San Fancisco, developed by Apple Computer.

[10] InfoWindow - an interactive video authoring system based on a hardware/software combination for specially equipped high-end IBM computers, developed by IBM.

[11] MacVideo - an interactive video authoring system for Macintosh systems with two monitors or overlay capabilities, developed by Edudisc, 1400 Tyne Boulevard, Nashville, TN.

[12] IconAuthor - a second generation interactive video authoring system for IBM machines, developed by Amtech Corporation, 77 Northeastern Boulevard, Nashua, NH.

[13] MacRecorder - a sound digitizing system for the Macintosh, developed by Farallon Computing, 2150 Kittredge Street, Berkeley, CA

[14]Audio F/X - a sound digitizing system for the IBM, produced by Forte, 72 Karenlee Dr., Rochester, N.Y.

Chapter 18
Collaboration in Hypermedia Environments

Martin Richartz
Digital Equipment Corp.
Tom D. Rüdebusch
Institute for Telematics
University of Karlsruhe, FRG

Keywords
Collaboration; hypermedia learning; authoring environment

Contents

Introduction ─────────────────

In order to achieve the goal of providing useful expert knowledge for any kind of electronic education or for accessing systems as sources of information, it is necessary to provide collaborative capabilities. The quality of the information stored in the system is dependent on the way all the information contributors can access and share their knowledge.

Traditionally, the process of assembling an encyclopedia or other high-level information source usually involves many people in geographically separate locations. We cannot expect

NATO ASI Series, Vol. F 67
Designing Hypermedia for Learning
Edited by D. H. Jonassen and H. Mandl
© Springer-Verlag Berlin Heidelberg 1990

that this situation will change in electronic environments. Today, knowledge is becoming increasingly complex, so that individuals are no longer able to be an expert in an entire knowledge domain. So collaboration is an essential prerequisite in making knowledge publicly available.

Conceptions of knowledge change as more people become involved as information providers. Therefore, methods of collaboration are needed which guarantee the quality of information, in any information system.

In general, collaboration should bring together people who have complementary skills and knowledge in order to more efficiently assemble information systems. Assembling teams of people increases the available source of information and motivates people to work, because they are interacting socially.

What is collaboration? _____

Collaboration, as we use the term here, takes place between humans only, regardless of whether they interact directly or they interact in an electronically mediated fashion. Collaboration is used in certain kinds of man-machine interactions, as in the Human Interface Tool Suite (1) developed by the MCC in Austin, Texas. There a user interface cooperates with the user in that it gives intelligent advice or help. Based on some rules, it tries to figure out the users actual needs and provides appropriate assistance. We call this type of interaction adaptive assitance rather than collaboration. The term collaboration should remain reserved for human interactions, no matter whether media are involved in the process or not.

Collaboration in an electronic information environment

Electronic environments are especially suitable for collaboration. They provide two major advantages:
- They allow members of a group to collaborate independent of time and space.
- The computer may act as a suitable tool for description, support, and control of collaboration.

DJ definition 1.3

The term information in hypermedia refers to data stored in a HyperInformation environment. The information chunks, like text, video, etc. that typically can be found in Hypermedia systems and also serve as anchors for HyperInformation links. The HyperInformation network built from the links established between the information chunks also constitutes information. Although collaborative capabilities are essential in HyperInformation systems, some systems provide only shared or distributed information bases rather than collaborative mechanisms between users. This is often due to the lack of technical solutions to this problem.

DJ results 2.8

Requirements: Easy to use, naturally embedded

Collaboration is useless if it is cumbersome and time consuming. Therefore, collaboration must be an intrinsic feature of any information environment and natural to use, in addition to the ease of use, which is an obvious requirement. When collaboration is available at all times, the user may not even notice that he or she is using collaborative features in his environment.

DJ explanation 9.7-8

Hence collaboration must not be restricted to dedicated collaboration tools. However, there may be additional tools available which facilitate the organization of collaboration as we will see in the forthcoming scenarios.

Some basic questions

Before we start with the presentation of design ideas for collaboration techniques, a number of questions should be asked.
  •At first glance we may ask: who are the partners in collaboration?
 Apparently there are already conceptions of roles in the instructional process. So we may derive different kinds of collaboration. There may be collaboration between
  •learners (there are various levels of skills among the learners),
  •learners and tutors,
  •learners and authors (feedback may be needed), or
  •authors (instructional experts and domain knowledge experts have to complement their skills).
Generally, we identify roles of information providers and information recipients.

  •How should collaboration be organized?

Is it sufficient to allow fully symmetrical, democratic collaboration, so that there is no longer a distinction between information providers and recipients? Is it necessary to have more sophisticated schemes with particular roles asigned to the participants, such as author, tutor, or learner? If too much protocol is imposed on the group members, does that restrict their informal interactions too severely?

•Is it necessary to distinguish the different roles in collaboration?

The answers may depend on the needs of the educational environment. In a more open environment, as can be found in universities, the boundaries between learners (the students), the authors, and the tutors cannot be clearly set. Therefore it does not make too much sense to distinguish these different types of collaboration. On the other hand, it may be useful to establish certain interaction patterns. Other environments, like primary education or training demand a sharper distinction of these roles. It may not be useful to allow learners, which undergo the instruction for gaining certain skills, to share the role of the authors or the domain experts, because of their lack of domain knowledge.

Scenarios for collaboration in a hyperinformation environment

Three collaborative scenarios with different levels of complexity can be conceived. The simplest allows fully democratic information sharing among the users. A slightly more complex one employs a hierarchical scheme of collaboration and therefore is somewhat restricted in its capabilities. The third scenario is a scheme that allows a much more subtle collaboration pattern inside an information environment. Such capabilities will be found in the NESTOR environment. All the kinds of solutions presented here require distributed access to the information base and thereby have a common technical requirement.

Fully democratic and anarchistic collaboration
This method of collaboration requires discipline of all participants and is suitable for a more or less utopian society of well educated humans. Also, this method seems the easiest to implement. The concurrency control of a distributed HyperInformation system fits all the technical needs of this scenario. This scenario comes close to Ted Nelson's vision of Xanadu [4]. Currently this scheme does not meet the needs of many commercial and public users, who do not want to rely on such a utopian society. Therefore this scenario is not considered further here.

Hierarchical approach to collaborative work

A hierarchical access scheme to the information base in not overly complex. In this approach various levels of information can be established which are superimposed from a user's point of view. At the lowest level there is the user's private information space. Transparently the user can also access the next higher information space level, the group information space. This continues until the root information space, which is the only information space global to all users, is found. The user transparently can access all information from all superimposed information spaces, but may be restricted in adding or modifying information in other than his or her own information space.

DJ parallel 11.2

If the user enters information, it is entered at a level specified by the user, by default this is the user's private information space.

If the new information shall be shared by the group, the information has to be entered into the group space. The user or a higher level instance may initiate information propagation from the private information space to a higher level information space. Here security aspects are involved. It may be desirable to prevent group members from altering the group or higher level information spaces, since this may override information from hierarchically higher information levels. But at least, the group members should be able to share their information in a direct, person-to-person manner. So, the capability to share information explicitly among group members or to 'mail' information from an individual information space to another is desired.

Although this approach will satisfy many needs, it lacks more 'intelligent' collaboration schemes. Here, only the roles of an information author/provider and a recipient are implemented. Only people in a provider role can make information shareable to other people, apart from individual information exchange mechanisms among partners, which may exist.

On the other hand, this method of "superposition" of information spaces might be very helpful in a more advanced collaboration scheme and might be integrated there.

Group collaboration by defining roles and tasks

In sophisticated learning and authoring environments the ability to establish more sophisticated collaboration policies is needed. Patterns of interactions have to be established which define in more detail the individual roles of the collaborating partners.

Such an approach is going to be implemented in the emerging NESTOR environment. However, these ideas are influenced by other research contributions [5]. Whether authoring, group learning or completing other tasks, NESTOR allows group structures and task structures to be established.

Group Structure. The group structure describes the overall interaction scheme to be applied in group communication. Schemes may range from a fully democratic group interaction which is required, for example, in brainstorming sessions, to strictly hierarchical schemes where individual responsibilities or roles are assigned to the different group members. Such hierarchical structures may be needed in an authoring process, where the planning and organizational responsibilities are assigned to a project leader.

It is necessary to have the capability to change the group structure dynamically, for example when a brainstorming session is needed in a project with assigned responsibilities.

Task Structures. The task structure allows the breakdown of the work into smaller units. Here quesitons may be answered like: How can a project be divided into subtasks, which later can be assigned to particular group members (in the group structure)? Information anchors for the subtasks may be specified as well as interaction points (e.g. with the project leader) and timelines. Other questions include: Can the subtasks be accomplished independently by different people, or do they have to work simultaneously on the same information? The granularity of interaction also has to be defined. Are the members collaborating at a very low level, so that they see the same information as their partners at the keyboard level, or does communication take place by exchanging messages that describe performed operations using electronic mail?

Finally, the relationship of the task structure to the group structure is to be established which specifies who is going to work on which (sub-) task and who is assigned which role. In a next step, who has to communicate with whom will be determined, along with which interaction points and timelines need to be monitored by the environment.

For the administration of group work, additional tools are needed like role editors, voting-tools, group and task editors, authorization, and registration tools.

Conclusion ─────────────────────────

Forthcoming HyperMedia environments have to offer sophisticated collaboration capabilities. Complex collaboration schemes must be available. As traditional systems offer little collaboration support, a lot of work has to be done until we can offer the capabilities described above.

Issues in human interfaces, communication and data storage have to be solved in order to overcome the shortcomings of today's existing information environments. These will be the subject of further research.

References ─────────────────────────

[1] Hollan, James et. al. (1988). *An Introduction to HITS: Human Interface Tool Suite*. MCC Technical Report No. ACA-HI-406-88.

[2] Yoder, E., Akscyn, R., McCracken, D. (1989). Collaboration in KMS, A Shared HyperMedia System. *CHI '89 Proceedings*.

[3] Mühlhäuser, M. *Hyperinformation Requirements for an Integrated Authoring/Learning Environment*. (This volume).

[4] Nelson, T. (1974). Dream Machines: New Freedoms through Computer Screens — A Mintority Report. *Computer-Lib: You Can and Must Understand Computers Now*. Chicago, IL: Hugo's Book Service.

[5] Winograd, T., and Flores, F. (Eds.) (1986). *Understanding Computers and Cognition: A New Foundation for Design*. Norwood, NJ: Ablex.

PART V

HYPERMEDIA DESIGN PROCESS

Chapter 19
The Hypertext/Hypermedia Solution—
But What Exactly is the Problem?

Alexander J. Romiszowski,
Syracuse University, USA

Keywords
Learning theory; educational technology; instructional systems

Contents

Learning, instruction and hypertext

Learning: Product and processes
We have come a long way in the last thirty or so years, from the general acceptance of the behaviorist definition of learning as a "specific change in behavior or capacity to behave", to cognitivist formulations that lay stress on the aquisition and internal organization of knowledge in the learner's mind. Recently, the development of schema theory has put particular stress on the internal organization of knowledge. Learning

AR explanation 4.5

is seen "as a process of change in the way that the individual views something, rather than the mere aggregation of facts," as Peter Whalley states in his chapter.

One should observe, however, that formulations such as Whalley's are still statements of the *outcomes*, or *products* of learning, rather than of the process itself. Such outcome statements are essential if we are serious about assessing the effectiveness of a given learning process. If we happen to wish to promote certain outcomes in preference to others in our educational system, then the outcome statements we formulate are our goals or objectives. They may no longer be specified in terms of observable behaviors. They may be stated with greater or lesser degrees of specificity. But they are nevertheless our objectives and in most real life projects that hope to succeed, it is a good idea to specify them up front with as much accuracy as is possible.

Much of the literature on the rationale for hypertext, however, seems to be based on a *process* definition of learning. Hypertext is "a good thing" because it "gives autonomy to the learner" to browse at will, or it encourages "informal, personalized, content-oriented information-seeking strategies" [1]. Other writers stress the supposed analogy between flitting from one node to another and the non-linear associative process of creative thinking [2,3] and suggest that hypertext enables learners to extend their intellects by using the "computer to collect, explore, and organize information just as you do in your mind" [4]. This process oriented philosophy, which seems independent of the specific goals or objectives of the learning activity, is seen by many authors to place hypertext

PD parallel 8.5

systems at a point diametrically opposed to CAL systems in a schema of educational applications of the computer.

There is, however, some doubt as to whether all these process oriented aspects of hypertext systems are necessarily "a good thing" in all manner of learning situations. The research on learner control of the learning process is, to say the least,

RK parallel 1.14
PWr comment Important point
DJ explanation 1.13

mixed. There is much evidence to suggest that learners, when free to select their own learning strategies, do not always select wisely (though there is also evidence, such as the classic experiment of Pask and Scott, [5] that under correctly planned conditions learners can identify and select optimal learning strategies).

The idea that a hypertext document is some sort of analogy for the semantic networks that supposedly exist in our minds is also rather shaky. Peter Whalley, in his chapter, makes the point that the rather simple webs of relatively large chunks of information, typical of most hypertexts, are something quite different from the much more complex, fine grained and contextually significant semantic networks of individual knowledge structures. Ray McAleese shows that by limiting node size to single-concept labels and by defining the types of links that connect one node to others in the network, one can represent a body of knowledge as an extremely fine-grained network. But does such representation help a reader to learn the topic quicker and better than linear text, or less fine-grained hypertext would? Or is such a network mainly helping the analysis of the topic in order to then author a more adequate (more chunked) message?

AR corroboration 4.3, contrast 6.14, DJ corroboration 4.3

Hypertext and learning

One might also make some observations on the relationship of hypertext to CAL. Helmut Niegemann sees in hypertext a way of closing "the wide gap between CBT and the single-student, single-teacher situation" by allowing the student "at least a limited possibility to ask questions of the system", by clicking on unfamiliar terms or unclear examples and accessing further levels of detailed explanation. This embedded "help system" is rather like the "resident hypertext program" described by Weidenfeld and Bruillard. Whereas this is quite an enhancement and can lead to the design of rather "lean" mainstream CBT sequences with most background and prerequisite information hidden from view until called up by the individual, it is hardly a new idea, being a common strategy in some forms of programmed instruction of the 60's (e,g, adjunct programs and the information mapping methodology). This form of application would best be classified as a structured information retrieval system backing up an existing instructional system.

Learning will be enhanced for specific learners insofar as they find in the hypertext the specific information that they are in need of and, furthermore, if that information is so presented that they find it understandable and relevant to their needs. These factors are aspects of the authoring of useful information resources designed for a heterogeneous user clientele, a topic we shall return to later in this chapter. The point to make at this time, is that we only know whether the information resources we have authored are in fact adequate, when some

RK example 3.3

effort is made to assess the outcomes of the reading/reference process in terms of the associated instructional system's learning objectives.

The views expressed by Terry Mayes et al are somewhat different. They make the point that, in bypassing all the prescriptive aspects of CAI and ICAI and handing almost all decision making to the learner, hypertext systems "are rightly called *learning systems*, rather than *teaching systems*". They continue, however, by arguing that there is an *instructional* theory or approach embedded in hypertext systems in that they "provide an environment in which *exploratory* or *discovery* learning may flourish". The juxtaposition of all the highlighted terms in one short paragraph may seem to introduce a number of other contrasts, while trying to make sense of the contrast between hypertext and CAI. Which, if any, of these terms are synonyms? Alternatively, what are the fine-grain differences between teaching and instruction, or between exploration and discovery? Mayes et. al. do not define all these terms explicitly, though the meaning they ascribe to some of them may be deduced from the rest of their text. Some reflection will, I hope, show that the clear definition of this terminology is more than a pedantic academic exercise.

AR definition 13.3

The use of the term *discovery learning* brings to mind yet another process oriented issue that has been with us for many decades. The controversy between the supporters of reception-learning (with David Ausubel as their guru) and the proponents of discovery-learning (e.g. Jerome Bruner and his followers) is well documented. However, many who use the term discovery-learning, apply it to any situation where students have to find something out for themselves. As a young boy, I was given a slide-rule with the words "I'm not going to teach you how to use it. Go and discover for yourself". So I asked an older schoolboy to show me. I remember it took quite some searching (exploration of my environment) to locate a student both knowledgeable and willing to show me. However I did finally "discover" such a student, but I did not "discover" how to use the slide rule. Similarly, users of hypertext systems "explore" the network till they "discover" a node that is of interest to them, but they do not discover the content that is stored in that node. We all learn the content of what we read through reception-learning.

RK parallel 12.11

There may be some educational value in the process of exploring a hypertext document, rather than reading a linear text, but the exploration does not guarantee discovery. Where discovery-learning, in the true meaning of the term, may occur is in the connections with previous experience and learning that may be made by the learners for themselves. Mayes et. al. are quite aware of this distinction. Indeed they make a point of quoting some disappointing learning results from the Intermedia system at Brown University, when used "passively rather than actively". This leads them to postulate that the appropriate *instructional* use of hypertext is for learners to *create* links for themselves, "making their own connections and integrations at the conceptual level".

AR results 13.3

Hypertext and instruction

So far,we have two distinct suggestions for the use of hypertext (or hypermedia) systems, as components of instructional systems. One is as information reference/retrieval systems to back up an instructional system (I would extend this to include not only hypertext backup to a "lean" CAI system, but also hypertext backup to any instructional system, whether computer-based or not). The other is as a system that facilitates and encourages learners to "discover" connections between ideas - some presented by the system and some generated by the learners themselves - and to "create" a structure of nodes and links that represents the conceptual structure they have discovered.

The question remains whether the structure that has been discovered and modelled is in fact admissible, or whether it contains conceptual errors or inconsistencies. Also one may ask whether the structure is a useful "tool to think with" or whether another way of viewing and organizing the knowledge structure may be more powerful. Only if such questions are addressed, criteria for judgement are defined and a process for evaluating the outcomes of the process is developed and used, are we, in my opinion, justified in considering such systems as instructional systems.

This last point serves to illustrate my own <u>definition of instruction, as a goal-oriented teaching process that is based on pre-planning and formative evaluation.</u>

AR implication 12.7

Not all teaching processes satisfy these three criteria. However, the absence of some or all of them does not necessarily invalidate the activity from an educational standpoint. A visit to the Louvre may not satisfy any of them to any great degree, yet may still be defended as educationally valuable. A surrogate visit, in a hypermedia environment, opens the experience to a much larger audience than could visit the real museum and may be similarly valuable if the simulated environment is a well designed replica and the user interface is troublefree. However, all this production planning may have given little thought to the specific learning goals expected, less still to the activities and information essential to the achievement of specific goals and none at all to the formative evaluation and revision of the system against specific learning goals. Giving students a reading list on a subject, with little study guidance and asking them to research the readings and form an opinion on the subject for later presentation at a seminar discussion, is an often practiced and strongly defended methodology, but is not instruction in the strict sense. Presenting the readings as a large database in a hypertext environment, may do much to facilitate the students' research task, cut time, increase the number of items of information accessed and presented,etc. But that alone does not make the exercise a better example of instruction.

However, both these cases could be transformed into examples of instructional systems by attention to the three criteria outlined earlier. Doing so would tend to ensure that certain specific learning goals are achieved. Not doing so, does not stop *some* learning from occurring, as Mayes et. al. point out in their distinction between *implicit* and *explicit* learning. Browsing hypertext systems, even when not related to specific learning goals, may result in a considerable amount of implicit learning. However, making this explicit, by means of some key questions up front to focus the search has been shown to not only increase the learning related to those key points and to reduce search time, but also to reduce navigation problems and increase levels of satisfaction with the system [6].

AR explanation 13.2
DJ explanation 13.3

Yet another application of hypertext systems in education, which is undoubtedly of value, but does not of itself satisfy the criteria for instruction, is the collaborative authoring of a document. Here, there may be no specific *learning* objectives set *by* or *for* the participating co-authors (though there are other types of objectives, related to the purpose of the document being authored and much incidental, implicit learning takes place through the sharing of ideas). Once again, it is possible to set learning goals for such an exercise and somehow to evaluate them by observing and analyzing the products of the collaborative work and also the collaboration process itself. This is the approach which is advocated by Duffy and Knuth in their description of the proposed Indiana University - AT&T Enriched Learning Environment. To the extent that this project uses a hypermedia collaborative authoring environ-

RK explanation 12.14
AR explanation 12.17-18

ment as a component of an educational program with explicit goals and a process of measurement and evaluation of results against these goals, it satisfies the conditions of an instructional system.

Hypertext as tool, tutor, and tutee

The various educational applications of hypertext and hypermedia systems outlined in the previous section are not unlike the examples quoted by other authors in this book. The scope of the examples is indeed quite similar to the four-category classification described by Duffy and Knuth. The emphasis here, however, has been to examine the applications with respect to whether they classify as instructional systems in their own right, as components of instructional systems, or as purely informational systems with no serious instructional pretensions. The outcome of this analysis suggests that hypertext systems, on their own, are never instructional systems in the full sense of this term, but are *informational* systems, designed to make information easy to retrieve, or to create, as networks of interconnected "documents". They can, however, be *components* of instructional systems, if designed to foster the achievement of specified learning goals, supported by the neccessary suplementary components (that define the goals, give practice that leads towards them and provide appropriate ways of measuring their achievement) and evaluated to assess how well they are achieving their goals.

It may be helpful, in this context, to borrow the classification first used by Taylor [7] in relation to the use of computers in education. He referred to the computer as *tool* (e.g. word processor), as *tutor* (e.g. CAI) and as *tutee*. This last category included tasks which the student undertook to program the computer (i.e. to teach it something) with the express purpose of learning something generalizable on the way (e.g. the powerful ideas that children are supposed to develop as a byproduct of using LOGO). I extended this classification into the area of intelligent and knowledge based systems , the "tool" class being exemplified by the use of expert advice systems as job-performance aids, the "tutor" class by ICAI systems and the "tutee" class by the use of projects that teach or reinforce the knowledge of a given domain by the construction of knowledge bases and simple expert systems capable of solving problems in the domain [8].

In the context of hypertext and hypermedia systems, the same classification system can be of value. The "tool" use is exemplified by the most common application of hypertext - its use

AR explanation 12.3-4

as an informational system for research and reference. As in the case of the other *tool* uses mentioned, this is not intrinsically instructional, but some implicit learning can be expected to occur through contact with the tool and the information stored in it.

SH parallel 23.22

At the other extreme, the *tutee* use is exemplified by using an empty hypertext *shell* to create, either individually or in a collaborative group exercise, a structured network of information on a domain, or to debate between each other multiple perspectives and viewpoints on a complex issue. Once more, just engaging in such an exercise is not explicitly instructional, though undoubtedly even more implicit learning will occur as a result of the dynamics of the process.

In the middle ground, we have the use of hypertext as *tutor*. As mentioned before, a hypertext or hypermedia system quite on its own, with total user control and no guidance or feedback, is not an instructional system, just like educational television programs, on their own, are not complete instructional systems. The informational system must be supplemented by:

- •systems that guide the learner towards the goals (whether the system or the learner selects the goals , the system must be able to provide guidance on how to reach them);
- •systems that provide appropriate practice to develop the skills and knowledge necessary to achieve the goals;
- •systems that can monitor, measure and evaluate progress towards the goals and, when it proves to be necessary can take or recommend remedial actions in order to reduce the gap between goal and reality.

Any of the different classes of hypertext applications can, in principle, be incorporated into instructional systems. The supplementary components listed above, may or may not be computer-based. As earlier examples suggest, transforming a *tool* hypertext database into an instructional system may sometimes be readily done by linking it to a CAI sequence. This approach makes sense in applications where the use of CAI makes sense. We can extend the range of theoretically possible applications by considering the linking of intelligent (or quasi-intelligent) tutoring systems to more complex, conceptually difficult databases. Such approaches are not all that new. Pask's CASTE system, that dates back over thirty years, has just such a configuration [9]. With the limitations of current developments in the field of ICAI however, it is reasonable to expect many systems for some time into the future to be "multi-media" with one of the essential monitoring, evaluation and remediation media being the teacher or professor.

In the case of the incorporation of hypertext shells in the *tutee* mode, for student collaboration on goal-directed learning projects, it is even more probable that the medium for monitoring and evaluating the process will be the professor or teacher. Indeed, in some areas of subject matter, the collaborative authoring effort may be so open ended and the evaluation process so much based on value judgements, empathy and feeling for the "spirit of the intent behind the letter of the message", that computer based methods may never become applicable. We may reach the limits of computability before we reach the limits of teachers' versatility as a monitoring and evaluation device in creative authoring tasks. Be that as it may, let us now turn to considering some aspects of the design of instructional systems that might employ hypertext systems as components.

Instructional systems design: Four levels —

Hypertext/hypermedia as a philosophy

The Instructional Systems Design and Development process may be viewed, in systems terms, as ocurring at several levels or degrees of resolution. Many authors refer to *macro* and *micro* aspects of the ISD process. The former is typically characterized as overall course or program design, curriculum development, etc. The latter is more concerned with the design of individual lessons or groups of related lessons, media and materials that are required to operationalize the lessons. These categories are still quite ambiguous, each containing sub-levels of detail. I have found it more helpful to visualize the process as ocurring at four easily distinguishable levels [10]:

Level 1. The overall supra- system, or client system that the instructional system will serve. This may be society, a specific corporate client organization, a conglomeration of vested interests, or all of these.

Level 2. The overall instructional system, typically a course, a program, or maybe a complex of interrelated programs and projects. The outcome of this level of design is a course outline or curriculum sufficiently detailed to define the major parameters of the instructional system.

Level 3. The instructional system components, or subsystems, typically lesson plans, exercise plans, progress tests, remediation plans, etc.

Level 4. The materials that have to be produced to implement the course and lesson plans. This is the level at which special media characteristics may have to be taken into consideration, message design details are defined, etc.

Any form of instructional design and development activity may be looked at in terms of these four levels of decision making. In the case of hypertext - based systems, in particular, it may help to identify some key points. We start at Level 1.

At the supra-system level, we generally see some strong pressures in play which facilitate or hinder the adoption of certain types of solution. The sources of these pressures may be theoretical, philosophical, political, religious, social, economic or a combination. Rarely are they predominantly technical "bottom-up" considerations. The decision to set up the Open University in Britain was driven largely by political (socialist policy) considerations. The overall media mix was dictated by economics and government control over certain mass channels of communication. The printed materials production and distribution system was dictated mainly on the grounds of convenience and vested interest (though the actual decision was later seen to play a vital role in the success and, indeed, survival of the Open University).

In the case of hypertext systems, we can see similar high level considerations as possible factors in favor of their adoption on a large scale. There are the philosophical positions of the founders of the movement. Both Vannavar Bush [2] and Theodor Nelson [11,12] have promoted the concept of extremely large interactive databases , linking many users in "literary communities". This is the concept that drives much of the popular support for hypertext-like environments -"if knowledge is power, then the more knowledge at our fingertips (at the click of a mouse), the more powerful and successful will be the society and the individuals who live there." In 1982, Roy Jenkins, at that time Minister of Education in Great Britain, wrote a preface to that year's issue of the World

Yearbook of Education (devoted to the subject of computers in education) in which he looked forward to the not-too-distant future when "the content of all the word's great libraries will pour through every living room in the land" [13]. I remember when I first read that phrase, it immediately conjured up the picture of the next day's newspaper headlines - "Information floods throughout the land. Millions drowned".

Apart from philosophical and political forces, there are possibly strong economic incentives for pursuing the promises of the proponents of large hypertext systems. It is said that the paper that is generated to support a modern jet fighter runs to over a million pages, and that information in these various manuals typically gets repeated on different pages between three and five times. Will hypertext reduce the volume of information to be authored by such a factor, as well as making it easier to access, to cross-refer and to update?

There are also the vested business interests, such as the "Education Utility" pressure group in the USA, currently (but probably temporarily) dormant due to lack of funds, which would make all educational materials available to all educational institutions via one large electronic network on a pay-as-you-use basis.

Then there are the believers in hypertext as an extension of the human brain, a belief promoted by much of the field's advertizing "hype". Will social and possibly even neo religious forces come into play (e.g. the new age movement, the left/right brain freaks, etc.) On the other hand there are real technical and financial limitations on what can really be achieve. And of course, there are the disbelievers, the late adopters, the gatekeepers, each of whom may have a myriad reasons to resist hypertext like they resist any innovation that changes the status quo, seems to threaten teachers' jobs, or looks like it might make for extra work.

Such factors and pressures form the backdrop to educational hypertext research, design and development. Although they may easily be evaluated and discounted or taken into consideration (as the case may be), they often do end up leading the research and development effort into directions which are not necessarily that fruitful. Most seriously, the excessive "hype" serves to get a bandwagon rolling so that soon everybody who is anybody is working with hypertext. It quickly becomes difficult to distinguish good hypertext from "cheap imitations". The imitations get the whole movement a bad name. The bandwagon grinds to a halt. Funding dries up. Another bright and promising technological innovation bites the dust. We have seen this all to often, with other educational innovations, such as instructional television and programmed learning.

RK parallel 4.2

Such supra-system considerations are of less concern to the scientist, researching the feasibility of new systems and new applications. But for the technologist, working on the solution of real world problems, these real-world pressures are of the utmost importance. Little has been said on these matters at this (scientific) conference. But they should be carefully considered by those who plan to use hypertext systems on a large scale.

The macro-design of hypertext systems

Products and approach of level 2. If the first level of decision making with respect to the design of instructional systems is principally driven by politics, philosophy, economics or emotion, the second level can be best characterized as the overall systems design, or strategic planning level. The products of this strategic planning stage are a full system specification, typically including

- specific goals or objectives derived from task,
- content and user population analyses,
- specification of the limitations of instruction as a solution to the problem together with suggestions of other complementary non-instructional actions that may be necessary,
- specification of the instructional sequence, structure, methods and media (this is where hypertext may appear if appropriate),
- necessary materials and equipment (including perhaps a specification of the hypertext workstation),
- estimates of time and costs (development and operational),
- implementation plans, evaluation plans, etc.

DJ comment It is not clear how constant or dissonant hypermedia design is from (ISD). See Jonassen, D.H. (in press). Hypertext and instructional design. *Educational Technology: Research and Development.*

Typically, instructional systems design (ISD) models, employ some form of *systems approach* to derive, by means of an iterative process, an optimal solution to the problem or opportunity that is being addressed. Actual design and development are preceded by analysis of the problem and its context and are followed (or accompanied) by tryout and evaluation, which may lead to further analysis, design and development cycles.

New product design and development does not necessarily
follow the same cycle. In particular, the analysis stage is
typically limited to assessing the market for the particular
product in mind, rather than analyzing the need for such a
product and the adequacy of other already existing products.
Once the product appears, independent researchers, as well as
some with vested marketing interests, get a program of
product field-testing under way. The research question is
"what can one do with this product". The process is often
characterized as "solutions in search of a problem".

GM comment Importantpoint.

The key focus of the conference. The focus outlined in the
last paragraph is in fact a very natural and necessary stage in
the development and dissemination process of a new product
or technique. Hypertext, although not a new idea, has only
recently become widely accessible due to the appearance of
PC based authoring environments and is therefore currently
going through such a dissemination stage. It is not surprising
that many of the chapters and much of the discussion at this
conference focussed more on the products than on the problems being addressed. There are some chapters which are
problem-centred, as for example Whalley's short but provoca-
tive paper, or the longer and more ISD flavored paper of
Duffy and Knuth. The majority of the chapters and especially
the discussions, however, focussed on the products and systems and what they were good for. Figure 1 presents a list of
the twelve most discussed aspects of hypertext systems design
and utilization strategy, each aspect illustrated by some examples laid out on a "dimension" that would appear to be
significant for the systems planner.

The twelve aspects listed in Figure 1 are not presented here as
an ideal or proposed model for the strategic planning of
hypertext systems. Other items could be added to the list.
These twelve are however the ones most frequently addressed
and most hotly discussed at this conference. Each of the
systems presented can be described by drawing its profile in
terms of where it lies on each of the twelve dimensions.

The first three dimensions are in fact to some extent problem-
centered, in that they address, respectively, the overall purpose
or goals of the system in question, the type of content to be
stored (and who will do the storing) and the characteristics
and range of potential users. These are similar to the three
dimensions for the classification of hypertext systems sug-

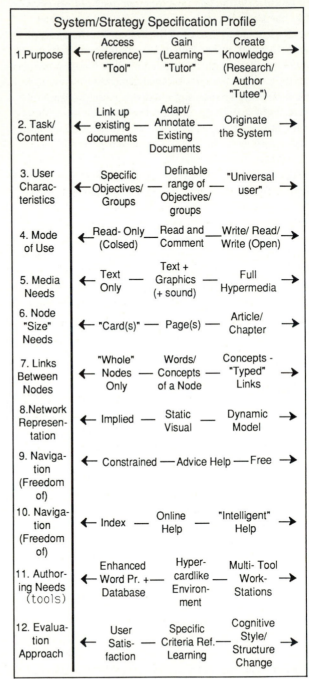

Figure 1.

gested by Halasz (1988) (see also the discussion in the chapter of Verreck and Lkoundi). They are also analogous to the three *classical* foci of initial analysis in the ISD process: Task, Content and Target Population. Note that *purpose* in Figure 1 is analogous to the *job* or *task* to be performed as an *outcome* of learning (the *objective* of learning) and *task/content* refers to what is to be stored in the system and what users do with this content during the *process* of learning. We may see therefore the same potential weakness in this as exists in the *classical* ISD model, which in effect tacitly assumes that instruction in job/task related content is indeeed necessary. Only recently has there been a shift in ISD towards the questioning of this tacit assumption, evidenced by the increasing practice of *Front-end Analysis* (at the front end of the project) to make absolutely sure that instruction is the most appropriate and only viable solution to the problem, need or opportunity that gave birth to the project in the first place. We might learn from this to consider whether some analogous "front-end" process of analysis should not be applied to question, in specific practical cases, whether hypertext /hypermedia is the appropriate solution for the underlying educational problem that is being addressed. This questioning really throws us back to examine the hidden assumptions and the pressures and preconceived solutions that are driving the project.

Some limitations of the focus. One pre-conceived mind-set, very apparent at the conference, was that in education hypertext is of particular use in creative, open-ended learning situations that aim to develop an understanding of the structure of a domain of knowledge. In fact, there is to date little research upon which to base this view. Research is sorely needed. There are, after all, other competitors with a similar claim: simulations and case studies for example. The time and cost factors of free browsing through a vast database, or collaborative authoring of a term paper, as opposed to standard texts with a study guide and advance organizer, have not been addressed. Peter Whalley was heard questioning whether the author's style in a well written conventional text might not better communicate the structure of a subject and lead to more and richer associative links being formed by the reader, than a non-linear hypertext version, but he was largely alone.

Also, little reference was made to the growing literature on the communication of structure by explicitly presenting concept maps, structural diagrams, computer generated graphics and the like. In defense of expository instruction for meaningful

WV explanation 15.2   19.15
AR definition 15.2

AR explanation 4.4

understanding, (even of structurally complex subject matter), there has been a marked swing in popularity towards discovery learning, experiential methods and learner control, which has not been accompanied by an associated research base that proves unequivocally that the swing is in the right direction. Perhaps Ausubel is right more often than we like to admit?

A related belief is that hypertext is less relevant to learning of basic concepts, facts, procedures and other routine subject matter. This would seem to be the domain of direct instruction, programmed instruction or the more conventional forms of CAI. Some have argued that one important use of hypertext systems may be as an adjunct to CAI in professional training situations, so that background and prerequisite knowledge may be available to those who require it, without cluttering up the main instructional sequence. Some contributors do admit, almost grudgingly, that it is probably true that a large proportion of real life applications of hypertext will be as closed systems, presenting a preplanned and prestructured knowledge base to a predefined user group for a predefined purpose. The case of aircraft documentation, mentioned earlier, may be a typical example.

Such applications may well outnumber the open, collaborative and learner-controlled types of applications that were so well represented at the conference. Depending on how one conceptualizes "hypertext", it is probable that at this time, such closed systems for reference and training are today many times more common than the open variety. It is certainly so if one includes in one's concept all the paper-based learning and reference systems (that nevertheless exhibit all the structural features of hypertext) that have been developed according to the Information Mapping™ methodology for the authoring of structured technical and training manuals. Back in the 1960's, when Theodor Nelson was developing the first open, collaborative systems, Robert Horn was developing a system for the authoring of non-linearly accessible manuals that could at one and the same time serve as learning or reference resources [14,15,16,17].

Whereas open, collaborative hypertext systems have been slow to catch on (principally no doubt because they really require a computer based system to work and relatively cheap systems have only recently become available), the Information Mapping ™ system was very rapidly adopted by many organizations, in many cases as the standard methodology for all

AR contrast 8.5

AR contrast 8.5, 3.4

technical writing and training manual development. Since the early 1970's, Horn has operated a company that produces such systems for clients (some 30 to 40 full time writers are employed) and has run regular training workshops which licence the participating organizations (somewhat like a franchise or software license) to use the patented course planning and materials authoring methods he has developed (hence the ™ for trade mark). I would estimate that many thousand such mapped information systems are in current use, mainly in the corporate training field. Most of these are paper based systems, though an increasing number are now being implemented on computers (the method was originally developed to be suitable for both paper and computer based implementation).

19.17

Why do these systems deserve to be considered here? Are they a form of hypertext/hypermedia? The presentation unit in this system is the *map*, which contains all relevant information on one topic within the domain. A topic is very discrete and well defined, being a single concept, a specific procedure, a principle, or a set of related facts. The information presented on such a unitary topic is itself sub- classified as to function and each type of information is set out in the map as a seperate paragraph, or *block* with a margin label defining the type of information. A complete taxonomy of essential and permissible information types for each topic type has been developed as a guide for authors. Thus the blocks in a map are like nodes in a very detailed network of information on a single topic, the links (margin labels) being in effect *typed*, as is now common in semantic networks. The maps (typically one or two pages of text only) are themselves interrelated by a *local index* printed on each map, giving pointers to all other maps with related information. Thus the the maps are the nodes of a less fine-grain network, that represents the author's schema of the domain of knowledge being communicated. Non-linear access is encouraged at two levels - the maps in the knowledge base and the blocks in a given map.

AR contrast 5.10

I have given quite a detailed description here of the Information Mapping ™ methodology, partly because its almost total omission from the papers presented at the conference illustrates the bias towards certain types of applications and certain types of delivery systems, that I mentioned earlier. Another reason is to illustrate that there is more of a theory base and research base for the design of hypertext systems than was perhaps implied by the papers and deliberations of the confer-

DJ comment I have conducted research where Information Mapping resulted in superior access times and accuracy.

JL corroboration 15.3,
example 13.14

DJ comment Like hypertext,
Horn has found that Information
mapping works best for very large
data bases of information.

AR explanation 7.4

ence. The principles and procedures of the Information Mapping ™ methodology are firmly based on learning theory and instructional design principles, albeit rather eclectically extracted from a range of theories and models. However, a very coherent and comprehensive set of authoring rules are the result [16]. The methodology has been subjected to formal research, not only in technical procedure training contexts, but also in academic content areas such as mathematics [18]. The many thousands of practical development projects executed over the years have themselves generated a <u>hypertext</u> database of several thousand maps about aspects of the mapping process, which are on file at Robert Horn's firm. These document successes and failures of different types of application of the approach, indicate factors for and against its adoption for specific types of content, etc. Experimental applications have been attempted across a range of improbable projects, including for example the documentation of the proceedings of a philosophically oriented conference [19], a task not unlike the one we are attempting in this book.

Completing the level 2 design schema. Where have we got to in our understanding of the factors that influence the design of hypertext systems? Having looked at the list of key points that drove the conference discussion (see Figure 1) and having examined some of the key aspects of the ISD process, it may be time to restructure/ network/schematize our point of view somewhat. Figure 2 presents a linked network of system or strategy design factors, created from the twelve key issues previously introduced. The links in this network are partly ones that are referred to in some of the conference papers and partly common sense.   They indicate only the principal interactions that exist between the twelve factors.

We might think of Figure 2 as a dynamic network rather like those discussed by Kommers in his chapter. A number of comments can immediately be made.

First, this is truly a network, or "entailment mesh" and not a flowchart of sorts. It is true that the numbers given to the nodes are in roughly numerical order from top-down, and this corresponds to the nominal sequence in which the decisions relating to the factors might be taken in an ideal (problem-oriented ISD model driven) world. However, in the real world, the first thing that often gets fixed is the hardware system available and this dictates the software options. Thus the delivery and authoring resources get defined first and

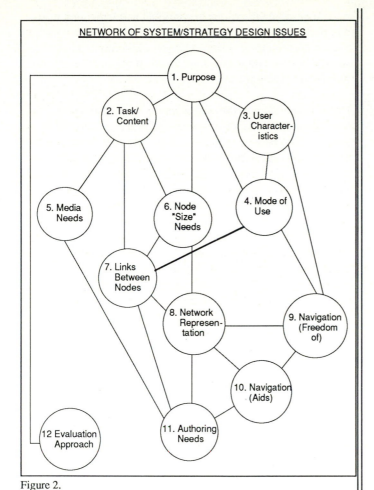

Figure 2.

these in turn limit the options on media, node size, types of links available, whether a network can be presented and how, navigation aids available, etc. In short, some real world projects work up the implied sequence of this network from bottom-up. As Leggett, Schnase and Kacmar state in their chapter, the hypertext system or model adopted defines what can be learned from the system. So try not to define the system or model before you have analyzed what is to be learned. Easier said than done, sometimes!

AR recommendation 20.7-20

A second observation is that the links themselves have meanings, in that they imply the existence of some linking rules and procedures that may allow one to explain exactly how, say the task/content affects decisions about media, node size and types of links. They imply the existence of, or rather the need for, a prescriptive design theory that would help us make the

AR explanation 7.4

necessary design decisions in a rational and integrated manner. If we imagine *zooming in* on a section of the network in Figure 2, (as Kommers suggests), we would hopefully find a second level of nodes and links, which represent the structure of this underlying theory.

Does such an underlying design theory exist? Parts of it do, but it would seem that we lack a comprehensive and integrated theory base for all our decisions. In the conference chapters, several authors suggest taxonomies of the purposes and uses of hypertext systems, but they give little prescriptive guidance as to the detailed design process of the system. Leggett, Schnase, and Kacmar address the questions of designing the nodes and links in hypertext. McKnight, Richardson, and Dillon show that some basically reference applications do not require much underlying design theory as the system paramenters are defined by the already existing materials that are to be stored and disseminated. Both Kommers and McAleese address the creation of sophisticated online networks as aids for the user to understand the structure of a knowledge domain. Several authors address different aspects of the navigation issue.

ARexplanation 16.13

AR example 7.6, 6.6

All in all, however, the underlying theory base is at best patchy and inconsistent, suggesting that much research is necessary in this field. The research and evaluation studies reported are, with one exception, rather global, comparing the hypertext system to some other form of presenting the information. Nielsen reports several such studies. Verreck and Lkoundi do the same, some case-observation data of a general nature. Marchionini suggests an evaluation methodology and framework. By and large, all these evaluation studies and suggestions are typical "level 2" approaches, that treat the details of the hypertext system as a *black box* and concern themselves principally with the neasurement and evaluation of the outputs and inputs. The one exception is the *keystroke/ screening journal* methodology, which Marchionini suggests and Mayes, Kibby and Anderson practice. We will come back to this in the next section.

AR results 9.12-13
AR results 15.9-10

AR recommendation 20.7-8

AR explanation 13.12-13

To conclude this section, we may take yet another peek at Figure 2 and consider some of the design questions to resolve that Jonassen and Grabinger list in their introductory chapter. It is possible to map some of these questions onto the links drawn in Figure 2 and other questions suggest other *background* nodes and the links to them. For example, there are many questions in their paper that refer to design issues of different types of hypertext structure (unstructured, structured, hierarchical) . It seems we should have a node labelled "type of network structure" with links from the task/content, purpose and user nodes, at least. This does not appear on my diagram, as the issue, though prompted heavily by Jonassen and Grabinger, was not effectively addressed by the conference participants. The reader might like to try, as an exercise, to identify other missing nodes and links, that can be identified from an analysis of the design questions listed by Jonassen and Grabinger. Maybe this will better integrate the *evaluation approach* node which is at present hanging out on its own branch, connected to nothing but the overall goals of the system.

One should note, however, that a large proportion of the design questions listed by Jonassen and Grabinger are concerned with the more detailed *micro-design* issues and therefore are not part of the "level 2" design schema. We shall address these *micro-design* issues in the next section.

Micro-design of educational hypertext

Products and approach of level 3. The third level of decision making in the instructional design/development process may be characterized as the *micro-design*, or *tactical* level. Typical products of this level include:
•Lesson plans for each individual lesson or session of the program planned in outline previously,
•specifications for the instructional materials that may have to be obtained or developed in order to teach each of the lessons,
•evaluation instruments, test items or exercises that will be used in class or in later practice, to measure whether expected learning has indeed taken place,
•remediation plans to deal with the inevitable slower student, or one who missed class, etc.

In the case of hypertext/hypermedia systems, this is the stage at which the network takes on its form, the content of each node is planned (possibly written) and key links between the nodes are defined. In the case of hypermedia systems, the specific medium for the content of each node is selected, specific shots, graphics or scenes from existing materials are identified, or, in the case of new materials to be produced, detailed specifications, storyboards, or scenarios are planned. The level of design detail at this stage may stop short of the

AR methodology 5.10

final scripting of scenarios, or the production of computer generated graphics, and similar tasks which require specialist production skills and knowhow and may, indeed, be delegated to specialists. The detail should however be sufficient for such specialists to be able to produce the final product with the minimum of further supervision by the designer. In the case of mainly textual material, which will in fact be written by the system designer, it is often the case that this stage of design is performed *on line* on the workstation, a prototype version of the final text content of each node being generated. However, experience shows that it is more effective and efficient to precede the generation of the final text by the development of a detailed outline of the content to be included in each node, as well as the provisional network of the nodes and links.

GM example 24.14

These items are all part of a *planned instruction* overall strategy. In the case of an open system, for student collaboration on the creation of a hypertext document, design of the system effectively is complete after the level 2 decisions have been taken, as from that point onwards it is the students who generate the input ideas, write the material for the nodes, as well as creating links between items as they are submitted by fellow collaborators. There may, in some cases be a need to design the outline or the stages that a group collaboration exercise should follow, and generally, when some definable and measurable learning outcome is expected, the evaluation system, may have to be designed at this stage.

In the case of a system created by an author, but from existing textual material, the design process is also somewhat simplified, in that no new text has to be generated. The existing text has to be analyzed and divided into nodes of the appropriate size and/or content, however, and this is often almost as complex a task as originating new text. Links have to be planned and in some instances, subsidiary bibliographic notes or footnotes may be generated as aids to the understanding of the content.

In most cases, the navigation aids that will be needed (indexes, graphical representations of the network, menus, hypermaps, etc.) will be generated towards the end of this stage of design, once the detailed structure of the system is more or less fixed. In the case of technically more complex navigation aids, as for example *intelligent help systems* or *dynamic interactive network representations*, the specifications of these components may be designed and the production delegated to specialists.

The approach to the execution of these design tasks may be highly theory-based or highly personal, based on intuition and past experience. Where we find ourselves on this dimension is a measure of whether we have a micro-design technology, or whether the process is more of an art form. As an instructional technologist, I tend to prefer the theory-based approach and, of course, argue that a sufficiently powerful and developed theory-base does in fact exist to allow one to claim that a design technology exists. If that is so, then the approach at the micro-design level follows a cycle similar to the one already described for macro-design:

1. Analysis of the goals/objectives of a specific portion of the overall system plan developed earlier
2. Application of relevant theory/principles to the design of a "blueprint" of the final hypertext system
3. Development of the details of this blueprint as far as is feasible without the use of specialized production skills, facilities, workstations, etc. (I am not referring here to hypertext design workstations that would be used as part of the design process, but rather to video or other special media)
4. Developmental testing and validation of the blueprints by peer critiquing, subject matter expert appraisal and simulated applications on individual students, etc.

Regarding the theory-base, opinions differ among instructional designers on what are the roots and the form of this base. One area of difference is the extent to which designers base their approach on behaviorist, cognitive or other theories of learning. We have seen from the conference, that the bulk of practitioners interested in utilizing hypertext in the educational context, tend to draw their theoretical base from the cognitive psychology schools (more precisely the areas of information processing and schema theory). Of late, a broader theory base has been growing in strength—cognitive science—this has extended the arena of cognitive psychology to include principles drawn from computer science, linguistics, general systems theory, neurology and many other disciplines. Whether this theory base is being effectively used is not that clear. Only a few of the papers presented at this conference addressed the practical implementation of a design methodology derived from a defined theory base.

DJ explanation 1.7-9

19.24

SH example 23.5,
DJ corroboration 5.4-5
AR explanation 23.5-6

AR explanation 23.12-13

DJ reference Landow, G. (1989). The rhetoric of hypermedia. *Journal of Computing in Education, 1,* 39-64., AR background 3.14-15

AR explanation 7.6, background 6.9

Micro-design models for hypertext. Instructional designers also differ on the question of how one should utilize one's theory base in the design process. One approach is to develop quite detailed prescriptive models for the design process, from the principles of the theory base being used. The various instructional design models that abound in the ISD literature, from the programmed instruction models of the 1960's to the more recent examples such as component display theory are examples of the prescriptive approach [20]. The other approach is to *work from first principles*, that is from a set of heuristics that are derived from the theory base, and are applied to specific design problems if in the judgement of the designer, they make sense in that specific case. This approach is characterized by a more loosely defined set of design steps and procedures, and much more exercise of the past experience, judgement and, maybe, creativity of the designer. (See [21] for an outline and defense of this approach).

By and large, the conference participants would seem to favor the latter approach. Whether this is by choice or default is not clear in all cases. Very few authors make any mention, however, of prescriptive design models for educational hypertext. Mention is made of several possibly relevant theory bases. For example Norbert Streitz uses theories of writing as their basis for the design of tools that might aid the authoring of contributions to a hypertext environment. Streitz draws on several theoretical positions and models of writing, as a basis for designing four mutually complementary planning spaces to be used by authors — the *planning space*, the *content space,* the *argumentation space* and the *rhetorical space*. This is one of the few detailed contributions to the development of models specifically for the design of hypertext systems. George Landow has also written on design aspects, which he calls the *rhetoric of hypertext and hypermedia*, based on his experience on the Intermedia project at Brown university. His approach has been to genetrate a series of general heuristic rules based partly on theory and partly on practical experience, to guide authors of hypertext.

Two contributors, Piet Kommers and Ray McAleese, base their approaches (principally to the design of hypertext networks) on Gordon Pask's Conversation Theory [22,23]. They both seem to use Pask's ideas as a theoretical framework and a source of some general design heuristics. Pask has, on the other hand, developed a fairly (though not to bindingly) prescriptive design model based on conversation theory, which is embodied in the CASTE system of conversational tutorial, an early example of a hypermedia system before that name was invented [9]. The nodes and links in a CASTE system are designed according to precise rules, derived from conversation theory, which control the interaction that a user may have with a given knowledge base in such a way that specific learning goals are achieved and learning sequence, though largely under student control, is not allowed to take paths which are quite invalid for the given learner at a given time. Approaches such as CASTE should have considerable value in the micro design of hypertext systems for learning in subject areas where different viewpoints exist and their analysis and discussion are part of the learning goals.

As mentioned earlier, the CASTE system has been used to investigate individual learning styles on computers and hypertext environments [25]. These were the famous *serialists* and *wholists* experiments, that stand out in the literature of research on lndividual learning styles and student's ability to identify and select an effective personal style.

Other research of this nature is relevant to the micro design of hypertext systems. Mayes, Kibby and Anderson report some results obtained through analysis of the trace files that log student paths through the Strathtutor hypertext system. One of my own students [24] performed a study of alternative control allocation (between student and system). Three versions of an instructional program on database concepts were prepared. Each of the versions had a common hypertext-like set of basic information screens. In one version these were annexed to a CAI sequence and had to be studied in a particular predetermined order and at predetermined points in the course. Two other versions of the course used the screens as a browsing database. Students had to attempt the same key questions that were embedded into the program, in order to have their learning measured, but in one case, pointers were supplied linking test items to specific screens, while in the other case there was no such coaching help and students had to organize their own learning sequence. The study was set up primarily to research the relationship of *locus of control* to success under these three systems. Some interactions were found, but in general, all student groups did best under the guided/coaching system. As an interesting byproduct of this study, it was found that more could be inferred from the path traces followed by different students, than from the official

AR results 13.12-13

DJ corroboration .113

independent/dependent variables.

A further recent study [6] compared the efficiency of using a hypertext document as a basis for free research on a topic with and without initial orientation on the structure of the hypertext and the purpose of the research. It was found that the more the students knew about the overall structure of the document and the purpose of their research, the less they browsed serendipiditiously, the more they used the document as a tradutional information resource and the more they liked the experience. Such research is beginning to show that for certain types of learning, under certain conditions, a more system controlled and prescriptive structure may be best.

Before leaving the question of micro design models, one should mention again the Information Mapping™ methodology. In addition to macro design principles, this methodology incorporates a fully developed micro design prescriptive model. It is based on an eclectic selection of principles from behavioral, social learning, cognitive, information processing and motivational schools, but knits them into a coherent set of practical procedures for the development of networks of single topic maps and the links between them. They have been shown to be effective, efficient, easy to write (even with the collaboration by non-computer means of several authors) and acceptable to a wide range of user groups [18,25,26].

Yet another promising approach that I am currently investigating is to adapt *Structural Communication* [27,28], a materials authoring technique developed to engage students in the deep processing of complex, multi-faceted subject matter , followed by analytical feedback on the connections and viewpoints that they have formed on key issues, to hypertext/hypermedia environments. An initial study of the effectiveness of an interactive videodisc simulation game (which has many of the structural characteristics of browsing hypermedia added to a CAI *backbone*, showed that the addition of a debriefing tutorial developed according to the prescriptions of structural communication, greatly enhanced the learning of general principles and theories that were implied (but not stated explicitly) in the scenarios of the simulation [29,30]. Current work is focussing on the creation of *case based interactive training* that will run in a hypermedia environment, with case data and scenarios stored as one network and theoretical discussion of decisions taken by the student stored in another, the two being linked by "problems for solution" set up in "structural communication" [31].

Where are we in micro-design? As mentioned before, there are two viewpoints on the use of theory as a basis for instructional design. The use of prescriptive models at the micro-design level is probably appropriate in some types of hypertext design exercises and not appropriate in others. However, the identification of the design principles as precisely and completely as possible is an essential step, whichever of the two approaches, prescriptive or heuristic, are adopted. It would seem that we have quite a way to go to achieve this goal. Duffy and Knuth, in their contribution, argue that "most of the thinking on hypermedia is instructionally atheoretical and technology based" (they mean computer technology based). They set about the task of putting this right at the macro-design level, by selecting their system design parameters that encourage what they consider to be the most promising potential contribution of hypertext/hypermedia to education, namely the promotion of "a pedagogy that emphasizes attending to relationships and demands it of students". The system is not yet operational, so they have no experience yet of trying alternative micro-design approaches. They appear to favor a *case based* approach and are not in favor of *traditional* approaches which have most often reflected the logical positivist position.

AR explanation 12.2

In the previous section, I have indicated some specific, more or less prescriptive, models for the development of instructional materials that benefit from running in a hypertext environment. Note the relative importance implied by this sentence: the materials or exercises come first and are designed to address a specific type of learning problem. They are the first aspect of the solution and only then do hypertext systems get identified as being the most convenient medium of delivery. All three of these systems of materials design have a long and fairly respectable history — Information Mapping ™ and Structural Communication were both first conceived in the late 1960's and developed in both paper and computer based implementations from the early 1970's on. Conversation Theory and the CASTE system have even earlier antecedents but due to the greater complexity of the CASTE system it was only experimentally implemented until the era of powerful microcomputers enabled it to be disseminated to a larger audience. All three of them are however little known, especially among hypertext practitioners, who might be the group that could best use them. Is this because they are outdated, or too *traditional*?

They were all developed as early reactions to some of the weaker aspects of programmed instruction, yet it is exactly that weaker, less cognitively based, and less challenging "traditional" programmed instruction methodology which is still the hidden theory base for the greater part of currently used computer based instrtuction. Should we not be making greater use of such relatively sound and successful micro-design methodology. Or, if we are for some reason not impressed by these, should we not be seeking or inventing some more acceptable approaches that espouse the learning theory principles we cherish while making rational use of hypertext environments as delivery vehicles?

Hypermedia materials development

Products and approach of level 4. The fourth level of instructional design and development is characterized as the very detailed and specialized work required to get a final working product out to the target students. Typical tasks in this stage are:

- the final scripting of audiovisual/video sequences and the validation of the scripts for both technical and pedagogical quality;
- the final revision of text to ensure that language and vocabulary are appropriate to the students, that examples and illustrations selected are meaningful and relevant to the students' reality;
- the input and screen design of CAL materials to ensure that best use is made of space, effects, color, sound, animation, etc;

By and large, the issues and the design principles at this stage are those that would relate to any media production for educational/instructional purposes. Hypertext and hypermedia may add a few extra special considerations, for example:

- in the case of text, the style of a node should be such that it can be read meaningfully irrespective of which of several other nodes had just been read previously;
- the use of graphics for compact communication of large amounts of interrelated information may be of special importance due to the restrictions imposed on node size by some systems;
- media selection takes on new meaning when the presentation may change from one medium to another with a frequency of seconds, as opposed to minutes in

conventional mediated instruction;
- •the effective use (and avoidance of misuse) of the special authoring tools offered by the various commercially available hypermedia authoring and creation packages - for example the appropriate use of icons and positioning of buttons.

These, and other similar considerations, may have become particularly important in the context of the authoring of hypertext and hypermedia, but they are not absolutely new and unresearched topics. The Information Mapping™ methodology offers an excellent *role model* for the authoring of non sequential chunks of text and the methodologies guidelines and training manuals are full of literally hundreds of suggestions for the packaging of different types of information in economical ways - tables of parts, compare/contrast, WHIF charts, etc. The media selection consideration has been a key issue in the short but busy history of the interactive video disc production industry and is a research topic that has already generated a rich and varied literature that will be of relevance to hypermedia system developers [32, 33]. The last consideration is of special importance and unique relevance to hypermedia developers. As such, the hypermedia community will have to develop its own research agenda and distribute findings in the form of guidelines and suggestions. This topic was one that many of the conference participants addressed, either in their papers, or in discussions and product demonstrations. It is clear that this research aspect is one that will not be overlooked.

AR example 14.3-4

Conclusion: Solution or problem? _____

It would seem, therefore, that by and large, the fourth level of instructional design is relatively well covered by current knowledge or ongoing research and development. We need have no great concerns at this level. However we should ensure that good production practices are publicized and widely disseminated, that new systems are evaluated with respect to production values of the type mentioned before they are made available on a large scale.

It is at levels 2 and particularly 3 that further fundamental research and theory building is required if the educational potential of this new non-linear multi-media methodology is to be fully realized. Potential applications, both large and small scale abound. Some appear to offer new and exciting possibilities for the promotion of deep level conceptual learning, for developing and evaluating the development of powerful conceptual schemata in the minds of large numbers of students, or for enhancing the power and the creativity of collaborative group work. Others appear to offer immense social or economic benefits by delivering the right information (not too little and not too much) to the right person at the right time and place.

However, similarly grand claims were made for other new technologies in the past. Most of such claims have not been realized to the extent that was expected (if at all). One commonly recurring reason for such failure to deliver, has been lack of an adequate theory-base to the design and development process. This has not always been due to a lack of sound theoretical principles. Sometimes it was more the failure to use the principles we had at our disposal. In this paper I have attempted to analyse the theory base to hypertext and hypermedia for educational purposes. It would seem that there are pockets of well tested principles in some areas of our field, possibly in the more traditional instructional situations. The novel ones, created as opportunities due to the invention of hypertext, are less well supported by research. We are still in the potential solution-seeks-compatible-problem stage of development.

One positive result of this conference has been to identify where we have a sound basis for our design decisions and where we do not. Hopefully, one outcome of this collection of papers will be to disseminate to a wide audience of would be users, designers and developers, the current "state of the technology" and identify where they as practitioners can rely on well founded principles and where they must tread warily, testing out their decisions as they go - and thus possibly contributing to the growth of the body of research upon which this field will be built.

Finally, let us also remember the importance of the first level. Although this is not strictly speaking a design and development issue, the initial conception of a project and its institutional support, together with later project planning, management ,control and evaluation issues, should not be overlooked or underrrated, More projects fail for reasons of managerial incompetence than because of technical inadequacy. Make sure your project is not among that illustrious group. In addition to wasting good technical resources and your own time on a project that is sick at the top level, all too often such failures reflect on the technology and not on the misguided clients or incompetent managers. Too many such failures in our field and we will all be viewed by our institutional colleagues as potential troublemakers rather than the saviours of education that we think we are. If we are not seen by others as an essential part of the solution, then we really are a part of the problem!

References

[1] Marchionini, G. and Schneiderman, B. (1987). Finding facts versus browsing knowledge. In *Hypertext Systems*. *IEEE Computer, 21*, (1), 70-80.

[2] Bush, V. (1945). As we may think. *Atlantic Monthly. 176*, (1), 101-108.

[3] Beeman, W. O., Anderson, K. T., Bader, G., Larkin, J., McClard A. P., McQuillan, P., and Shields, M. (1987). Hypertext and pluralism: from lineal to non-lineal thinking. In *Proceedings of the Hypertext '87 Conference*, (67-88). University of North Carolina at Chapel Hill.

[4] Apple Computer (1987). *Hypercard: freedom to associate.* Apple Computer Inc., Cupertino, Ca.

[5] Pask, G., and Scott, B. C. E. (1972). Learning strategies and individual competence. In *International Journal of Man-Machine Studies, 4,* (3).

[6] Romiszowski, A J. (1989). *Communicating and developing cognitive structures through CBI: The tools of creativity.* Proceedings of the 31st. International conference of the Association for the Development of Computer-based Instructional Systems (ADCIS), November 1989, Washington, DC.

[7] Taylor, R. P. (Ed.) (1980). *The Computer in the School: Tutor, Tool, Tutee.* New York: Teachers College Press.

[8] Romiszowski, A. J. (1987). Artificial intelligence and expert systems in education: Potential promise or threat to teachers? *Educational Media International* (Journal of the International Council for Educational Media), *24*(2) 96-104.

[9] Pask, G. and Scott, B. C. E. (1973). CASTE: A system for exhibiting learning strategies and regulating uncertainties. *Journal of Man-Machine Studies, 5,* (1).

[10] Romiszowski, A. J. (1981). *Designing instructional systems.* (Chapter 13, pages 269-280, gives an overview of the author's four-level ISD model). London: Kogan Page.

[11] Nelson, T. H. (1981-1987) *Literary machines.* A hypertext book, regularly updated and reissued by the author. Project Xanadu, San Antonio, Texas.

[12] Nelson, T. H. (1988). *Managing immense storage.* Byte Magazine, January, 255-238.

[13] Megarry, Walker, D. R.F., Nisbet, S., and Hoyle, E. (Eds.) (1982). *World yearbook of education 1982/83: Computers and education.* (Preface by Roy Jenkins, M.P.-page 10) London: Kogan Page.

[14] Halasz, F. G. (1988). Reflections on Notecards: Seven issues for the next generation of hypermedia systems. *Communications of the ACM, 31*(7), 834-844.

[15] Horn, R. E. (1969). *Information mapping for learning and reference.* Lexington, Mass.: Information Resources Inc.

[16] Horn, R. E. (1976). *How to write information mapping.* (A non-sequentially organized manual, regularly updated and expanded since 1972) Lexington, Mass.: Information Resources Inc.

[17] Romiszowski, A. J. (1986). *Developing auto instructional materials.* (Chapter seven is devoted to an update on Information Mapping). London: Kogan Page.

[18] Romiszowski, A. J. (1976). *A study of individualized systems of mathematics instruction at the post-secondary levels..* Unpublished doctoral dissertation. University of Technology, Loughborough, UK.

[19] Horn, R. E. (Ed.) (1983). *Trialectics: Toward a practical logic of unity.* Lexington Mass.: Information Resources Inc.

[20] Reigeluth, C. M. (Ed.) (1983). *Instructional design theories and models: An Overview of their current status.* Hillsdale, New Jersey: Lawrence Erblaum.

[21] Winn, W. (1989). Toward a rationale and theoretical basis for educational technology. *Educational Technology Research and Development (ETR&D) Journal, 37*(1). 35-46.

[22] Pask, G. (1976). Conversational techniques in the study and practice of education. *British Journal of Educational Psychology, 46,* 12-25.

[23] Pask, G. (1984). Review of conversation theory and a protologic (or protolanguage), Lp. *Educational Communications and Technology Journal (ECTJ), 32,* (1). 3-40.

[24] Ferguson, H. (1988). *The effect of locus of control on achievement and preference in CAI tutorial systems, which vary in terms of system control, learner control with coaching and learner control with no coaching.* Unpublished doctoral dissertation, Syracuse University, Syracuse, New York.

[25] Arce, J. F. and Romiszowski, A. J. (1985). Using a relational database as a means of integrating instructional and library materials in a computer- managed course. *Proceedings of the 26th, ADCIS International Conference. Association for the Development of Computer-based Instructional Systems.*

[26] Romiszowski, A. J. (1986b). Applying the new technologies to education and training in Brazil. In Rushby, N and Howe, A (Eds.), *Aspects of educational technology XIX: Educational, training and information technologies-Economics and other realities.* London: Kogan Page.

[27] Hodgson, A. M. (1971). An experiment in computer-guided correspondence seminars for management. A*spects of Educational Technology V.* London: Pitman.

[28] Hodgson, A. M. (1974). Structural communication in practice. In A. J. Romiszowski (Ed.), *APLET yearbook of educational and instructional technology 1974/75.* London: Kogan Page.

[29] Romiszowski, A. J. (1988). *Structural communication enhancements to an interactive video simulation-game: in search of reflective learning. Aspects of educational technology XXII.* London: Kogan Page.

[30] Romiszowski, A. J., Grabowski, B., and Damadaran, B. (1988). *Structural communication, expert systems and interactive video: A powerful combination for a non-traditional CAI approach*. Paper presented at the 1988 Annual Convention of the Association for Educational and Communications Technology, New Orleans, January.

[31] Romiszowski, A. J. and Grabowski, B. L. (1989). Interactive video and cognitive structures: A technique for enhancing the effectiveness of interactive simulations and games. *Proceedings of the Seventh Conference on Interactive Instruction Delivery*. Society for Applied Learning Technology (SALT), Warrenton, Va.

[32] Grabowski, B. L. (1989). Reflections on why media comparison studies continue to be conducted-with suggested alternatives. *Proceedings of selected research paper presentations at the 1989 Annual Convention of the Association for Educational Communications and Technology*, (123-130).

[33] Slee, E. (1989). A review of the research on interactive video. *Proceedings of selected research paper presentations at the 1989 Annual Convention of the Association for Educational Communications and Technology*, (149-166).

Chapter 20
Evaluating Hypermedia-Based Learning

Gary Marchionini
University of Maryland, USA

Keywords

Evaluation; research methods; quantitative design; qualitative design; pattern analysis

Contents

Introduction

Each time a new technology is applied to teaching and learning, questions about fundamental principles and methods arise. Television and computers, for example, have raised issues related to learning theory, curricula (content, sequence) and methods (delivery, evaluation). Educational technologists are forever reconciling the tensions between learning theory and the practical applications of technology to instruction [1]. The current interest in hypermedia as an educational technology once again raises these issues. The purpose of this paper is to propose a multi-faceted approach to evaluating hypermedia-based learning with particular emphasis on the learning process. This approach is aimed at projects that

NATO ASI Series, Vol. F 67
Designing Hypermedia for Learning
Edited by D. H. Jonassen and H. Mandl
© Springer-Verlag Berlin Heidelberg 1990

assume that learning is a constructive process that includeds hands-on activities as well as traditional expository methods. The methods discussed apply to a variety of hypermedia systems and are meant to help designers and instructors assess the effectiveness of hypermedia-based learning.

Characteristics of hypermedia: Access, control, and collaboration

Hyperdocuments permit and encourage authors and readers to work with non-linear organizations of textual, graphic, and audio information. Hypermedia systems use highly interactive interfaces to combine features from text processing, database management and graphic design. Three key characteristics of hypermedia systems make them attractive for information processing in general, and for teaching and learning in particular: they can integrate varied formats and voluminous amounts of information; they are enabling rather than directive systems; and they facilitate interactions among people and machines as well as among groups of people. These characteristics raise issues of *access, control*, and *collaboration* which offer opportunities and challenges to learners and instructional designers alike [2].

PD contrast 8.2

Effects of hypermedia on learners

DJ parallel 1.18

Learners must acquire a new type of *literacy* to benefit from the new opportunities for learning that hypermedia offers. Issues of access, control, and collaboration present conceptual and physical tradeoffs for learners. First, hypermedia offers quantitative and qualitative differences in access to information. Huge amounts of material in a variety of formats can be instantly accessed by learners, thus providing them with both breadth and depth for their information needs. However, comprehensive access requires sophisticated information seeking skills, and developing and applying these skills demands cognitive resources. The effective use of large collections demands the use of indexes and guides to navigate in a sea of connected information.

RK explanation 12.5

Second, hypermedia is an enabling technology rather than a directive one, offering high levels of user control. Learners can construct their own knowledge by browsing hyperdocuments according to the associations in their own *cognitive structures*. As with access, however, control requires responsibility and decision making. Undisciplined traversal of a hyperdocument is entertaining at best and may be disorienting and confusing. There is an inherent pedagogical tension in providing a medium that allows learners great latitude in choosing how they use that medium, since they may not choose to learn what the teacher expects them to learn. Such a medium may be limited to open-ended instructional goals like learning how to learn and synthesizing concepts rather than easier to measure goals at the fact acquisition or comprehension levels. Ross & Morrison [3] discuss the many studies in which high levels of learner control lead to less learning and argue that learner control may be most appropriate for capable learners, *higher order skills*, and familiar content and for determining the presentational features of instruction.

Third, hypermedia facilitates timely and iterative interactions with the system and with other humans. Interaction with hypermedia offers the usual advantages noted in the computer-based instruction literature (e.g., immediate feedback, individualized and unbiased attention, consistent instructional sequences, non-passive learning). In addition, user-modifiable hypermedia systems allow users to add to or change hyperdocuments. Students can "collaborate" with the system by downloading segments and by annotating and editing them to produce their papers and reports. Students can create their own paths through the hyperdocument, save and annotate them as interpretations of the content, and share these traversals and notes with teachers and fellow students. As shared paths are added to the hyperdocument, author/reader and instructor/learner relationships begin to blur, opening new possibilities for teacher-learner collaboration and interaction. The potential of computers to facilitate group work is an active area of research [4] and requires careful examination in learning environments. Of course, group work is not appropriate for all learning activities and problems of integrity of information in an evolving hyperdocument and assessing individual learning must be considered. At a more individual level, a hyperdocument can help a learner study, i.e., interact with him/herself. Highlighting ideas on paper while reading is a common practice that allows learners to study—reflect on previous learning experiences. Saving and reviewing paths through a hyperdocument can serve a similar function in helping learners reflect on their learning and easily diverge from previous routes through the content.

Effects of hypermedia on designers

Designers can gain both pedagogical and production benefits from hypermedia systems. They can show explicit relationships among various concepts; apply the dynamic features of

---

20.3

DJ explanation 1.16-17

PWr contrast 8.7

SH parallel 23.22

SH parallel 23.9

moving images, graphics, and sound to illustrate concepts and skills; and collaborate with colleagues in developing and organizing concepts. Designers can also apply word processing and graphic design tools to facilitate the production of hyperdocuments and can modularize *authoring* so that key modules can be used in a variety of products.

Designers must, however, cope with new challenges. A major challenge is the need to develop new organizational patterns for writing instructional materials in addition to struggling with the usual problems of language, sequence, and style [5]. For example, key decisions must be made about the size of text fragments, number and type of links per screen/window, and standardization of vocabulary through which links are made. See Kearsley [6], Marchionini, Liebscher, & Li [7], Shneiderman [8], and Wright [9] for discussions of authoring hyperdocuments and Jonassen [10] for a discussion of logical structures of hyperdocuments. Furthermore, production is often constrained by the expense of new technology; lack of marketing experience on the part of publishers; and poor authoring tools for creating, managing, and editing links and for managing versions of hyperdocuments [11]. Additionally, teachers who include hyperdocuments in their instruction have few precedents for assigning, managing, and evaluating student use of these documents. Hypermedia requires a new type of authoring literacy consistent with the new types of instruction it makes possible.

RK parallel 3.3

To learn and teach effectively with hypermedia systems, both learners and designers must thus acquire new levels of information literacy that will enable them to take advantage of the new types and levels of learning and teaching that hypermedia makes possible. One key aspect of this information literacy is the notion that units of information are not discrete, but rather that all units of information are related. This practical form of connectionism must be internalized by both learners and designers if they are to take full advantage of electronic information systems in general and hypermedia in particular.

Effects on the evaluation process

From an instructional design point of view, the central problem in evaluating learning is to state the *goals and objectives* clearly and to develop criterion measures for assessing learning in light of these goals and objectives. This problem is particularly acute for learning at the problem solving or strategic levels of cognitive processing, since our current understanding of these processes is rather poor [12] and since their outcomes do not readily lend themselves to quantification. A second challenge to evaluation of learning based on predefined goals is that it is limited to directed learning. Many learning theorists accept the Piagetian notion that learning is a constructive process (see [13] or [14] for illustration and discussion). One approach to instruction based on a constructionist view of learning is to provide rich environments in which learners can actually construct their own knowledge. Some designers view technology as one way to implement such environments [15,16]. If learners are allowed or encouraged to determine their own learning goals, then evaluation of their learning must be based on those individual goals. Streibel [17], for example, argued against implementing learning in formal systems in general and computer-based systems in particular and for encouraging learning to take place in informal, social settings controlled by learners.

Regardless of whether goals and objectives are difficult to state and measure or whether learning should be based on learner-determined goals and experiences, evaluation of students interacting with instructional environments must be conducted. Where possible, such evaluations should link instructor specified goals to outcomes and, in other cases, assess both the process and products of learning longitudinally and in a way which is consistent with the goals set by the learner.

The characteristics of hypermedia affect the evaluation process in a variety of ways. First, the newness of the medium will affect learning outcomes because designers are inexperienced using it. Because there is such a limited experience base for creating and using hyperdocuments in educational settings, there is a need for establishing baseline data about the effects of such applications. More importantly, many of the pedagogical decisions designers must make are choices about the degree of access, control, and collaboration to build into products and there are no clear research principles for making such decisions. Student learning ultimately depends on the interaction of individual learner characteristics and the results of these choices. Jonassen [10] presented a procedure for designing hyperdocuments that entails identifying and mapping key concepts before organizing and linking them. Having such specifications in hand may help in conducting evaluations of use, since, at the very least, the number of visits

RK parallel 12.19
DJ explanation 1.7-8

to concepts could be easily counted. In systems with large amounts and varied formats of information, a major evaluation problem is noting what is accessed. In systems that provide high levels of learner control, the major evaluation problem is assessing how learners manage this control and freedom as they learn. In dynamic, collaborative systems, the salient evaluation problem is who does what as well as how it is done.

Evaluation of learning at knowledge acquisition or skill levels must be driven by goals and objectives. However, highly interactive, open systems may facilitate learning at levels that resist well-defined goals and objectives. Moreover, they may facilitate learning distinct from goals and objectives defined by the designer but that are valuable and appropriate nonetheless. The essential problem of evaluating highly interactive systems is in measuring both the quality of the interaction as well as the product of learning. Evaluations of hypermedia-based learning must address both the process of learning and the outcomes of learning.

The solution to these problems of evaluation is to take a multifaceted approach to evaluation. First, in the early applications of a new technology, special attention must be given to collecting baseline data that is extensive and varied. Such data can be used for building precise experiments and for explaining the outcomes of other facets of the evaluation. Second, the fact that there are no proven methods for assessing the process of learning suggests that we observe and analyze the behavioral patterns exhibited during learning from several perspectives. By comparing the results of these observations, we search for corroboration among methods and results, thus amassing both tools and evidence that may be generalizable. Finally, because the aim is to examine process as well as product, evaluation must observe and assess the process at many stages, not just its completion. Data collection thus becomes more of a "real-time", analog process rather than a discrete set of measures applied at carefully arranged intervals. Thus, if evaluation is to address the processes as well as the products of learning with a new technology, a variety of methods must be used. One important advantage that the medium itself offers is the potential to capture many of the interactions between learner and system. Computer-monitored data collection methods should be included in the evaluator's repertoire of methods, and figure prominently in the general framework below.

A multi-faceted approach to evaluation requires incremental and systematic views across task domains, systems, and users. For hypermedia-based learning, a dimension particular to the characteristics of hypermedia must be added to the evaluation design. This dimension includes variables related to the process of learning affected by access, learner control, and collaboration.

The following table (Table 1) summarizes methods and data types useful in a multi-faceted evaluation design. Although the first method, document and product analysis, is really an assessment of the design process rather than of the learning process, it affects the learning process and so is included as a baseline method for evaluations of learning. Since data types can be used across methods, discussions of data types and methods follow in separate sections.

Data Types

A multi-faceted approach to evaluation applies a variety of measures. While the data types for document/product analysis (e.g., benchmarks like *readability levels*, *access speeds*, *display rates*, or checkoffs for program features) are an important aspect of the evaluation process, they are well described in the instructional system design literature and are not further discussed here. First, measures used as indicators of learning having taken place (i.e., outcome measures) are discussed, followed by discussion of indicators of the process of learning.

Outcome Measures. Learner performance on tests or assignments are typically used to judge the quality and quantity of learning. For well-defined objectives at skill or knowledge acquisition levels of learning, teacher-made tests or standardized tests are considered valid and reliable indicators of learning. For open-ended objectives and higher levels of learning, essays or projects are generally used for evaluation. Because evaluating such products involves judgment rather than simple scoring, panels of judges are sometimes used to improve the reliability of results. In any case, a priori criteria sets should be developed to improve validity.

Evaluation Methods and Data Types

Data Collection Methods	Costs	Data Types Interval	Data Types Ordinal/Nominal
Document/Product Analysis	low	benchmark results	inclusions/ exclusions
Observations	high	#moves? time? #errors?	success patterns notes error types
Keystroke/ Screen Journal	very low	time #moves #errors	success patterns error types
Think Aloud	high	time? #moves #errors	success patterns explanations/notes error types
Interview	high	time? #moves? #errors	success patterns explanations/notes satisfaction
Questionnaire	low	scores	satisfaction
Performance	low	scores	grades content analyses

Table 1. Note: Data types with "?" suffixes may be impractical to collect.

One advantage of performance scores is that they are typically interval or ratio values (or can be transformed as such) and can thus be used with powerful inferential statistical analyses that allow generalizations to be made about uniform impact [18]. Performance tests provide the best measures of learning outcomes and all summative evaluations should strive to include such measures in their research toolkits.

Success is a useful measure of learning outcomes in situations in which skill or fact acquisition is the aim of instruction. Success is often difficult to scale and typically yields dichotomous data values. Many of the potential outcomes of learners using hyperdocuments require complex judgments about success and must be treated like essays and projects to assure validity and reliability. Learner satisfaction is often used to assess the impact of learning. The high levels of control provided by hypermedia environments force learners to take responsibility for their actions, which presumedly leads to higher self-satisfaction. Assessing this expected increased satisfaction may be problematic since it appears to compare "apples to oranges". In general, satisfaction, while it may be correlated with learning, is the weakest evidence for learning because it is removed from observable behavior. Moreover, anyone who learns something from an activity must be somewhat satisfied, since it is impossible to know what one did not learn.

Process Measures. Many researchers use number of actions taken and latency between actions as indicators of performance. Egan [19] compared collections of human-computer interaction studies in three task domains (text editing, information retrieval, and programming) by analyzing ranges of response times across users. He was able to use his findings to illustrate human-computer interaction effects across tasks and users. Numbers of actions taken during learning can be used as indicators of individual differences as well as system effects. Marchionini [20-21] has distinguished between physical moves and conceptual moves and used the latter in analyzing search strategies of children using full-text electronic search systems. Numbers of moves and time to make them are advantageous for analysis since they are measured on a ratio scale. They are useful indicators of the efficiencies of learning but may not be indicators of effectiveness of learning.

Another important measure of both system and user performance are the number and type of errors. Error analysis can be especially useful during formative evaluations of designs, when it can be used to develop error trapping strategies for future versions [22]. Furthermore, in summative evaluations of learning, error counts can be used to make comparisons across learners or tasks. Error types can be used to suggest patterns of cognitive processing in individual learners and thus can be useful in evaluations of the learning process.

Norman [23] has noted that errors can be simple mechanical slips (e.g., typos, letter reversals, etc.) or thought errors (e.g., misunderstandings, overgeneralizations, etc.). Perkins and Simmons [24] provided a thoughtful taxonomy of thought errors across three task domains. Although both types of errors can be used to evaluate systems and learning with those systems, it seems reasonable to focus on thought errors when assessing the learning process. However, thought errors are particularly difficult to address since they require evaluators to make inferences about cognitive activity.

A somewhat global measure that directly addresses the process of learning is the "pattern of use". A "pattern of use" is a classification assigned by the evaluator that is based on a set of strategies exhibited by learners over several learning sessions. Each strategy is composed of a set of tactics a learner applies when using the system. Such classifications can be built from analyses of user self-reports and observer notes, or from behavioral traces collected on audio or video tapes or by the computer itself. Marchionini [20] analyzed conceptual moves as tactics when exploring the information-seeking strategies of elementary students. Patterns can be used to classify individuals for comparative purposes or to make inferences about the cognitive processes used by individuals. Patterns of use can also provide designers with information on system features during formative evaluations. Patterns are, however, difficult to collect and analyze. Collection requires judgments to be made when discrete actions (e.g., a keypress or mouseclick) are coded as tactics and again when tactics are classified into strategies. Moreover, strategies are inherently temporal and variable in length, making coding and analysis difficult. Although analysis of user states and transitions has been used to assess tactics and determine strategies [20,25], new methods of analyzing such data are needed. In the meantime, it seems prudent to apply the incomparable pattern recognition capabilities of the human mind directly to the process of learning in order to make direct inferences about learning patterns.

Evaluation methods

A multi-faceted approach to evaluation must necessarily apply a variety of methods of data collection. Such an approach takes the best from both quantitative and qualitative methodologies. This discussion includes methods that begin with instructional product evaluation (summative design), focuses on learning process methods, and culminates with learning product methods.

Summative design. Document analysis and product testing—methods that have been used by industry to evaluate the marketability of products and by consumers to make judgments about product purchases—can be applied to the assessment of instructional products [26]. In education, product testing underlies most of the evaluation procedures used to evaluate instructional software. Many forms and procedures for conducting software evaluation have been developed and applied (e.g., EPIE, Microsift) but there is little reliability among the qualitative judgments reached by applying such forms to the same software [26]. Five key criteria used in software evaluation are: environment requirements (e.g., prerequisite skills, hardware requirements, program cost), capability (program features), usability (interface design), reliability, and performance. For instructional software, measures of reliability and performance are usually limited to the software-computer effects (e.g., number of bugs, access and display speeds, etc.) rather than learner-software effects, which are more difficult to assess. Product evaluations serve a useful role in establishing a context for evaluation of learning and perhaps in aiding in the selection process, but they must be augmented by procedures that directly address student learning.

Learning process. Empirical evidence is the hallmark of scientific inquiry, and behavioral observations are obvious methods for conducting inquiries about human learning with technology. An important assumption underlying the use of such methods is that human behavior reflects cognitive processing. Observations may be intrusive or unobtrusive, random or systematic, brief or longitudinal, and formal or informal. Data can be collected by one or multiple observers who make mental, written, audio-taped, or video-taped notes. See Verreck and Lkoundi [28] for examples of using videotape to study adult learning in a hypertext environment. Two central problems with observational techniques are defining what to observe (what categories of cognitive activity are of interest and how to disambiguate the indicators of these categories from the stream of observable behavior) and controlling for the observer as instrument. Kerlinger [29] discusses the need to categorize observations and argues that passive observations do not interfere with subject performance after a brief adaptation period. He argues for proper planning and control as a prelude to increased use of observational techniques for conducting generalizable educational research. Other educational researchers believe that the complexities of human behavior defy generalization across individuals. They reject causal explanations for behaviors, and seek rather to understand the interactions between the individual and their learning environment [30]. They argue for observations that are both intensive and extensive, focusing on the details of individual behavior rather than gross indicators across many individuals. Neuman [31] argues for the use of naturalistic methods in computer based education because the theory and methodology match the nature and needs of interactive learning.

When learning takes place in a computer environment, it is easy to program the machine to capture behavioral traces of the human-computer interaction [32]. Keystrokes, mouse clicks, and screen touches can be easily captured and time-stamped; and all screen transactions (including mouse moves) can be recorded for immediate or subsequent analysis. These serve as behavioral traces of learner performance and thus are forms of observational data. Most significantly, having the computer collect observational data controls one of the main problems of observation—observer as instrument—because the computer operates in an unobtrusive, unbiased, and consistent manner. Moreover, such data collection efforts are very inexpensive. The tradeoff, of course, comes with the other central problem of observation—mapping the data to categories of cognitive activity. One approach is to code computer-monitored data to conceptual moves related to the cognitive task [20-21]. This approach depends on the creation of a set of all possible conceptual states a user can encounter and making judgments about how sequences of keypresses move users from state to state. Such coding of paths through a hyperdocument is under investigation in several studies at the University of Maryland. A major problem is that the coding from the keystrokes/mouseclicks to the conceptual states requires human interventions and is therefore subject to the problems associated with human coding. The coded data, of course, requires even more complex analysis. Transition matrix analyses have been used to detect patterns in performance, and state-by-state comparisons across user samples have been computed to compare system or user effects. An approach currently under investigation is to produce graphic representations (both static and dynamic) of the data to allow visual comparisons to be made by people. Machine-monitored data collection techniques have been used by many researchers in human-computer interaction [33-34] and they should prove valuable in studies of the hypermedia-based learning process. Regardless of its value in detecting patterns of learning, such data serves as a record of events that can be reconstructed when evaluators are conducting analyses of other types of data.

Interviews with learners and instructors can yield valuable data about the learning process [31]. Interviews may be conducted in groups (focus groups) or with individuals and can take place before, during, and after learning takes place. They can be aimed at either the process or product of learning, or at both. In any case, interviews should be guided by carefully constructed schedules that direct the interviewer and facilitate subsequent coding and analysis.

A combination of observation and interview known as "think aloud" has been used effectively to probe human cognitive activity. Ericsson & Simon [35] provide the classic discussion of this technique which requires the observer to train and encourage the subjects to verbalize their thoughts as they learn. A variation on the technique is to elicit learner commentary at critical decision points. The observer must thus be thoroughly aware of these critical decision points and able to initiate unanticipated questions as opportunities arise. Moreover, the subjects must be able and willing to verbalize thoughts as they participate in the research. "Think aloud" methods have also been criticized because the subject may not be consciously aware of all the processes which guide their behavior or that the very process of verbalizing their cogitations may affect their learning. Nonetheless, "think aloud" methods have been effective in theory building and surely should be included in the multi-faceted methodologist's toolkit. Another variation, known as *constructive interaction* has been used by Mayes [36] to assess learning with the StrathTutor system. This method pairs users and collects their verbal interactions for subsequent analysis. These methods are very expensive, since they require highly trained participant observers and extensive, individualized sessions. They directly address the cognitive process, however, and may be useful in generalizable evaluations when augmented by other methods.

DJ explanation 13.14-18

Learning products. Questionnaires are attractive instruments for collecting data because they can be used with large numbers of subjects at relatively low cost. Questionnaires should be carefully worded, not too long, and thoroughly pilot tested before use. One problem with questionnaires is that return rates may be low, thus violating the representativeness of the sample. A more basic problem with questionnaires is whether they actually elicit truthful and serious responses from respondents. Questionnaires are best used as supporting instruments for a comprehensive evaluation project.

The best method for determining the outcome of a learning task is to measure learner performance on tests for that task. For well-defined learning tasks, like knowledge acquisition or motor skill development, performance tests are easily constructed and applied. For higher-order learning, however, tests of learning are more subjective and require additional steps to assure validity and reliability. Performance tests for hypermedia-based learning where user control and collaboration are minimized may be possible if proper controls for the newness of the medium can be applied. If the greatest potential of hypermedia lies in access, learner control, and collaboration, then the performance tests that are used must be sensitive to these features. Such tests may include criterion-based measures that are created or selected by the learner rather than the teacher. Although such lack of measuring control may be dissatisfying for generalizable evaluation, perhaps learner-directed (created) performance tests can yield generalizable results if large enough numbers of results can be collected and compared.

Implementation of an evaluation plan ⎯⎯

Evaluation of instructional products and the learning that takes place through these products is challenged by emerging media that are highly interactive. The interactivity of hypermedia provides learners with access to vast and varied information, control over the process of learning, and potential for collaboration with the system and other people. Such empowerment of learners forces evaluators of learning to adopt a broad-based set of methods and criteria to accommodate self-directed learning. A multi-faceted approach to evaluation of hypermedia-based learning that focuses on the learning process seems reasonable at this early stage in the evolution of interactive electronic technology.

Individual methods are currently being applied in several investigations of hypermedia-based learning [e.g., 37-38] and a large-scale evaluation based on the overall framework is planned for the Perseus Project [39-40] over the next four years. The Perseus Project is a hypermedia environment for the study of the ancient Greek world. Based on HyperCard, the system will provide access to multiple media stored on optical discs that students in a variety of courses will purchase in lieu of or in addition to traditional printed materials. It will contain Greek and English versions of Greek literary works; images of works of art, maps, and architecture; collections of secondary works; and sets of tools for learning and analyzing the Greek language and culture. Each year, a new version of the materials will be produced, augmented by new articles and works contributed by scholars of classical Greek culture. Thus, Perseus is planned as a medium for teaching, learning, and electronic publishing. The evaluation plan [40] focuses on four groups of questions related to content, system, instruction, and learning. The evaluation for the first year will be formative in nature, aiming to influence the development of future releases of Perseus. Subsequent phases will be increasingly summative, aiming to assess the impacts of the materials on teaching, learning, and scholarly research. Many of the methods described in the framework for evaluation presented here will be used at various times and in various settings that include large and small public and private universities. For the first year of the evaluation, the questions related to learners focus on determining the tactics and strategies students use and how these develop into patterns of learning. In subsequent years, as behaviors and perceptions are identified and classified, comparisons across populations and courses will be made, and distinctions among traditional and Perseus-supported learning assessed.

Acknowledgements

The author wishes to acknowledge the helpful comments and suggestions made by Delia Neuman and Peter Evans in the preparation of this paper.

References

[1] Clark, R. (1989). Current progress and future directions for research in instructional technology. *Educational Technology Research and Development, 37*(1), 57-66.

[2] Marchionini, G. (1988). Hypermedia and learning: Freedom and chaos. *Educational Technology, 28*(11), 8-12.

[3] Ross, S. & Morrison, G. (198). In search of a happy medium in instructional technology research: issues concerning external validity, media replications, and learner control. *Educational Technology Research and Development, 37*(1), 19-33.

[4] Winograd, T. & Flores, F. (1986). *Understanding computers and cognition.* Norwood, NJ: Ablex Publishing.

[5] Landow, G. (in press). The rhetoric of hypermedia. In D. Jonassen & H. Mandl (Eds.), *Designing Hypertext for Learning.*

[6] Kearsley, G. (1988). Authoring considerations for hypertext. *Educational Technology, 28*(11), 21-24.

[7] Marchionini, G., Liebscher, P., & Lin, X. (1989). Authoring hyperdocuments: designing for interaction. Paper presented at the 1989 Mid-Year Meeting of the American Society for Information Science, San Diego, Ca.

[8] Shneiderman, B. (1989). Reflections of authoring, editing, and managing hypertext. In E. Barrett (Ed.), *The society of text.* Cambridge, MA: MIT Press.

[9] Wright, P. (in press). *Interface alternatives for hypertexts. Hypermedia.*

[10] Jonassen, D. (1986). Hypertext principles for text and courseware design. *Educational Psychologist, 21*(11), 269-292.

[11] Halasz, F. (1988). Reflections on notecards: Seven issues for the next generation of hypermedia systems. *Communications of the ACM, 31*(7),836-852.

[12] Alexander, P., & Judy, J. (1988). Domain-specific and strategic knowledge. *Review of Educational Research, 58(*4), 375-404.

[13] Lochhead, J. (1979). An introduction to cognitive process instruction. In J. Lochhead & J. Clement (Eds.), *Cognitive Process Instruction.* (pp. 1-4) Philadelphia, PA: The Franklin Institute Press.

[14] Vosniadou, S., & Brewer, W. (1987). Theories of knowledge restructuring in development. *Review of Educational Research, 57*(2), 51-67.

[15] Dwyer, T. (1980). Heuristic strategies for using computers to enrich education In R. Taylor (Ed.), *The computer in the school: Tutor, tool, tutee,* (pp. 87-103). New York: Teachers College Press

[16] Papert, S. (1980). *Mindstorms: Children, computers, and powerful ideas.* New York: Basic Books.

[17] Streibel, M. (1986). A critical analysis of the use of computers in education. *Educational Communications and Technology Journal, 34*(3),137-161.

[18] FIPSE Technology Study Group. (1988). Ivory towers, silicon basements: *Learner-centered computing in postsecondary education.* McKinney, TX: Academic Computing Publications.

[19] Egan, D. (1988). Individual differences in human computer interaction. In M. Helander (Ed.), *Handbook of human-computer interaction*, (pp. 543-568). New York: Elsevier.

[20]. Marchionini, G. (1989). Information-seeking strategies of novices using a full-text electronic encyclopedia. *Journal of the American Society for Information Science, 40*(1), 54-66.

[21]. Marchionini, G. (1989). Making the transition from print to electronic encyclopedias: Adaptation of mental models. *International Journal of Man-Machine Studies, 30,* 591-618.

[22] Carroll, J., & Aaronson, A. (1988). Learning by doing with simulated intelligen help. *Communications of the ACM, 31*(9), 1064-79.

20.17

[23] Norman, (1988). *The psychology of everyday things*. New York: Basic Books.

[24] Perkins, D. & Simmons, R. (1988). Patterns of misunderstanding: An integrative model for science, math, and programming. *Review of Educational Research, 58*(3), 303-326.

[25] Penniman, W.D., & Dominick, W. (1980). Monitoring and evaluation of on-line information system usage. *Information Processing and Management, 16*, 17-35.

[26] Scriven, M. (1981). Product evaluation, In N. Smith, (Ed.), *New techniques for evaluation*. Beverly Hills, CA: Sage Publications.

[27] Jolicoeur, K. & Berger, D. (1986). Do we really know what makes educational software effective? A call for empirical research on effectiveness. *Educational Technology, 26*(12), 7-11.

[28] Verreck, W. & Lkoundi, A. (in press). From instructional text to instructional hypertext. In D. Jonnasen & H. Mandl, (Eds.), *Designing hypertext for learning*.

[29] Kerlinger, F. (1973). *Foundations of behavioral research (2nd Edition)*. New York: Holt, Rinehart & Winston.

[30] Guba, E. & Lincoln, Y. (1982). Epistemological and methodological bases of naturalistic inquiry. *Educational Communication and Technology Journal*, 30, 233-252.

[31] Neuman, D. (in press). Naturalistic inquiry and computer-based instruction: Rationale, procedures, and potential. *Educational Technology Research and Development*.

[32] Rice, R. & Borgman, C. (1983). The use of computer-monitored data in information science and communication research. *Journal of the American Society for Information Science, 34*(4), 247-256.

[33] Card, S., Moran, T. & Newell, A. (1983). *The psychology of human-computer interaction*. Hillsdale, NJ: Erlbaum Associates.

[34] Singley, M. & Anderson, L. (1988). A keystroke analysis of learning and transfer in text editing. *Human-Computer Interaction, 3*(3), 223-274.

[35] Ericsson, K. & Simon, H. (1984). *Protocol analysis: Verbal reports as data.*
Cambridge, MA: MIT Press.

[36]. Mayes, T., Kibby, M. & Anderson, T. (in press). Learning about learning from.hypertext. In D. Jonassen & H. Mandl (Eds.), *Designing hypertext for learning.*

[37] Harris, M. & Cady, M. (1988). The dynamic process of creating hypertext literature. *Educational Technology, 28*(11), 33-39.

[38] Jones, T. (1989). Incidental learning during information retrieval: A hypertext experiment. Paper presented at the International Conference on Computer Assisted Instruction, Austin, Texas.

[39] Crane, G. (1988). Redefining the book: Some preliminary problems. *Academic Computing, 2*(5), 6-11.

[40] Marchionini, G., Neuman, D. & Morrell, K. (1989). *Perseus Evaluation Plan Perseus Project Working Paper Number 5.* Harvard University, Cambridge, MA.

PART VI

CONCEPTUAL FOUNDATIONS FOR DESIGNING HYPERMEDIA SYSTEMS FOR LEARNING

Chapter 21
Some Examples of Hypertext's Applications

Eric Bruillard, Gérard Weidenfeld
SOFTIA
Paris, FR

Keywords

Computer assisted learning; viewpoint; hypermedia systems; help systems; learning by doing

Contents

Introduction

Hypertext or more generally hypermedia fits various applications. The general idea of three dimensional reading appears in a software engineering application as well as in a teaching program. Of course, the hypertext structures dedicated to both applications differ greatly.

Since effective uses of hypertexts have not been adequately documented we can offer no typology, but we will try to present some models of different uses of hypertexts in very

NATO ASI Series, Vol. F 67
Designing Hypermedia for Learning
Edited by D. H. Jonassen and H. Mandl
© Springer-Verlag Berlin Heidelberg 1990

different situations. The material in the first part of this chapter is based upon training applications first initiated by Softia :

- •Hypertext linked with a prolog kernel for a prolog training environment.
- •Conjunction of hypertext and problem solver in a mathematical training programm
- •Two programs which enable a wide exploration of a choice of poetry or philosophical french texts

A first system was developed as HyperInfo. One of it's main characteristics is memory residence which makes it usable at the same time as other software. Hypertext functions as a help facility, complementary to other task or other educational software. A number of products have been designed with this system. A survey of these applications will be made with a special interest on an intelligent authoring *system* including a version of this hypertext : Bull's Starguide. We conclude by briefly explaining improvements we want to add and describe a complete Hypermedia system.

The evolution of training programs ‗‗‗‗‗

SEVE system

The first version of hypertext was the SEVE system [1, 2, 3]. It is constructed in Prolog with a set of window facilities which provides the hypertext interaction. The initial purpose of this system was to facilitate the use of administrative documents by different kinds of people for different purposes: explaining words, expressions or what they have to write in the fields, and verify the correctness of their assessments. But this system has mainly been used for creating computer assisted learning programs. This system enables the author to combine guided and discovery sequences. The bridges between these two kind of sequences are often related to some critical aspects of learning processes :

- •Give sense to an assessment : what it means, some examples,...
- •Make the messages of the system more explicit : at least two main situations :
  - •Indications (for instance, what is the formal way for.....)
  - •Comments about errors. Here the use of hypertext gives some flexibility to the diagnostic system : a cooperative process occurs in which the student has opportunity to make a

rather general message more explicit.
•Add domain knowledge to the software.

The principles underlined by the SEVE system are linked to
many *assumptions about learning* :

> •We don't know precisely what learning is, but we think
> that it is a dynamic process based upon actions and
> problem solving (generally speaking, *learning by
> doing*),
>
> •A learning process can be viewed, in a hypertext sense,
> as the creation of links between general knowledge
> and different tasks or problems.

DJ explanation 1.8-9

These assumptions describe the kind of learning programs we
intend to do: environments that can be freely explored by
learners, in which they have tasks to perform, and contextual
access to knowledge displayed in a hypertext format. Thus,
hypertext is a supplementary resource in which learners can
extract information they need for solving problems or for
understanding their mistakes.

Examples of training programs
We can briefly describe four products that have been built :

Apilog. Apilogis a Prolog software engineering tool which
offers an information environment ("hyper-book" about
Prolog), a syntactic analysis module which makes a first
diagnosis about a student's errors, a Prolog interpreter, and a
set of examples and goals. An important feature of Apilog's
hypertext is the two level explanation network devoted respectively to beginners and advanced students. This property,
however, does increase the amount of work for the author,
who must keep count of the cards common to both points of
view and build two browsers with some common functions.

ARRIA. This system enables the user to build geometrical
proofs in a controlled environment. Arria is not really a
problem solver although it functions similarly. They are three
important features in these system.

> •The use of hypertext for explaining errors. Errors are
> detected by the control system and a message is
> displayed in an hypertext format.
> •Access to a mathematical course while solving the
> problem.
> •Explicit assessments of proofs.

LYRE and Textes Philosophiques. These two programs enable a wide exploration of a choice of poetry or philosophical French texts. The main technical improvement in these programs is an extensive use of "viewpoint". A text is shown on the screen and the student has opportunity to choose a way of "reading" this text. A guided mode is also available. The user may look at the poetical analogies used or the poetical techniques used (alliteration, musicality, ...). Each of these categories is a "viewpoint". There are also other kinds of viewpoints, for instance, what is related to nature, death, color.... in a poem. The selection of any viewpoint highlights the parts of the text relative to that viewpoint. When the cursor is moved over such a highlighted word, an explanation of this word, according to the given viewpoint is displayed in a window. Again some words are highlighted in the window and are linked to explanations, always according to the selected viewpoint. Seemingly everything occurs as if several hypertexts were nested together. In fact, the situation is much more complicated because their is some "arithmetics" on viewpoints. A word may be attached with several viewpoints. In that case it has the same meaning according to any of the related viewpoints. This property has a concrete visualization : the word belonging to viewpoint 1 appears in some color, those belonging to viewpoint 2 appears in an other color and those belonging both to viewpoint 1 and viewpoint 2 appears in a third color. The ability to cross viewpoints enables a very deep, fascinating text exploration.With very slight technical changes, hypertext is used to give a flat (but colored) description of a three dimensional phenomena; which is a quite unusual. It would be interesting to extend these programs in allowing the user to *explore links between several texts* .

Viewpoints in hypertext

This notion of viewpoint that we have just described is an important feature of the system and is extremely important for several reasons. It allows more contextual access to hypertext based on contexts such as:

- •the task
- •the general knowledge of the user
- •the history of the activity

You will notice that the last, history of activity, is dynamic and the others are mostly static. According to a task, the notion of viewpoint is related to what is called "plural readings." Poetry can be considered as a compacted hypermedia because of the links between formal aspects and internal meaning (sounds, pictures, rhythm, etc...). The teacher's job is to explain and show these hidden links. As a reader or listener, we just have to click in our head. That is evident for poetry or philosophical texts, but it is also true for writing Prolog programs. Such a program can have different meanings according to the instantiation of the variables. Another point is that words or expressions that signal links are highlighted. Changing the viewpoint has a visual effect on the current text. This feature can be used to see directly the important points in a given viewpoint. For example, in solving a classical word problem with several questions, a student may experience difficulties in attending to the relevant information in the statement of the problem. Here, links can be more important than content, since the dynamic process of changing the viewpoint according to the question is very useful.

To summarize, our use of hypertext in the SEVE system is not very different from a help system. The goal of a help system is to give the right information at the right moment (in trying to understand user's intention), and in a learning environment, we try to give an access to relevant informations for performing a current task (teacher's intention). This can lead to a *usability metric of an hypertext* in a goal driven system: how many operations (or links?) are needed for a user in a given context to get the right information for performing a task.

Hypertext authoring systems

All the programs discussed previously were, as pointed out, programmed in Prolog, which permits "intelligent tutoring system's capabilities. The next section describes briefly an intelligent authoring system which includes hypertext.

Hypertext in an intelligent authoring system
The Starguide system was developed at Bull MTS by Gerard Claes and his staff. A precise description of the system may be found in [4]. Basically, it includes an authoring system with a student modeller, a teacher modeller, and the features (expert systems, oriented object language kernel) needed to account for these models in pedagogical processes.

Another nice feature of Starguide is that it offers the opportunity to stand beneath a software application (for instance text editor or spreadsheet) and react to actions performed by the student in the application. Inside this system, hypertext has

JL comment Very important!

the precise objectives pointed out previously: to provide information to the student, explain errors and assessments, and help online.

The last feature of Starguide suggests that a *good user's interface for learning about some software is this software itself*. This was the primary idea for designing HyperInfo.

Resident hypertext—HyperInfo

Technical description of HyperInfo. Let us first recall that on a PC computer a "resident program" is a program which may be loaded into memory and reside there while another program runs and until some action (usually the stroke of a particular key) is performed. The resident program is active until the user leaves it temporarily. This is one of the important technical features of HyperInfo, which can provide textual explanation cards to the user for any software that runs on a DOS system. Cards possess the usual properties: they are displayed in a window; and in each card, some keywords are highlighted to give access to further information. At each node the user may enter more deeply in the explanation graph or come back to the previous card or leave the hypertext and come back to the main software. There are three ways in which the user may switch from the application to the hypertext .

1. Strike a key and *access the table of contents*, then stroll through the hypertext.

2. Strike another key and *access directly the card of the word under the cursor*

3. Move a special cursor to *any word or sentence on the screen* and access its card.

The two last points are made possible with a special inner structure of the hypertext: each card is referred to by it's name (in fact one of it's possible names), and what is more important, the stack of cards is independent of the front end. In other words, once you build an application (or stack using Hypercard's vocabulary), it may be used in conjunction with any software, without needing further development. A useful analogy is a dictionary : once created it applies to any text relative to it's domain.

Main applications of HyperInfo

As explained previously, HyperInfo was designed for providing online help. Obviously it does this, but we were fortunate to discover that, sometimes with slight changes, it can be applied to other kinds of applications. Here are some examples.

- •Explaining computerized procedures: How to fill some kind of documents? how to write a dedicated letter? These are typical problems that can be solved with an HyperInfo application. In fact you may at the same time, provide training and online help, that is, learning by doing.
- •Comments on computer programs: Too many comments in a program make it unreadable and too few are insufficient for understanding it.Resident hypertext with contextual access provides a simple efficient solution. Comments are developed as necessary, and may be consulted as needed.
- •Computer aided presentation. HyperInfo is a useful environment for authoring linear presentation displays.
- •Patching CAL programs. Some CAL would benefit from a layer of information making messages more explicit or more dedicated to some devoted public. Once again, HyperInfo provides an easy to build solution that enables the program to make sense in a particular context to existing inadequate educational software. It is also a convenient way of sharing information between the different actors of the computer aided educational process. The author provides more information through hypertext, or the trainer or teacher may adapt the program to a particular training environment or student type,or students may add their comments individually or collectively.
- •Dealing with unorganized data - cooperation with databases

This point will not be developed here. It is only a brief look at the other (than educational) application of hypertext: documentation. Two principal ways of accessing information are provided:

- •Query: if you know what to ask, then use a data base and some devoted language, like SQL.
- •Wander: if you don't exactly what you need. Then use hypertext.

The fact that HyperInfo is resident allows us to have, at the same moment, access to structured information (database) and less structured information. Further works are in progress for making better connections between these two ways of accessing information. Probably some applications to learning or training may evolve from this.

HyperInfo for authors

The conception of HyperInfo applications leads us again to some resolution of the access problems. The authoring problem is to transfer an expository kind of knowledge into a non-linear but direct access. From an organizational viewpoint, we have to cut a large amount of information into small pieces, with cross-referencing. At any time, the user needs only a small amount of information, and must not be obliged to conduct a long search to get it. We have experimented with this problem with school teachers in order to create an orthographical French grammar in the HyperInfo format. The initial results show that the removal of perspective seems to be very hard. We do not yet have a sufficient methodology for the conception of such hypertexts. <u>It is very different to create a hypertext for yourself and for other people.</u>

Conclusion: From hypertext to hypermedia

In HyperInfo, the content of the cards is basically text, although the graphics screens may be accessed. This results from the primary technical choice of making the hypertext resident, i.e. using as little memory as possible in order run at the same time as other software. If the hypertext is intended to be used alone (which is the usual way), there is much more flexibility, and the cards may include other data types :

- •Graphics: full screen pictures (created with drawing programs or scanners) in which any number of zones provides easy access to other hypermedia cards.

- •Programs: Any program may be run from any sensitive zone of any card. This feature provides access to external world such as, videodisk, speech generation, sensors or to other processes. The only limitation is memory available on the computer.

- •Texts: HyperInfo is of course compatible with that hypermedia program. That means that text windows, displayed in a graphical format may be accessed from everywhere.

•Rules: This feature is under development. Basically, a link, instead of being static, may became dynamic. The invocation of such a card activates a set of rules (partly local to the given card and partly global or context dependent).

Hypermedia applications

Most of the previous applications also apply in an improved form. We will mention briefly some "canonical" domains for the use of hypermedia.

1. Technical documentation: based on pictures, you point a part of a schema and get the appropriate description: new picture or text.

2. Interactive information: In public places, museum, department stores,halls,.... hypermedia is easy to use and very responsive.

3. Some "CAL" programs: CAI programs built around hypermedia provide increased learner control. These programs often deal with technical features

4. Patching CAL programs: The way in which these programs may be enhanced by hypermedia is a bit different than was described earlier. Hypermedia acts as an integrator. The student starts with exploration and then has a CAL sequence to perform.

Notice that we did not, in the previous description, mention the applications of simultaneous use of usual artificial intelligence techniques and hypermedia. Some projects are under development and will at least yield two new kinds of applications: contextual help for the use of software and contextual help for building and browsing a hypertext. Our focus in this chapter was on existing systems. Of course AI is a major focus and we will describe some improvements in the future.

References

[1] Brouayue, P., Bruillard, E., Marchal, G., and Weidenfeld, G. (1987). SEVE *Actes du congrès francophone sur l'Enseignement assisté par ordinateur.* Cap d'Agde

[2] Weidenfeld, G. (1987) *Third International Conference on Artificial and Education*. Pittsburgh, PA.

[3] Ferrett, E., and Weidenfeld, G. (1987). Exploratory environments and Intelligent Tutoring Systems. *Deutch Journal for Education* .

[4] Claes, G. (1988). *Contribution à l'application de l'Intelligence Artificielle pour l'Enseignement Assisté par Ordinateur* Thèse soutenue à l'Université Paris-sud (ORSAY).

[5] MULTIMEDIA JOURNAL 1 (1989). *De la création à l'utilisation de produits éducatifs conçus à l'aide de nouvelles technologies*. Publication DELTA, phase exploratoire.

Chapter 22
Hyperinformation Requirements for an Integrated Authoring/Learning Environment

Max Mühlhäuser
Telematics Group
University of Kaiserslautern, FRG

Keywords

Hypertext; hypermedia; hyperinformation; computer aided instruction; multimedia; integrated environment

Contents

NATO ASI Series, Vol. F 67
Designing Hypermedia for Learning
Edited by D. H. Jonassen and H. Mandl
© Springer-Verlag Berlin Heidelberg 1990

Introduction ————————————

Overview

This chapter reports about the mutual influences of hypermedia technology and integrated computer supported authoring/learning. It presents a set of recommendations for adaptations and extensions of hypermedia systems, leading to a "hyperinformation system" suitable as a design center for integrated authoring/learning environments.

In the beginning, a vision will be presented of how the authoring/learning process can be supported in such an integrated environment. This view forms the context in which subsequent sections of the chapter have to be seen. The next section will describe the evolution of systems based on the "hyper..." paradigm. Recommendations will be given about how to construct an appropriate base system adhering to the "hyper..." paradigm. The base system can be used as a generic "virtual machine" on which to build integrated authoring/learning environments. The final section will very briefly sketch an overall architecture for such an environment.

Background

The work in this chapter has been carried out in the context of a project called NESTOR. This project is undertaken jointly by the University and the Digital Equipment Campus-based Engineering Center (CEC) in Karlsruhe, and by other universities. The field of research is the use of networked multimedia workstations for computer supported authoring/learning. A major project goal is to implement a prototype authoring/learning environment on a network of multimedia workstations, focussing on the following topics:

- a framework for integrating and customizing toolsets for authoring and learning in a common environment,
- computer support for instruction, e.g., for the generic formal description, selection, incorporation, and execution of instructional methods and strategies;
- seamless integration and synchronization of media;
- distribution aspects (collaborative authoring/learning, distance learning, media communication, distribution in hyperinformation, etc.).

Instruction processes: Tradition and vision

We want to provide an understanding both of known approaches to instruction and of our vision of new approaches, which we want to call "computer supported authoring/learning." In this part of the chapter, we will outline this vision technically and from an "instructional" perspective. First of all, however, we must introduce some understanding and terminology as a common foundation. Talking about a multidisciplinary problem domain always covers the problem of coping with different terminologies and "world models". Computer supported authoring/learning touches computer science as well as different disciplines: pedagogy, psychology, didactics, instructional design. In the remainder, terms and processes related to computer supported authoring/learning will be described in an informal way, abstracting from details, but trying to find a synthesis of all the "world models" related. This must mean, however, that a member of one of the disciplines will find terms used in a way that he is not exactly used to.

Principles of instruction

This section will provide an idea of how we basically understand instruction and authoring/learning. Corresponding terms will be introduced in the way we want to use them in the remainder. *Boldface italic* denotes terms, **boldface** denotes explanations.

Category is one of the most fundamental terms for understanding instruction, even thinking in general. Our learning and thinking is related to our ability to build categories, i.e. to **unite and distinguish** things, to recognize similarities and differences, and to relate new things to those we know by including or excluding them from categories we know. We build subcategories and supercategories, assign several categories to the same thing, and relate categories to one another. In biology, the ability to learn and the ability to build categories are integrated. We want to take the view that everything we learn is understood by its adherence or non-adherence to previously known categories. This simplistic view will help us to define and understand terms, the conclusions we draw are however not bound to this view.

22.4

DJ explanation 6.6-7

Concept shall denote the **representation of a category** in our mind.

DJ explanation 1.7-8

We can now understand *instruction* (seen as the combination of teaching and learning) as the **intention to convey concepts**. It can be seen as a valuable goal to make the process of instruction (of conveying concepts) efficient. "Efficient" here may mean economical (fast, easy, cost-effective...), and it may mean that we want to avoid misconceptions which are due to the process of conveying the concepts. We may well want to accept misconception—or better: the diversity of concepts— as a natural, evolutionary and sociologically desirable effect. Diversification of concepts should however not arbitrarily occur due to uncontrollable "transmission losses" in the process of conveying concepts, but rather be restricted to conveyance procedures which conserve the relevant aspects of concepts, such as the evoked behaviour or the adherence to ethical rules.

Information is some **symbolic representation** which can **evoke a concept** in our mind. Nothing is said about the size of the information, the kinds of symbols used, or whether the information can directly or only indirectly (after a "transformation") evoke a concept. Gestures, a light going on, and shelves full of books are all information, as is the computer scientist's intuition of information as "meaningful data."

Model is defined as information which **exhibits** some **behavioral analogy** to the concept it represents. Lab experiments, miniature models, and computer programs may be examples for models. Experimenting with models is well accepted as a good way of learning about concepts.

Technical resources denote means for **non-volatile storage**—possibly additionally **manipulation** and **transmission**—of information. The most noticible technical resources are textbooks and computer systems.

A *course* is a self-contained unit of information produced intentionally for instruction. *Courseware* denotes a course stored, manipulated, and presented **using a computer system**.

Document shall be the term for an **information as a "Gestalt"** when presented to the learner, e.g., for textual information in the sum of the actual text, the layout, color, presentation medium (paper, computer screen), font, size, and other context of the presentation (even hour of day etc.).

Recording media/storage media/transmission media/presentation media are used when an author generates information/ when information is stored/transmitted/provided to the learner. Respective examples are: a camera with a tape recorder/a videotape/a fibre optics computer networks/a holographical device.

Information media denote the "kind of symbols" used to form the information, e.g., audiovideo, audio, text, graphics. *Media* shall be a short term for information media. *Teachers* and *authors* are humans who **produce information** with the (primary) intention of teaching.

Learners are humans who **consume information** for the same reason.

Teachers require learners to be relatively **close in time and space**: information is provided primarily in volatile form (e.g., using speech) and often transmitted within small distances (e.g., within a single room).

Authors typically produce information in a non-volatile form, making storage, replication, and transmission over long distances easy, **reducing time and space constraints** to the triviality that learning cannot occur before authoring (but way after, and at any place), and allowing better evaluation of the information provider (the author).

Tutors shall be defined as humans **assisting** learners in **consuming authored information.**

Historically, we have seen a shift from teaching/learning to authoring/learning, i.e. the authoring/learning process is increasingly important. This is partly due to the advantages mentioned, especially the freedom in time/space.

In the last several hundred years, the shift to authoring/learning was largely geared by the tremendously increasing use of the *textbook* (in a broad sense as textual, graphical, and image information on paper, written with the intend of instruction) as a technical resource.

Technical vision

With the advent of the computer as a technical resource, multiuser systems with terminals and PCs were used for instructional purposes. Severe ergonomical drawbacks and an essential lack of hardware and software features made them largely infeasable for this purpose.

More recent advances open a number of opportunities for substantially increasing the efficiency of the process of conveying concepts in an authoring/learning environment (in the above defined meaning).

We see the need for a *multifacetted computer system*, comprised of powerful workstations, capable of coping with multiple information media, integrated in a distributed system, and providing an online information space:

- Powerful workstations must be available to authors, tutors, and learners, with advanced high resolution graphics, "direct manipulation" interfaces, virtual memory multitasking, exhaustive local storage and provisions for seamless network integration.
- Information media must be introduced on workstations, including motion video, sound, and high quality image—ultimately stored in digitized format—to be integrated, transmitted and processed without cost-intensive add-on hardware.
- Distributed systems must show a high level of integration and sophistication: *realtime media communication*, *distributed processing support* not restricted to client/server architectures ("access" traffic) but allowing *dynamic irregular topologies* ("balanced n-party" traffic), and *computer mediated collaboration* support for the authoring and learning processes as described below.
- Online information space has to make most of the "secondary" information used along with the provision and consumption of a course available online. More and more, contents of courses will not be recorded to a computer processible medium intentionally for a specific course, but be retrieved at authoring time from *multimedia libraries*. Today we find mostly textual databases, but offline multimedia libraries starting to evolve already. Their online accessability will take a few more years to be technically feasible, at least over wide area networks.

Multiuser and *multilevel* support has to be offered to authors and learners: courses must be extracted from, related to, merged with the residual online information space, consisting of parts which may be private, group based, organization wide, or pertaining to another organization. *Courseware reusability*, based on modular courseware, dedicated tools, and copyright regulations, is required, introducing "cut & paste" authoring techniques analogous to those practiced with hardware lecture notes.

Instructional vision

Multifaceted computer systems (computers, for short) as described in above can help in many ways in instruction; many of their features have not yet been sufficiently explored in this context. We want to briefly sketch the envisioned influence of computers on courseware, authoring, and learning.

Computer support in courseware. The traditional form of courseware has often been characterized as "presentation CAI" as it usually presents units of information to the learner, then interacts with him/her to determine (guess) his/her level of understanding, and branches to the next unit of information according to the results of the interaction. In order to understand how courseware on a multifaceted computer system should function. We want to describe the capabilities of the system to store, manipulate, and present information:

- *Flexible gestalt:* as the Gestalt of the information is of great importance for the learners performance, the flexibility and power of a multifacetted computer system should be used to keep the Gestalt of the information—in its broadest sense—as flexible and adaptive as possible. Layout, information media used, flow of information (granularity, sequence, iterations...) can be varied and driven by authors, tutors, and/or learners. Even "lower level concepts" may be kept variable to augment the learners' performance in understanding the important "higher level concepts" (imagine, e.g., an automatic translation system used in a multilingual environment; there it could be desirable to sacrifice "literal translation" of sentences for better achievement of "translation of meaning").
- *Use of models:* the processing power of a computer can help to make much better use of models, (e.g., simulations). The relevant classes of models to be incorporated and used are:
- *Concept models*, i.e. models of concepts to be conveyed (see Principles of Instruction).
- *Instruction models*, i.e. instructional strategies, rules, and methods.

•*Student models*, i.e. models reflecting the envisioned student population.

•*Human centering:* The biggest advantage of teaching/ learning lays in the flexibility which is inherent in human-human interaction. In order for authoring/ learning to make use of this advantage, too, "human centered" authoring/learning and tutor assistance must be considered. Human centered authoring/ learning must try to keep the motivation of authors and learners high and to reflect the individual differences of different humans using a system.

Computer supported authoring. Most organizations producing computer-based instruction use well defined procedures to reach in a production cycle. Goal selection, content assessment, determination of objectives, scripting/storyboarding, prototyping, production, formative and summative evaluation, and delivery are some of the steps of the processes that must be completed. The traditional approach, however, has two principal disadvantages:

•It is badly computer supported. While the end product (courseware) is a computer program, the production, up to the actual generation of the computer program itself, is only marginally influenced by the use of computer programs. This is especially true when authoring *languages* are used. The use of existing authoring *systems*, on the other hand, introduces computer use somewhat earlier in the production cycle, but at the same time often restricts the possibilities of the instructional designer in an intolerable way: courses usually have to adhere to one single, predefined, rigid instructional strategy which the authoring system is built around, the strategy being often a derivative of presentation-CAI based on few types of building blocks.

•It is either inflexible or poorly controllable. The "paper based" procedures used in many organizations can only be changed with difficulty. Especially uncommon processes, like one where authors and learners are the same group of persons, are difficult to introduce. Cooperation among groups either follows ethical rules or is bound to restrictive procedures.

We suggest a process approach that overcomes these deficiencies:

- *Computer supported authoring* should be provided throughout the process, integrating tools which guide the developer through the steps, producing computer-readable data which can be reused in subsequent steps/tools. Special emphasis should be placed on:
- Computer support for *instructional aspects,* i.e. for formally describing flexible instructional strategies and rules (enabling reuse), and for incorporating them into a course;
- Computer support for *collaboration* among authors, between authors and learners, and among learners.
- *Flexibility of the authoring process* should be provided through flexible, customizable tools, user-accessable and easily changeable descriptions of the process formed around a toolset.
- Tool support is to be provided for *exhibiting the possible features* of integrated courseware and a computer supported learning process.

Computer supported learning. The frustration with traditional presentation-CAI infers that the computer system can be better used, with a strong emphasis on the student model. This suggests an "intelligent tutoring systems" (ITS) approach, trying to couple courseware with a model as complex and complete as possible of the potential learner, allowing reactions to questions and to the way s/he answers questions or drives the courseware. The enormous complexity of a human, a good model of which is hard to build, and the resulting vulnerability and lack of general applicability of ITS systems developed, recently seem to have lead to a second frustration phase. More and more, people believe that models (student models, instruction models, sometimes even concept models) are largely impossible and should not be tried. Rather, students should organize the information and should be provided as much freedom and as little "determinism" as possible, helping to make the "free journey" through information as easy as possible. This vision prompted the introduction of "hypertext systems" into instruction.

DJ corroboration 4.3

Our vision, however, is that of *staggered guidance.* The flexibility offered by a hypertext-like organization of information should not lead to a new religion, preaching totally unguided walks through vast amounts of information. Rather, systems should allow flexible combinations of information with instruction models, student models, and concept models, more or less "guiding" the user through the information space.

Free and *unguided* should not be mixed up. Freedom is necessary because models can never be complete and can never predetermine each and every facet of the "reality" they model, but guidance is necessary because everybody who ever learned knows the possible stimulation that can come from a teacher who, in the broadest sense, provided external motivation and evaluation. The emphasis should be laid on avoiding "bad teacher" behavior.

Rather than exaggerating the disadvantages of authoring/learning, we must reduce them. The worst characteristic of author-based instruction is its "distribute and forget" nature, i.e. authors produce documents, "dump" them onto the learners, and forget about the learners. Many distance learning efforts suffer this syndrome. Over the last years, electronic mail channels from learners to authors (and among learners) have become popular. This feedback channel is much too "thin" (it takes too big an effort to overcome a learner's problem), and it is totally decoupled from the courseware. These disadvantages have to be overcome, too.

Hyperinformation requirements _____

Related work

An excellent overview about major open issues—from a technical (computer science) perspective—is given in [2]. The use of hypertext/hypermedia in the instructional context is discussed in [4], an excellent practical system in this respect, called IDE (a follow-on project being called Alexandria), is presented in [5,6].

DJ example 24.1-19

Major *technical* open issues identified in the literature comprise
- the need for different access patterns and concepts, like query-based access and (hypermedia) link-based access;
- the impacts of the use of hypermedia within a community, such as concurrency, distribution, collaborative work issues, etc.;
- the impacts of extensive day-to-day use such as configuration and scaling support (versioning, hierarchical structuring).

Major *instructional* aspects discussed in the literature show
- how knowledge can be treated in the context of hypertext, the basic suggestion being to represent knowl-

edge as semantic networks and to map those onto hypertext structures, and

- how IDE supports the representation of (mostly factual) knowledge as hypertext and how it supports the whole authoring/learning processes around hypermedia-based information.

The following list of research directions is a synthesis of issues stated (explicitly or implicitly) in the above cited and related literature, in project NESTOR.

DJ corroboration 6.9-10   22.11

Evaluation of hypertext/hypermedia systems

The evaluation of hypertext was in the past driven by a requirement for a more flexible Gestalt of information. We will show how increasing flexibility was introduced, what goals where missed, and how our vision of "Hyperinformation Processing" can help to lay the ground for the vision stated at the beginning of the chapter.

We want to distinguish *hypertext/hypermedia*—information from *hypertext/hypermedia systems* (systems which allow the creation and/or manipulation and/or consumption of hypertext/hypermedia).

Hypertext

What was added: structure. Hypertext added *explicit nonlinearity* to "text", i.e. textbook-like information (cf. above). Textbooks had already had many ways of helping the reader to organize his/her own path through the information:

- relations between pieces of information: references to "primary sources" (within the text) and to "secondary sources" (citations)...
- different abstraction levels: tables of contents, abstracts, plain text, footnotes, in-depth chapters...
- support for alternative learning processes: verbal, formal, example-based descriptions...

DJ comment Such as the annotations and reference sitations in this book.

Hypertext eschewed predefined paths through the information, made relations, abstractions, and alternatives explicit, and allowed the references to "secondary sources" to become "primary" by directly connecting to the secondary source instead of to a citation. Doing this, formerly independent pieces of information were accumulated in larger information sets.

With the hypertext idea as described, three generic building blocks of hypertext fell into place:
> •**nodes** (or cards): atomic—from the point of view of the hypertext system—pieces of information
> •**collections:** sets of nodes; also: sets of abstractions
> •**links:** references between nodes and/or abstractions

Hypertext was possible only through the shift from textbooks to computer-based storage media, but we will see that hypertext did not take advantage of many of the essential features offered by multifaceted computer systems.

What was left out: Categories. Early hypertext systems did not provide explicit support for categorization, an essential structuring means:
> •Nodes and links could not be assigned categories in the sense that system support would be given for treating members of a category equally (this informal definition will be refined in below).
> •Collections were really only sets of nodes (or of abstractions), i.e., pure "envelopes" around elements, and did not exhibit information and/or behaviour of a more abstract level than that of the contained elements.

What was lost: guidance. Freedom without guidance is essentially undesirable. Not only the problem of "getting lost in hypertext" is to be avoided (there is a controversy about whether this problem seriously exists), "goal-directed learning" and "motivation and evaluation" also imply some level of guidance at learning time. Hypertext provides more freedom, but guidance through the information space is partly lost. Most of the steps described in the remainder of the chapter tried, as one of their goals, to reintroduce guidance.

DJ definition 1.13

Hypermedia
What was added: media. The advent of multiple media on the computer opened a new opportunity for more flexible Gestalt of information: nodes could be based on the most appropriate media, alternative media could be used, time-variant concepts could be better transformed into information using time-based media like audio or video.

What was left out: media synchronization. The difficulty in coping with multiple media is that of synchronizing different media in order for them to jointly form integrated multimedia information instead of just "multiple media". For example, if audiovidual information is accompanied by textual information and by animated graphics, it should make no difference what "surface" of the multimedia information the learner interacts with. Whether he enters text (e.g., to be searched in the textual information), manipulates the audiovidual player or a graphical equivalent of it on the screen, or manipulates the graphical animation, in any case the whole integral multimedia information should "adapt" to the manipulation.

Briefly, the hypertext system should offer means for composing different media into "integrated multimedia" and for integrally manipulating them. Hypermedia systems to date offer too little support—the best known system in this regard being Athena Muse [3]. Too much "handcrafting" is still required when developing individual hypermedia in order to achieve some of the synchronization/integration functionality described.

Intelligent hypermedia
What was added: "Intelligence." Early in hypertext/hypermedia development, the need for representing notions of "artificial intelligence" within hypertext was raised. The "bubbles-and-arcs" structure and static nature of hypertext qualified semantic networks as the most appropriate concept of AI. Indeed, semantic networks can be expressed relatively easily with hypertext/hypermedia systems, some systems even provide special support for this. Concept modelling, instruction modelling, and student modelling can be realized to a certain degree on this basis.

DJ contrast 4.3

DJ contrast 4.3, corroboration 6.9-10

What was left out: "Reasoning." Out of the basic approaches to AI programming, "semantic networks" is only one. Rule-based programming (like, e.g., with PROLOG) and functional programming (like, e.g., with LISP) are other ones, and they have their competitive edge over semantic networks in much better possibilites to express dynamic behaviour, i.e., to "reason" at runtime. Exisiting authoring systems which include sophisticated instruction and student modelling (IDE, see above) therefore combined hypertext/hypermedia systems (including semantic networking) with other "AI programming" capabilities (IDE is written in LISP), yet without making functional (or rule-based) programming capabilities part of the hypertext/hypermedia system.

Hypermedia processing

What was added: Dynamics. A major strength of a computer system is without doubt its *processing* capability. Plain hypertext concentrates on the *storage* capability of computer systems and makes little use of the processing capability, except just for executing the basic functions like "follow link", "display node", and "display hypertext network". But these basic functions could easily be hardwired into an "electronic book" (MIT media lab is one of the institutes which pursues this idea), the flexible programmable power of a computer is not needed here. "True" dynamics in hypertext/hypermedia means that links and nodes are "computable." The possible links to be followed from a starting node are computed at the time the learner "wanders" through the network, and nodes may be programs instead of static information elements. In addition to computable links and nodes, computable networks should be possible.

What was lost: Static structure. Of course, HyperCard™ provides programmable links and nodes. To achieve this, however, static structuring was reduced to the single building block of the "card" (basically HyperCard's notion of a node). Static links, static collections, static "network structures" do not exist; the only existing and visible hypertext/hypermedia structure is that of "the network a learner created up to now as he wandered through the network".

What was left out: Common semantics. Programming a node, if allowed, today occurs in programming languages. Programming a link, if possible, like with systems like HyperCard, occurs in a special language (in the Hypercard case: Hypertalk) associated with the hypertext system. Therefore an author has to know several "semantic worlds": the semantics for node creation (layout, "buttons", etc.), the semantics for the creation of the actual information element (either using an editor for static nodes, or a programming language for programmable nodes), the semantics for link description, the semantics for "reasoning." What is missing is an integral semantic framework for talking about dynamics and statics, about nodes, links and whole networks, about structure and contents (still, of course, with the possibility to refer to "imported" static or dynamic information elements).

The vision: Hyperinformation

What is to be added: a) Collaboration. The constant change of a learner's (and also an author's) concepts due to interaction with his/her environment has to be reflected in the way information is treated. This means that mutual access to and change of information by different humans, i.e. collaborative manipulation of information, is to be supported. Many existing hypertext/hypermedia systems are still designed for single-node, single-thread, single-user access. The few existing distributed extensions like KMS [1] do not support individualized policies for the organization of mutual access. Distribution is either supported only in a client/server-access sense, or by allowing to distribute selfcontained hypertext/hypermedia networks over a computer network. In the envisioned hyperinformation system, frequently changing combinations of computer network nodes and different hyperinformation networks should be able to be interferred with one another, exhibiting a certain degree of network transparency while keeping the distinctions of personal/restricted/public/global view and access. A "side effect" of this move from individual to collective knowledge is the move from moderate size information bases (whose organization is determined largely by a single individual) to very large sizes, whose organization is determined largely by many individuals and/or by machines; this fact will reemphasize the "getting lost" problem.

What is to be added: b) Everything "left out" and "lost" before. A visionary integrated hyperinformation system comprises all of the features defined as "added" above but also integrates what was "left out" or "lost" there.

The result: A hyperinformation processing system. The envisioned system continues to follow a node/link paradigm (or bubbles-and-arcs, or object/method-call, or entity/relationship, whatever one prefers) in the broadest sense, with the following features:

> •**Nodes:** nodes can be assigned categories ("types" or "classes" in computer science terminology), the system offering predefined and user-definable class operations. Nodes can be static or dynamic information elements or abstractions. Abstractions can have their own behaviour/contents in addition to the sum of their contents, and can be used for true information hiding. An example of an abstraction is a (synchronized, integrated) multimedia object, where the system provides means and semantics for synchronization/integration. Programming of dynamic nodes follows the object-oriented programming paradigm.

22.15

DJ explanation 18.4-6

•**Links:** links can also be assigned categories (types, classes). Link types/classes can be used in the more elaborate concept of a "space", (e.g., continuous one-dimensional space "time" in a historical hyperinformation, discrete one-dimensional space "depth" in explanatory information, continuous two-dimensional space "geography" etc.). Categories and spaces simplify orientation and guidance. Links can be static or dynamic, and can be instance-, set- and class-based (with respect to the nodes they relate). Dynamic links follow the "method–call" paradigm of object-oriented systems or can be more implicit (following the rule-based paradigm when "reasoning" about nodes, node types etc.).

•**Webs:** Networks and self-contained subnetworks of nodes and links compose "webs" (the notion of a web is often used with relation to hypertext/hypermedia networks, in different meanings). The dynamic behaviour of and access to a web is expressed using two relevant concepts:

• **Scripts:** scripts describe the dynamic guidance through a web of nodes and links, using procedural semantics (following the object-oriented programming paradigm), using rule-based/functional "reasoning", and/or using associative means (queries about contents).

• **Policies:** policies regulate cooperative access to webs by groups of people. Policies consist of "rules" and "roles", where roles in turn are sequences of "actions", described via scripts, and of "role interactions". Individuals and "threads" (which are similar to operating system processes) may take roles at runtime.

The envisioned hyperinformation system can be characterized as an intelligent hypermedia processing system, including categories, media synchronization, reasoning, dynamics, structure, and common semantics.

Hyperinformation and computer-supported authoring/learning

A hyperinformation system as described earlier is a powerful "virtual execution environment" which turns the hardware of a multifaceted computer system (a network of multimedia workstations) into a sophisticated authoring/learning "base system".

This base system offers a unique semantic and operational framework for building an authoring/learning environment. It offers both

- •the semantics for the authoring/learning environment, and
- •the semantics for courseware itself.

Related to the first function, policies and scripts allow the system builder/manager to configure specific "preconfigurations" (an "authoring station", a "tutoring station", a "learning station"), and user-accessable policies/scripts allow modification of existing preconfigurations and tools into user-specific individual configurations; experienced users may use the hyperinformation base system to create new tools. The author usually does not get direct access to the hyperinformation base system, but rather uses tools to author courseware.

The overall architecture of an integrated authoring/learning system, according to the evaluation so far, has the following levels (top to bottom):

- •**Toplevel: Courseware.** The actual "applications" of the system are the courses in their different stages at definition, design, development, and delivery/execution time.
- •**Platform level: Authoring/learning environment.** According to the initial goal, courses are built using an authoring/learning environment, set up and individually configured on top of the hyperinformation base system with utilities, policies, and scripts.
- •**Base system level: Hyperinformation system.** A hyperinformation system as described earlier, forms a sophisticated authoring/learning base ("virtual machine") and hides technology dependencies from the platform level. It integrates processing (dynamics), storage (statics), reasoning, and network wide collaboration in a common semantic framework, following extended paradigms of "hyper...", "object-oriented", and "collaborative".
- •**Ground level: Multifacetted computer system.** Below these specific levels, there is a common "technical" level of an advanced network of multimedia workstations as described earlier.

Conclusion

Requirements and architectural and conceptual issues have
been discussed for a next-generation hyperinformation system
to be used as a basis for a networked multimedia authoring/
learning environment. The thoughts presented were developed
as part of a project for targetting a prototype authoring/learn-
ing environment. The project is considered a step of many on
the path from today's common "course hacking" to a widely
accepted courseware engineering methodology and to related
standards.

Acknowledgements

I would like to take this opportunity to thank Martin Dürr,
Gerold Blakowsi and Tom Rüdebusch (University of
Karlsruhe), Kathleen Coyle, Josef Dirnberger, Burkhard
Neidecker-Lutz, Martin Richartz, Joachim Schaper, Florin
Spanachi, Paul Tallett, and Igor Varsek (Digital CEC
Karlsruhe) for their manifold fruitful contributions to this
chapter.

References

[1] Akscyn, R. M., McCracken, D. L., and Yoder, E.A. (1988).
KMS: A distributed hypermedia system for managing knowledge in organizations. *CACM 31*(7) 820 - 835.

[2] Halasz, F. G. (1988). Reflections on Notecards: Seven
issues for the next generation of hypermedia systems. *CACM
31* (7) 836-852.

[3] Hodges, M. E., Sasnett, R. M., and Ackerman, M. S.
(1989). A construction set for multimedia applications. *IEEE
Software,* January, 37 - 43.

[4] Jonassen, D. H. (1989). Designing Hypertext for Learning.
In:M. Scanlan, .and T. D O'Shea, (Eds.),*New Directions in
Educational Technology.* New York: Springer Verlag.

[5] Russell, D. M., Burton, R. R., Jordan, D. S., Jensen, A. M.,
Rogers, R. A., Cohen, J. (1988). *Creating Instruction with
IDE: Tools for Instructional Designers..* Xerox PARC, Report
No. P88-00076.

[6] Russell, D. M. (1987). The Instructional Design Environment: Interpreter. In J. Psotka, L.D. Massey, and Mutter, S.A.(Eds.),*Intelligent tutoring systems: Lessons learned*. Hillsdale, NJ: Lawrence Erlbaum.

Chapter 23
Elaborating Arguments: Writing, Learning, and Reasoning in a Hypertext Based Environment for Authoring

Norbert A. Streitz
Jörg Hannemann
GMD-IPSI
Darmstadt, FRG

Keywords

Cognitive compatibility; authoring; writing theories; structure of arguments; elaboration; improving reasoning; activity spaces; knowledge-based support

Contents

NATO ASI Series, Vol. F 67
Designing Hypermedia for Learning
Edited by D. H. Jonassen and H. Mandl
© Springer-Verlag Berlin Heidelberg 1990

Introduction ━━━━━━━━━━━━━━━━━━

The topic of this workshop focused on the applications of hypertext/hypermedia for learning. Addressing research on hypertext this way raises a classical question of designing instructional material: What kinds of tools and concepts of learning do the authors have for preparing material to be used in the learning situation? This question is especially relevant for the construction of computer-based learning environments where the learner is confronted with the kind of tutoring or coaching situation found in intelligent tutoring systems [1,2,3]. In any case, we consider the learning situation as one where the author of the material wants to communicate knowledge about a given subject. While publishing is a means of communicating knowledge, writing is the activity of producing knowledge. Authors working on a subject start with some initial ideas, formulate and reformulate their ideas and their wording, retrieve and incorporate related work, design, compose and redesign documents in a nested, cyclic publishing process. With hypermedia we consider a learning situation where the learning material is not a printed book or a standard computer-assisted instruction program. Hypermedia offers innovative ways for designing learning materials as well as interactive learning situations. Two main features of hypertext - machine supported links and interactive branching facilities [4]— introduce the kind of interactivity for which instructional authors have been waiting for a long time. The resulting learning materials constitute a special category of hyperdocuments. But qualitative new products demand innovative tools. In this paper, we discuss the design of tools which support authors in the process of creating hyperdocuments in a cognitively adequate way. Our approach addresses the new kinds of final products as well as the situation for creating and learning from these new products.

DJ contrast 4.3

From our point of view [5], writing is a complex problem solving and design activity with multiple constraints. The final product, in terms of a hyperdocument, can be viewed as an externalized representation of internal knowledge structures which have been developed by the author. Thus, authoring tools which are especially geared to the preparation of hyperdocuments will offer much better facilities for conveying the message and intention of authors. In this way, they can communicate knowledge in a format which is closer to their knowledge structures than was possible with traditional documents. Integrating additional information about the author's intentions and knowledge structure and conveying them to the learner as part of an electronic document (author-provided structured elaborations) facilitates more comprehensive processing by the learner. Documents produced with these tools maintain the authors' knowledge structures by preserving their argumentative and rhetorical structures. This improves not only reader comprehension, but also text analysis from machine translation or automated abstracting.

Another starting point for our research is the observation that few hypertext systems offer active (intelligent) support to the author by providing feedback, advice, or guiding. Of course, the realization of this goal requires the integration of knowledge-based capabilities into a hypertext system. This implies that the architecture of the authoring tool includes components which permit monitoring and analysis of the author's activities. They are necessary to build up knowledge bases about authors and semantic structures of documents. But existing systems do not provide such facilities

Based on this assessment of the current situation of hypertext systems, we are developing an active, knowledge-based authoring and idea processing tool for creating and revising hyperdocuments. The system - SEPIA: Structured Elicitation and Processing of Ideas for Authoring - will represent a major portion of the functionality we expect from an author's workbench of the future. The research presented in this paper represents only some part of it and must be viewed within this framework.

System design and prototype development of SEPIA is based on two main objectives. Our first and overall objective is to build a cognitively adequate system. To accomplish this, we employ the approach of user-oriented and task-driven system design based on the principle of cognitive compatibility [6]. This is based upon results derived from models about cognitive processes in writing and problem solving. The second more ambitious objective is to build an active system. In order to do this, it was necessary to reduce the complexity of the general problem of active systems. We selected a finite but non-trivial subset of authoring activities and document types: argumentation and argumentative texts. The activity as well as the document type are very well defined and exhibit structures which offer excellent starting points for monitoring and guiding.

DJ comment An appearently lost art in formal public education.

DJ definition 1.8-9

The cognitive foundation of our hypertext-based authoring system has two main reference points. The first is the rich body of research on text comprehension which provides a foundation for learning aspects. The second one is the widely neglected but now growing body of research on the process of text production which serves as a basis for the authoring process. Our adaptation of the concepts and models of these two research areas to the problems of writing and learning in the hypertext domain is just beginning.

Designing and creating hypertext _____

Two general problems for authoring in hypertext environments can be identified. First, the problem of *cognitive overhead* [4] which results from having to label nodes, links and structural relationships at a very early stage. Experiences with NoteCards [7] show that this often results in premature organization. This conflicts with the users natural way of generating ideas and writing initial segments of text when structures are less definite in the beginning. Most of the time, they are not explicitly spelled out; they exist only in the mind of the author and evolve in a flexible way much later. Second, almost all authoring tools for hypertext involve rather passive storage and retrieval systems, i.e. they do not provide active support compatible with the activities of the authors. By active we mean that the authoring tool should be able to monitor and guide authors in their problem solving activity.

DJ parallel 1.18

In general, the issue of providing cognitively adequate support for authors of hypertext documents has not been addressed as much as is desirable. One exception is the approach taken with the development of the Writing Environment (WE) [8,9]. In this case, design decisions were based on a cognitive framework of writing. This approach is a very promising one, but the specific implementation lacks some features of the full hypertext concept. Although WE provides a linking mechanism in the network mode, the resulting structure is not preserved in the final document. Research does not really address the crucial problem that writing a non-linear text may require very different process of creating, revising, and composing documents, which require different kinds of support. On the other hand, publishing to date demanded hypertext as the final document structure. This is evidenced in reports of authors using NoteCards for idea processing and structuring but turning to outlines and traditional text processing tools when writing the final document [10].

Theories of writing as a basis for authoring tools _____

The construction of writing tools is mainly based on intuition and first-order task analysis. What is lacking is a sound theoretical foundation for building cognitively compatible interfaces which provide intelligent support for writing. Kintsch [11] forecasts that the progress in this field will remain restricted unless a sufficient cognitive theory of writing is developed. This deficit is not surprising because the cognitive processes of writing have been a largely unexplored field in cognitive science. Although this situation is beginning to change, existing models of writing only emphasize a small section of this complex problem solving activity. We still do not know what is going on in authors' minds when they progress from "chaos to order," as Brown has characterized this process [12].

The widely cited model of Hayes and Flower [13] emphasizes the problem-solving aspect of writing. Based on the analysis of think aloud protocols, it identifies three main subprocesses (planning, translating, and reviewing) and their organization in the overall composing activity. Results from experimental research [14] confirm this distinction and indicate that these processes are not subsequent stages but that they show up during the whole course of writing - although at different times with different frequency.

A model which reflects fundamental differences between novice and expert writers has been proposed by Scardamalia and Bereiter [15]. It emphasizes the role of knowledge in the writing process and distinguishes between a knowledge telling and a knowledge transformation strategy. Knowledge transformation is conceived as an interaction between two problem spaces: the content space and the rhetorical space. While the content space is meant to be the space for generating and structuring the author's knowledge about the domain of the intended document, planning and organization of the document structure takes place in the rhetorical space. This is also the place where decisions on including, excluding, sequencing and reformulating information are made.

Another theory which will foster the development of authoring systems stems from van Dijk and Kintsch [16,17]. For our purposes, different levels of text organization (micro- and macrostructure) and the corresponding operations (macroop-

SH explanation 5.5

411

erators) for mapping transitions between them are important. Whereas this is basically a semantic organization, we also adopt a more syntactic differentiation proposed by Collins and Gentner [18] between a global text level, a paragraph level (global sequencing) and the sentence or word level (local sequencing). At the global level we refer to the concept of superstructures [16]. An example of such a structure is the organization of a scientific report consisting of hierarchically ordered elements, like introduction, method, results, etc.

The case of argumentation

When designing instructional material, the content and the method of presentation of the content should be convincing for the learner. This implies that the author has to use arguments and to apply appropriate rhetorical structures. The creation of argumentative texts is a special case of writing. Although it seems fairly obvious to relate models of writing to research on argumentation, this is still lacking. On the other hand, there is a long tradition and a variety of schools of thought on what the basic elements of argumentative structures are [19,20,21]. Systems which are designed to support argumentation have to adopt a specific argumentation model. The gIBIS-system [4] is based on Rittel´s ideas of Issue Based Information Systems (IBIS)[25]. Especially geared to computer-aided reasoning is ARL, a special argumentation representation language, proposed by Smolensky et al. [23] which is used as the basis for the development of EUCLID - a system meant to support argumentation. Argumentation has been investigated to some extent, although with a focus different from ours. One example is the OpEd-system [24], an implementation of a model of argument comprehension.

For the representation of arguments, we adopt a schema proposed by Toulmin [19]. Figure 1 shows all of the different elements of a complete argument. While datum and claim are mandatory constituents, warrant, backing and rebuttal are optional. The relation so links a datum to a claim, constituting the following argument which states: "The farmer who does without fertilizer and herbicides in the field and without hormones and tranquilizers in the pigsty has to work much harder than a chemistry farmer" —so—> "it is not worthwhile to produce natural food". Since we are dealing with common sense argumentation instead of formal logical reasoning, an argument is more readily accepted if one can provide a warrant which legitimates the so relation via the since relationship. The warrant provides a general rule which justifies the so conclusion. In a further step, this warrant can be backed by providing evidence for the validity of this rule. In order to handle exceptions from the rule one can use the element rebuttal which questions the claim. Although the original version of the Toulmin schema does not account for the concept of a backing for the unless relationship, our analysis shows that this should be included in a complete schema.

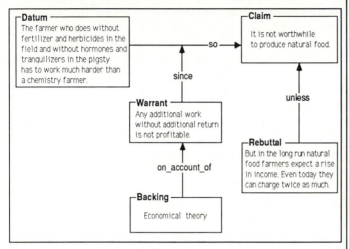

Figure 1. Example of a Toulmin Argumentation Schema

Whereas the Toulmin schema provides an analysis at the micro level, we also need a representation of argumentation at the macro level. Kopperschmidt proposes a hierarchical organization of argumentation resulting in different levels of abstractions [21]. We adopt this idea but use our own abstraction hierarchy which shares some features with the IBIS-approach [25,26] and with subsequent refinements by PHIBIS [27]. This approach distinguishes between three types of elements: issues, positions, and arguments. An issue describes the initial question to be answered by the argumentation. The main issues can be divided into subissues. For each subissue one can state at least two positions which can be supported or attacked by a number of arguments.

Perspectives on learning and reasoning ——

Focussing our system on the production of argumentative and persuasive texts, we are interested in learning that goes beyond the introductory level that is typical for school learning. Spiro et al. [28] have called this form of learning "advanced knowledge acquisition". This advanced form of learning will

SH explanation 12.19

provide the basis for a new paradigm of lifelong learning. Acquiring a deeper understanding of concepts, using them for reasoning, and applying them flexibly in diverse domains have been identified as the central characteristics which distinguish advanced learning from introductory learning. In the following section on learning aspects of our system, we concentrate our discussion on the first two topics: *getting a deeper understanding* and *improving reasoning*.

Any discussion of these aspects has to take into account the critical factor of advanced learning: The *active involvement of the learner*. Under the label *elaborative processing*, the active role of the learner in knowledge acquisition is emphasized in research on text processing. Because learning from text is still a prototypical situation for today´s advanced forms of learning, the construct *elaboration* seems to be a good starting point for developing a sound cognitive foundation for learning in hypertext environments.

Improving comprehension and retention

It is widely recognized that the reader of a text passage does not passively store the input sentence strings. Rather, the reader is obliged to make many inferences to connect different parts of the text and to relate the text with his prior knowledge. This activity has been called *elaborative processing*. Elaborations are additional facts about material to be remembered that are thought about at the time the material is studied. A basic hypothesis related to this concept is that memory for targets will be enhanced to the extent that more contextual information is encoded with each target. Anderson [30,31] provides a theoretical foundation to explain the effect of better recall performance for target items that are elaborately processed.

A framework for learning in hypertext-based environments. The elaboration model of Anderson [31] assumes that long-term memory is a network of interconnected propositions. When a person reads a passage, new propositions are added to this memory network. Any particular newly encoded proposition is weak. For this reason, it is uncertain whether a subject will be able to activate the presented proposition when he needs it. But if the subject encoded multiple propositions that were partially redundant with the target, she or he would have a much better chance of recall it if this information is relevant. Anderson distinguishes three reasons for better recalling. The first is that elaborations redirect the activation away from interfering paths to the target path. Second, elaborations can provide additional concepts from which the activation spreads. This result in a greater chance that the relevant content unit will be activated. Third, if a content unit could not be stored in the network it can be reconstructed or inferred using elaborations.

There is a wide range of literature supporting the elaboration hypotheses reviewed and discussed by Reder [32,33]. This research has led to the conclusion that learning central ideas of a text is more efficient if the subject generates elaborations during comprehension. At first glance, hypertext/hypermedia systems with their potential for associative idea linking may provide a rich and interesting context to foster these multiple elaborations. This is a frequently found form of self-directed exploration in hypertext environments. We call it learning by *associative elaboration*. But the quantity of elaborations is not the whole story. The notion that only the number of elaborations improves retention of the main ideas of a text must be questioned in the light of recent research. The results of several experimental studies demonstrate that the quantity of the elaborative context which an author provides to the reader may not exclusively determine the enhancement of comprehension and memory for some target information. The quantity of elaborations is only important if it bears certain qualitative relationships to the target information [32]. That is, effective author-provided elaborations involve activation of information that clarifies the significance or relevance of concepts. The usefulness of elaborations really depends on whether they help to constrain the interpretation of the main points of a text [34].

According to this elaboration model, an author should provide valuable elaborations to the learner which are accurate, diverse, and interesting [33]. In hypertext environments, using the potential of explicit linking and preserving a generated structure, an author has a better opportunity to fulfill these criteria.

A necessary prerequisite for the generation of a context fostering useful elaborations by the learner is an organization scheme. Such an organization scheme may take the function of an *ideational scaffolding* inducing elaborations that clarify and constrain main ideas in a document. Starting with Toulmins´s model of argumentation we have developed such a

SH corroboration 4.5, parallel 6.12

scheme for our hypertext authoring system. As this framework will aid the author in explicitly structuring his ideas and arguments it will provide the reader with a recurrent structure focussing his elaborations on critical parts and elements of the argumentation. We call this form of learning *structured elaboration* and derive two different elaboration strategies supported by our system.

Improving the mastery of learning

One central issue of research on elaborative processing in text comprehension is its emphasis on the *active role of the learner*. Recognizing that "we can unleash a new Renaissance of discovery and learning," John Scully [29] has raised the active role of the learner in his stimulating vision on new and diverse educational experience coming up with this Renaissance: " What tomorrow´s student will need is not just mastery of subject matter, but mastery of learning. Education will not be simply a prelude to career, but a lifelong endeavor" (p.1057).

But education and students are not well prepared today unleashing this second Renaissance. This is the reason why we are currently bearing on more author-provided structures for elaborations. But the future should give more system-independence to the learner. <u>Therefore the development of higher cognitive skills that enable students to be independent learners and independent, creative problem-solving users of their knowledge has become a very important challenge for future education</u>. As Nickerson [35], one of the most well known proponents - puts it, we have to add a fourth R to the list of the three basics of education: reading, ´riting, and ´rithmetic. For him a candidate would be *reasoning*. Therefore he calls for more attention to the question of how to teach reasoning explicitly. Proposing the evaluation of informal arguments as central to this question, he argues for the development of more systematic programs improving argumentative skills. Currently we cannot offer such a systematic program. But, by converting the learner to an author we will not only provide a tool for analyzing and structuring argumentation but also an environment for a learner to get more practice in argumentation. Supposing that this training will result in an improvement of reasoning skills, we also regard this environment as a vehicle gathering data for the development of more systematic programs that foster thinking and reasoning in hypertext environments.

We describe two examples of elaboration strategies and the training concept for argumentative reasoning in more detail

DJ corroboration 3.2

after we have introduced our concept of activity spaces dedicated to diverse subtasks of writing as a central design decision for building authoring systems.

Cognitive compatibility, externalization, and activity spaces

As indicated before, the idea of cognitive compatibility [6] is our prime principle and guides our system design. This implies that the environment offered to the author corresponds to properties inherent to different cognitive activities and structures of writing. Specifically, we assume that providing different representations which allow easy mapping of internal structures to external task structures and vice versa is a fundamental prerequisite for task-oriented system design [5]. Second, we adopt the principle of *externalization*. Here, we argue that different skills and additional knowledge can be brought to bear on external representations than on internal ones. External representations are open to modification and reinterpretation in more transparent ways than internal representations. This suggests the guideline to provide means which enable the author to externalize as many internal or mental states and intermediate products as possible. Implementing this principle provides the author with different means for structured *thought dumping*. Thus, externalization reduces mental load, especially memory load, which overcomes the limits of internal representations.

Observation of authors shows that for outlining with paper and pencil they make extensive use of scribbles and drawings with idiosyncratic notations in order to express part of their internal structures. A standard text editor does not provide space to do this. There, an author has to write words and sentences - line by line. Usually, something like a scratch pad is not provided. Scratch pads that do exist offer only standard graphics tools. But our argumentation is not aiming at providing sophisticated graphic capabilities. Rather we recommend providing room for specialized notational schemata that consist of elements and relations (leading to node-link hyperstructures) and to provide operations on these structures which correspond to generic mental operations of writing and arguing.

This goal is achieved by providing a variety of *activity spaces* realized by dedicated windows which differ in their structural setup and their inherent functionality. The number of activities supported and the extent of this functionality is identified on the basis of cognitive models of writing and task-specific features. Examples are modes for generating and structuring ideas for the content domain (content space), for the type/structure of the target document (rhetorical space), and the style/procedure of the argumentation (argumentation space). Our idea of activity spaces originates from Newell's [36] extension of the problem space to be the fundamental organization unit of all cognitive activities and the notion that more than one problem space can be generated during problem solving [37]. Accordingly, we decompose the overall writing activity into a number of specific activities and assign a special space to each of them. Elements of activity spaces are not problem states. Instead, they function as objects of the problem solving activity and are presented to the problem solver who can manipulate them directly. This conceptualization results in a design which somewhat resembles the *rooms metaphor* of Card & Henderson, an interface that supports fast task switching [38]. Furthermore, the idea of activity spaces is similar to the concept of having different windows for different cognitive modes in the WE-system [9]. By distinguishing between network mode, tree mode, edit mode, and text mode, WE focuses mainly on the stages of preparing traditional (linear) documents. Our approach stresses additional cognitive features of the authoring activity, e.g. planning, argumentation, and rhetorical transformations.

Examples of activity spaces

Decisions about the number and the functionality of our activity spaces are based on a rationale that integrates results from different models of writing and text production[1] . Details and specifications of these spaces follow from there.

First, we adopt the general idea of Scardamelia & Bereiter and distinguish between a *content space* and a *rhetorical space* and corresponding activities [15]. We expand their notion by viewing these spaces as two instantiations of our more general idea of activity specific problem spaces.

Second, we employ Hayes & Flower's analysis of identifying at least three main subprocesses of the writing activity: planning, translating, and reviewing, especially their differentiation of the planning process [13]. Since planning is central to each phase of writing and its results coordinate and guide all

---

[1] We are also developing an integrated cognitive model of writing, but there is no space in this paper to give more details of it.

other subprocesses, authors need an opportunity for externalization, monitoring, and revision of their plans and goals whenever necessary. Therefore, we propose a third space: the planning space.

Third, we have to take into account that our specific activity and document, i.e. argumentation, requires a separate *argumentation space* as a platform for constructing networks of argumentations. This activity is different from generating and structuring elements of the content domain of the intended document and is different from organizing the structure of the document in terms of rhetorical decisions. In summary, our system design is based on these four spaces shown in Figure 2.

Although each activity space is defined by its specific characteristics, there are still some common features to all of them. These are derived from our analysis of invariant features of the activities to be supported. First, we provide some generic operations: creating, deleting, copying, naming, renaming nodes and links. Second, it is possible to activate and *open* a node which results in the creation of a window to be used for writing and editing the content (e.g. text) of the node. Links are also objects which can be activated and edited. The *content* of a link depends on its type. Example: activating and opening the *so link* in the argumentation space results in displaying the warrant and backing structure of this link.

DJ parallel 18.4

Furthermore, we introduce in all spaces the concept of *level*. For example, subgraphs of the network in the argumentation space are embedded in a hierarchy which reflects different degrees of abstraction and which are typical for argumentative texts. On the other hand, there are other relationships within each level so that the total structure is non-linear. The level concept is motivated for text-like representations by the distinction between micro- and macrostructure proposed by van Dijk and Kintsch [16] and encompasses also *superstructures* which indicate organizations for larger documents adhering to specific sequencing of chapters and paragraphs.

In the following section, we provide a brief description of the four spaces: planning, content, argumentation, and rhetorical space. For more details - especially on the argumentation and the rhetorical space, refer to Streitz et al [39].

Planning space

This space serves to support the author in setting up an agenda and in coordinating the whole authoring activity which again requires that the author keeps track of what he is doing (personal monitoring). The function of this space can best be characterized as supporting but also stimulating an authors meta-planning activity. One key to the development of a global structure of an argumentative document is the specification of the main issue ("Does natural food save us ?") in a hierarchy of subissues ("Is our food noxious?", " Is it worthwhile to produce natural food?") (see Figure 2). These subis-

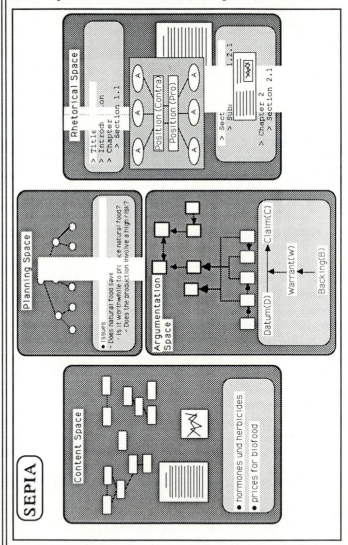

Figure 2. Activity spaces.

sues are then taken as topics for working on an argumentation network in the argumentation space. The agenda of interesting questions is not only a planning device for idea generation but at the same time a structured list of topics which can be transformed into the structure of chapters to be used later in the rhetorical space. The planning space functions as a switchboard between the other three spaces. Thus, it contains the overall goal structure and plans for writing. Although an author might stay with his original intentions for quite a while, he is free to change and modify his initial decisions in the sense of what has been called *opportunistic planning* [40].

Content space

Having identified the domain of the intended document, an author turns to the content space. In this space, she/he acquires and collects information about the selected domain which is indicated by the issues identified in the planning space. This can be achieved in two ways. First, an author can start to generate ideas about the domain at a concept level, relate them to each other, e.g. as part-whole relationships, and structure them in a semantic network (see Figure 2). The purpose here is to obtain a representation of the objects and their mutual relationships involved in the domain of the document.

DJ parallel 6.3-10

Second, an author can access additional information. This may include documents produced by him before or which come from external sources, e.g. fact and bibliographic data bases, on-line encyclopedias, or multi-media knowledge bases. The latter information consists of more or less complete documents where an author can copy parts and use them in the same or in a modified form in his new document. It might also be the case that he receives some stimulation for a new chain of arguments he has not thought of before. Again, this space exhibits different levels ranging from short notes on an idea and sketches of semantic networks to complete multimedia documents which can be viewed and included in the intended document.

Argumentation space

The argumentation space serves as the medium for generating, ordering, and relating arguments for specific issues working at one issue at a time. The representation of the argumentation space in Figure 2 provides an impression of the overall structure of this space. The argumentative activities result in a network with different levels of abstraction and of the following node and link types.

•**Nodes**: statements (attributes: name, position, claim, datum, level)
•**Links**: so (attributes: warrant, backing), contradicts, contributes to (same notation as in Figure 3)

The nodes of the network represent statements generated by an author during the development of his argumentation. Each node is an object which is characterized by four attributes, we call 'position', 'claim', 'datum', and 'level'. Nodes are mainly connected by the 'so' relationship. Besides, the relation 'contradicts' can be used to connect two statements at one level of the network. But contrary to 'so', this link always connects statements of the same type, i.e. a datum with a datum, a claim with a claim and a position with a position. It therefore describes the relationship of mutual opposition. Relations between different levels of the net are represented by the relation 'contributes-to'. Figure 3 shows an example of an argumentative network with three levels.

Different operations are provided to an author to build an argumentative structure consist of the generated elements:

•**Operations**: generate, support, object to, justify, negate, generalize, specialize

These operations serve either as a means to incrementally develop and expand arguments at a given level of abstraction or to specify or generalize arguments or parts of arguments thus establishing different levels of abstraction in an argumentation.

The data types (nodes, links) as well as the operations described in this paragraph form a useful basis for supporting authors in their attempt to construct sophisticated argumentations. The operations in the space obey to the principle of cognitive compatibility and the proposed network gives a clear view of the argumentative structure, thereby preserving the different levels typically found in more complex argumentations. Therefore, we think that this space considerably facilitates the writing of argumentative documents.

Rhetorical space

When writing an argumentative document, even for use in a learning situation, the author's intention is not only to communicate his ideas, but also to communicate knowledge in a convincing way. This is not only a matter of content and

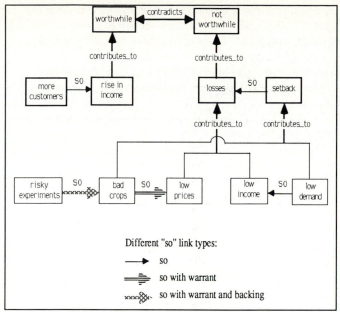

Figure 3. A network resulting from argumentation.

argument structures but above all a matter of rhetorical structuring. Thus, in this space more directly the learning perspective is important.

Considering rhetorical aspects, an author imposes a document structure on his ideas and arguments which he has explicated and elaborated in the content and argumentation space, as well as an argumentative strategy or line of argumentation. For this task we propose another separate activity space, called rhetorical space. The problems to be solved in this space require:

- •decisions on the global outline of the document
- •decisions on the rhetorical reorganization of positions and arguments for each subissue
- •decisions on writing coherent sentences

Thus we have to provide functionality for making these decisions in the rhetorical space. This is achieved by distinguishing between an outline mode, an argumentation strategy mode, and a text edit mode (cf. Figure 2). Using these three different rhetorical modes, the author gets support for arranging positions, counterpositions, and arguments into a convincing format (*argumentation strategy*), embedding it into the structure of a complete enriched document and expanding parts of it into a coherent text.

The results of operations on the structural level are demonstrated in Figure 4. It represents a section of an article dealing with the main issue "Does natural food save us?" and corresponds to the previously described argumentation net in Figure 3. Part 1 of Figure 4 shows a section of the issue structure of the article, part 2 describes the rhetorical structure of subissues.

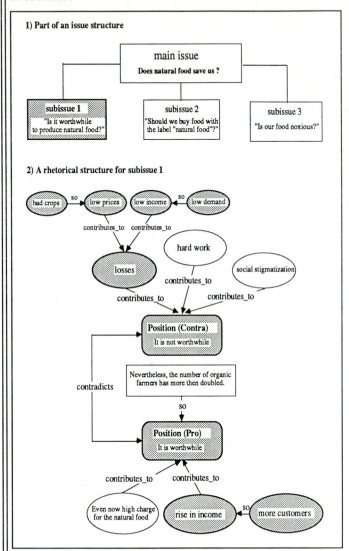

Figure 4. Example of a rhetorical structure.

As the rhetorical space provides a means to reorganize and enrich selected parts of the argumentative network and to place them in a rhetorically rearranged hierarchy of subissues, different types of documents can be produced on this basis with respect to different goals and issues of learning. We only mention two examples: (1) a *guided tour* through the argumentation network. Starting with a selected issue, the recipient is guided through the original line of the author's argumentation leading to a spelled-out position. (2) In general, the result of the rhetorical transformations is a coherent full text document having either a linear or a non-linear structure with respect to the *surface information* about facts and statements. In either case, the document is a hyperdocument providing not only the factual information for a learner but also access to the underlying argumentation structure. Therefore, even while reading a *traditional* document, she or he gets the exciting possibility of going back to the sources, i.e. to early and intermediate products of the authoring process. In this way, the learner can duplicate the author's argumentation at a more detailed level. Later on, we will present learning strategies partly using these different rhetorical transformations.

Travelling activity spaces _____

Empirical research on the writing process of mature authors has shown that production and transformation of knowledge during writing is not done in a linear sequence of stages from idea generation to text generation. There is a constant interaction between levels of text representation as well as among different subtasks. For instance, problems in formulating an argument clearly and convincingly might result in the subgoal "generate an example illustrating this argument". Let us translate this situation into our world of activity spaces. Although the rhetorical space is always the final destination, an author's train of thought is not heading there in a straightforward way. Instead, we expect heavy traffic between the spaces. This resembles the interaction of cognitive processes when locating the solution of different subproblems in different problem spaces which can be mapped to the proposed activity spaces.

> •Information flows from the *planning space* to the other three spaces: Issues specified in the planning space set topics for the content space, direct the structuring in the argumentation space, and are transformed into an outline in the rhetorical space. On the other hand, information flows from these three spaces back to the planning space: Operations in each of them may result in new insights leading to the formulation of new goals or to the specification of new subissues in the planning space ("opportunistic planning").

- Structured knowledge, elicited or generated in the *content space* may be translated into argumentative statements in the argumentation space or into a nonargumentative text passage in the rhetorical space.

- There is a close relationship between the *argumentation space* and the rhetorical space because the argumentation space functions as a quarry for the rhetorical space. The argumentation graph or parts of it must be reorganized according to an argumentation strategy in the rhetorical space. In addition, the need for explication of an argument often results in operations in the content space discovering new insights and thus reducing the original fuzzyness.

- The detection of deficits in the *rhetorical space* leads to the formulation or specification of new arguments in the argumentation space. It may also require certain operations in the content space, such as searching for missing knowledge or elaborating facts generated so far.

Promoting advanced learning and thinking

Elaboration strategies

There has been a considerable amount of research on how to improve the reader's ability to elaborate a passage. Most of this work has been concerned with adjunct aids like adjunct questions. Perhaps the most influential work was that on advanced organizers by Ausubel [41]. Ausubels's conceptualization of learning as assimilation is extended in Mayer's [42] theory of *assimilation to schema* and the theory of *web teaching* by Norman [43].

All these approaches advocate starting learning with general-level knowledge that subsumes the content presented in the following ongoing course of knowledge acquisition; the remainder of the instruction is then a process of successive differentiation. For example, one could start a history course by summarizing the major events in history, then proceed to provide a little more detail about each of those events adding a few of the next important events, until the desired level of detail is reached. In the context of argumentation, we can start with the main line of argumentation and then sucessively expand this macro-unit.

According to our argumentation model an incremental expansion can be realized in three different ways:

- subdividing each element of the macro-unit in more details (node expansion)
- providing evidence (warrant, backing) supporting the ´so´-relations (link expansion)
- continuing the macro-unit on one level as a causal sequence which has to be shown as providing effective elaborations (chain of arguments)

These are extensions which have well defined relations to elements of a main argument. They should induce elaborations which help to clarify the main point according to the results of the qualitative analysis of author-provided elaborations. Helping to ensure that the learner is always aware of the context and importance of the argumentative details and their relations, this incremental extension-strategy acts against the problem of decontextualization recognized in several hypertext applications [26]. This strategy allows learners to make a more informed decision about the following steps in his course of knowledge acquisition from hypertext. Therefore, it can facilitate the learner to control an issue which is always problematic in an interactive computer supported learning environment.

The elaboration strategy which mainly relies on a *general-to-detail* procedure may be supplemented by a more flexible one. It is based on a metaphor which Spiro et. al. [28] called the "metaphor of landscape exploration." They characterize this knowledge acquisition strategy as follows: "Deep understanding of a complex landscape will not be obtained from a single traversal. Similarly for a conceptual landscape. Rather, the landscape must be criss-crossed in many directions to master its complexity and to avoid having the fullness of the domain attenuated. The same sites in a landscape (the same cases or concepts in a knowledge domain) should be revisited from different directions, thought about from different perspectives, and so on" (p. 379).

This concept of multiple points of view is very important for learning in a hypertext environment and especially for the evaluation and understanding of controversal and ill-structured topics. Promoting a healthy skepticism in terms of Scully's requirements for a new learning paradigm [29] multiple points of view are neccessary for building up your own position. In getting a deeper understanding of the pro and

GL comment Important point.

con positions related to a special issue, developing it is not enough for the learner to follow one line of argumentation but rather she/he should encounter several lines of argumentation. These lines of argumentation can be realized as multiple paths (guided tours) through a full and carefully developed argumentative structure.

This potential of useful structured elaborations can not only be increased by a combination of the two strategies but also by a careful assignement of goals, priming questions, examples, illustrations and multiple analogies which are well arranged on a screen. Trigg [44] has used the term *remote deictic reference* denoting the spatial layout of extensions and explications refering to a central node. Developing guidelines for these deictic references are one of the main tasks of a new rhetoric of hypertext.

Improving reasoning skills

Reconstructing argumentation. A first step improving reasoning skills could be the analysis and reconstruction of argumentation generated by other individuals in different domains using a common structure of arguments. This is the approach of Toulmin et. al. [45]. One main assumption of the book is that an emphasis on variations of arguments from field to field , despite a common structure, seems likely to foster transfer. Although this is a very promising approach for improving thinking skills, it does not use the full potential of hypertext systems especially designed for argumentation.

SH corroboration 12.8 see footnote SH results 13.18

DJ explanation 18.4-6

Constructing new arguments. One essential feature of hypertext systems is the blurring of the distinction between authors and readers. A learner could be an author modifying (revising) a given (bad) argument or constructing new arguments of his own (i.e. supporting a counterposition), rather than simply analyzing those of others.

Though there is a serious lack of knowledge about the teaching of reasoning skills, we agree with Nickerson [35 p. 368] "that teaching students about reasoning is not really enough. If reasoning skills are truly skills in the usual sense of the word, they are probably improved most effectively by practice." Providing a set of computer-supported operations for generating, ordering, relating and rhetorically restructuring arguments as in the SEPIA system we are developing, is a step in this direction. Using these operations, a learner can incrementally build up an argumentative structure as an author. Making his assumptions, claims, warrants, backings and positions and their relations explicit in a common framework, a user will get intensive experience in detecting inconsistencies, incompletenesses, ambiguities, and confusions in his argumentation. Such a practice in structuring arguments will enable a student to focus more on critical factors in problems, to take different points of view and, to evaluate positions of others critically. In this way he will get more independence in exploration and problem solving which prepares him better for the lifetime of learning and discovery coming up in the 21st century. Thus this approach opens a new perspective for learning in hypertext environments which goes beyond the conventional route of augmenting human cognition by providing a dynamic medium for information storage and presentation. An additional advantage of such a system is that learning a specific subject matter and improving thinking skills can be well integrated.

The development of such a tool is experimental. More data for testing our assumptions should result in the development of more precise models and effective approaches to enhance the acquisition of cognitive skills. This development must take into account the research on psychological factors that lead to faulty argumentation and reasoning [46]. Research is more important if we want to realize our goal described below: Making our hypertext system active. This active part does not only extend the support for an author by monitoring and guiding his activities but also provides active feedback to a learner making the learning of cognitive skills more effective.

This wider perspective opens the door to the world of intelligent tutoring systems. Megarry [47] claimed that intelligent tutoring methods and systems are a step in the wrong direction. According to her,

> a false trail has been laid by intelligent tutoring systems that try to create a model of the student . . . To treat the learner as a dumb patient and the computer system as an omnicient doctor is both perverse and arrogant" (pp. 173).

Let´s try to free him from his patient role. Improving his reasoning skill effectively is certainly the right way.

Embedding activity spaces in SEPIA _____

This section provides an overview of the complete system we are currently developing. In order to realize the active part of the SEPIA system (see Fgure 6),we conceived the following components and knowledge bases. First, in order to provide feedback to an author (whenever we use the term author we also mean a learner), the system has to acquire knowledge about the author's original goals and plans, intended topic domain, document type, writing strategy, target group, etc. These data are acquired via a Knowledge Elicitation Component employing an interactive dialog technique. They form the basis of the system's model about the author (the initial author model).

Second, in order to be active at an appropriate point of time, the system has to monitor the author's writing behavior. The Monitoring Component provides protocol data about an author's activities in different windows (i.e. activity spaces). These data are used to update a dynamic part of the author model which obviously has to be distinguished from a rather static part corresponding to an author's initial profile. In order to use this information in a coherent way for guiding the process, we will provide a mechanism which integrates the data coming from different information sources. A future goal for the monitoring component is to make use of results from research on text analysis in order to employ a semantic analysis of an author's input.

Third, a guiding component processes the integrated information about the author's activity (i.e. the dynamic author model), compares it to information about the earlier acquired author's profile (on goals and plans, etc.) and to information stored in a script knowledge base. The script knowledge base contains knowledge about document types (e.g. hypertext structures) and argumentation structures. In a more advanced version, the system will also use additional knowledge about the content domain. Thus, the system has objective knowledge of rules of discourse (argumentation) and rules and facts of the domain. On the other hand, it has subjective knowledge of the author, i.e. of the author's mental model of the domain and the author's mental model of discourse (especially argumentation). Based on the result of the comparison of the objective knowledge to subjective, the system provides feedback and active support/advice to the author/learner following

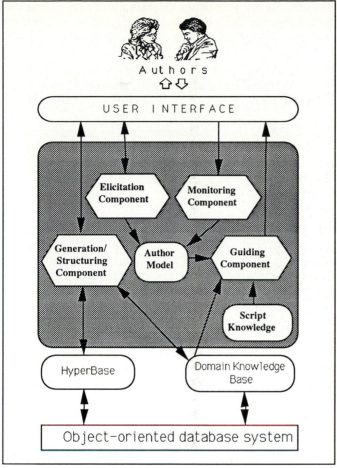

Figure 5. Architecture of the knowledge-based authoring/learning tool
SEPIA (Structured Elicitation and Processing of Ideas for Authoring)

a specific guiding/didactic strategy. Of course, these additional
features need much more detailed considerations which will
be reported elsewhere.

Conclusions and recommendations ⎯⎯⎯⎯

In this section, we summarize our ideas within a more global
framework and make some recommendations for the design of
future hypertext systems. The availability of innovative
technology for the production and reception of electronic
documents raises the question of how to improve the quality
of these documents. There are at least two aspects of the
notion of quality. The first refers to additional multi-media

features, e.g. high-resolution graphics and images, animation and simulation, video including sound, etc. The second is the extent to which the document contains additional structural information which can be used for further processing, e.g. in learning situations. Although multi-media features are of course desirable for hyperdocuments, we want to stress the second aspect.

The traditional situation is characterized by predominantly linear documents - on paper as well as in electronic format. An additional level of structure can be found in currently produced hyperdocuments. Unfortuately in most cases, it is restricted to simple 'points to' links. A general hypertext model should go beyond this and rather employ the full capability of multiple types of nodes and links, including composites as an augmentation of the basic node and link model [7]. The analysis and specification proposal in this paper has identified how one can enrich hyperdocuments with special links and nodes. We have demonstrated this for argumentative and rhetorical structures. The enrichment of hyperdocuments is reached by preserving structural information created and used by an author in his composing activity. The information concerns the final structure of the document as well as that of transient intermediate products. It has to be noted that this additional structure can be accessed by the author as well as the learner if he has the permission to do this. It thus facilitates structured elaborations fostering the comprehension of the intended message. Another advantage of this approach is that these links are also machine processible.

Additional information of this kind is only available if an author is provided with tools which allow him to generate structures and to make them part of the hyperdocument. Our approach led to the concept of activity spaces and the heavy utilization of externalizing subjective knowledge structures based on the author's mental models. Activity spaces implemented as dedicated windows with activity specific functionalities can be viewed as a natural metaphor for supporting cognitive processes in any interactive problem solving activity. Thus, this concept is applicable to a wide range of interactive systems and not restricted to hypertext systems.

A further and logical step in the development of authoring tools in hypertext environments is to extend the support by knowledge-based components as given in the description of the SEPIA-system. It has to be pointed out that this kind of support is possible because monitoring of an author's externalized behavior provides the system with information that can be used to guide his subsequent activities.

Addressing the authoring and not merely the browsing aspect of hypertext systems we open new and promising perspectives for learning, especially for the improvement of cognitive skills. Getting support not only in the reconstruction of knowledge but also in constructive activities as an author, a learner can use the system to get systematic practice in reasoning. We think this is a necassary step to empower the mastery of lifelong learning in a complex web of rapidly changing knowledge for which hypermedia becomes a core technology as Scully [29] puts it.

Acknowledgements

Thanks are especially due to our colleagues Jörg Haake, Werner Rehfeld, Helge Schütt, Wolfgang Schuler, and Manfred Thüring working in the WIBAS-project. The ideas presented in this paper have greatly profited from our dicussions with them and their stimulating comments.

References

[1] Sleeman, D., & Brown, J. S. (Eds.) (1982). *Intelligent tutoring systems*. New York, NY: Academic Press.

[2] Wenger, E .(1987). *Artificial intelligence and tutoring systems - Computational and cognitive approaches to the communication of knowledge*. Los Altos, CA: Morgan Kaufman.

[3] Mandl, H. & Lesgold, A. (1988). *Learning issues for intelligent tutoring systems*. New York: Springer.

[4] Conklin, J. (1987). Hypertext: An introduction and survey. *IEEE Computer* , *20*(9), 17-41.

[5] Streitz, N. A. (1988). Mental models and metaphors: Implications for the design of adaptive user-system interfaces. In H. Mandl & A. Lesgold (Eds.), *Learning issues for intelligent tutoring systems,* (pp. 164-186). New York: Springer.

[6] Streitz, N. A. (1987). Cognitive compatibility as a central issue in human-computer interaction: Theoretical framework and empirical findings. In G. Salvendy (Ed.), *Cognitive engineering in the design of human-computer interaction and expert systems,* (pp. 75-82). Amsterdam: Elsevier.

[7] Halasz, F. G. (1988). Reflections on Notecards: Seven issues for the next generation of hypermedia systems. *Communication of the ACM, 31*(7), 836-852.

[8] Smith, J. B., Weiss, S. F., & Ferguson, G. J. (1987). A hypertext writing environment and its cognitive basis. In *Proceedings of the Hypertext '87 Workshop,* (pp. 195-214.) Chapel Hill, NC.

[9] Smith, J. B., & Lansman, M. (1988). *A cognitive basis for a computer writing environment.* (Technical Report). Chapel Hill, NC.: University of North Carolina, Department of Computer Science.

[10] Trigg, R. H., & Irish, P. M. (1987). Hypertext habitats: Experience of writers in NoteCards. In *Proceedings of the Hypertext '87 Workshop*, (pp. 89-107). Chapel Hill, NC..

[11] Kintsch, W. (1987). (Foreword of C. Bereiter, & M. Scardamelia), *The psychology of written composition,* (pp. 9-12). Hillsdale, NJ: Lawrence Erlbaum.

[12] Brown, J. S. (1986). From cognitive to social ergonomics and beyond. In D. Norman, & S. Draper (Eds.), *User-centered system design: New perspectives on human-computer interaction*, (pp. 457-486). Hillsdale, N.J.: Erlbaum.

[13] Hayes, J. R., & Flower, L. S. (1980). Identifying the organization of writing processes. In L.W. Gregg, & E.R. Steinberg (Eds.), *Cognitive processes in writing,* (pp. 3-30). Hillsdale, NJ: Lawrence Erlbaum.

[14] Kellog, R.T. (1987). Effects of topic knowledge on the allocation of processing time and cognitive effort to writing processes. *Memory & Cognition, 15*(3), 256-266.

[15] Scardamalia, M., & Bereiter, C. (1987). Knowledge telling and knowledge transforming in written composition. In S. Rosenberg (Ed.), *Advances in applied psycholinguistics: Vol. 2. Reading, writing, and language learning*, (pp. 142-175). Cambridge: Cambridge University Press.

[16] Dijk, T. A. van, & Kintsch, W. (1983). *Strategies of discourse comprehension*. New York, NY: Academic Press.

[17 Kintsch, W. (1988). The role of knowledge in discourse comprehension: A construction integration model. *Psychological Review*, *95*(2), 163-182.

[18] Collins, A., & Gentner, D. (1980). A framework for a cognitive theory of writing. In L.W. Gregg, & E. Steinberg (Eds.), *Cognitive processes in writing: An interdisciplinary approach*, (pp. 51-72). Hillsdale, NJ: Lawrence Erlbaum.

[19] Toulmin, S. (1958).*The uses of argument*. Cambridge: Cambridge University Press.

[20] Wunderlich, D. (1980). *Arbeitsbuch Semantik*. Frankfurt: Athenaeum.

[21] Kopperschmidt, J. (1985). An analysis of argumentation. In T. A. van Dijk (Ed.), *Handbook of discourse analysis: Vol. 2. Dimensions of discourse*, (pp. 159-168). London: Academic Press.

[23] Smolensky, P., Fox, B., King, R., & Lewis, C. (1988). Computer-aided reasoned discourse or, how to argue with a computer. In R. Guindon (Ed.), *Cognitive Science and its application for human-computer interaction*, (pp.109-162). Norwood, NJ: Ablex.

[24] Alvarado, S. J., Dyer, M. G., & Flower, M. (1986). Editorial comprehension in OpEd through argument units. In *Proceedings of the 5th National Conference of Artificial Intelligence - AAAI '86 (Vol. 1)*, (pp. 250-256). Los Altos, CA: Kaufmann.

[25] Kunz, W., & Rittel, H. (1970). *Issues as elements of information systems* (Working paper 131). Berkeley, CA: University of California, Center for Planning and Development Research.

[26] Conklin, J., & Begeman, M.L. (1988). gIBIS: A hypertext tool for exploratory policy discussion. *ACM Transactions on Office Information Systems*, *6*(4), 330-331.

[27] McCall, R., Schaab, B., & Schuler, W. (1983). An information station for the problem solver: system concepts. In C. Keren & L. Perlmutter (Eds.), *Applications of mini- and microcomputers in information, documentation and libraries.* New York: Elsevier.

[28] Spiro, R. J., Poulson, R. L., Feltovich, P. J., & Anderson, D. K. (1988). Cognitive Flexibility Theory: Advanced knowledge acquisition in ill-structured domains. In *Proceedings of the Tenth Annual Conference of the Cognitive Science Society*, (pp. 375-383), August 17-19. Montreal, Quebec, Canada. Hillsdale, NJ: Lawrence Erlbaum.

[29] Scully, J. (1989). The relationship between business and higher education: a perspective on the 21st century. *Communications of the ACM*, *32*(9), 1056-1061.

[30] Anderson, J .R. (1980). *Cognitive psychology and its implications.* San Francisco, CA: Freeman.

[31] Anderson, J. R. (1983). *The architecture of cognition.* Cambridge, MA: Harvard University Press.

[32] Reder, L. M. (1982). Elaborations: When do they help and when do they hurt? *Text*, *2*(1-3), 211-214.

[33] Reder, L. M, (1985) Techniques avaible to author, teacher, and reader to improve retention of main ideas of a chapter. In S. F. Chipman, J. W. Segal, & R. Glaser,. *Thinking and learning skills, Vol. 2: Research and open questions,* (pp.37-64). Hillsdale, NJ: Lawrence Erlbaum.

[34] Stein, B. S., & Brandsford, J. D. (1979). Constraints on effective elaborations: Effects of precision and subject generation. *Journal of Verbal Learning and Verbal Beahavior*, *18*, 769-777.

[35] Nickerson , R. S. (1986). Reasoning. In R.F. Dillon & R.J. Sternberg (eds.), *Cognition and instruction*, (pp. 343-373). Orlando: Academic Press.

[36] Newell, A. (1980). Reasoning, problem solving, and decision processes: The problem space as the fundamental category. In R.S. Nickerson (Ed.), *Attention and performance VIII*, (pp. 693-718). Hillsdale, N.J.: Lawrence Erlbaum.

[37] Kant, E. & Newell, A. (1984). Problem solving techniques for the design of algorithms. *Information Processing & Management*, *20*(1-2), 97-118.

[38] Card, S. K., & Henderson, A. (1987). A multiple, virtual-workspace interface to support user task switching. In Carroll, J. M., & Tanner, P. P. (Eds.), *Proceedings of the CHI und GI '87 Conference on Human Factors in Computing Systems*, (pp. 53-59).Toronto. New York: ACM.

[39] Streitz, N.A., Hannemann, J., & Thüring, M. (1989). From ideas and arguments to hyperdocuments: Travelling through activity spaces. In N. Meyrowitz (Ed.), *Proceedings of the ACM Confernce: Hypertext ´89 Workshop*. (pp 343-364). New York: ACM.

[40] Hayes-Roth, B., & Hayes-Roth, F. (1979). A cognitive model of planning. *Cognitive Science*, *3*(4), 275-310.

[41] Ausubel, D. P. (1963). *The psychology of meaningful verbal learning*. New York, NY: Grune and Stratton.

[42] Mayer, R. E. (1979). Can advanced organizers influence meaningful learning. *Review of Educational Research*, *49*, 371-383.

[43] Norman, D. A. (1973). Memory, knowledge, and the answering of questions. In R. Solso, *Contemporary issues in cognitive psychology*. New York: Winston.

[44] Trigg, R. (1988). Guided tours and tabletops: Tools for communicating in a hypertext environment. *ACM Transactions on Office Information Systems*, *6,* (4), 398-414.

[45] Toulmin, S., Rieke, R., & Janik, A. (1979). *An introduction to reasoning*. New York, NY: Macmillan.

[46] Nisbett, R. & Ross, L. (1980). *Human inference: Strategies and shortcomings of social judgment*. Englewood Cliffs, NJ: Prentice Hall.

[47] Megarry, J. (1988). Hypertext and compact discs - the challenge of multimedia learning. *British Journal of Educational Technology, 19*, 172-183.

Chapter 24
Alexandria: A Learning Resources Management Architecture

Daniel M. Russell
Institute for Research on Learning
Xerox Palo Alto Research Center

Keywords

Hypermedia; integrated learning environment; situated learning; embedded systems

Contents

What is Alexandria? _____

The original library at Alexandria was the repository for all the accumulated knowledge and wisdom of the ancient world. Founded by Ptolemy I in the third century B.C., Alexandria represented the ultimate resource for scholars of its day.

This time around, we propose to construct a new Alexandrian library, not with all of the known-earth encompassing view of the original, but similar in intent. The new Alexandria is a

NATO ASI Series, Vol. F 67
Designing Hypermedia for Learning
Edited by D. H. Jonassen and H. Mandl
© Springer-Verlag Berlin Heidelberg 1990

world for the student to explore; a world that provides a rich set of computational and media systems for a student to work with, work through, and to discover. The goal of Alexandria is not to create another prescriptive tutoring system, but to build an information center that integrates with the student's daily work and study activities. As computer workstations become more prominent in the classroom, we feel a need to devise a strategy to embed workstation learning materials into everyday experience. The goal is to provide an architecture that can provide resource access within a subject domain that is rich enough to draw a student to use it, detailed enough to provide substantial learning experiences, and pragmatic enough to begin building Alexandrias for many different domains.

Accordingly, Alexandria is an architecture — a specification for the kinds of components, and how they hook together — rather than a strict specification of one application. An Alexandria architecture describes a mechanism for providing access to learning materials, and and for composing within a workstation environment.

This discussion of Alexandria is divided into two components: the Alexandria architecture *per se,* and the instructional approach that motivates many of the architectual decisions.

The Alexandria architecture provides the following capabilities:

> •*A uniform interface and access to a large number of learning resources*. There is enormous value in creating a common access mechanism to many resources. The common model of computer-based learning systems portrays the host machine's operating system as a necessary evil to be negotiated in order to get to the learning materials. A better approach is to dedicate the machine to navigating through *learning space* — focusing on student goals and instructional plans — rather than distracting a student with multiple invocation methods for different resources.[1] Contrast this with other large computer-centered

---

[1] By "resource" I don't mean the collocation of programand data that Apple© does. Rather a "resource" is any body of materials or instructional activity on the workstation that can plausibly be construed as educational. Aresource is a packet, possibly active, possibly even offline, that forms a chunk of instruction.

systems (e.g., PLATO) which require that the learner already know what materials exist, when they are appropriate to use, and how to invoke them to run.

•*Integration of resources.* Not only are the resources accessible via a common interface, but they are also *integrated* within a hypermedia *background.* That is, a student can easily branch from one resource to another, adding links between resource "places" and hypertext media fragments (e.g., linking a document currently being written to a syntax checker; or linking from a frame of a video sequence into a simulation).

•*Navigation and resource management..* The *kernel* — the central organizing resource in Alexandria — helps the student understand what other resources are available for both learning new material and accomplishing work. The kernel provides management facilities for the student to move easily between resources.

•*Learning advice.* Finally, Alexandria's kernel also gives advice to the student about what resources are appropriate to accomplish a specific learning objective. In this capacity, the Alexandria kernel assists the student to achieve his instructional objectives by creating an instructional plan, which the student may follow or alter as desired.

The Alexandria architecture is driven by several key issues in teaching and learning.

•*Learning is highly contextualized.* We know from cognitive studies of learning that what is learned is in many ways keyed to the situation in which it is learned and the context in which the skills and knowledge are used. [e.g. 1]. As a consequence, Alexandria accentuates integration between learning resources and doing work within a domain. That is, by integrating learning with working resources, Alexandria blends the distinction between the object of learning and the way learning about the domain happens [2].

•*Conceptually rich environments.* It is becoming increasingly clear than in order to be a viable computer-based learning system, a rich environment is required to illustrate how elements of the subject matter interrelate [3]. The power of a computer-based instructional system lies in its ability to provide effective learning situations that are unavailable in other media, while retaining the ability to manipulate the elements of the subject matter directly. In other words, a computer is not best used as a page-turner, but works best when presenting information in forms that are not directly reproducible by other media. In general, these are computational, hands-on manipulable, multi-media kinds of presentations, such as the SHERLOCK tutor [4].

•*Direct participation in the subject matter.* Not only is learning contextualized and thus best provided in a richly represented environment, but learning is also best when not abstracted away from its use. Ideally, a computer-based teaching system will allow the learner to work within the subject matter, thereby not only learning the subject *per se*, but also the means and ways of acting as a practitioner within the domain [1,2].

•*No single universal learning/teaching strategy.* With differently motivated students in different circumstances, it is difficult to imagine a single instructional paradigm that is appropriate under all possible circumstances. Alexandria allows for a wide variety of instructional strategies, driven either by the learner or by the system.

In addition, as a practical matter, the Alexandria architecture must be:

•*Portable* — a system that can be used in many different locations, on easily available machines.

•*Robust* — Alexandria should keep on working, or in the event of failure, should provide work-around functionality. We want Alexandria to feel as robust as paper.

•*Domain independent* — the ideas of Alexandria are, we feel, powerful enough to be useful in many domains, from use by students in a technical training context, to students trying to understand and acquire a second language and culture.

•*Media-rich* — video, sound, text, hypertext, data bases, and community exchange of knowledge.

•*Simple to use* — for success, Alexandria needs a short learning curve; students must be able to quickly get into using Alexandria for practical purposes. We want Alexandria to fade away, becoming only the name of a place to get work accomplished.

•*Extendable* — We cannot predict what components will go into an Alexandria system, but it must be relatively easy for users to extend the range of resources available in Alexandria.

Finally, the Alexandria design is based on three fundamental assumptions about its use:

•*Self-directed learners* — While Alexandria could be tailored for beginners, or for directive teaching, our current view is that it will be primarily for adults that are self-motivated, and not requiring much direction for education. (We do not address issues of motivation or control.)

•*Community* — Although Alexandria can be used in isolation, one of the important advantages of Alexandria is the incorporation of a like-minded community to share and exchange information. Ideally, as part of a larger Internet, Alexandria could be the access portal for a learner into a resource system, including community social resources (through sharing of work, comments, activities across local groups and distant / distributed communities).

•Technology base — Alexandria assumes that the computer workstation is one of the primary tools of the learner. While Alexandria is not processor dependent, it does rely on the learner using the workstation on a regular and ongoing basis. That is, the workstation is a constant in the learner's work/study life, and is not seen as an extraordinary place where learning occurs independent of day-to-day activities.

Alexandria in use

Alexandria is primarily a system for workstation oriented users. In our view, such workstations should be ubiquitous for many learning situations, and placed in a variety of locations — a student's dorm room, a centralized study area, a library, and so forth. Such workstations, and Alexandria as an element of these workstations are, in Jef Raskin's word, an *information appliance*, intended to be used in an everyday sort of way.

To the student, the kernel is the *common spot* in the system from which learning activities are initiated and work utilities used. In a sense, the kernel **is** the system to a user — it is the place where work starts and stops, and it is the location where access to work tools, educational advice, and navigation is found.

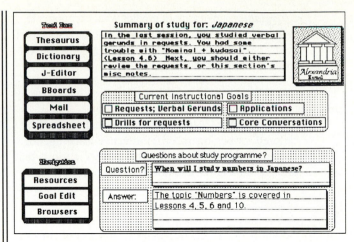

Figure 1. The Alexandria kernel interface gives centralized access to a set of tools (e.g. a Thesaurus or dictionary), a recap of the work performed to date (in the upper center), fast access to the currently suggested learning resources is through the central menu ("Current Instructional Goals") with navigation information in the lower left. "Resource" lets the student see what resources are available, "Goal Edit" alters the current instructional goals of Alexandria, and browsers creates graphical maps to view what resources the student has used, and what resources are planned. Ideally, the student will be able to ask simple questions about what will be (or what has) learned through a dialog box at the bottom.

So, when the student begins work and boot the Alexandria machine, the screen might appear as in Figure 1. From this kernel screen, the student may directly access either tools of the workstation (in the Tool Box, upper left corner), or may access any of the learning resources through either direct access (e.g., the current instructional goals can be accessed by clicking on the resource checkbox in the screen center) or by interacting with the domain advisor. The domain advisor can create instructional sequences of resources in response to stated objectives or can provide single one-time lessons on a topic of particular interest, assuming that sufficient resources exist in the system database.

Whether directed by the advisor, or out of simple interest, the student may select a resource and launch the resource from the kernel. The student works with the resource and returns to the kernel as desired, perhaps to continue his/her daily work. The kernel keeps track of what resources the student currently is using, and helps navigate the student back to the original task or not. To mitigate the common feeling of being lost in hyperspace, the kernel provides a set of navigation tools. The content browser shown in Figure 2 is the most common, but it is not the only such mechanism.

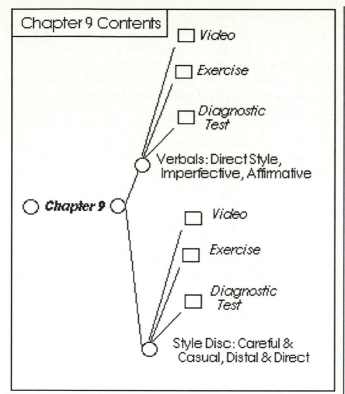

Figure 2. A content browser from the resource navigator. Using such a graphical display, a student can easily examine the resource set, searching for a particular resource to teach a topic, or to answer a specific question.

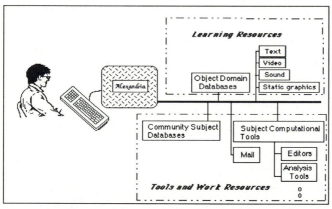

Figure 3. Alexandria provides centralized access to a wide variety of learning resources and tools to support the learner in everyday work activities. To the student, Alexandria brings together a rich set of resources materials and systems under the kernel. By interacting with the kernel, the student may be directed to any of the resources. The kernel tracks student resources use and can make recommendations to the student about which resources might prove useful.

The Alexandria architecture

In essence, Alexandria is an infrastructure that ties together a wide variety of learning resources within a single, integrated access mechanism for the student. Specifically, the central idea of the Alexandria architecture is a coordinating kernel that provides basic services to the student and manages a set of learning resources.

The kernel. The Alexandria kernel coordinates the management and use of learning resources by the student. The kernel provides basic navigation through the resource materials, recording the student's progress through the resource materials, giving assistance in accessing and managing the resources, and consultation services. Beyond simple coordination and centralization, the Alexandria kernel acts somewhat like a reference librarian answering questions like "Where can I learn about the Japanese Tea Ceremony?" and somewhat like a academic counseler "What should I do next?".

Thus, for simple resource navigation tasks, the kernel provides:

- *resource browsers* — to show what resources are available for use; especially when filtered by learning specific predicates (e.g., level of difficulty; types of resources; etc. See Figure 2.)
- *the ability to answer questions* — about what the student has done to date. What resources has the student used? How did she/he perform on them? Which resources should be redone to achieve mastery? Which resource would the student like to review? What were the last three resources the student worked with?
- *maintain user profile* — As a student uses the system, the kernel not only tracks what the student has done (history), but also determines what important characteristics of instruction the user seems to prefer. The kernel will use this information to modify future suggestions of resources to use.
- *provide access* — to work tools and resources. An Alexandria system must embed — that is, provide learning resources at the learner's work site — in this case, the online workstation environment. Naturally, the tools and resources will vary from setting to setting. In a scholastic environment, for example, the kernel must provide access to task-specific tools such as text editors, graphics packages, mailing lists (e.g.,

an interest group on a specific topic), on-line bulletin boards, communal databases and access to people willing to act as resources. This provides work tools to the learner and extends the notion of a resource to include people, databases and workgroups.

Finally, the kernel also:

•*provides representation interoperability*— Alexandria is supposed to be an annotatable, flexible, user-tailorable medium. Resources must participate in a hypermedia-style protocol to allow for annotation and modification by the learners (on a purely local, user modifcation copy basis). As students annotate the resource base, the kernel must maintain individual student modifications to the base, and integrate each in a smooth fashion. [2]

Without the kernel, Alexandria is simply a large hypermedia database with integrated tools that are appropriate to the learning task. With a kernel, Alexandria provides a layer of mediation for the student between the task (learning) and the many resources available within Alexandria.

What kinds of resources? ⎯⎯⎯⎯⎯

Resources are defined as packets of computation that are dealt with as though they are hypermedia nodes. Broadly speaking, Alexandria resources are virtually anything that might be of use to a student that can be packaged or accessed via a computer-based system. Typically, a resource will either be a microworld-style environment that a student can enter and participate within (e.g., a simulation or role-playing game), or it may be a utility for the student to use in the course of doing work in the domain (for instance, a database or text editor). Ideally, resources should have a limited *grain size* — that is, neither too large (teaching many concepts) nor too small (a small hack that teaches a tiny fragment). A resource should

JL recommendation 6.17
DJ explanation 6.3

---

[2]In addition to standard hypermedia links between resources, we have come to believe that process state is as much a hypermedia anchor as well as a text location. Alexandria thus extends the hypetext model sloghtly to incorporate process links to *process states i.e.,* following a link may invoke a process (e.g., a simulation or game); while exiting the process returns the student to the point (context) from which the process was invoked.

ideally teach a small number of coherent skills or concepts, or provide practice, experience, or useful functionality.

Examples of resources: include:
- *simulations* — e.g. STELLA simulations or models of specific devices [4]
- short *programmed instruction* segments for specific instruction
- *diagnostic segments* for students to test their understanding by answering questions and responding with an analysis of their specific problem areas
- *dynamic problems* - to situationally embed a student in a problem solving situation (a la "No Recuerdo" of the Athena project)[5].
- a *technical lexicon* shared among an interest group
- a *subject-indexed video library* to find appropriate video segments based on interest (RDBMS with pointers into video library, after video kit from the MIT Media Lab) [6].
- linguistic packages — for example, syntax checkers (e.g., AT&T's Writer's Workbench) or flexible lexicon creation/sharing for shared dictionaries)
- database that allow a student to manipulate data sets, create hypotheses and experimentally verify them.

However, in Alexandria, a resource is not limited to purely computational activities. Because of our emphasis on contextualized use and socially mediated understandings, a resource might also be a reference to an individual (perhaps through electronic mail), a network discussion group on a domain-related topic, an active electronic bulletin board, or a publically accessible community database. A resource is a part of Alexandria when it can be described in terms of what it can do or teach, how to access it, and to what extent it participates in the full Alexandria protocols (described below). Hence, people or community activities can act as resources and become part of the entire learning experience for an Alexandrian student.

For the most part, Alexandria resources may refer to each other explicitly by linkages. They may be sequenced together by the kernel to create a coherent whole in response to a student question or instructional goal. The role of the Alexandria architecture is to provide an environment in which individual resources can be represented, manipulated and synthesized into an effective teaching presentation for the student.

By participating in an Alexandria environment composed of many resources that can by interlocked via the kernel, a resource can leverage its effectiveness by not having to take on all the problems of a completely detailed, all inclusive Intelligent Tutoring System. A single resource need achieve only a single instructional goal. Intra-goal management is managed by the kernel, and needn't be dealt with at the resource level.

Part of the motivation for this resource library design (independent units, cross-linked and synthesized into a presentational *whole cloth* by the kernel) lies in our recognition that no one educational software manufactory can easily produce an entire set of resources to satisfy a learner's instructional objectives. In this architecture, many resources from a variety of authors can be available to the learner.

How does Alexandria work?

This section shows how Alexandria works from the programmer's perspective. The technical requirements of the kernel functionality are determined, and the behavior of resources (how the resources function as hypermedia entities) are described. From a system-building perspective, the challenge for Alexandria is how to provide access for the student, with the ability to integrate resources and also allow synthesis of instructional sequences. The answer is to define a set of protocols each resource must follow, and then describe the basic functions of the Alexandria kernel.

Alexandria resource protocols

A resource is essentially a packet of instruction that Alexandria deals with as a hypermedia node. That is, each resource implements a basic protocol in order to function as a member of the resource set.

To participate fully, each Alexandria resource must (a) be invocable from the kernel, (b) be suspendable (and continuable or restartable), (c) accept links to it from other resources, (d) allow links coming from it, (e) allow for a clean termination of the resource, and (f) be described to the kernel in terms of the resource description language. In short, a resource should participate in an *open hypertext model* [7] and be describable in terms in an agreed-upon language that can be used by the various Alexandria functions. [3]

A resource allows a student to make annotations, which are kept as either overlays on top of resources (i.e., they do not modify the resource source but modifies the student's view of the resource). If the entire resource is a local copy, then the student can modify the resource directly by creating links to and from the resource.

Kernel functions

The kernel supplies a set of basic functions that allow the individual resources to work as an ensemble, rather than as disjoint individuals interconnected in a maze.

As outlined above, the kernel provides the following functions:

1) *Tracking* — recording student use of resources . By tracking student resource use, a history list is constructed of student activity. From this, the instructional advisor can determine what modules have been seen, when, the duration of use, and what instructional goal was being satisfied.

2) *Instructional advice* — the ability to answer simple questions from the student about what to do next. To do this, the kernel contains some knowledge about instruction in general (e.g., prerequisite structures, preferences for teaching style for domains) and knowledge about the domain as represented in the resource set available for use.

3) *Navigate* — tools to help the student navigate through the resource space. Provide a common ground for users, with navigation aids and work monitors to answer the questions: "What's available?" and "What instructional goal am I doing now?".

4) *Coordination* — resources must be able to call and refer to one another. By supplying a linking mechanism between resources, the kernel allows the resources to be described and linked together as whole units, rather than at the individual hypermedia unit level. Some links not only link-to but also cause some computational process to become active (e.g., a simulation).

---

[3]Note that not all resources are able to fully inplement the protocol. Some resources, such as human tutors available thourgh electronic mail, do not support program suspension or linking-to or linking-from. These resources are, from this point of view, partial resources.

How does the kernel operate?

For the most part, kernel functions are student-driven. The student may create a browser to examine a portion of the available resource set or might ask a question about what lessons might occur next. However, there is a representation issue to resolve.

A central mechanism in the Alexandria system is the kernel's description of the available resources. For the navigation and advisor functions to operate, the kernel must describe each available resource in terms of what the resource teaches, what concepts and skills it assumes as prerequisites, and what system resources are required to run the resource. For example, a resource database would minimally have records with the following fields:

Resource Database:

    Name — *name of resource*

    InvocationParams — *calling sequence, parameters needed to launch resource*

    Level Taught — *"level of difficulty / complexity" of the entire resource*

    Concepts taught — *concepts / skills taught or practiced by this resource (roughly, what can be learned from this resource)*

    Skills req'd to use — *prerequisite concepts, skills*

    Resources req'd to run — *a list of the systems needed to use this resource (physical, software, access privledges, etc.)*

The relations and terms used to describe resources in this database define a *resource description language* (RDL). Naturally, each Alexandria will have a different RDL depending on what resources are devised for a given system, and according to what local belief about the educational content of resources can be. Of course, the resources described by the RDL need not be directly callable resources. Individuals and new group communities accessible over the network might be described as resources having particular kinds of expertise. They are also described in the resource database in the same RDL.

The student can also state explicit instructional goals to the kernel. By using a standard planning mechanism, it is often possible to create a sequence of resources that will fulfill that objective, as described in the operation of the IDE-Interpreter. As Figure 1 illustrates, the instructional sequence of resources that satisfies the instructional objective becomes available with a summary of instruction activity to date to the student for explicit instruction.

Alexandria as an integrated system

In use, Alexandria pulls together daily work on a computer work-station with learning activities. Ideally, all tools within the workspace should be integrated into the architecture in order to provide seamless workstation use. Just as many currently available text editors have built-in word spelling correctors, or dictionary access mechanisms, Alexandria attempts to integrate domain resources (both reference and learning) into the patterns of daily work life. Just as a work-station user now accesses an on-line dictionary to resolve questions about phrasing of a particular text passage or to discriminate fine meanings of words in context, Alexandria will provide tools to answer questions about a wider range of topics. In addition, without ever having to leave the electronic workspace, an Alexandria can deliver focussed domain instruction that fits into a larger sequence of instruction (much as going to a classroom does) or in response to specific workplace driven demands. By placing a modest amount of knowledge about the resource set into the kernel of Alexandria, we believe that a powerful learning and access tool can be made available to students.

The IDE-Interpreter: An Alexandria-class tutoring system

Although our current work is still very much in progress, Alexandria is an architecture which is based on our experiences with similar systems. The current design grows directly from our experience with an early instance of the Alexandria architecture called the IDE-Interpreter. The IDE-Interpreter is described as an intelligent tutoring system that creates an instructional plan to satisfy a set of instructional goals[8]. Experience with the IDE-Interpreter altered our expectations and understanding of what needed to be supplied in a hyper-media tutorial environment. It is a nearly complete example of an Alexandria-class tutoring system, although not a truly "open" hypertext environment. All resources are not fully interlinkable, and the navigation tools are incomplete. Nevertheless, it does have a fully-functional instructional sequence advisor, the ability to link and launch resources, and the ability to have partial resources integrated into the instructional sequence.

Description

The IDE-Interpreter is built on top of Notecards [9] and implements many of the Alexandria architecture features by extensions to that hypermedia system. The IDE-Interpreter creates an instructional plan and guides the student through the plan. The plan is implemented by primitives termed Instructional Units (resources in Alexandria), which present instructional materials, pose questions, and interact with the student. The student's interaction with the instructional unit is recorded and analyzed to update a student model. The planner uses the updated student model to modify the instructional plan, constantly updating its plan to achieve the instructional goals.

Creating and running an instructional plan

The IDE-Interpreter cycles through four modules to create, execute, and monitor an instructional plan. Each cycle corresponds to planning and implementing a single instructional goal. Goals are represented as the grain size of a single instructional interaction (a presentation of a page or two of material), asking the student a few questions, or presenting an open work / study environment. The four modules are (1) an Instruction Problem Solver that creates instructional plans for the student to follow, (2) an Instructional Unit Selector in

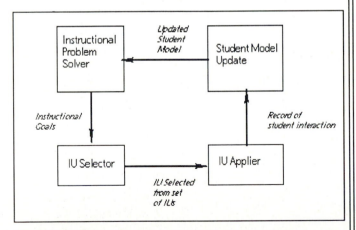

Figure 4. The IDE-Interpreter's main cycle first builds an instruction plan from a set of instructional goals, then selects an IU that can satisfy the current goal from the plan, then applies that IU (presents it to the student), and finally updates its student model before restarting the cycle.

charge of finding (or creating) an instructional unit for the student to run, (3) an Instructional Unit Applier that actually delivers the unit to the student, moderating all interactions with the student, and (4) the Student Model Update, which records all student interactions and modifies an overlay / issue-based student model.

The IDE-Interpreter creates and dynamically modifies an instructional plan for the student to follow. The plan is used to sequence instructional units into a single, coherent instruction stream for the student. While interacting with the instructional units, student behavior is monitored, and the Student Model is updated to reflect inferences about student understanding. The IPS uses the Student Model and its rule base to modify the current instructional plan, and the cycle repeats. As in Alexandria, a language is defined to form an RDL to describe each of the instructional units to the central planner (IPS).

Instructional Units as resources

An Instructional Unit is an isolable fragment of instruction, the elements comprised of an instructional sequence. An instructional unit, in simple systems, corresponds to an extended *frame* in other tutoring environments. That is, an instructional unit encapsulates information to be presented, or questions to be asked. A typical instructional unit encompasses a page or two of text, perhaps with accompanying graphics, presenting a (small) set of concepts. However, an instructional unit can also include complex questions, simulations, interactive game settings, and exploratory environments. Any display or interaction with a pedagodical goal, implementable within the computational environment and described in terms of the KS, can form an instructional unit. An instructional unit can be a generator for a class of instructional interactions. For example, an instructional unit that poses algebra problems may be implemented by a problem generator, for example [10]. This way, one instructional unit could be used repeatedly, each time creating a new interaction for the student. Ideally, all instructional units should be generated by the system in response to the instructional goals created. Our use of *canned instructional units* is a computational (and manpower) compromise. In this approach there is a certain amount of course consistency as it is delivered to different students. With a sufficiently rich set of instructional units, course delivery is very adaptable to individual learning behaviors (all students need not be taught the same material in the same sequence) and individual learning styles (all students need not be taught in the same way)

Using the IDE Interpreter as a tutoring system

The Interpreter creates an instructional plan based on the initial instructional goals, the KS, the Student Model and the Strategy rules. It synthesizes a sequence of IUs, but also revises each cycle, depending on the state of the Student Model. The Interpreter delivers the instructional units with the student. At each step, the student's interactions are examined, and the Student Model updates its Instructional Issues as required. The instructional plan is then re-examined, and repaired or updated as needed based on new information. This cycle continues until the Interpreter has determined that the instructional objectives have been satisfied, or that the initial instructional goals cannot be met.

In our limited testing of the system, we found the IDE-Interpreter to be effective at constructing interesting and useful sequences of IUs from the set available. Despite the quantized nature of the plan produced, with fairly simple engineering, it was possible to produce instruction sequences that were smooth in transition and useful to the student.

Current work on Alexandria ⎯⎯⎯⎯⎯

Currently, at the Institute for Research on Learning, we are investigating ways to construct viable Alexandrias. Our initial focus is on second language instruction, in particular, Japanese for English speakers.

Teaching Japanese is an especially difficult domain since so much of the knowledge needed to function is embedded in the culture, and not easily susceptible to traditional computer-based instruction. It is our hope that building a learning system that puts learning directly into the work/study environment will have significant effects on learning. Students will not only be able to increase time-on-task but do so in a way that is intrinsically richer due to the increased accessibilty of appropriate resource information when needed. As a part of Alexandria, we believe that the emphasis on communal interactions through on-line tutors, community databases, public discussion bulletin-boards, all of which are tied into the Alexandria resource set, will support learners in coming to understand the language.

Satisfying all of the goals described here is a large task. It relies largely on our ability to create an infrastructure that can support (simultaneously) intra-resource linkages, multimedia and multi-language displays, together with all of the kernel functions. As a consequence, we are still largely at this design phase with only a few actual working products. Based on our experiences with the IDE-Interpreter, and with other large-scale resource linking activities (e.g., MediaWorks, [11]), we are planning to construct a functional Japanese Alexandria in the near term.

Summary

Alexandria is an architectural specification for a class of learning systems that are *embedded* (in work), *integrated* (by intra-resources protocols to allow annotation) and *mediated* (by the kernel) for navigation and sequencing of presentation. Our goals are primarily to construct systems that enable learning; doing so by placing the learning activity in a use context, in as rich an environment as possible, and by simplifying the use and access of the learning materials.

The power of an Alexandria system comes about through permitting access, but also because of the abillity of individual resources to interlock, each providing a piece of instruction, and relying on the kernel for system-level support and instructional guidance. This partitioning of concerns seems to make Alexandria an ideal architecture for a variety of domains, and in our particular application, for transmitting a complex and rich set of understandings to the student.

References

[1] Lave, J. (1988). *Cognition in practice: Mind, mathematics and culture in everyday life*. New York: Cambridge University Press.

[2] Brown, Collins, and Duguid (1989). Situated cognition and the culture of learning. *Educational Researcher, 18 ,(1)* 32-42.

[3] Burton, R. R. (1989). The environment module of intelligent tutoring systems, in M. C. Polson and J. J. Richardson, (Eds.), *Foundations of intelligent tutoring systems*. Hillsdale, NJ: Lawrence Erlbaum Associates.

[4] Lesgold, A. (1988). *Sherlock: A coached practice enviroment for an electronics troubleshooting job.* Tech. Reprt. Pittsburgh: University of Pittsburgh, LRDC.

[5] Murray, J. (1987). Humanists in an institute of technology: How foreign languages are reshaping workstation computing at MIT. *Academic Computing*, (September).

[6] Brondma, H. P. & Davenport, G. (1989). *Creating and viewing the elastic Charles — A hypermedia journal..* Hypertext II, University of York, York, UK (June).

[7] Pearl, A.(1989). *S*un's Link Service: A protocol for linking. *Proccedings of Hypertext '89.* New York: ACM.

[8] Russell, D. M. (1989). IDE: The interpreter. in J. Psotka, L. D. Massey, and S. A. Mutter, (Eds.), *Intelligent tutoring systems: lessons learned.* Hillsdale, NJ: Lawrence Erlbaum Associates.

[9] Halasz, F., Moran, T. P., Trigg, and R. H. (1987). Note-Cards in a nutshell. *Proceedings of ACM CHI + GI '87 Conference.* Toronto, Canada (April, 1987).

[10] McArthur, D., Stasz, C., Hotta, J. Y., Peter, O. and Burdorf, C. (in press). *Skill-oriented lesson control in an intelligent tutor for basic algebra.* The RAND Corporation.

[11] Pea, R. (1990) Design spaces for hypermedia composition tools. In B. Bowen (Ed.), *Designs for learning.* Apple Press.

NATO ASI Series F

Including Special Programme on Sensory Systems for Robotic Control (ROB)

NATO ASI Series F

NATO ASI Series F